Project Management Mastery Question Bank

Comprehensive practice questions for project management excellence

Rakesh Kumar Verma

www.bpbonline.com

First Edition 2026

ISBN: 978-81-67080-011

**To View Complete
BPB Publications Catalogue
Scan the QR Code:**

www.bpbonline.com

Dedicated to

My beloved parents:

Shri S.P. Verma and Smt. S. Verma

My beloved parents-in-law:

Shri B.K. Verma and Smt. P. Verma

My wife Nidhi and my daughter Eshani Verma

About the Author

Rakesh Kumar Verma is a project management professional with more than 18 years of experience delivering high-impact transformation programs across the global telecom industry. His career has taken him through diverse and challenging roles at organizations such as Nokia, LTIMindtree, Reliance Jio, and ZTE, where he has led multi-vendor, multi-technology projects involving 4G, VoLTE, IMS, and emerging 5G networks.

Over the years, Rakesh has built a reputation for bringing structure, clarity, and predictability to complex delivery environments. He has managed cross-functional engineering teams, navigated demanding stakeholder ecosystems, and ensured that mission-critical projects meet stringent quality and regulatory standards. His work reflects a blend of technical depth, disciplined execution, and a calm, solution-oriented leadership style.

As a PMI-PMP **Authorized Training Partner Instructor** (**ATPI**), Rakesh has trained and mentored close to 1,000 PMP aspirants from various industries. Learners value his ability to simplify concepts, connect PMI frameworks with real project scenarios, and provide practical guidance that builds confidence for the exam. His mentorship has helped hundreds of professionals achieve their PMP certification on the first attempt.

Rakesh is also committed to continuous learning. He holds several globally recognized certifications, including PMI-CPMAI, PMI-PMP, SAFe POPM, PSM-I, PRINCE2 Practitioner, BCAA-CAIO, PMI-PMP-ATPI, and IITLv3(F). These credentials reflect his ongoing curiosity and his dedication to staying aligned with evolving project management practices, agile frameworks, and emerging technologies.

In his current role as a technical project manager – applied R & D at Nokia, he leads large-scale transformation projects for Tier-1 telecom operators, ensuring seamless integration, predictable delivery, and operational excellence in environments where reliability and precision are essential.

This Project Management Preparation Guide is an extension of his passion for teaching and mentoring. Through this question bank, Rakesh aims to provide a learning resource that captures the latest trends and updates from the Project Management domain, helping learners prepare with clarity, confidence, and a structured approach.

Acknowledgement

First and foremost, I want to extend my heartfelt thanks to the **Project Management Institute** (**PMI**) for providing early access to PMBoK v8, PMI-ATPIs (authorized training partner instructors) and the PMP aspirants. It is your real-world perspective that ensures the questions are relevant and aligned with the current practices in the field.

I am also deeply appreciative of the dedicated team of BPB publications for being supportive enough to provide me with quite a long time to finish the book. Their constructive feedback and thoughtful suggestions have been invaluable in refining the content. It is their meticulous attention to detail that has helped shape this resource into a more effective tool for learners.

I would also like to acknowledge the unwavering support of my wife and my little daughter. Thank you for your patience and understanding during the long hours spent working on this project. Your support has been a pillar of strength, and I am grateful to have you by my side.

It is my hope that this question bank fosters a deeper understanding of project management principles. Thank you all for your contributions and support; it has truly been a collaborative effort that I cherish.

Preface

Welcome to your essential practice companion for mastering project management concepts. This question bank is specifically designed to help you transform the reader's theoretical knowledge of project management into practical insights

Pursuing a project management is about developing a mindset that allows one to navigate complex organizational challenges. While textbooks provide a solid foundation, true readiness comes from hands-on practice. This curated question bank serves as your bridge, helping you turn theoretical principles into actionable skills through targeted questioning.

To align with the latest project management standards, we have organized this question bank into twelve focused chapters, each comprising a set of questions across three main sections:

Section I: Standard for Project Management

Chapter 1: Introduction to Project Management — This chapter sets the stage with questions that cover essential principles, terminology, and the integration of predictive, agile, and hybrid methodologies. It emphasizes the importance of aligning projects with organizational goals.

Chapter 2: System for Value Delivery — Here, you will find questions that explore how organizations can structure their project systems to maximize benefits and deliver real value, highlighting practices that ensure alignment with strategic objectives.

Chapter 3: Project Management Principles — This chapter includes questions focusing on key principles like leadership, accountability, and adaptability that guide ethical and effective project decisions. The questions also stress the critical role of stakeholder engagement.

Chapter 4: Project Lifecycles — In this chapter, you will encounter questions that cover various life cycle models, predictive, adaptive, and hybrid, to help you choose the right approach based on specific project needs.

Section II: Project Management Practices

Chapter 5: Project Management Performance Domain — This chapter focuses on questions related to essential operational areas, such as team performance and stakeholder engagement, that directly impact project success. The questions will help you understand how to monitor and improve performance in these domains.

Chapter 6: Tailoring — Here, you will find questions about customizing processes, tools, and practices to meet the unique constraints of an organization or project, highlighting the importance of flexibility in project management.

Chapter 7: Inputs and Outputs — This chapter examines questions about the flow of information, resources, and requirements into processes, leading to the deliverables produced. Understanding these elements is crucial for effective project execution.

Chapter 8: Tools and Techniques — You will encounter questions that introduce practical methods and systems that project teams use to plan, monitor, and execute their work effectively.

Section III: Practice Sets

Chapters 9 to 12: Practice Sets 1 to 4 — These chapters provide four full-length practice sets containing situational, multiple choice, and scenario-based questions. This allows you to apply your knowledge in a realistic setting.

To get the best out of this question bank, tackle each chapter thoughtfully. Engage with the questions not just to find the right answer but to analyze the distractors and understand why one approach is more effective than others. Each chapter features questions designed to reflect the psychological and intellectual demands of the respective topics, helping you build critical thinking skills. Think of this question bank as your supportive partner in identifying knowledge gaps, refining your reasoning, and boosting your confidence. Embrace the process, learn from your mistakes, and prepare consistently.

Coloured Images

Please follow the link to download the
Coloured Images of the book:

https://rebrand.ly/wv3ckuv

We have code bundles from our rich catalogue of books and videos available at **https://github.com/bpbpublications**. Check them out!

Errata

We take immense pride in our work at BPB Publications and follow best practices to ensure the accuracy of our content to provide an indulging reading experience to our subscribers. Our readers are our mirrors, and we use their inputs to reflect and improve upon human errors, if any, that may have occurred during the publishing processes involved. To let us maintain the quality and help us reach out to any readers who might be having difficulties due to any unforeseen errors, please write to us at:

errata@bpbonline.com

Your support, suggestions and feedback are highly appreciated by the BPB Publications' Family.

Piracy

If you come across any illegal copies of our works in any form on the internet, we would be grateful if you would provide us with the location address or website name. Please contact us at business@bpbonline.com with a link to the material.

If you are interested in becoming an author

If there is a topic that you have expertise in, and you are interested in either writing or contributing to a book, please visit www.bpbonline.com. We have worked with thousands of developers and tech professionals, just like you, to help them share their insights with the global tech community. You can make a general application, apply for a specific hot topic that we are recruiting an author for, or submit your own idea.

Reviews

Please leave a review. Once you have read and used this book, why not leave a review on the site that you purchased it from? Potential readers can then see and use your unbiased opinion to make purchase decisions. We at BPB can understand what you think about our products, and our authors can see your feedback on their book. Thank you!

For more information about BPB, please visit www.bpbonline.com.

Join our Discord space

Join our Discord workspace for latest updates, offers, tech happenings around the world, new releases, and sessions with the authors:

https://discord.bpbonline.com

Table of Contents

SECTION- I

Standard for Project Management

CHAPTER 1
Introduction to Project Management

Introduction

The set of questions in this chapter exclusively focuses on the fundamentals of project management. These questions are designed to help the reader grasp the essential ideas that are crucial for understanding how modern project management works. The questions are organized into several types to make learning easier. For example, *multiple choice questions* with one correct answer, *multiple-answer questions* with more than one correct option, *fill-in-the-blank questions* that require completing the sentences with the right words, and *matching questions* where the reader is expected to connect terms with their correct definitions.

After completing this chapter, the reader will gain a clear understanding of why project management is important, the key terms commonly used in this field, the special features that make projects different from regular tasks, and how effective project management helps an organization achieve its goals.

Overall, this chapter aims to build a strong foundation in project management that will benefit in making a solid understanding of the fundamentals of project management.

Objectives

The main objective of this chapter is to help project management aspirants and learners:

- Understand and recall the definitions and roles of fundamental project management terms.
- Recognize what distinguishes projects from operations and why these differences matter.
- Appreciate how project management supports organizational strategy, value delivery, and change.

This chapter is designed to provide learners with a solid foundation in project management. The main objective of this chapter is to introduce the learners with the essential terms used in the discipline and clarifying the purpose and role of each concept, enabling readers to build a strong vocabulary for further study. Using the different types of questions, this chapter, also explains the key differences between projects and ongoing operations, emphasizing why these distinctions influence how work is planned, executed, and controlled within an organization. In addition, it highlights the broader significance of project management by showing how well-managed projects contribute to organizational strategy, support value creation, and enable purposeful change. By engaging with these ideas, learners gain a deeper appreciation of why project management is a critical capability in today's dynamic business environment.

Use this question bank to brush up your knowledge on the fundamentals of project management in line with the project management field.

Single select multiple choice questions

1. **What is the main purpose of The Standard for Project Management ?**
   a. To define project scheduling tools
   b. To provide a basis for understanding project management and how it facilitates intended outcomes
   c. To focus on operations only
   d. To eliminate all project risks

2. **Which of the following is not listed as a way in which project management enables organizations?**
   a. Compete more effectively
   b. Ensure long-term sustainability and growth
   c. Guarantee project profit
   d. Drive positive change

3. **Which of the recent shifts influencing the projectmanagement landscape is not identified as a shaping factor?**
   a. Climate change
   b. Technological advancements such as AI
   c. Daily resource leveling
   d. Geopolitical instability

4. **What is the role of adaptive project management approaches?**
   a. They always replace predictive approaches
   b. They enable teams to tailor strategies to meet unique challenges and dynamic conditions
   c. They focus on eliminating all documentation
   d. They apply only to IT projects

5. **What is a 'project'?**
   a. An ongoing routine operation
   b. A temporary initiative in a unique context undertaken to create value
   c. A type of portfolio
   d. A recurring program

6. **Which of the following is an explicit benefit of applying The Standard for Project Management?**
   a. Eliminating the need for organizational governance
   b. Supporting organizations in navigating complexities and ensuring consistency and effectiveness in delivery
   c. Focusing solely on product development
   d. Mandating one universal methodology for all projects

7. **What do organizations expect projects to deliver?**
   a. Only outputs
   b. Outcomes that create value
   c. Fixed profit margins
   d. Unlimited resources

8. **In the key terms, what is the difference between a product and an artifact?**
   a. Artifacts are always tangible, products are intangible
   b. Product refers to tangible or intangible items produced, and artifacts are documents or items created to help manage the project
   c. All artifacts are products
   d. There is no difference

9. **Which describes a "unique context" for a project?**
   a. Projects can be managed the same way as operations
   b. Each project differs due to goals, environment, stakeholders, or other dimensions
   c. Projects and operations are identical
   d. Projects never interact with their environment

10. **Which of the following is not a reason for a project ending, per the Introduction?**
    a. Objectives achieved
    b. Resources depleted

c. Change in external environment

d. Routine updates completed

11. **Which factor is not included as causing shifts in project management?**

a. Resource constraints

b. Geopolitical instability

c. Advances in artificial intelligence

d. Tax law changes

12. **From the given options, identify a major reason for updating definitions of project management concepts.**

a. To reduce documentation

b. To reflect global accessibility and language

c. To eliminate stakeholder engagement

d. To mandate a single methodology

13. **What term refers to a document or item created during a project to help manage it and provide information?**

a. Outcome b. Artifact

c. Benefit d. Value

14. **Which project element is described as quantifiable and may be an end item or a component item?**

a. Output b. Product

c. Benefit d. Artifact

15. **What is the primary way projects support organizational change?**

a. By creating deliverables

b. By enabling a transition from a current state to a future state

c. By eliminating operational work

d. By focusing only on outputs

16. **Which of the following is not explicitly listed as a characteristic that distinguishes projects from operations?**

a. Temporary nature

b. Defined objectives

c. Routine processes

d. Unique context

17. **Which is not a responsibility associated with organizational governance?**

a. Enforcing legal and compliance requirements

b. Defining ethical responsibilities

c. Setting personal project manager goals

d. Facilitating decision-making for value delivery

18. **Which of the following is cited as a key difference between programs and projects?**

a. Projects are always larger

b. Programs integrate the scope of component projects and subprograms

c. Projects last longer

d. Programs are temporary

19. **Which among the following best describes "organizational work"?**

a. Only ongoing operations

b. Both operations and projects

c. Strictly benefits realization

d. Only product delivery

Multi-select multiple choice questions

20. **Organizations expect projects to deliver which two of the following?**

a. Value

b. Guaranteed profits

c. Outcomes

d. Only physical outputs

21. **Which two statements are true about the project manager's role?**

a. Project managers are expected to align project outcomes with organizational strategic objectives

b. Project managers only perform technical tasks

c. Project managers require excellence in a wide array of disciplines
d. Project managers avoid using technology

22. **From the given options, select two reasons for the temporary nature of projects.**
a. Project objectives have been achieved
b. Changes in strategy or environment eliminate the need
c. Projects never end
d. Projects are always routine

23. **Which two are considered the main distinctions between projects and operations?**
a. Projects are temporary
b. Operations are ongoing
c. Projects are always part of daily routines
d. Operations produce unique deliverables

24. **Which two are cited as ways project management enables organizations to create a positive impact for society?**
a. Delivering outputs
b. Driving positive change
c. Responding to changes in the business environment
d. Focusing only on financials

25. **Which two are considered as "foundational elements of project management"?**
a. Differences between operations management and project management
b. The role of artificial intelligence
c. The link between organizational and project governance
d. The history of project management

26. **Which two of the following are listed as possible endpoints for a project?**
a. Achieving objectives
b. Termination for legal, regulatory, or compliance issues
c. Repeating the same deliverables
d. Ongoing resource allocation

27. **What are two main functions of organizational governance?**
a. Ensuring transparency and resiliency
b. Managing team performance only
c. Enforcing compliance with policies
d. Creating project charters

28. **Which two are functions of project governance?**
a. Defining accountability and communication protocols
b. Setting only the project budget
c. Prioritizing initiatives and allocating resources
d. Focusing solely on documentation

29. **Which two options are explicitly listed as project artifacts or outputs?**
a. Documents created during a project
b. Project Management Office policies
c. Tangible items such as products
d. Ongoing operational reports

30. **Which two statements describe the temporary nature of projects?**
a. Projects have a defined beginning and end
b. Projects are always ongoing
c. Projects end when objectives are achieved, or resources are exhausted
d. Projects continue until operations are finished

31. **Select two options as possible reasons for project termination?**
a. Legal, regulatory, or compliance issues
b. Change in strategy, priorities, or external environment
c. Project team fatigue
d. Customer satisfaction

32. **Which two are listed as project management expectations in modern organizations?**
a. Alignment with organizational strategy
b. Excellence in a single technical discipline
c. Navigating complex environments
d. Avoiding all change

33. **Which two are considered part of the organizational environment influencing projects?**
    a. Governance
    b. Random chance
    c. Culture
    d. Unplanned events only

Fill-in-the-blanks

34. **A ____ is defined as a collection of programs, projects, and operations managed as a group to maximize overall value delivery and achieve strategic objectives.**
    a. Portfolio b. Project
    c. Program d. Operation

35. **_____ is defined as a product, result, or service generated by a process.**
    a. Output b. Portfolio
    c. Team d. Benefit

36. **The project management defines __ as a set of individuals performing the work of the project to achieve its objectives.**
    a. Project team b. Sponsor
    c. Customer d. Stakeholders

37. **A __ is a gain or asset realized by the organization and other stakeholders as the result of outcomes delivered.**
    a. Benefit b. Output
    c. Portfolio d. Product

38. **__ is the application of knowledge, skills, tools, and techniques to project activities to meet or exceed the intended value.**
    a. Portfolio management
    b. Project management
    c. Operations management
    d. Product development

39. **A __ is a temporary initiative in a unique context undertaken to create value.**
    a. Program b. Project
    c. Operation d. Portfolio

40. **The ______ is the person assigned by the performing organization to lead the team responsible for achieving the project objectives.**
    a. Project sponsor b. Program manager
    c. Project manager d. Portfolio director

41. **The projects enable organizations to align their deliverables to ______ and associated goals.**
    a. Regulatory compliance
    b. Business strategy
    c. Market share
    d. Customer complaints

42. **______ is defined an end result or consequence of a process or project.**
    a. Output b. Outcome
    c. Artifact d. Benefit

43. **A ______ is a collection of programs, projects, and operations managed as a group to maximize value delivery.**
    a. Program b. Portfolio
    c. Project d. Artifact

44. **_______is the application of knowledge, skills, tools, and techniques to project activities to meet or exceed intended value.**
    a. Portfolio management
    b. Project management
    c. Operations management
    d. Benefits realization

45. **The ______ is the person assigned by the performing organization to lead the team responsible for achieving project objectives.**
    a. Project sponsor
    b. Project manager
    c. Operations manager
    d. Program coordinator

46. **A ______ is a group of related projects and program activities managed in a coordinated way.**
    a. Portfolio b. Program
    c. Operation d. Benefit

47. **Organizational ______ helps ensure transparency, oversight, compliance, and adaptability for stakeholders.**
    a. Governance b. leadership
    c. Strategy d. Communication

48. **The ______ nature of a project indicates a beginning and an end to the project work.**
    a. Predictive b. Temporary
    c. Continuous d. Routine

49. **______ management is distinct from formal project management and focuses on efficient production of products or services.**
    a. Resource b. Operations
    c. Schedule d. Risk

50. **The ______ state is the organization's status before the project begins.**
    a. Final b. Future
    c. Current d. Desired

51. **______ management involves selecting, prioritizing, managing, and optimizing programs and projects to align with strategic goals.**
    a. Project b. Portfolio
    c. Benefits d. Stakeholder

Match the following

52. **Match each concept (Table A) to its definition (Table B):**

Table A	Table B
a. Outcome	i. Excess of benefits over investment
b. Artifact	ii. Tangible or intangible item produced by a project
c. Value	iii. Temporary initiative to create value
d. Product	iv. End result or consequence of a process/project
e. Project	v. Document or item created during a project

53. **Match the term in Table A to its definition in Table B:**

Table A	Table B
a. Portfolio	i. Excess of benefits over investment
b. Program	ii. Application of knowledge, skills, tools, and techniques
c. Product	iii. Group of related projects and program activities managed together
d. Project management	iv. Artifact produced, quantifiable, tangible, or intangible
e. Value	v. Collection of programs, projects, and operations managed as a group

54. **Match each role (Table A) with its correct description (Table B):**

Table A	Table B
a. Project manager	i. Coordinates multiple related projects
b. Project team	ii. Is affected by or can affect project outcomes
c. Portfolio manager	iii. Manages a collection of programs and projects
d. Program manager	iv. Leads the project team to achieve objectives
e. Stakeholder	v. Performs work to achieve project objectives

55. **Match the type of management (Table A) with its primary purpose (Table B):**

Table A	Table B
a. Project management	i. Aligning all projects and programs to the strategy
b. Program management	ii. Providing direction, control, and compliance
c. Portfolio management	iii. Achieving defined objectives in a unique context
d. Operations management	iv. Ensuring ongoing product/service delivery
e. Governance	v. Managing related projects for synergy

Concept-based objective questions and answers

56. **What is "value delivery system" as defined in the introduction?**

    It is a collection of strategic business activities aimed at building, sustaining, and/or advancing an organization, including portfolios, programs, projects, and operations. This system enables organizations to align work with strategic objectives and achieve desired outcomes.

57. **What is the primary difference between projects and operations?**

    Projects are temporary and unique, undertaken to create value, while operations are ongoing and repetitive.

58. **Why is it important to understand the relationship between portfolio, program, and project management?**

    Understanding these relationships helps organizations coordinate resources, align with strategic goals, and maximize value.

59. **Define a "project management team"?**

    The members of the project team are directly involved in project management activities.

60. **What does the term "outcome" encompass?**

    The end result or consequence of a process or project, including long-term effects or value generated, positive (benefits) or negative (disbenefits).

61. **How are project management and other management disciplines related?**

    Project management interacts with disciplines like product management and is influenced by organizational governance and culture.

62. **What is meant by "project success"?**

    It refers to the consensus view that a project delivered value worth the effort and expense.

63. **Why emphasize stakeholder involvement in defining project success?**

    This is because project success is a consensus view across beneficiaries, stakeholders, and participants regarding delivered value.

64. **What is the main purpose of organizational governance?**

    Providing support, direction and control through policies, processes, and decisions to meet strategic and operational goals.

65. **Distinguish between project management and operations management?**

    Project management focuses on temporary initiatives creating value; operations management ensures ongoing efficient production of products and services.

66. **Why is it important for organizations to coordinate portfolio, program, and project management?**

    To allocate resources efficiently, avoid competition for resources, and maximize value delivery in alignment with strategy.

67. **What is a "benefit"?**

    A gain or asset realized by the organization and stakeholders as a result of outcomes delivered.

68. **Why must project outcomes be evaluated?**

    To determine how effectively a project achieved its objectives and to understand its overall impact.

69. **What is the "future state" in the context of project management?**

The desired result of the change driven by the project represents the organizational goal after project completion.

70. **What is the impact of early engagement of operations teams in projects?**

It facilitates the seamless integration and sustainability of project outcomes in the organization's operational framework.

71. **In what way do portfolios, programs, projects, and operations interact?**

They are interconnected components that help organizations achieve goals and manage change, sometimes competing for the same resources.

72. **Why is project management now considered a "strategic competency"?**

This is because it enables organizations to achieve objectives, drive change, and maintain competitiveness in a complex environment.

73. **How can project management support organizational sustainability and growth?**

By aligning deliverables with strategy, enabling adaptation to change, and facilitating value creation.

74. **What is the relationship between project outcomes and organizational value?**

Effective project outcomes contribute to organizational value by achieving intended objectives and benefits.

75. **How does organizational governance facilitate value delivery in portfolios and projects?**

By promoting alignment with strategic objectives and enabling decision-making for value creation.

76. **What is the primary difference between a product and an outcome?**

A product is an artifact produced by a project, while an outcome is the result or consequence (positive or negative) of the project.

77. **How do project and operations teams interact during a project lifecycle?**

They may transfer deliverables, resources, and knowledge at various points to ensure successful implementation and sustainability.

78. **Define the "value" that projects are expected to deliver, and why is this perspective important for project managers?**

Value is defined as the excess of financial and non-financial benefits over the investment gained from achieving goals. This perspective is important because it encourages project managers to focus on organizational and stakeholder benefits, not just completing tasks or deliverables. Understanding value ensures that projects are aligned with broader business objectives and deliver meaningful results.

79. **What is meant by the temporary nature of projects? How does it impact project management practices?**

The temporary nature means every project has a defined start and end, requiring focused planning, monitoring, and closure. It impacts management by ensuring clear objectives, resource allocation, and attention to transitioning deliverables or outcomes to operations after completion. Moreover, recognizing this helps avoid treating projects as ongoing operations and promotes accountability for results.

80. **What is the distinction between "outputs" and "outcomes" in project management?**

Outputs are products, results, or services produced by the project, while outcomes are the end results or consequences, positive (benefits) or negative (disbenefits) that reflect the impact or value created. This distinction guides project managers to measure not just what is delivered, but the real-world effects of those deliverables.

81. **In what way does organizational governance support project success?**

Organizational governance provides direction, controls, and oversight through policies, processes, and decision frameworks, ensuring projects are aligned with strategic objectives and deliver value. This structure helps maintain consistency, transparency, and compliance, enabling better decision-making and value delivery.

82. **Why should project management be seen as a "strategic competency" in organizations?**

    Project management enables organizations to achieve strategic goals, adapt to change, drive innovation, and maintain competitiveness. Treating it as a strategic competency elevates its importance beyond task management to a key driver of long-term organizational success. Also, this perspective ensures project management is integrated into business strategy and value creation.

83. **Explain the importance of tailoring project management approaches.**

    Tailoring ensures that project management practices fit the unique context, environment, and requirements of each project, rather than applying a "one size fits all" approach. It increases effectiveness and relevance, helping to address specific challenges and opportunities for each project.

84. **What is meant by "unique context" in project management, and how does it affect project execution?**

    "Unique context" refers to the specific conditions, goals, stakeholders, and environment that distinguish one project from another, requiring customized management and execution strategies. It ensures that each project is approached according to its particular needs, increasing the likelihood of success.

85. **How do portfolios, programs, and projects interact within an organization's value delivery system?**

    Projects may be stand-alone or grouped into programs for coordinated management, and both can belong to portfolios that are managed to maximize strategic value and align with organizational objectives. It should be noted that this layered structure enables prioritization, resource optimization, and alignment with strategy.

86. **Why emphasize stakeholder consensus in defining project success?**

    Project success is based on the consensus of stakeholders and beneficiaries that the delivered value justifies the effort and cost, ensuring diverse needs and expectations are addressed. This approach promotes stakeholder engagement and satisfaction, not just technical completion.

87. **Describe the role of a project manager.**

    The project manager leads the team responsible for achieving project objectives, facilitates work, manages processes, and enables value delivery in alignment with organizational goals. This role requires a balance of leadership, management, and strategic alignment.

88. **What is the significance of integrating project, program, and portfolio management with operations management?**

    Integration ensures smooth transition of deliverables, knowledge, and resources, supports sustainability, and avoids conflicts in resource allocation, aligning projects with ongoing business operations. This helps maintain long-term benefits from project outcomes.

89. **How can a change in organizational strategy lead to project termination?**

    If the organization's strategy shifts and the project no longer supports new objectives, it may be terminated to reallocate resources where they add more value. This demonstrates the importance of strategic alignment for project continuation.

90. **Why is early engagement of operations teams recommended during project planning?**

    Early engagement ensures smooth handover, adoption, and sustainability of project outcomes in the operational environment. This reduces the risks of failed implementation and maximizes value realization.

91. **Explain how projects create value through organizational change.**

    Projects are undertaken to move an organization from its current state to a desired future state, driving change that produces tangible or intangible value for stakeholders. It must be noted that change is at the heart of value creation in project management.

92. **Discuss the importance of understanding both the benefits and potential disbenefits of project outcomes.**

Recognizing both benefits (positive outcomes) and disbenefits (negative outcomes) allows for better evaluation, risk management, and informed decision-making regarding project value. This holistic view helps project managers manage expectations and impacts.

93. **Define a "portfolio" and what is its purpose?**

A portfolio is a collection of programs, projects, and operations managed as a group to maximize value delivery and achieve strategic objectives. Managing collectively enables prioritization and resource optimization.

94. **Why is it critical for project managers to align project activities with the organization's system for value delivery?**

Alignment ensures that projects contribute to strategic objectives, deliver intended benefits, and make efficient use of organizational resources. This alignment is key to organizational growth and stakeholder satisfaction.

95. **What is the impact of the external and internal environment on projects?**

Both environments influence project success by providing context, constraints, and opportunities that must be understood and managed for effective project delivery. Environmental awareness helps in risk identification and tailored planning.

96. **Describe how organizational governance can influence project priority and resource allocation.**

Governance structures set policies and decision-making protocols that help prioritize projects and allocate resources in line with strategic objectives. This ensures resources are directed to where they add most value.

97. **What is the impact of AI in project management?**

AI offers advanced tools for analysis, prediction, and automation, improving outcomes when used responsibly and with human oversight, depending on input quality. Responsible AI use can enhance project management effectiveness.

98. **What is the difference between "project management team" and "project team"?**

The project management team is directly involved in management activities, while the project team includes all individuals performing project work. This distinction clarifies roles and responsibilities.

99. **Why is "value delivery system" a central concept?**

It integrates all project-related activities—portfolios, programs, projects, and operations—into a system that aligns work with strategy and desired outcomes, maximizing organizational value. This holistic approach supports adaptability and sustainable success.

Conclusion

In this chapter, we covered the foundation that is required to understand project management. Through the different types of questions in this chapter, we've learned not just the definitions, but also how projects connect with programs, portfolios, and day-to-day operations. We have also seen how governance helps keep all work aligned with the organization's goals.

Let us keep these basic ideas in mind, as they are the starting point for everything else in project management. A better understanding of these fundamentals makes it easier to learn the next chapters and to apply project management practices confidently in any organization.

In the very next chapter, we will explore a bit more with a similar approach (using different flavours of questions) in the areas related to value creation, project environment, product management considerations, functions associated with the project, and project management roles.

References

1. Project Management Institute (PMI). *The Standard for Project Management – Introduction*. PMI, 2024. Referred to for understanding the purpose, structure, and overarching framework of the Standard, including its alignment with modern project delivery and organizational strategy.
2. Project Management Institute (PMI). *A Guide to the Project Management Body of Knowledge (PMBOK® Guide)* – Eighth Edition. Project Management Institute, 2024. Primary source for foundational concepts, terminology, value delivery systems, and project management principles used throughout the question bank.
3. PMI Lexicon of Project Management Terms. Project Management Institute. Used to ensure consistency and accuracy in the definitions of key project management terms included in the question bank.

Answers

Q. No.	Answers
1	b
2	c
3	c
4	b
5	b
6	b
7	b
8	b
9	b
10	d
11	d
12	b
13	b
14	b
15	b
16	c
17	c
18	b
19	b
20	a, c
21	a, c
22	a, b
23	a, b
24	b, c

Q. No.	Answers
25	a, c
26	a, b
27	a, c
28	a, c
29	a, c
30	a, c
31	a, b
32	a, c
33	a, c
34	a
35	a
36	a
37	a
38	b
39	b
40	c
41	b
42	b
43	b
44	b
45	b
46	b
47	a

Q. No.	Answers
48	b
49	b
50	c
51	b
52	a-iv b-v c-i d-ii e-iii
53	a-v b-iii c-iv d-ii e-i
54	a-iv b-v c-iii d-i e-ii
55	a-iii b-v c-i d-iv e-ii

CHAPTER 2

System for Value Delivery

Introduction

This chapter guides the readers through a series of questions on how value is created, delivered, and sustained within an organization. The reader will gain a clear understanding of what value means in project management, and get an in-depth understanding of how projects, programs, portfolios, and everyday business operations all connect and support each other to achieve strategic goals. Also, readers will discover how different parts of an organization, such as people, processes, and technology, work together as a system to achieve these goals. The chapter also explains the important roles played by internal and external factors, including organizational culture, policies, and the wider business environment.

By the end of this chapter, the reader will be able to build a solid foundation about value creation, what all are contributing factors, and what role internal and external factors play.

Objectives

This chapter aims to help learners understand how value is created and delivered through project work. Even though the content is presented as questions and answers, the goal is to build a practical understanding of what *value* means in project management and why it matters. The chapter also helps learners see how different roles, teams, and organizational structures work together to support value delivery.

Through the questions, readers become familiar with the key functions, resources, and processes that help projects move forward successfully. The chapter also highlights how feedback, coordination, and ongoing improvement keep the value delivery system healthy and effective. By working through this material, learners strengthen their ability to think about projects not just as tasks, but as contributors to meaningful outcomes.

Single select multiple choice questions

1. **Which of the following best describes "business value"?**
   a. The total cost of project resources
   b. The net quantifiable benefit (tangible or intangible) that supports the health and well-being of the organization
   c. The number of completed deliverables
   d. The duration of the project lifecycle

2. **What is the main purpose of a value delivery system within an organization?**
   a. To complete projects faster
   b. To maximize and sustain value by aligning portfolios, programs, projects, products, and operations with strategy
   c. To reduce the number of projects
   d. To focus only on financial returns

3. **Which of the following is an example of an intangible business value?**
   a. Stockholder equity
   b. Infrastructure capabilities
   c. Brand recognition
   d. Utility

4. **Which condition is not an example of an enterprise environmental factor (EEF) internal to the organization?**
   a. Organizational culture and governance
   b. Geographic distribution of resources
   c. Marketplace conditions
   d. Information technology systems

5. **What is meant by 'organizational process assets' (OPAs)?**
   a. Only financial data
   b. Internal plans, processes, templates, and knowledge repositories that influence project management
   c. External legal requirements
   d. Project team's personal devices

6. **Which of the following would not typically be found in an organization's internal environment?**
   a. Organizational culture
   b. Government regulations
   c. Infrastructure
   d. Information technology systems

7. **Which of the following is a key output of the information flow within a value delivery system?**
   a. Only project deliverables
   b. Performance analysis and strategic updates
   c. Employee payroll
   d. Product backlog

8. **Which of these is not an example of a knowledge repository?**
   a. Issue and defect management data
   b. Project files from previous projects
   c. Marketing advertisements
   d. Historical information and lessons learned

9. **Which organizational structure type is most likely to provide a project manager with high authority and resource availability?**
   a. Functional (centralized)
   b. Organic or simple
   c. Project-oriented
   d. Multidivisional

10. **What is a primary reason for tailoring guidelines within organizational policies?**
    a. To eliminate standard processes
    b. To adapt standard processes to the specific needs of a project
    c. To avoid compliance requirements
    d. To use only external templates

11. **Which of the following is a direct example of a project contributing to environmental sustainability?**
    a. Increasing quarterly profits
    b. Reducing carbon emissions in a new facility
    c. Hiring new staff
    d. Launching a marketing campaign

12. **What is the primary benefit of using preapproved supplier lists and contract templates in projects?**
    a. Enforcing project deadlines
    b. Enabling standardized and efficient procurement processes
    c. Eliminating stakeholder communication
    d. Increasing project costs

13. **Which knowledge repository is most helpful for tracking the resolution of project issues and defects?**
    a. Configuration management
    b. Issue and defect management data
    c. Financial data
    d. Performance metrics

14. **Which organizational structure type provides moderate to high project manager authority and usually a full-time, designated job role?**
    a. Functional (centralized)
    b. Matrix—strong

c. Organic

d. Virtual/network

15. **What is one of the main reasons for updating knowledge repositories during and after a project?**

    a. To comply with legal requirements only

    b. To capture lessons learned and enable continuous improvement

    c. To advertise products

    d. To finalize project accounting

16. **What is the typical impact of not tailoring organizational policies, templates, and procedures to the specific needs of a project?**

    a. Reduced project management effort

    b. Increased risk of misalignment and inefficiency

    c. Guaranteed project success

    d. Elimination of all documentation

17. **Who within the organization is primarily responsible for providing vision and clarifying direction during a project?**

    a. End user

    b. Portfolio manager

    c. Facilities staff

    d. Resource manager

18. **Which of the following is a key function that can be performed by both individuals and teams to ensure effective project delivery?**

    a. Provide oversight and coordination

    b. Secure legal advice

    c. Approve annual budgets

    d. Design company logos

19. **Which of the following is a key function associated with projects?**

    a. Scheduling only

    b. Providing oversight and coordination

    c. Marketing outreach

    d. Auditing only

20. **What is the primary role of a business analyst in a project setting?**

    a. Approving budgets

    b. Gathering and documenting requirements

    c. Managing project risks

    d. Overseeing procurement

21. **Which example best illustrates a project's contribution to community development?**

    a. Launching a new marketing campaign

    b. Constructing a community park

    c. Filing annual taxes

    d. Conducting employee evaluations

22. **From the given following options, who is ultimately responsible for securing resources for a project?**

    a. Project team members

    b. Portfolio managers and project sponsors

    c. End users

    d. Product owners

23. **What is a common trait of hybrid organizational structures?**

    a. They never change

    b. They combine features from multiple structure types

    c. They only use virtual teams

    d. They are exclusive to large organizations

24. **Which of the following best describes the intended use of organizational project closure guidelines?**

    a. To guide the process for ending and documenting project work

    b. To select new vendors

    c. To report daily project status

    d. To evaluate staff performance

25. **What is one of the main purposes of a stakeholder register template as an organizational asset?**

    a. To track project expenses

    b. To systematically record and manage stakeholder information

c. To assign project team roles

d. To schedule project meetings

26. **Which statement about the relationship between product, program, and project management is most accurate?**
    a. They work independently with no overlap
    b. Product management provides vision while programs and projects execute and deliver value
    c. Programs manage only financial data
    d. Projects always outlast products

27. **How does adaptive (agile) project coordination typically differ from predictive approaches?**
    a. Adaptive uses only virtual teams
    b. Adaptive emphasizes self-organization and continuous feedback
    c. Predictive avoids planning
    d. Predictive uses no documentation

28. **Which project function specifically helps ensure that customer and end-user input is directly integrated into ongoing development activities?**
    a. Providing resources
    b. Soliciting and managing feedback
    c. Performing work
    d. Issuing contracts

29. **Which of the following is not an example of organizational knowledge repository content?**
    a. Completed schedules
    b. Lessons learned
    c. Marketing slogans
    d. Risk reports

30. **What is the primary purpose of having progress monitoring processes in place?**
    a. To enforce attendance
    b. To ensure project performance meets or exceeds the value proposition
    c. To update office layouts
    d. To allocate parking

31. **Which competency involves applying problem-solving techniques and dealing with enterprise politics to deliver value?**
    a. Social responsibility
    b. Power skills
    c. Results
    d. Ways of working

32. **Which of the following is most likely to be included in preapproved supplier lists managed as part of OPAs?**
    a. Individual team resumes
    b. Contract templates
    c. Stakeholder engagement plans
    d. Company holiday schedules

33. **Which project characteristic is most influenced by the organization's geographic distribution of resources?**
    a. Project scheduling
    b. Team structure and collaboration methods
    c. Number of deliverables
    d. Project profitability

34. **Which type of organizational structure is most likely to have part-time project managers with low authority?**
    a. Matrix—strong
    b. Project-oriented
    c. Functional (centralized)
    d. Hybrid

35. **What is one benefit of maintaining issue and defect management data repositories?**
    a. Reducing product features
    b. Tracking and resolving problems efficiently
    c. Encouraging repeated mistakes
    d. Limiting stakeholder input

36. **How is "employee capability" treated as an internal EEF?**
    a. Employee satisfaction
    b. Skills, expertise, and specialized knowledge within the organization
    c. Number of employees
    d. Team social events

37. **What distinguishes a virtual/network organizational structure?**
    a. All work is done in one physical office
    b. Networked nodes at points of contact and flexible roles
    c. Only temporary employees are used
    d. Projects never use virtual teams

38. **Why is it important that project teams regularly update organizational knowledge repositories?**
    a. To ensure lessons learned and performance data are available for future projects
    b. To increase paperwork only
    c. To advertise the project
    d. To reduce the need for planning

39. **Which aspect of the project environment may require special consideration when managing international projects?**
    a. Organizational culture only
    b. Legal restrictions and country-specific regulations
    c. Project team size
    d. Project color scheme

40. **What is a practical benefit of using standardized project templates?**
    a. Reducing flexibility in all projects
    b. Ensuring consistency, efficiency, and compliance across projects
    c. Limiting team communication
    d. Increasing project complexity

41. **How can financial considerations as external EEFs affect project planning?**
    a. By determining only the project's color scheme
    b. By influencing cost estimates, budgets, and funding availability
    c. By setting team meeting times
    d. By eliminating project risks

42. **Which project function is most closely associated with aligning project team efforts, removing obstacles, and maintaining focus?**
    a. Performing work
    b. Oversight and coordination
    c. Providing resources
    d. Applying expertise

43. **What is a core reason for organizations to maintain knowledge repositories for metrics?**
    a. To store outdated information
    b. To collect and analyze measurement data for processes and products
    c. To advertise the organization
    d. To register patents

44. **Which project role is primarily responsible for gathering and documenting requirements to ensure alignment with business needs?**
    a. Project sponsor
    b. Business analyst
    c. Functional manager
    d. Resource manager

45. **What is the main function of service-level agreements (SLAs) in projects?**
    a. To define roles in the project team
    b. To set expectations for service quality and performance
    c. To replace project contracts
    d. To schedule vacations

46. **What is a typical reason for a project management team to engage with executives and business unit leaders before project initiation?**
    a. To plan the office party
    b. To advance strategic objectives and improve performance alignment
    c. To assign parking spots
    d. To select project colors

47. **Which organizational process asset is most likely to help a project manager with estimating project costs?**
    a. Product backlog
    b. Historical information repository
    c. Customer feedback forms
    d. Market analysis report

48. **What is a primary benefit of decentralized coordination in project teams, especially in agile environments?**
    a. Increased bureaucracy
    b. Enhanced team self-organization
    c. Slower decision-making
    d. Reduced project flexibility

49. **Which of the following is a key input to most project management planning processes?**
    a. Enterprise environmental factors (EEFs)
    b. Final project deliverables
    c. Customer purchase order
    d. Media releases

50. **Which function is most closely associated with removing obstacles and maintaining team focus during a project?**
    a. Stakeholder management
    b. Oversight and coordination
    c. Product management
    d. Contract negotiation

51. **What is a common feature of "organizational knowledge repositories"?**
    a. They are always external
    b. They store lessons learned and performance metrics
    c. They track only financial transactions
    d. They replace project documentation

Multi-select multiple choice questions

52. **Which two of the following are considered tangible business value elements?**
    a. Goodwill
    b. Profitability
    c. Employee well-being
    d. Market share
    e. Environmental awareness

53. **Which two statements accurately describe the role of operations in the value delivery system?**
    a. Operations support portfolios, programs, and projects
    b. Operations are stand-alone and do not influence projects
    c. Operations interact dynamically with other components to enable strategic outcomes
    d. Operations exist only for payroll functions
    e. Operations function separately from organizational strategy

54. **Which two of the following are examples of organizational knowledge repositories?**
    a. Financial data repositories
    b. Project files from previous projects
    c. Stakeholder meetings
    d. Brand awareness campaigns
    e. Team-building exercises

55. **Which two roles often provide organizational direction and insight on projects?**
    a. Portfolio manager
    b. Project sponsor
    c. Team member
    d. End user
    e. Office administrator

56. **Which two are positive examples of project outcomes that create business value?**
    a. Improved efficiency and productivity
    b. Missed regulatory deadlines
    c. Environmental sustainability achievements
    d. Repeated process errors
    e. Failure to meet stakeholder needs

57. **Which two of the following are considered OPAs?**
    a. Earned value data
    b. Country-specific tax laws
    c. Project templates
    d. Marketplace competition
    e. Public health protocols

58. **Identify two examples of external EEFs:**
    a. Social and cultural influences
    b. Resource availability

c. Government or industry standards
d. Information technology systems
e. Employee skill levels

59. **Which two roles often facilitate and support project work in adaptive/agile projects?**
a. Scrum master
b. Product owner
c. Receptionist
d. Facility manager
e. Security guard

60. **Which two factors are critical considerations when determining an optimal organizational structure for project delivery?**
a. Organizational size
b. Preferred vendor list
c. Strategic objectives
d. Office color scheme
e. Team's lunch schedule

61. **Which two are key responsibilities of a project management team?**
a. Facilitating and mentoring the project team
b. Managing external market trends
c. Managing processes to deliver outcomes
d. Handling only procurement contracts
e. Avoiding stakeholder communication

62. **Which two of the following are considered knowledge repositories in organizations?**
a. Issue and defect management data
b. Social media profiles
c. Historical performance information
d. Personal contact lists
e. Tax returns

63. **Which two functions are described as supporting project delivery beyond the project team's work?**
a. Applying expertise
b. Performing work
c. Organizing team lunches
d. Providing organizational direction and insight
e. Scheduling travel

64. **Which two roles are often responsible for guiding a project's direction in adaptive or hybrid development environments?**
a. Portfolio manager
b. Product owner
c. Scrum master
d. Facilities manager
e. Security guard

65. **Which two examples best represent tangible deliverables in project management?**
a. Infrastructure capabilities
b. Market share
c. Goodwill
d. Employee well-being
e. Public benefit

66. **Which two are examples of policies, processes, and procedures within organizational process assets?**
a. Change control procedures
b. External government standards
c. Product backlog
d. Resource assignment management
e. Social media guidelines

67. **Which two organizational roles often secure project resources at the highest level?**
a. Portfolio managers
b. Project team members
c. Project sponsors
d. End users
e. Business analysts

68. **Which two items should be updated in organizational knowledge repositories during a project?**
a. Lessons learned
b. Team lunch schedules
c. Performance metrics
d. Personal calendars
e. Office supply lists

69. **Which two functions are specifically mentioned as helping teams adapt and improve performance?**
    a. Facilitation
    b. Issue and defect management
    c. Support
    d. Social events
    e. Product branding

70. **Which two factors are most likely to require tailoring of project management processes?**
    a. Organizational culture
    b. Color of project team t-shirts
    c. Project complexity
    d. Office furniture arrangement
    e. Weather outside

71. **Which two organizational process assets are most likely to improve stakeholder engagement?**
    a. Stakeholder register templates
    b. Earned value analysis tools
    c. Project closure guidelines
    d. Communication plan templates
    e. Risk data from previous projects

72. **Which two statements describe the benefits of providing resources throughout the project lifecycle?**
    a. Ensures continuous progress
    b. Guarantees the elimination of all project risks
    c. Allows for quick response to changing needs
    d. Reduces the need for end-user feedback
    e. Limits need for organizational oversight

73. **Which two roles are likely to be directly involved in supporting feedback cycles in adaptive projects?**
    a. Product owner
    b. Scrum master
    c. External auditor
    d. Facilities manager
    e. Finance director

74. **Which two project functions can directly contribute to benefits realization after project closure?**
    a. Oversight and coordination
    b. Issue and defect management
    c. Project closure guidelines
    d. Benefits sustainment activities
    e. Team-building exercises

Fill-in-the-blanks

75. **__ are internal to the organization and may include plans, templates, and historical information that influence project management.**
    a. Enterprise environmental factors
    b. Organizational process assets
    c. Risk registers
    d. Product backlogs

76. **The __ is the desired result or consequence of a process or project, which may be positive (benefits) or negative (disbenefits).**
    a. Product
    b. Outcome
    c. Output
    d. Procedure

77. **__ refers to the conditions not directly controlled by the project team that can enhance or constrain project management options.**
    a. Organizational process assets
    b. Enterprise environmental factors
    c. Project policies
    d. Lessons learned

78. **__ is the integration of people, data, processes, and business systems to create, develop, and maintain a product throughout its lifecycle.**
    a. Product management
    b. Portfolio management
    c. Project management
    d. Operations management

79. **Project __ is the set of individuals performing the project's work and directly responsible for achieving objectives.**

    a. Sponsor b. Team

    c. Management office d. Customer

80. **__ is the process of providing oversight, coordination, and support to align efforts and maintain team focus in a project.**

    a. Facilitation

    b. Oversight and coordination

    c. Risk management

    d. Procurement

81. **__ are conditions not controlled by the project team that can impact or constrain project activities, both internally and externally.**

    a. Knowledge repositories

    b. Enterprise environmental factors

    c. Project assets

    d. Product backlogs

82. **The __ provides decision leadership outside of the project management team's authority and supports project alignment with business objectives.**

    a. Project sponsor

    b. Scheduler

    c. Team member

    d. Facilities manager

83. **__ is responsible for assigning the right personnel, equipment, and expertise to project teams for resource optimization.**

    a. Functional/resource manager

    b. End user

    c. Project customer

    d. Business analyst

84. **The __ is responsible for gathering and documenting requirements to ensure project scope and product functionality match business needs.**

    a. Project sponsor

    b. Business analyst

    c. Project manager

    d. Facilities coordinator

85. **The __ is the set of individuals responsible for performing project work and achieving objectives.**

    a. Project team

    b. Sponsor

    c. End users

    d. Functional manager

86. **__ is the process of contributing specialized knowledge, vision, and skills in a specific subject area within a project.**

    a. Facilitation

    b. Applying expertise

    c. Resource allocation

    d. Product management

87. **__ is a competency that includes adaptability and emotional intelligence, essential for project management teams.**

    a. Ways of working

    b. Business acumen

    c. Power skills

    d. Results orientation

88. **Project __ is a competency related to the application of strategic thinking and aligning projects within the organizational context.**

    a. Leadership b. Acumen

    c. Governance d. Knowledge

89. **A __ is a formal or informal document that provides guidance for how project work should be performed in the organization.**

    a. Policy b. Milestone

    c. Output d. Deliverable

90. **__ are artifacts, practices, or knowledge from the performing organization used to execute or govern a project.**

    a. Organizational process assets

    b. Project deliverables

    c. Project scope statements

    d. Product features

91. **__ is a competency involving the application of standards, methodologies, and frameworks to execute projects.**
   a. Ways of working
   b. Power skills
   c. Social responsibility
   d. Results orientation

92. **__ are government-imposed regulations or requirements that must be considered as external EEFs.**
   a. Organizational procedures
   b. Public health and safety regulations
   c. Templates
   d. Internal policies

93. **The __ may initiate projects at any point in the product lifecycle to create or enhance product components.**
   a. Facilities manager
   b. Product management
   c. Project sponsor
   d. Procurement office

94. **A __ is generally established by the PMO or another function and guides project work, often updated only via organizational policy.**
   a. Work authorization
   b. Policy, process, or procedure
   c. Product feature
   d. Stakeholder meeting

95. **__ is a critical function that helps teams resolve conflicts, build consensus, and advance project objectives in a supportive manner.**
   a. Facilitation
   b. Procurement
   c. Marketing
   d. Auditing

96. **__ are roles that interact with the project management team to address strategic issues impacting a project or product.**
   a. Customers and sponsors
   b. Receptionists
   c. External regulators
   d. Office suppliers

Match the following

97. **Match each item in Table A with the correct description from Table B:**

Table A	Table B
a. Portfolio management	i. Storing and retrieving project and organizational knowledge
b. Organizational structure	ii. Assigning resources and authority in projects
c. Organizational process assets	iii. Internal plans, templates, and historical info used in projects
d. Knowledge repositories	iv. Framework linking strategy to execution
e. Product management	v. Creating, developing, and maintaining products throughout their lifecycle

98. **Match each concept (Table A) to its definition (Table B):**

Table A	Table B
a. Outcome	i. Excess of benefits over investment
b. Artifact	ii. Tangible or intangible item produced by a project
c. Value	iii. Temporary initiative to create value
d. Product	iv. End result or consequence of a process/project
e. Project	v. Document or item created during a project

99. **Match each internal or external project influence in Table A with its correct example in Table B:**

Table A	Table B
a. Internal EEF	i. Organizational culture and structure
b. External EEF	ii. Country or local laws and regulations
c. OPA - Policies	iii. Project closure guidelines
d. OPA - Templates	iv. Risk register template
e. Knowledge repository	v. Lessons learned database

100. **Match each function or role in Table A with its correct description in Table B:**

Table A	Table B
a. Oversight	i. Ensuring project team alignment and removing obstacles
b. Resource manager	ii. Assigns personnel and expertise for the project
c. Business analyst	iii. Gathers and documents requirements
d. Facilitation	iv. Encourages collaboration and consensus on solutions
e. End user	v. Provides feedback and verifies project deliverables

101. **Match each knowledge repository in Table A with the correct contents in Table B:**

Table A	Table B
a. Configuration management	i. Project documents and standards baselines
b. Financial data	ii. Incurred costs and budgets
c. Historical information	iii. Project closure documentation
d. Issue management	iv. Status and resolution of defects
e. Metrics data	v. Performance measurement information

102. **Make correct pair by matching options in Table A with the options given in Table B:**

Table A	Table B
a. Policies	i. Guidelines for conducting project work
b. Procedures	ii. Step-by-step instructions for processes
c. Templates	iii. Standardized project documents and forms
d. Knowledge repositories	iv. Storage of lessons learned and historical data
e. Preapproved supplier list	v. Set of approved vendors for procurement

103. **Match each concept (Table A) to its definition (Table B):**

Table A	Table B
a. Power skills	i. Adaptability and emotional intelligence
b. Social responsibility	ii. Ethical standards and giving back to society
c. Business acumen	iii. Strategic thinking and industry knowledge
d. Ways of working	iv. Applying standards, methodologies, and frameworks
e. Results	v. Achieving tasks and using problem-solving techniques

Concept-based objective questions and answers

104. **How does a value delivery system help organizations achieve strategic alignment?**

A value delivery system integrates portfolios, programs, projects, products, and operations, ensuring that all activities are coordinated and aligned with organizational strategy. This system allows organizations to prioritize efforts, allocate resources efficiently, and adapt to changing needs, maximizing value creation.

105. **Why is it necessary to assess both project outcomes and project management process efficiency when measuring project success?**

Focusing solely on process efficiency might deliver a project on time and on budget, but if the outcomes do not deliver expected value or benefits, the project cannot be considered successful. Conversely, even a project with a strong result can be marred by inefficient or costly management. Both dimensions are essential for real, sustainable success.

106. **What role do enterprise environmental factors (EEFs) play in tailoring project management processes?**

EEFs, both internal and external, shape the choices available to project managers and may require processes to be adapted (tailored) to fit the specific organizational context, constraints, and opportunities. By considering EEFs, project managers can better align their approach to the realities of the environment.

107. **How does continuous feedback from end users and stakeholders contribute to project value?**

Continuous feedback ensures that the evolving needs of end users and stakeholders are integrated into the project, reducing the risk of delivering a product or service that doesn't meet expectations. This approach increases alignment, credibility, and satisfaction, ultimately enhancing the value delivered.

108. **Why is tailoring organizational process assets important for project management success?**

Tailoring OPAs, such as templates and checklists, allows project teams to adapt best practices to their project's unique needs, increasing efficiency and relevancy, and improving the likelihood of achieving desired outcomes.

109. **How do organizational knowledge repositories benefit ongoing and future projects?**

They store and make accessible critical data, lessons learned, performance metrics, and historical information, allowing teams to avoid repeating mistakes and leverage proven solutions, ultimately raising project success rates.

110. **What is the value of engaging end users and stakeholders continuously throughout the project lifecycle?**

Continuous engagement helps ensure that deliverables remain relevant, requirements are accurately captured, and stakeholder satisfaction is achieved, reducing the risk of rejection or missed expectations at project closure.

111. **Describe how program and project management work together within a product lifecycle.**

Program management may oversee related projects within a product lifecycle, ensuring coordination and synergy, while project management delivers specific features or improvements. This collaboration supports comprehensive development and efficient value delivery.

112. **How does providing organizational direction benefit a project's outcome?**

Organizational direction helps set priorities, clarify requirements, and align project efforts with strategic value, which maximizes the project's contribution to organizational goals.

113. **What is the significance of integrating product management within a portfolio?**

Integrating product management ensures product investments align with business strategy, prioritizes high-value initiatives, and enables efficient allocation of resources across multiple product lines.

114. **Why is it important for organizations to maintain both policies and knowledge repositories as part of their process assets?**

Policies provide consistent guidance and structure for conducting project work, while knowledge repositories capture ongoing learning, lessons, and performance data. Together, they help standardize practices and encourage continuous improvement.

115. **Explain why project management teams need a mix of skills and leadership styles.**

Projects involve diverse people, challenges, and situations; a mix of skills and leadership styles enables teams to respond effectively to changing needs and stakeholder expectations, enhancing the likelihood of project success.

Conclusion

This chapter provided readers with a comprehensive look at how value is delivered within organizations through effective project management. By engaging with various question formats, aspirants have developed a deeper understanding of how projects, programs, portfolios, and operations interact as part of a unified system.

Value delivery stands at the core of project management practice. Whether through increased efficiency, enhanced stakeholder satisfaction, or positive social and environmental outcomes, each element discussed in this chapter contributes to meaningful and lasting impact.

As readers progress to subsequent chapters, these concepts form a strong foundation for further study. A clear grasp of value delivery principles will enable aspirants to tailor their project management approach to diverse environments and better support organizational objectives.

The next chapter, will continue to build on these fundamentals, focusing on the project environment, product management, core project functions, and critical roles that all play a part in achieving successful value delivery.

References

1. Project Management Institute (PMI). A Guide to the Project Management Body of Knowledge (PMBOK® Guide) – Eighth Edition. Project Management Institute, 2024. Used as the primary source for concepts related to value delivery, organizational systems, and the principles that guide effective project management.
2. Project Management Institute (PMI). The Standard for Project Management . PMI, 2024. Consulted for its structured explanation of performance domains, system interactions, and the broader framework that supports value-driven project delivery.
3. Project Management Institute (PMI). The Standard for Project Management – System for Value Delivery. PMI, 2024. Referred to for understanding how organizations design, operate, and improve their value delivery systems, and how projects function within that system.
4. PMI Lexicon of Project Management Terms. Project Management Institute. Used to ensure accuracy and consistency in the terminology applied throughout the question bank.

Answers

Q. No.	Answer(s)
1	b
2	b
3	c
4	c
5	b
6	b
7	b
8	c
9	c
10	b
11	b
12	b
13	b
14	b
15	b
16	b
17	b
18	a
19	b
20	b
21	b
22	b
23	b
24	a
25	b
26	b
27	b
28	b
29	c
30	b
31	c
32	b
33	b
34	c

Q. No.	Answer(s)
35	b
36	b
37	b
38	a
39	b
40	b
41	b
42	b
43	b
44	b
45	b
46	b
47	b
48	b
49	a
50	b
51	b
52	b, d
53	a, c
54	a, b
55	a, b
56	a, c
57	a, c
58	a, c
59	a, b
60	a, c
61	a, c
62	a, c
63	a, d
64	b, c
65	a, b
66	a, d
67	a, c
68	a, c

Q. No.	Answer(s)
69	a, c
70	a, c
71	a, d
72	a, c
73	a, b
74	a, d
75	b
76	b
77	b
78	a
79	b
80	b
81	b
82	a
83	a
84	b
85	a
86	b
87	c
88	b
89	a
90	a
91	a
92	b
93	b
94	b
95	a
96	a
97	a - iv b – ii c - iii d - i e - v

Q. No.	Answer(s)
98	a - iv b - v c - i d - ii e - iii
99	a - i b - ii c - iii d - iv e – v
100	a - i b - ii c - iii d - iv e – v
101	a - i b - ii c - iii d - iv e – v
102	a - i b - ii c - iii d - iv e – v
103	a - i b - ii c - iii d - iv e – v

CHAPTER 3
Project Management Principles

Introduction

This chapter presents a comprehensive set of questions and answers designed to help learners engage deeply with the foundational principles that guide modern project management. The PMI standard emphasizes that project management is not merely a collection of tools, templates, or processes; it is a mindset shaped by beliefs, behaviors, and ways of thinking that influence how project teams interpret situations and respond to challenges. The principles outlined in the standard, such as adopting a holistic view, focusing on value, embedding quality, leading with accountability, integrating sustainability, and building an empowered culture, serve as broad, flexible guidelines that can be applied across industries, project types, and organizational environments.

By working through this question bank, learners gain exposure to how these principles operate in practice and how they support the proactive, ownership-driven, and value-focused mindset described in the standard. The questions encourage learners to think about the interconnected nature of project components, the importance of systems thinking, and the role of leadership and culture in shaping project outcomes. This chapter aims to make these concepts accessible, relatable, and easier to internalize, helping learners build confidence as they prepare for real-world project responsibilities.

Objectives

This chapter will help learners develop a clear and practical understanding of the core principles that guide effective project management. Through a structured set of questions and answers, this chapter encourages readers to explore how these principles shape the mindset required for modern project work, one that is proactive, grounded in ownership, and consistently focused on delivering value. The material aims to deepen learners' appreciation of why adopting a holistic view is essential for navigating complexity, how value becomes the central measure of project success, and why embedding quality into both processes and deliverables strengthens outcomes. It also highlights the importance of accountable leadership, empowered team culture, and the integration of sustainability across all project areas. By engaging with these questions, learners gain insight into how principles connect with performance domains such as governance, scope, schedule, finance, stakeholders, resources, and risk. Ultimately, the chapter seeks to equip learners with the ability to interpret these principles not just as theoretical ideas but as practical guides that influence everyday decisions and behaviors within project environments.

Single select multiple choice questions

1. **Which statement best describes the nature of project management principles?**
    a. There are strict rules to be followed in every project
    b. They provide guidance and reinforce a mindset for project professionals
    c. They are only relevant for large organizations
    d. They are optional suggestions with no real impact

2. **Which of the following is not one of the six principles of project management?**
   a. Adopt a Holistic View
   b. Integrate Sustainability Within All Project Areas
   c. Maximize Profit at All Costs
   d. Embed Quality into Processes and Deliverables

3. **What does the "project management mindset" emphasize?**
   a. Only following checklists
   b. A set of beliefs, ways of thinking, and habits that enable value, adaptability, and strategy
   c. Avoiding change in any form
   d. Relying on a single leadership style

4. **Which principle is most closely associated with systems thinking and managing interdependencies within a project?**
   a. Be an Accountable Leader
   b. Adopt a Holistic View
   c. Focus on Value
   d. Build an Empowered Culture

5. **Which project management principle centers on maximizing return for the organization, customer, and stakeholders?**
   a. Embed Quality into Processes and Deliverables
   b. Focus on Value
   c. Integrate Sustainability Within All Project Areas
   d. Build an Empowered Culture

6. **Which principle promotes the integration of environmental, social, and economic considerations into all project areas?**
   a. Be an Accountable Leader
   b. Focus on Value
   c. Integrate Sustainability Within All Project Areas
   d. Adopt a Holistic View

7. **The "ownership" dimension of the project management mindset primarily integrates which two principles?**
   a. Adopt a Holistic View and Embed Quality
   b. Focus on Value and Integrate Sustainability
   c. Be an Accountable Leader and Build an Empowered Culture
   d. Embed Quality and Focus on Value

8. **What is a key impact of applying the "Embed Quality into Processes and Deliverables" principle?**
   a. Projects will always be completed faster
   b. Deliverables consistently meet stakeholder needs and acceptance criteria
   c. Teams can ignore stakeholder requirements
   d. Only the final product is evaluated

9. **What is an example of the principle of Be an Accountable Leader in action?**
   a. Ignoring team feedback
   b. Leading cross-team discussions to resolve conflicts and improve collaboration
   c. Delegating all decisions to external consultants
   d. Avoiding difficult decisions

10. **Which principle encourages the creation of a team environment where individuals feel safe to contribute and collaborate?**
    a. Embed Quality into Processes and Deliverables
    b. Build an Empowered Culture
    c. Focus on Value
    d. Integrate Sustainability Within All Project Areas

11. **Which of the following best describes the value-driven dimension of the project management mindset?**
    a. Repeating past practices regardless of results
    b. Focusing on delivering outcomes that align with strategy and sustainability
    c. Limiting project objectives to cost reduction
    d. Avoiding stakeholder involvement

12. **In which principle is the concept of "psychological safety" most emphasized?**
    a. Be an Accountable Leader
    b. Embed Quality into Processes
    c. Integrate Sustainability
    d. Build an Empowered Culture

13. **Which of the following best supports the continuous improvement of project processes?**
    a. Accepting initial process designs as final
    b. Regularly reviewing and refining processes based on lessons learned
    c. Avoiding stakeholder feedback
    d. Ignoring process efficiency

14. **Which leadership trait is not emphasized in the Be an Accountable Leader principle?**
    a. Integrity
    b. Self-awareness
    c. Openness to feedback
    d. Domineering control

15. **What is the direct benefit of integrating sustainability into project decision-making?**
    a. Increased short-term costs only
    b. Contributing to long-term organizational resilience and innovation
    c. Limiting team diversity
    d. Reducing attention to stakeholder needs

16. **Which principle is best demonstrated by encouraging diverse perspectives and open participation?**
    a. Adopt a Holistic View
    b. Embed Quality
    c. Build an Empowered Culture
    d. Be an Accountable Leader

17. **What is a core goal of embedding quality into both deliverables and processes?**
    a. To speed up all project phases
    b. To ensure acceptance criteria are met or exceeded
    c. To focus only on compliance
    d. To reduce stakeholder engagement

18. **Which performance domain benefits most directly from a strong focus on value?**
    a. Governance
    b. Schedule
    c. Risk
    d. All domains

19. **What does "shared leadership" mean in project management?**
    a. Only the project manager makes decisions
    b. Leadership is exercised by different team members as needed
    c. Leadership is assigned by vote
    d. Only executives lead

20. **What is the main purpose of linking project management principles to organizational and ethical values?**
    a. To ensure strict rule-following
    b. To help project managers drive positive and sustainable changes
    c. To focus only on financial outcomes
    d. To reduce documentation

21. **Which principle is especially important for preventing scope creep and misalignment?**
    a. Embed Quality into Processes
    b. Adopt a Holistic View
    c. Build an Empowered Culture
    d. Integrate Sustainability

22. **What is a practical way to demonstrate the Focus on Value principle in an adaptive project?**
    a. Focusing only on technical outputs
    b. Collaborating with stakeholders to determine valuable features iteratively
    c. Avoiding customer input
    d. Prioritizing speed over quality

23. **Which prinziple is best demonstrated when a team regularly updates its processes to reflect feedback and lessons learned?**
    a. Build an Empowered Culture
    b. Embed Quality into Processes and Deliverables

c. Be an Accountable Leader

d. Focus on Value

24. **What is the chief benefit of integrating sustainability goals into project documentation?**

a. Short-term cost reduction

b. Ensuring sustainability is monitored and achieved throughout the project

c. Avoiding stakeholder involvement

d. Limiting innovation

25. **A project team is struggling with balancing environmental goals and tight budget constraints. Which principle should guide their decision-making to ensure both long-term and short-term organizational objectives are met?**

a. Be an Accountable Leader

b. Focus on Value

c. Integrate Sustainability Within All Project Areas

d. Build an Empowered Culture

26. **During a project review, the team realizes that stakeholder expectations have shifted due to changing market conditions. What is the most appropriate principle to address this situation?**

a. Embed Quality into Processes and Deliverables

b. Adopt a Holistic View

c. Focus on Value

d. Be an Accountable Leader

27. **A project manager encourages team members to bring up potential risks early and to suggest improvements to processes. Which principles are most closely applied?**

a. Focus on Value and Be an Accountable Leader

b. Embed Quality and Adopt a Holistic View

c. Adopt a Holistic View and Build an Empowered Culture

d. Integrate Sustainability and Focus on Value

28. **A team faces a major setback due to a supplier failure. The project manager organizes a lesson-learned session and invites team members to suggest changes for future resilience. Which principle is most directly demonstrated?**

a. Be an Accountable Leader

b. Focus on Value

c. Integrate Sustainability

d. Embed Quality into Processes

29. **Which principle would be most helpful in ensuring that a new training program is designed to meet both current organizational needs and future talent development objectives?**

a. Integrate Sustainability

b. Adopt a Holistic View

c. Embed Quality into Processes and Deliverables

d. Focus on Value

Multi-select multiple choice questions

30. **Which two principles are most strongly reflected in a project management mindset that balances people, profit, and planet?**

a. Adopt a Holistic View

b. Integrate Sustainability Within All Project Areas

c. Focus on Value

d. Be an Accountable Leader

e. Embed Quality into Processes

31. **Which two of the following are key characteristics of projects managed with a holistic view?**

a. Integrated decision-making

b. Enhanced communication

c. Eliminating all project risks

d. Maximizing gold plating

e. Ignoring stakeholder input

32. **Which two principles are closely tied to the "proactive" dimension of the project management mindset?**
    a. Be an Accountable Leader
    b. Embed Quality into Processes and Deliverables
    c. Focus on Value
    d. Adopt a Holistic View
    e. Build an Empowered Culture

33. **Which two are cited as impacts of embedding quality into project processes and deliverables?**
    a. Reduced need for rework
    b. Greater use of unskilled labor
    c. Improved decision-making and process improvement
    d. Ignoring customer feedback
    e. Lower morale

34. **Which two attributes are key to accountable leadership as described in the standard?**
    a. Integrity, honesty, and fairness
    b. Self-awareness
    c. Avoiding feedback
    d. Rigid leadership style
    e. Delegating all authority

35. **Which two benefits are associated with integrating sustainability across all project areas?**
    a. Increased employee satisfaction
    b. Decreased shareholder trust
    c. Improved relationships with stakeholders
    d. Higher consumption of resources
    e. Reduced legal compliance

36. **Which two factors are fostered by building an empowered culture in project teams?**
    a. Clarity on roles and responsibilities
    b. Proactive stakeholder collaboration
    c. Ignoring diversity
    d. Mandating rigid processes
    e. Complete elimination of risk

37. **Which two project management principles support accountability and psychological safety in teams?**
    a. Be an Accountable Leader
    b. Build an Empowered Culture
    c. Embed Quality into Processes
    d. Focus on Value
    e. Ignore feedback

38. **Which two actions are examples of a value-focused approach in project management?**
    a. Continually evaluating project alignment with business objectives
    b. Customizing products to maximize features regardless of need
    c. Terminating projects unlikely to deliver intended value
    d. Focusing only on deliverables
    e. Avoiding stakeholder feedback

39. **Which two characteristics are most closely associated with a holistic approach to project sustainability?**
    a. Quantifying both positive and negative contributions
    b. Avoiding stakeholder engagement
    c. Considering environmental and social impacts
    d. Focusing only on financial returns
    e. Ignoring compliance requirements

40. **Which two principles are most closely linked to enabling stakeholder satisfaction?**
    a. Embed Quality into Processes
    b. Focus on Value
    c. Build an Empowered Culture
    d. Integrate Sustainability
    e. Ignore feedback

41. **Which two attributes are characteristics of a growth mindset in project management?**
    a. Willingness to adapt
    b. Avoiding new ideas
    c. Continual learning
    d. Sticking to old habits
    e. Limiting team input

42. **Which two are impacts of a lack of commitment to quality in project management?**
    a. Poor project outcomes
    b. Increased rework
    c. More stakeholder engagement
    d. Improved efficiency
    e. Enhanced morale

43. **Which two are actions an accountable leader takes?**
    a. Fosters team trust
    b. Adapts leadership style to the situation
    c. Ignores stakeholder concerns
    d. Delegates without direction
    e. Avoids personal reflection

44. **Which two benefits are directly linked to empowered project teams?**
    a. Higher morale
    b. Increased innovation
    c. Lower stakeholder trust
    d. Less communication
    e. More rigid processes

45. **Which two dimensions are essential for embedding sustainability within project management?**
    a. Social equity
    b. Ignoring environmental impact
    c. Environmental stewardship
    d. Limiting communication
    e. Financial focus only

46. **Which two attributes are necessary for high-performing project teams in an empowered culture?**
    a. Clarity of roles
    b. Openness to diverse perspectives
    c. Rigid hierarchy
    d. Avoiding collaboration
    e. Focus on short-term gains

47. **Which two practices support a proactive project management mindset?**
    a. Anticipating challenges
    b. Waiting for problems to escalate
    c. Planning ahead
    d. Ignoring risks
    e. Delaying decisions

48. **Which two principles are most supported by the resource and risk performance domains?**
    a. Embed Quality into Processes
    b. Be an Accountable Leader
    c. Integrate Sustainability Within All Project Areas
    d. Adopt a Holistic View
    e. Build an Empowered Culture

49. **Which two elements are emphasized in team agreements for empowered project cultures?**
    a. Behavioral expectations
    b. Collaborative practices
    c. Non-participation
    d. Individual competition
    e. Avoiding feedback

50. **Which two benefits are directly linked to accountable leadership in project teams?**
    a. Higher trust and morale
    b. Reduced need for communication
    c. Improved decision-making
    d. Elimination of feedback
    e. Increased team conflict

51. **Which two are outcomes of integrating sustainability within all project areas?**
    a. Improved brand value
    b. Increased legal risks
    c. Reduced operational waste
    d. Greater stakeholder resistance
    e. Less resilience

52. **Which two actions would most support building an empowered culture in a virtual project team?**
    a. Promoting open communication
    b. Encouraging shared leadership
    c. Restricting team input
    d. Ignoring time zone differences
    e. Centralizing all decisions

53. **Which two principles work together to align project execution with organizational strategy and stakeholder needs?**
    a. Focus on Value
    b. Embed Quality Into Processes
    c. Be an Accountable Leader
    d. Integrate Sustainability
    e. Build an Empowered Culture

54. **Which two factors should project teams consider when defining team agreements for empowered cultures?**
    a. Clear roles and responsibilities
    b. Rigid assignment of work
    c. Behavioral norms
    d. Limited stakeholder engagement
    e. Competition for leadership

55. **A large global project team is distributed across several countries, with varying local regulations, work cultures, and stakeholder expectations. Which two principles are essential for supporting project success in this context?**
    a. Adopt a Holistic View
    b. Focus on Value
    c. Rigid leadership
    d. Integrate Sustainability
    e. Ignore stakeholder feedback

56. **A project sponsor wants to know how the project will avoid rework and unnecessary costs while ensuring stakeholder satisfaction. Which two principles should the project manager highlight?**
    a. Embed Quality into Processes and Deliverables
    b. Build an Empowered Culture
    c. Focus on Value
    d. Integrate Sustainability
    e. Be an Accountable Leader

57. **A company wants to roll out a new product quickly but faces concerns about long-term environmental impact and regulatory compliance. Which two principles are most directly relevant to guide the project team?**
    a. Integrate Sustainability Within All Project Areas
    b. Focus on Value
    c. Be an Accountable Leader
    d. Embed Quality into Processes
    e. Build an Empowered Culture

58. **A project manager is tasked with leading a high-stakes project that involves shifting customer requirements, regulatory uncertainty, and multiple stakeholder groups. Which two principles should be prioritized to enable success?**
    a. Adopt a Holistic View
    b. Focus on Value
    c. Embed Quality into Processes
    d. Integrate Sustainability
    e. Be an Accountable Leader

59. **In a project post-mortem, the team identifies that unclear roles and lack of trust led to communication breakdowns. Which two principles could have best prevented this?**
    a. Build an Empowered Culture
    b. Adopt a Holistic View
    c. Focus on Value
    d. Be an Accountable Leader
    e. Embed Quality into Processes

Fill-in-the-blanks

60. **The project management mindset is composed of three dimensions: proactive, ownership, and __.**
    a. Value-driven b. Risk-averse
    c. Compliance d. Hierarchical

61. **The principle that involves understanding projects as interconnected systems is called _.**
    a. Adopt a Holistic View
    b. Focus on Value
    c. Be an Accountable Leader
    d. Embed Quality

62. **The principle that focuses on achieving organizational objectives, societal benefits, and customer needs is __.**
    a. Focus on Value
    b. Embed Quality
    c. Build an Empowered Culture
    d. Be an Accountable Leader

63. **The principle of __ ensures that project deliverables consistently meet acceptance criteria and stakeholder expectations.**
    a. Embed Quality into Processes and Deliverables
    b. Integrate Sustainability
    c. Focus on Value
    d. Build an Empowered Culture

64. **A(n) __ leader is responsible for decision-making, ethical behavior, and fostering trust.**
    a. Accountable b. Passive
    c. Hierarchical d. Task-oriented

65. **Integrating __ within all project areas means considering social, environmental, and economic impacts across the lifecycle.**
    a. Sustainability b. Quality
    c. Value d. Risk

66. **Building an __ culture involves mutual trust, clear roles, and proactive collaboration.**
    a. Empowered b. Isolated
    c. Traditional d. Rigid

67. **The principle of Focus on Value requires constant evaluation and __ of project alignment with business objectives.**
    a. Adjustment b. Elimination
    c. Delay d. Standardization

68. **Projects managed with a(n) __ view are more likely to align with organizational strategy and achieve integrated outcomes.**
    a. Holistic b. Linear
    c. Simplistic d. Isolated

69. **The __ mindset in project management is fundamental for adaptability, value, and strategy.**
    a. Growth b. Static
    c. Risk-averse d. Rigid

70. **Integrated decision-making is a hallmark of the __ principle.**
    a. Adopt a Holistic View
    b. Focus on Value
    c. Embed Quality
    d. Be an Accountable Leader

71. **The triple bottom line in project management refers to people, profit, and __.**
    a. Planet b. Planning
    c. Procedures d. Policies

72. **The ability to consistently meet acceptance criteria and stakeholder expectations is central to the principle of __.**
    a. Embed Quality into Processes and Deliverables
    b. Integrate Sustainability
    c. Focus on Value
    d. Build an Empowered Culture

73. **Effective leaders in project management demonstrate __ by adapting their style to the situation.**
    a. Flexibility b. Rigidity
    c. Avoidance d. Indifference

74. **Ensuring that all project components contribute positively, or that negative contributions are quantified, is part of a __ approach.**
    a. Holistic b. Linear
    c. Top-down d. Minimalist

75. **The principle of __ Within All Project Areas encourages responsible use of resources and consideration for future generations.**
    a. Integrate Sustainability
    b. Embed Quality
    c. Focus on Value
    d. Adopt a Holistic View

76. **__ is a leadership attribute that involves understanding motives, values, and strengths.**
    a. Self-awareness b. Compliance
    c. Rigidity d. Passivity

77. **A(n) __ culture is characterized by open collaboration and mutual trust.**
    a. Empowered b. Isolated
    c. Competitive d. Rigid

78. **The principle of Focus on Value encourages teams to continually __ alignment with business objectives and intended outcomes.**
    a. Evaluate b. Ignore
    c. Delay d. Standardize

79. **The principle of __ encourages teams to see beyond immediate deliverables and consider the full impact of project decisions.**
    a. Adopt a Holistic View
    b. Focus on Value
    c. Embed Quality
    d. Be an Accountable Leader

80. **Focusing on __ helps ensure that projects deliver benefits that justify investment.**
    a. Value b. Schedule
    c. Risk d. Compliance

81. **The principle of __ requires meeting or exceeding customer and stakeholder expectations as a routine part of project work.**
    a. Embed Quality into Processes and Deliverables
    b. Integrate Sustainability
    c. Adopt a Holistic View
    d. Build an Empowered Culture

82. **Effective project leaders demonstrate __ by being open to feedback and supporting their teams' needs.**
    a. Humility b. Rigidity
    c. Indifference d. Competition

83. **Integrating __ means considering the well-being of people, planet, and profit in all project decisions.**
    a. Sustainability b. Risk
    c. Quality d. Compliance

84. **When a project team applies systems thinking to address interdependencies and unforeseen impacts, they are practicing the principle of __.**
    a. Adopt a Holistic View
    b. Embed Quality
    c. Focus on Value
    d. Integrate Sustainability

85. **A team regularly adjusts their work based on stakeholder feedback and changing business needs, demonstrating the principle of __.**
    a. Focus on Value
    b. Build an Empowered Culture
    c. Be an Accountable Leader
    d. Integrate Sustainability

86. **Proactively managing risks and anticipating challenges throughout the project lifecycle is a key part of the __ dimension.**
    a. Proactive b. Ownership
    c. Value-driven d. Sustainability

87. **When leadership is shared and adaptively exercised by different team members as the situation demands, the principle of __ is being applied.**
    a. Be an Accountable Leader
    b. Build an Empowered Culture
    c. Focus on Value
    d. Embed Quality

88. **Effective use of feedback loops and quality gates throughout a project is central to the principle of __.**
    a. Embed Quality into Processes and Deliverables
    b. Focus on Value
    c. Integrate Sustainability
    d. Adopt a Holistic View

Match the following

89. **Match each concept (Table A) to its definition (Table B):**

Table A	Table B
a. Adopt a Holistic View	i. Maximizing return and aligning outcomes with goals
b. Focus on Value	ii. Managing projects as interconnected systems
c. Embed Quality into Processes	iii. Guiding with integrity and responsibility
d. Be an Accountable Leader	iv. Fostering trust, collaboration, and open contribution
e. Build an Empowered Culture	v. Meeting or exceeding acceptance criteria

90. **Match each concept (Table A) to its definition (Table B):**

Table A	Table B
a. Proactive dimension	i. Belief in adaptability and learning
b. Ownership dimension	ii. Fosters accountability, collaborative teams
c. Value-driven dimension	iii. Integrates sustainability and stakeholder value
d. Systems thinking	iv. Considers interdependencies and root causes
e. Growth mindset	v. Anticipates challenges, plans ahead

91. **Match entries in Table A with the options provided in Table B:**

Table A	Table B
a. Adopt a Holistic View	i. Maximizing return and aligning outcomes with goals
b. Focus on Value	ii. Guiding with integrity and responsibility
c. Embed Quality into Processes	iii. Managing projects as interconnected systems
d. Be an Accountable Leader	iv. Fostering trust, collaboration, and open contribution
e. Build an Empowered Culture	v. Meeting or exceeding acceptance criteria

92. **Match entries in Table A with the options provided in Table B:**

Table A	Table B
a. Proactive dimension	i. Belief in adaptability and learning
b. Ownership dimension	ii. Considers interdependencies and root causes
c. Value-driven dimension	iii. Integrates sustainability and stakeholder value

Table A	Table B
d. Systems thinking	iv. Fosters accountability, collaborative teams
e. Growth mindset	v. Anticipates challenges, plans ahead

93. **Match each knowledge domain in Table A with the correct contents in Table B:**

Table A	Table B
a. Governance domain	i. Alignment with objectives and requirements
b. Scope domain	ii. Transparency and accountability
c. Schedule domain	iii. Proactive identification and mitigation
d. Finance domain	iv. Realistic timelines and adaptive planning
e. Risk domain	v. Efficient resource allocation and cost control

94. **Make the correct pair by matching the options in Table A with the options given in Table B:**

Table A	Table B
a. Environmental sustainability	i. Listening and collaborating with all parties
b. Social responsibility	ii. Establishing clear task completion methods
c. Economic sustainability	iii. Reducing carbon footprint and resource use
d. Stakeholder engagement	iv. Improving community well-being
e. Process definition	v. Direct cost savings and long-term value

95. **Match each concept (Table A) to its definition (Table B):**

Table A	Table B
a. Proactive habit	i. Shared behavioural expectations
b. Shared leadership	ii. Anticipating challenges
c. Value-driven mindset	iii. Multiple people exercising leadership skills
d. Team agreement	iv. Ongoing process refinement
e. Continuous improvement	v. Focus on outcomes and sustainability

96. **Match each concept (Table A) to its definition (Table B):**

Table A	Table B
a. Integrity	i. Harnessing varied perspectives for project value
b. Self-awareness	ii. Moral principles and honesty
c. Flexibility	iii. Enabling proactive team collaboration
d. Empowerment	iv. Understanding motives and strengths
e. Diversity	v. Adapting leadership style to the situation

97. **Match each concept (Table A) to its definition (Table B):**

Table A	Table B
a. Sustainability benefit - Financial	i. Clear task and work assignment methods
b. Sustainability benefit- Operational	ii. Listening and collaboration
c. Sustainability benefit- organizational	iii. Employee satisfaction and improved relationships
d. Stakeholder engagement	iv. Cost savings and sustainable investment
e. Process definition	v. Innovation and productivity improvements

98. **Match entries in Table A to their suitable meaning in Table B:**

Table A	Table B
a. Performance	i. Do processes maintain consistency?
b. Conformity	ii. Do customers give valuable feedback?
c. Reliability	iii. Do deliverables function as intended?
d. Satisfaction	iv. Are outputs maximized for input?
e. Efficiency	v. Are deliverables aligned with specifications?

Concept-based objective questions and answers

99. **Why are project management principles described as "complementary" and "supplementary" in the standard?**

    Project management principles are complementary because they support and reinforce each other without contradiction. They are supplementary because each principle adds value and guidance in different areas, helping project professionals navigate complex and interconnected project environments.

100. **How does the proactive dimension of the project management mindset contribute to project success?**

    The proactive dimension encourages forward-thinking, anticipates potential challenges, and ensures appropriate planning at every stage. This leads to better preparation, risk mitigation, and alignment with strategic objectives.

101. **What is the significance of "integrated decision-making" in projects managed with a holistic view?**

    Integrated decision-making considers diverse perspectives and the interconnection of project elements, leading to more sustainable, effective, and well-aligned outcomes.

102. **Why is it important for project teams to shift their focus from deliverables to intended outcomes?**

    Focusing on intended outcomes ensures that the project achieves its vision or purpose and delivers value, not just outputs.

103. **How can embedding quality into both processes and deliverables impact project outcomes?**

    Embedding quality leads to deliverables that meet or exceed acceptance criteria, minimizes rework, improves efficiency, and enhances customer and stakeholder satisfaction.

104. **In what way does accountable leadership influence project teams and results?**

    Accountable leaders build trust, ensure ethical behavior, and motivate teams, resulting in higher performance, better decision-making, and resilience in facing challenges.

105. **How does integrating sustainability into project management benefit organizations and stakeholders?**

    It supports long-term value by balancing social, environmental, and economic outcomes, improving reputation, and opens new opportunities while meeting regulatory and stakeholder demands.

106. **What does "empowered culture" mean in the context of project management, and why does it matter?**

An empowered culture means teams and stakeholders trust each other, collaborate proactively, and are clear on roles and agreements, which enables higher engagement, innovation, and project success.

107. **How do the project management principles relate to performance domains?**

Principles provide the mindset and foundational guidance, while performance domains describe the practical arenas where that mindset is applied to create the outcome.

108. **How do the project management principles relate to performance domains?**

The principles serve as the mindset and foundation that inform and guide all project management practices, while the performance domains provide the practical mechanics and structure for effective project delivery. By linking principles with performance domains, practitioners ensure their actions are rooted in the right mindset and values, leading to well-rounded and effective project management.

109. **What is the practical value of systems thinking for a project manager applying a holistic view?**

Systems thinking enables project managers to see the interdependence within a project, anticipate ripple effects, and make decisions that account for the overall system, not just isolated parts. This leads to better risk management, communication, and alignment with organizational strategy.

110. **Why should project managers consider both short-term and long-term value when making decisions?**

Considering both ensures that immediate gains do not undermine future benefits or sustainability, supporting the organization's strategic goals and stakeholder interests over time.

111. **How does the principle of "Embed Quality" help reduce risk in project management?**

By focusing on quality in both processes and deliverables, teams can prevent defects, reduce rework, and catch issues early, thereby lowering the likelihood and impact of risks throughout the project lifecycle.

112. **What is the difference between leadership and authority in the context of project management?**

Authority is the formal position or control given to individuals, while leadership is about inspiring, influencing, and motivating others—regardless of official roles. Effective project management relies on both, but leadership is essential for cultivating trust and driving positive outcomes.

113. **Why is stakeholder engagement considered critical in almost every project management principle?**

Engaging stakeholders ensures their needs, perspectives, and feedback are considered, which increases buy-in, alignment, and the chance of successful project outcomes.

114. **How does the principle of integrating sustainability create opportunities for innovation in projects?**

By prioritizing sustainable solutions, teams are encouraged to find new, resource-efficient methods, materials, and approaches that not only meet project goals but also deliver environmental and social benefits.

115. **What is the role of team agreements in building an empowered culture?**

Team agreements establish shared norms, expectations, and behaviors, promoting trust and accountability. This foundation supports proactive collaboration and enables teams to work more effectively together.

116. **Why is it important for project managers to adapt leadership styles based on the situation?**

Different challenges, teams, and project phases may require different approaches; flexibility in leadership ensures that the project manager can respond effectively to varying needs and circumstances, supporting team performance and project success.

117. **How does continuous improvement support the principle of embedding quality?**

Continuous improvement involves regularly assessing and refining processes and deliverables, which helps maintain quality standards, reduce waste, and increase efficiency throughout the project lifecycle.

118. **What are the key benefits of fostering diversity in project teams?**

Diverse teams bring varied perspectives, skills, and experiences, which enhance creativity, problem-solving, and the ability to address complex challenges collaboratively.

119. **How do the project management principles support the achievement of organizational strategy?**

By guiding decision-making, promoting alignment with strategic goals, and fostering a mindset that values sustainability, quality, leadership, and empowerment, the principles help ensure that projects contribute meaningfully to the broader organizational mission.

120. **How does the principle of holistic view enhance risk management?**

By considering interdependence and the broader project ecosystem, risks can be identified earlier and managed more effectively, minimizing disruptions and strengthening project resilience.

121. **Why is stakeholder diversity valuable in empowered team cultures?**

Diverse stakeholders bring different perspectives, which enrich problem-solving, increase innovation, and improve project outcomes through inclusive collaboration.

122. **What is the relationship between continuous improvement and stakeholder satisfaction?**

Continuous improvement ensures processes and deliverables adapt to stakeholder feedback and evolving needs, leading to higher satisfaction and project success.

123. **In what way does integrating sustainability affect financial performance in projects?**

It can lead to cost savings, reduced risks, access to sustainable financing, and enhanced long-term value for the organization.

124. **How does shared leadership contribute to project team morale?**

It empowers team members, distributes responsibility, and fosters a sense of ownership, which increases trust, motivation, and resilience.

125. **Why is adaptability important in project management leadership?**

Different challenges, teams, and environments require different approaches; adaptability ensures leaders can respond effectively to any situation.

126. **What is the key benefit of embedding quality into project scope management?**

It ensures deliverables meet requirements and prevent rework, leading to greater efficiency and stakeholder satisfaction.

127. **How does integrating sustainability into governance promote long-term value?**

It aligns decision-making with environmental, social, and economic goals, ensuring projects contribute to the organization's strategic mission responsibly.

128. **Why is psychological safety vital in project management teams?**

It enables open communication, risk-taking, and learning from mistakes, which are essential for innovation, collaboration, and effective problem-solving.

129. **How do project management principles support continuous learning and development?**

They encourage adaptability, proactive improvement, reflection, and knowledge sharing, which help teams and organizations grow and achieve better results over time.

130. **How can the integration of all six project management principles support organizational agility in a rapidly changing market?**

By fostering a proactive and collaborative mindset, promoting ongoing learning and adaptation, focusing on stakeholder value, embedding quality and sustainability, and enabling distributed leadership, all six principles together help organizations respond swiftly to change while maintaining alignment with strategic goals and delivering sustainable results.

131. **In a situation where a project must balance conflicting stakeholder interests, which principles and practices should the project manager apply to achieve a fair and effective outcome?**

The project manager should apply Adopt a Holistic View to understand interdependencies, Focus on Value to keep efforts aligned with strategic benefits, Build an Empowered Culture for inclusive dialogue, and be an Accountable Leader to ensure ethical and transparent decision-making.

132. **What strategies can teams use to ensure quality processes are sustained in highly adaptive or hybrid project environments?**

Teams should establish clear acceptance criteria, use frequent feedback loops, embed continuous improvement, and empower all members to identify and address quality issues proactively.

133. **How does the value-driven dimension of the project management mindset help resolve resource allocation disputes among departments?**

By focusing on what delivers the greatest value to the organization and stakeholders, resource decisions are made transparently and objectively, reducing conflict and supporting the best outcomes.

134. **Why is it important for project managers to continuously align project activities with the broader organizational strategy, even if the original business case was clear?**

This is because organizational priorities, market conditions, or stakeholder needs may evolve during project execution, ongoing alignment ensures the project remains relevant, valuable, and responsive to change.

Conclusion

This chapter concludes by reaffirming that project management principles are the compass that guides project teams through uncertainty, complexity, and change. They provide a stable foundation that helps project professionals remain adaptable, thoughtful, and value-driven in diverse environments. The questions and answers in this chapter are designed to deepen learners' understanding of these principles and encourage them to think critically about how mindset influences project outcomes.

By exploring how principles connect with performance domains such as governance, scope, schedule, finance, resources, stakeholders, and risk, learners gain a clearer picture of how theory translates into practice. The chapter reinforces that successful project management is not about rigid adherence to processes but about applying principles with judgment, awareness, and a commitment to delivering meaningful results. The insights gained here prepare learners to approach future chapters and real project scenarios with greater confidence and clarity.

With this foundation strengthened, the transition to the next chapter becomes a natural progression, moving from why projects should be managed a certain way to how those principles unfold across different phases and development approaches. This shift helps the reader see how principles influence life-cycle selection, adaptability, and execution flow, creating a smooth bridge between understanding intent and applying it in practice.

References

1. Project Management Institute (PMI). The Standard for Project Management . Project Management Institute, 2024. Primary reference for the principles, mindset dimensions, and performance domain interactions that form the foundation of this chapter's question bank.
2. Project Management Institute (PMI). The Standard for Project Management – Project Management Principles. PMI, 2024. Used extensively to explain the six project management principles, their intent, their practical application, and their influence on project behaviour and outcomes.
3. Project Management Institute (PMI). A Guide to the Project Management Body of Knowledge (PMBOK® Guide) – Eighth Edition. PMI, 2024. Consulted for supporting concepts related to performance domains, quality, value delivery, and the broader project management framework.
4. PMI Lexicon of Project Management Terms. Project Management Institute. Referred to for maintaining consistency and accuracy in terminology across the question bank.

Answers

Q. No.	Answers
1	b
2	c
3	b
4	b
5	b
6	c
7	c
8	b
9	b
10	b
11	b
12	d
13	b
14	d
15	b
16	c
17	b
18	d
19	b
20	b
21	b
22	b
23	b
24	b

Q. No.	Answers
25	c
26	c
27	c
28	d
29	a
30	b, c
31	a, b
32	b, d
33	a, c
34	a, b
35	a, c
36	a, b
37	a, b
38	a, c
39	a, c
40	a, b
41	a, c
42	a, b
43	a, b
44	a, b
45	a, c
46	a, b
47	a, c
48	c, d

Q. No.	Answers
49	a, b
50	a, c
51	a, c
52	a, b
53	a, d
54	a, c
55	a, d
56	a, c
57	a, d
58	a, b
59	a, d
60	a
61	a
62	a
63	a
64	a
65	a
66	a
67	a
68	a
69	a
70	a
71	a

Q. No.	Answers
72	a
73	a
74	a
75	a
76	a
77	a
78	a
79	a
80	a
81	a
82	a
83	a
84	a
85	a
86	a
87	a
88	a
89	a -ii b -i c -v d -iii e -iv

Q. No.	Answers
90	a -v b -ii c -iii d -iv e -i
91	a -iv b -i c -v d -ii e -iv
92	a -v b -iv c -iii d -ii e -i
93	a -ii b -i c -iv d -v e -iii
94	a -iii b -iv c -v d -i e -ii

Q. No.	Answers
95	a -ii b -iii c -v d -i e -iv
96	a -ii b -iv c -v d -iii e -i
97	a -iv b -v c -iii d -ii e -i
98	a -iii b -v c -i d -ii e -iv

CHAPTER 4
Project Lifecycles

Introduction

This chapter introduces learners to the foundational concept of the **project lifecycle**, a core element of modern project management practice. Every project, regardless of its industry or complexity, progresses through a series of phases and activities from initiation to closure. Understanding this lifecycle is essential because it shapes how project managers plan, execute, monitor, and deliver outcomes that align with organizational strategy. This chapter, with the help of a variety of questions, explains how project phases, development approaches, delivery cadence, and project management focus areas come together to form a structured yet flexible framework for managing work. It also highlights how different lifecycle models, predictive, adaptive, and hybrid, respond to varying levels of uncertainty, stakeholder involvement, and scope stability. This question bank is designed to help learners internalize these ideas through more than a hundred questions that encourage deeper reasoning rather than simple recall.

Objectives

The objective of this chapter is to strengthen learners' understanding of how project lifecycles operate and why they matter in real-world project environments. Through the questions provided, learners will explore how phases are structured, how phase gates support decisionmaking, and how cost, risk, and stakeholder influence evolve over time. The chapter also aims to clarify the distinctions between predictive, adaptive, and hybrid development approaches, helping learners recognize when each approach is most appropriate based on factors such as requirements stability, innovation level, regulatory constraints, and organizational culture. By engaging with these questions, learners will gain insight into how delivery cadence, integrated baselines, iterative planning, and flow-based scheduling influence project outcomes. Ultimately, the goal is to help learners develop the ability to evaluate project conditions and select or recommend a lifecycle approach that maximizes value, reduces uncertainty, and supports effective governance throughout the project's duration.

Single select multiple choice questions

1. **Which statement best captures the primary distinction between a project lifecycle and a product lifecycle as outlined in the standard?**
   a. The project lifecycle only applies to adaptive approaches, while the product lifecycle is used in predictive projects.
   b. The project lifecycle provides the framework for managing a project from start to closure, while the product lifecycle focuses on outcomes produced by the project.
   c. The project lifecycle is limited to closing processes, whereas the product lifecycle is ongoing.
   d. The project lifecycle is determined by the product owner; the product lifecycle is determined by the project team.

2. **In a hybrid project, which scenario most accurately represents the use of both predictive and adaptive approaches simultaneously?**
   a. The project starts adaptively and switches fully to predictive after requirements stabilize.
   b. The project uses adaptive methods for one deliverable and predictive for another, with both running in parallel.
   c. The project only uses predictive approaches after the planning phase.
   d. Predictive methods are chosen, but adaptive elements are never applied.

3. **Select the one attribute that is not a typical characteristic used to define a project phase.**
   a. Duration
   b. Entrance criteria
   c. Stakeholder's personal preference
   d. Resource requirements

4. **What is the primary function of a phase gate in the project lifecycle?**
   a. To launch the next project
   b. To formally review and determine if the phase outcomes and exit criteria have been met before progressing
   c. To double project resources
   d. To reduce the number of project phases

5. **In the context of adaptive approaches, which constraint is typically the most flexible?**
   a. Cost
   b. Schedule
   c. Scope
   d. All constraints are fixed

6. **Which scenario best illustrates the use of flow-based scheduling within an adaptive approach?**
   a. Delivering a full product only at project closure
   b. Limiting work in progress and maximizing deliverable flow based on team capacity
   c. Setting all scope, schedule, and cost at project start
   d. Reusing traditional organizational structure

7. **In the standard, what is the recommended project management response when the integrated baseline must evolve due to increased requirements uncertainty?**
   a. Freeze the baseline and avoid changes
   b. Use an adaptive approach with periodic reviews and evolving baseline
   c. Terminate the project
   d. Focus solely on cost reduction

8. **Which delivery cadence is most aligned with continuous integration and deployment practices in software projects?**
   a. Single delivery
   b. Multiple sequential deliveries
   c. Periodic delivery
   d. Continuous delivery

9. **According to the standard, when is the ability of stakeholders to influence project scope typically the highest?**
   a. At the end of the project
   b. During project closure
   c. At the start of the project or phase
   d. After all deliverables are completed

10. **What is the primary benefit of progressive elaboration in project planning?**
    a. Reduces planning time
    b. Allows for ongoing refinement of plans as more information is gathered
    c. Fixes all requirements up front
    d. Avoids stakeholder involvement

11. **When using a predictive approach, what is the primary advantage of delivering a product incrementally rather than as a final release?**
    a. It eliminates planning needs.
    b. It allows stakeholders to use and benefit from parts of the product before the full project is done.
    c. It reduces the importance of change control.
    d. It avoids the need for phase gates.

12. **According to the standard, which element is most likely to remain fixed in an adaptive project using an inverted triangle of constraints?**
    a. Scope
    b. Schedule
    c. Project team composition
    d. Stakeholder roles

13. **Which of the following is not a potential decision outcome at a phase gate?**
    a. Continue to next phase
    b. Continue with modification
    c. Park the project temporarily
    d. Automatically increase the project budget

14. **Which delivery cadence is most likely to be selected for a project where regulatory submissions are required at set milestones?**
    a. Single delivery
    b. Multiple deliveries (sequential)
    c. Continuous delivery
    d. Randomized delivery

15. **Which project attribute is most likely to influence the choice between a predictive and adaptive approach when safety requirements are paramount?**
    a. Degree of innovation
    b. Safety requirements
    c. Team size
    d. Geographic location

16. **According to the standard, what distinguishes a project phase from a project management Focus Area?**
    a. A phase always covers all Focus Areas
    b. A phase is a time-based division, while Focus Areas are sets of actions that can overlap and repeat within phases
    c. Focus Areas are only for closing projects
    d. Phases and Focus Areas are synonymous

17. **When planning for a hybrid project, what is a key consideration in sequencing adaptive and predictive streams?**
    a. Always start with predictive streams
    b. Consider which deliverables require flexibility versus stability and sequence accordingly
    c. Complete all adaptive work before any predictive work
    d. Ignore dependencies between streams

18. **The standard identifies which factor often necessitates the use of a predictive approach for a deliverable?**
    a. High product innovation
    b. Stringent safety requirements
    c. Team preference
    d. Desire for rapid change

19. **What is the primary function of progressive elaboration in adaptive project planning?**
    a. To freeze the plan early
    b. To allow for ongoing, detailed planning as the project progresses and information emerges
    c. To shorten every project phase
    d. To minimize stakeholder involvement

20. **In the context of Focus Areas, what is the key role of the Initiating Focus Area?**
    a. Tracking project performance
    b. Defining the project or phase, aligning stakeholders, and securing authorization
    c. Only closing the project
    d. Allocating resources for procurement

21. **What is the principal reason for using a timeboxed cadence in adaptive project approaches, according to the standard?**
    a. To reduce the need for stakeholder engagement
    b. To provide regular opportunities for feedback and planning based on completed work
    c. To eliminate the need for monitoring
    d. To maximize up-front documentation

22. **According to the standard, how does the cost of changes typically behave across the project lifecycle in a predictive approach?**
    a. Cost of changes stays constant
    b. Cost of changes decreases over time
    c. Cost of changes increases as the project progresses
    d. Cost of changes is highest at project completion

23. **In an adaptive approach, when are requirements typically refined or changed?**
    a. Only during the planning phase
    b. At the end of the project
    c. Iteratively, throughout the project, based on ongoing feedback
    d. Only during project closure

24. **What is the role of the project manager and team in selecting the project lifecycle according to the standard?**
    a. Always dictated by the PMO
    b. They may advise management or select the cycle based on project needs
    c. They must select adaptive methods for all projects
    d. Only the sponsor can choose

25. **Which project characteristic is most likely to necessitate the use of an iterative planning approach?**
    a. Well-known, stable requirements
    b. High degree of uncertainty and evolving requirements
    c. Fixed regulatory submission schedule
    d. No need for stakeholder input

26. **In a scenario where a project team must repeatedly revisit planning as new information emerges, which planning technique is most strongly recommended by the standard?**
    a. Progressive elaboration
    b. Freeze planning at the start
    c. Planning only at phase closure
    d. Finalize all plans post-initiating

27. **Which is the most likely risk if a project lifecycle is chosen without considering the nature of deliverables?**
    a. The project will always finish early
    b. The development approach may not align with the project's requirements, leading to inefficiency
    c. Stakeholders will be more satisfied
    d. Project cost will be unaffected

28. **When a hybrid approach is used, what must be managed carefully to avoid integration failure?**
    a. Team compensation plans
    b. Handoffs and dependencies between adaptive and predictive streams
    c. Only stakeholder communication
    d. The physical workspace design

29. **The standard highlights which attribute is critical for an adaptive approach to be successful in a digital project?**
    a. Low stakeholder involvement
    b. Frequent iterative feedback and scope evolution
    c. A single delivery at project closure
    d. Complete scope freeze at project start

30. **Which Focus Area is most likely to address detecting performance variances and recommending corrective actions?**
    a. Executing
    b. Planning
    c. Monitoring and Controlling
    d. Initiating

31. **In which scenario does the standard suggest that a predictive approach may still benefit from phased incremental delivery?**
    a. When stakeholder engagement is low, and requirements are unclear
    b. When the overall scope is well understood, but phased delivery offers value due to complexity or risk
    c. When regulatory requirements prohibit all increments
    d. When the team is not co-located

32. **What is the main advantage of having Focus Areas interact dynamically rather than sequentially, as described in the standard?**
    a. It eliminates the need for planning
    b. It allows for more responsive and adaptive project management across phases and iterations
    c. It ensures all resources are allocated up front
    d. It minimizes the need for monitoring

33. **What is the impact of not updating the project management plan during execution when significant changes occur, as described in the standard?**
    a. The project will always finish on time
    b. The plan may become misaligned with objectives, increasing the risk of failure
    c. Stakeholders will be more satisfied
    d. Change requests are unnecessary

34. **According to the standard, what is the key advantage of using a rolling wave planning approach in a complex project?**
    a. It locks down the scope early
    b. It enables detailed planning for imminent work and high-level planning for later work, supporting adaptability
    c. It eliminates the need for monitoring
    d. It prevents stakeholder changes

35. **In a scenario where a project team is managing multiple, parallel deliverables that do not have to be completed sequentially, what delivery cadence is most appropriate?**
    a. Single delivery
    b. Multiple, parallel deliveries
    c. Waterfall
    d. Continuous delivery only

Multi-select multiple choice questions

36. **Which two scenarios most accurately require a hybrid development approach according to the standard?**
    a. A construction project with a fixed foundation and a user interface that will evolve through feedback
    b. A project with all requirements defined before kickoff
    c. An infrastructure project with regulatory requirements and a separate agile software module
    d. A project where incremental delivery is not allowed
    e. A project with no interdependent deliverables

37. **According to the standard, which two variables about deliverables most strongly influence the choice of project development approach?**
    a. Requirements certainty
    b. Degree of scope stability
    c. Project manager's personal style
    d. Stakeholder's vacation schedule
    e. Marketing budget

38. **Which two factors about organizational culture and structure may guide teams to select an adaptive approach?**
    a. Preference for network-oriented structure
    b. Hierarchical structure with rigid authority
    c. Culture that values flexible thinking and innovation
    d. Focus on minimizing stakeholder involvement
    e. Prohibition of remote work

39. **Which two project variables are most likely to make iterative or adaptive approaches preferable?**
    a. Significant stakeholder involvement and evolving requirements
    b. Fixed schedule and cost
    c. Highly regulated environment
    d. Small, co-located teams
    e. Value from delivering work early, even if incomplete

40. **According to the standard, which two actions are most relevant during the Monitoring and Controlling Focus Area?**
   a. Tracking and measuring project performance
   b. Adjusting the project management plan as needed
   c. Approving marketing budgets
   d. Finalizing business case
   e. Team-building events

41. **Which two statements best describe the relationship between project Focus Areas and project phases, as outlined in the standard?**
   a. Focus Areas are sequential, never overlapping
   b. Focus Areas can overlap and interact within and across project phases
   c. Project phases divide time, Focus Areas provide action structure
   d. Focus Areas are only for predictive projects
   e. Focus Areas must always align with the product lifecycle

42. **In an adaptive project, which two practices help maintain alignment with evolving stakeholder needs?**
   a. Frequent feedback loops
   b. Strict up-front planning with no changes
   c. Iterative planning and execution
   d. Ignoring incremental delivery
   e. Freezing requirements after the first iteration

43. **According to the standard, which two factors are most critical for selecting a project development approach for a global, distributed team?**
   a. Organizational structure
   b. Team location
   c. Team member's food preferences
   d. Project sponsor's vacation
   e. Project color scheme

44. **A hybrid approach is particularly beneficial when which two conditions are present?**
   a. The project has both highly stable and highly uncertain deliverables
   b. The organization prohibits all change
   c. One stream is adaptive, the other is predictive
   d. All requirements are fixed and known
   e. All stakeholders want the same delivery cadence

45. **Which two project Focus Areas are most likely to require participation at every phase of both predictive and adaptive lifecycles?**
   a. Initiating
   b. Monitoring and Controlling
   c. Closing
   d. Planning
   e. Executing

46. **Which two statements best describe how monitoring and controlling activities are implemented in adaptive projects, according to the standard?**
   a. Monitoring and controlling are performed only at project closure
   b. These activities may occur more frequently or less consistently due to the need for ongoing adjustments
   c. Monitoring and controlling is a separate, stand-alone Focus Area
   d. Monitoring and controlling often overlap with execution in adaptive projects
   e. Monitoring and controlling should be avoided in iterative cycles

47. **According to the standard, which two best describe the nature of project phase attributes?**
   a. They may be unique and measurable for each phase
   b. They are always the same for all projects
   c. They include entrance and exit criteria
   d. They must be determined by external regulators
   e. They are only relevant in closing

48. **Which two aspects are important when selecting an adaptive approach for a digital project as described by the standard?**
    a. The need for frequent feedback and the likelihood of changing requirements
    b. Deliverables are always fixed
    c. The need for up-front, detailed planning
    d. Project is in a heavily regulated environment
    e. Partial delivery and scope evolution are expected

49. **Which two factors should guide the use of an incremental approach within a predictive lifecycle?**
    a. Overall scope is well understood
    b. Phased delivery offers advantages due to size or risk
    c. All requirements are unknown
    d. Stakeholder feedback is not valued
    e. Regulatory review is not required

50. **The standard describes four patterns of hybrid project management. Which two are illustrated by the figures in the text?**
    a. Adaptive phases followed by predictive rollout
    b. Only predictive phases
    c. Simultaneous use of adaptive and predictive approaches
    d. Adaptive followed by adaptive
    e. Predictive with no adaptation

51. **Which two statements best explain why organizations often standardize a few project lifecycles rather than using a new one for every project?**
    a. Standardization increases consistency in project management practices
    b. It supports efficiency in training and resource allocation
    c. It is mandated by all regulatory bodies
    d. It reduces stakeholder involvement
    e. It eliminates the need for any tailoring

52. **According to the standard, which two practices are critical for project teams using adaptive approaches to maximize value and manage uncertainty?**
    a. Frequent review and planning based on feedback
    b. Documenting all requirements at the project start
    c. Allowing requirements to evolve
    d. Fixing scope at project initiation
    e. Avoiding stakeholder input

53. **Which two types of project variables are most likely to influence the selection of delivery cadence?**
    a. The nature of deliverables and stakeholder expectations
    b. Project team size only
    c. The color scheme of the project documents
    d. Resource allocation only
    e. Amount of required regulatory oversight

54. **Which two factors most significantly increase the need for Focus Areas to overlap in modern project management?**
    a. Iterative, adaptive approaches and complex, multi-phase projects
    b. Lack of stakeholder engagement
    c. Waterfall-only methods
    d. Prohibition of rolling wave planning
    e. Projects with no monitoring

55. **Hybrid Level 2, as described in the standard, is characterized by which two conditions?**
    a. Predictive and adaptive approaches both contribute significantly
    b. Only predictive methods are used
    c. Adaptive approach is dominant with minor predictive elements
    d. Both approaches are balanced and critical to success
    e. Hybrid method is only used in closing

56. **Which two best describe why the Focus Areas model is applicable regardless of project lifecycle approach?**
    a. It provides a flexible structure for managing key actions
    b. It is only used in predictive approaches
    c. It supports tailoring to specific project and organizational needs
    d. It requires sequential execution only
    e. It cannot be applied in adaptive environments

57. **Which two challenges are mitigated by using phase gates at both the start and end of each phase?**
    a. Ensuring project readiness before starting a phase
    b. Preventing unplanned resource allocation
    c. Guaranteeing all project changes are accepted
    d. Confirming exit criteria have been met before progressing
    e. Mandating adaptive approaches for all projects

58. **Which two variables are most likely to be optimized by flow-based scheduling in an adaptive approach?**
    a. Work in progress (WIP)
    b. Frequency of phase gates
    c. Flow of deliverables
    d. Requirement of upfront documentation
    e. Rate of change control board meetings

59. **Which two project types are most suited for an adaptive or hybrid approach according to the standard?**
    a. Projects with high requirements uncertainty
    b. Projects driven by innovation and need for rapid feedback
    c. Projects with all requirements defined and fixed
    d. Projects with minimal stakeholder involvement
    e. Projects requiring no change during execution

60. **The standard describes multiple approaches for hybrid projects. Which two patterns are not considered hybrid according to the figures in the standard?**
    a. Adaptive phase followed by predictive rollout
    b. Predictive phase with no adaptive component
    c. Simultaneous adaptive and predictive streams
    d. Largely predictive with a minor adaptive element
    e. Largely adaptive with no predictive component

61. **Which two Focus Areas are most directly responsible for ensuring a project's value proposition is achieved as project conditions change, according to the standard?**
    a. Planning
    b. Executing
    c. Monitoring and Controlling
    d. Closing
    e. Initiating

62. **Which two statements best capture the standard's guidance on tailoring project lifecycles?**
    a. Tailoring optimizes outcomes for the project's unique context
    b. Standardizing all elements removes the need for project manager expertise
    c. Tailoring supports the integration of Focus Areas with industry or organizational needs
    d. Tailoring is discouraged in adaptive approaches
    e. Tailoring increases project inflexibility

63. **Which two variables, if ignored, can cause a project's development approach to fail to achieve its objectives?**
    a. Deliverables' nature and requirements certainty
    b. Project manager's attire
    c. Organizational structure and culture

d. Color of project Gantt charts
e. Stakeholder engagement

64. **Which two challenges are best addressed by using a hybrid approach combining predictive and adaptive elements?**
    a. Managing mixed stability and uncertainty in deliverables
    b. Ensuring that all work is completed by one team
    c. Adapting to evolving business needs while maintaining control over stable elements
    d. Avoiding all change
    e. Mandating only a single cadence

65. **Which two statements describe the impact of not performing phase gate reviews as described in the standard?**
    a. Risks of proceeding without meeting criteria increase
    b. Opportunities for early problem detection are missed
    c. Project cost will always decrease
    d. Planning becomes unnecessary
    e. Stakeholder engagement is maximized

Fill-in-the-blanks

66. **The project lifecycle provides the foundational __ for managing a project, regardless of the specific work or approach.**
    a. Framework b. Product
    c. Deliverable d. Contract

67. **A __ is a collection of logically related project activities that culminate in one or more deliverables or outcomes.**
    a. Phase b. Charter
    c. Sprint d. Iteration

68. **During a __, a review is conducted to verify exit criteria and decide on next steps, such as continuation, modification, or closure.**
    a. Phase gate b. Daily standup
    c. Product release d. Deliverable check

69. **The __ approach is suitable when requirements are highly uncertain and subject to frequent change.**
    a. Adaptive b. Predictive
    c. Hybrid d. Waterfall

70. **Progressive __ refers to ongoing planning and refinement as more information becomes available throughout the project.**
    a. Elaboration b. Delivery
    c. Closure d. Feedback

71. **In a(n) __ approach, work is reviewed at regular intervals, and the integrated baseline evolves based on stakeholder feedback.**
    a. Adaptive b. Predictive
    c. Waterfall d. Incremental

72. **Projects with a high degree of __ often benefit from an adaptive or hybrid approach, as noted in the standard.**
    a. Complexity b. Routine
    c. Regulation d. Simplicity

73. **The __ Focus Area consists of processes or actions to formally complete or close a project, phase, or contract.**
    a. Closing b. Executing
    c. Planning d. Monitoring

74. **The __ approach is characterized by planning most work up front and controlling changes through phase gates.**
    a. Predictive b. Adaptive
    c. Hybrid d. Incremental

75. **A(n) __ delivery cadence is common in agile software projects for frequent value release.**
    a. Periodic b. Single
    c. Sporadic d. Static

76. **A(n) __ approach is particularly useful when the final features of the product are refined based on market needs during the project.**

a. Adaptive b. Predictive
c. Hybrid d. Waterfall

77. **The __ Focus Area includes actions for coordinating resources, managing engagement, and performing project activities.**

a. Executing b. Planning
c. Initiating d. Closing

78. **A project team considering team size, colocation, and remote work as variables for selecting a development approach is addressing __ considerations.**

a. Organizational b. Regulatory
c. Stakeholder d. Contractual

79. **__ is the practice of incrementally delivering value to production on an ongoing basis, emphasizing automation and frequent deployments.**

a. Continuous delivery
b. Periodic delivery
c. Single delivery
d. Predictive delivery

80. **__ refers to the iterative process of updating and refining the project plan as more information becomes available.**

a. Progressive elaboration
b. Waterfall planning
c. Scope freezing
d. Adaptive closure

81. **In a(n) __ project approach, the cost and staffing levels are usually lowest at the start, increase during work, and drop at the end.**

a. Predictive b. Adaptive
c. Hybrid d. Incremental

82. **When a project is divided into phases with unique attributes and specific entrance and exit criteria, these are known as __.**

a. Project phases b. Focus Areas
c. Deliverable gates d. Iterations

83. **_ is the method of scheduling that aims to maximize the flow of deliverables and minimize waste, popular in adaptive approaches.**

a. Flow-based scheduling
b. Predictive resource allocation
c. Waterfall planning
d. Scope freezing

84. **In predictive approaches, the integrated baseline is typically established early and includes scope, schedule, and __.**

a. Cost b. Feedback
c. Regulation d. Agile team roles

85. **In adaptive approaches, a cycle of __ is essential for refining both the plan and the deliverables.**

a. Feedback
b. Budgeting
c. Freezing requirements
d. Regulatory approval

86. **In the standard, projects that are designed to deliver value to production on an ongoing basis using automation are described as having __ delivery.**

a. Continuous b. Periodic
c. Single d. Multiple

87. **The variable that refers to the degree to which a project's scope is stable throughout execution is called __ stability.**

a. Scope b. Cost
c. Schedule d. Risk

88. **__ approaches require significant up-front planning to ensure safety compliance, especially in products with rigorous safety requirements.**

a. Predictive b. Adaptive
c. Incremental d. Hybrid

89. **When project requirements are not fully defined up front, and partial deliveries are expected, the standard recommends a(n) __ approach.**

a. Adaptive b. Predictive
c. Waterfall d. Integrated

90. __ cycles are used in adaptive projects to enable ongoing feedback and incremental delivery.
    a. Iterative
    b. Predictive
    c. Closing
    d. Waterfall

91. The standard states that in adaptive approaches, __ is often used to limit work in progress and optimize delivery flow.
    a. Kanban
    b. Waterfall
    c. Stage gate
    d. Predictive sequencing

92. According to the standard, project team size and __ are important organizational variables when selecting a development approach.
    a. Location
    b. Project color scheme
    c. Product backlog
    d. Stakeholder voting

93. The standard identifies __ as a management philosophy that focuses on identifying and addressing the most significant limiting factor to achieving a goal.
    a. Theory of constraints
    b. Kanban
    c. Agile
    d. Waterfall

94. According to the standard, the __ approach is optimal when the cost of iterating far exceeds its value, such as in certain construction projects.
    a. Predictive
    b. Adaptive
    c. Incremental
    d. Hybrid

95. In the standard, __ are described as checkpoints to compare project performance to expectations and decide future action.
    a. Phase gates
    b. Sprints
    c. Daily standups
    d. Focus Areas

Match the following

96. Match the project development approach with its most appropriate scenario:

Table A	Table B
a. Predictive	i. High uncertainty and evolving requirements
b. Adaptive	ii. Requirements are clear and stable
c. Hybrid	iii. Product delivered in usable segments
d. Incremental	iv. Maximizes deliverable flow, limits WIP
e. Flow-based	v. Separate streams need different approaches

97. Match each Focus Area with its primary purpose:

Table A	Table B
a. Initiating	i. Track, measure, and regulate performance
b. Planning	ii. Develop/refine objectives and course of action
c. Executing	iii. Complete work as per the current plan
d. Monitoring and controlling	iv. Formally complete or terminate the project/phase
e. Closing	v. Align stakeholders and authorize the project

98. **Match each cadence type with its best project example:**

Table A	Table B
a. Single delivery	i. Drug development with sequential trial submissions
b. Multiple deliveries	ii. Cloud services are deployed daily
c. Periodic delivery	iii. Security system upgrades in different locations
d. Continuous delivery	iv. Process roll-out at project completion
e. Parallel deliveries	v. Internal software releases every 2 weeks

99. **Match each phase gate location with its primary benefit:**

Table A	Table B
a. End of phase gate	i. Checks alignment with business documents
b. Start of phase gate	ii. Evaluates options for next steps
c. Iteration review	iii. Validates incremental value and feedback
d. Decision point review	iv. Ensures resources and planning are in place
e. Stage gate	v. Confirms deliverable completion and readiness

100. **Match each development approach with its best-matching characteristic:**

Table A	Table B
a. Predictive	i. High uncertainty, iterative feedback cycles
b. Adaptive	ii. Fixed scope, planned up front
c. Incremental	iii. Visual limit of WIP, continuous improvement
d. Hybrid	iv. Early partial delivery, phased outcomes
e. Flow-based	v. Mixes predictive and adaptive approaches

101. **Match each Focus Area with a key artifact or process:**

Table A	Table B
a. Initiating	i. Performance measurement
b. Planning	ii. Transition to operations
c. Executing	iii. Project charter
d. Monitoring	iv. Road-mapping
e. Closing	v. Coordinating resources

102. **Match each project variable with the best-matching recommended approach:**

Table A	Table B
a. Well-known requirements	i. Predictive
b. Highly innovative deliverable	ii. Predictive
c. Project with both stable and evolving parts	iii. Adaptive
d. Strict safety requirements	iv. Adaptive
e. Significant stakeholder participation	v. Hybrid

103. **Match each Focus Area to a typical challenge managed within that area:**

Table A	Table B
a. Initiating	i. Confirming achievement of business goals
b. Planning	ii. Aligning stakeholder expectations
c. Executing	iii. Detecting performance variances
d. Monitoring	iv. Rolling wave adjustments
e. Closing	v. Coordinating and optimizing resources

104. **Match each project management Focus Area with a key risk it helps to manage:**

Table A	Table B
a. Initiating	i. Incomplete transition to operations or benefits
b. Planning	ii. Unaddressed performance variances
c. Executing	iii. Failure to complete work as planned
d. Monitoring	iv. Failure to align the project with strategic goals
e. Closing	v. Inadequate definition of objectives

105. **Match each delivery cadence to its description:**

Table A	Table B
a. Single delivery	i. Regular, fixed interval releases
b. Multiple deliveries	ii. Ongoing, incremental value to production
c. Periodic delivery	iii. All outcomes at project end
d. Continuous delivery	iv. Simultaneous work on separate deliveries
e. Parallel deliveries	v. Components delivered at different times

106. **Match each hybrid level to its characterization:**

Table A	Table B
a. Hybrid Level 1	i. Change-driven, iterative, and incremental
b. Hybrid Level 2	ii. Adaptive dominant with key predictive elements
c. Hybrid Level 3	iii. Plan-driven, fixed scope
d. Adaptive	iv. Predictive dominant, adaptive reduces pain points
e. Predictive	v. Both approaches contribute significantly

107. **Match each scenario to the most suitable development approach:**

Table A	Table B
a. Stable requirements, high upfront certainty	i. Incremental
b. Evolving requirements, high uncertainty	ii. Hybrid
c. Both stable and evolving deliverables	iii. Flow-based
d. Phased value delivery, planned increments	iv. Predictive
e. Maximizing flow and limiting work in progress	v. Adaptive

Concept-based objective questions and answers

108. **Why is it recommended to place phase gates not only at the end but also at the start of project phases?**

Placing phase gates at the start of phases (pre-phase gates) ensures proper alignment, adequate planning, resource allocation, and addressing of risks before progressing. This checkpoint enhances project control and increases the likelihood of success by verifying readiness and alignment before significant work begins.

109. **Why hybrid approaches are increasingly necessary for modern projects, and provide an example of how they might be employed.**

Hybrid approaches combine elements of both predictive and adaptive methodologies, allowing flexibility to address both stable and uncertain areas of a project. This is necessary because most projects have components with differing requirements, stability, and risk. For example, in a smart building project, construction may follow a predictive approach, while IT integration uses adaptive methods.

110. **A project team is determining the best development approach for a new product. The requirements are unclear, stakeholders desire frequent feedback, and regulatory oversight is minimal. Which approach should they choose, and why?**

The team should use an adaptive approach because it is best suited for projects with high uncertainty, evolving requirements, and a need for frequent stakeholder feedback, especially when regulatory demands do not require rigid up-front planning.

111. **What is the significance of delivery cadence, and how does it relate to the choice of development approach?**

Delivery cadence, whether single, multiple, periodic, or continuous—determines how and when value is delivered. Adaptive approaches favor periodic or continuous cadence for regular feedback and adjustment, while predictive favors single or multiple (planned) deliveries. The choice of cadence supports the team's ability to meet business objectives and respond to change.

112. **Discuss how the Focus Areas differ from project phases and why this distinction matters for managing projects as per the standard.**

Focus Areas (Initiating, Planning, Executing, Monitoring and Controlling, Closing) are sets of actions that can occur iteratively and overlap within and across project phases. Project phases are time-based divisions in the project lifecycle. This distinction matters because Focus Areas provide structure for actions that may not align linearly with phases, supporting flexibility and adaptation in management.

113. **Why is it important for large, complex projects to consider using both incremental and hybrid approaches?**

Large, complex projects often have deliverables with different requirement certainty and risk profiles. Using incremental and hybrid approaches allows teams to manage each stream with the most effective method, optimizing value, stakeholder engagement, and risk management. Ignoring this increases the risk of delayed value delivery, missed requirements, and inflexibility in responding to change.

114. **Explain how the relationship between the Focus Areas and project phases supports flexibility and control in both predictive and adaptive lifecycles.**

Focus Areas provide a structure for essential project management actions that may overlap or repeat within and across phases, regardless of the development approach. This flexibility ensures that planning, execution, monitoring, and closing can be tailored and iterated as needed, supporting responsiveness to change and control over project outcomes.

115. **Adaptive approaches use both iterative and incremental methods. Explain the practical differences and benefits of each within the adaptive framework.**

Iterative methods focus on refining and improving the solution through repeated cycles, while incremental methods deliver the product in usable segments that build on each other. Together, they allow for ongoing feedback and early value delivery, enabling the team to adjust to stakeholder needs and reduce risk.

116. **When might a project team choose to "park" a project at a phase gate, and what factors should guide this decision according to the standard?**

A project may be parked if another urgent business initiative arises or if alignment with organizational goals is temporarily lost. The decision should be guided by reviewing current performance, resource availability, and the project's continued alignment with business objectives, as outlined at phase gates.

117. **Explain the role of phase gates in increasing project control. When should they be used for maximum effectiveness?**

The phase gates act as formal checkpoints to review whether exit criteria for a phase have been met; they support informed decisions about project continuation, modification, or closure. They increase control by verifying alignment with objectives and readiness for the next phase. Using phase gates at both the start and end of phases maximizes effectiveness by ensuring readiness before and after each phase.

118. **The progressive elaboration is essential for planning in both predictive and adaptive approaches. Explain why this is important and how it supports project objectives.**

Progressive elaboration allows plans to be refined and expanded as new information emerges, supporting accuracy and adaptability. In predictive projects, it helps avoid over-specification early; in adaptive projects, it enables ongoing response to stakeholder feedback and changing conditions, ensuring objectives are met efficiently.

119. **In a hybrid project, how does the team ensure that predictive and adaptive streams interact effectively, according to the standard?**

By identifying dependencies, sequencing appropriately, and using clear communication for handoffs and integration points, teams ensure that adaptive and predictive streams support each other and deliver integrated project value.

120. **Why delivery cadence selection is a major factor in achieving a project's business objectives.**

Delivery cadence determines how and when project outcomes are delivered. Selecting the right cadence (single, multiple, periodic, or continuous) ensures timely value realization, aligns with stakeholder needs, and enables responsiveness to feedback or shifting priorities, directly supporting business objectives.

121. **How do Focus Areas support effective project management across different industries and development approaches?**

Focus Areas offer a flexible structure for managing key project actions (initiation, planning, execution, monitoring, and closing) that can be tailored to the context of any industry or development approach, supporting effective management, adaptation, and stakeholder alignment.

122. **Define the relationship between delivery cadence and stakeholder satisfaction, and what are the implications for selecting a project lifecycle?**

Delivery cadence affects how frequently stakeholders receive value or feedback. Regular, predictable deliveries (periodic or continuous) allow for ongoing input and adjustments, which is especially important in environments with high uncertainty or evolving needs. Selecting a lifecycle with the appropriate cadence supports greater satisfaction and alignment.

123. **The standard recommends tailoring Focus Areas for each project. Explain why this is necessary.**

Tailoring Focus Areas ensures the project management structure fits the unique needs, complexity, and development approach of the project. If not tailored, the project may become inefficient, misaligned, or unable to respond effectively to change, increasing the risk of failure.

124. **What is the main advantage of having phase gates at both the start and end of phases in a highly regulated project?**

Start gates ensure readiness—plans, resources, and risks are addressed before work begins.

End gates verify that all criteria are met and compliance is achieved. This dual use increases control, ensures compliance, and minimizes risk of late-phase failures.

125. **Why might a project team select an incremental approach within a predictive lifecycle, and what are the key benefits and challenges of this choice?**

Incremental approaches allow for phased delivery when the overall scope is well understood, but early, partial delivery provides stakeholder value or manages risk. Benefits include earlier value realization and more manageable work packages. A challenge is maintaining alignment and integration as increments are added.

126. **How does the standard describe the integration of adaptive and predictive methods within a single hybrid project, and what factors ensure their successful coordination?**

Integration is achieved by assigning adaptive methods to streams with evolving requirements and predictive methods to stable streams, ensuring clear boundaries and communication. Success depends on identifying dependencies, sequencing work appropriately, and managing handoffs.

127. **It is recommended to integrate stakeholder feedback loops in adaptive projects. Discuss the risk if feedback is only collected at project closure and the benefits of ongoing feedback.**

If feedback is only collected at closure, stakeholder needs may be missed, and costly rework or dissatisfaction may arise. Ongoing feedback allows early course correction, better alignment, and increased satisfaction.

128. **Explain why resource allocation decisions should be reevaluated at phase gates in large, multi-phase projects.**

Resource needs and priorities may change during each phase. Reevaluating at phase gates ensures alignment with objectives, prevents resource waste, and supports project viability.

129. **A project is executed in a highly regulated industry with mandatory reviews at each milestone. Describe how phase gates and Focus Areas should be integrated, and the likely consequences if these controls are omitted.**

Phase gates must be placed at key milestones to review compliance, ensure exit criteria are met, and make go/no-go decisions. Focus Areas must be tailored to emphasize compliance, monitoring, and stakeholder alignment at each phase. Omitting these controls increases the risk of undetected noncompliance, rework, and project failure.

130. **Explain how guidance on progressive elaboration and rolling wave planning supports risk management in large, complex projects.**

Progressive elaboration and rolling wave planning allow teams to plan in detail for immediate work while keeping long-term plans flexible, enabling teams to respond to emerging risks and new information, thus reducing exposure to unforeseen threats.

Conclusion

This chapter concludes by reinforcing the idea that project lifecycles are not rigid templates but adaptable frameworks that guide how work is organized and delivered. The questions in this section encourage learners to think critically about how different lifecycle choices influence project performance, stakeholder engagement, and the ability to respond to uncertainty. Whether a project follows a predictive path with stable requirements or an adaptive path with evolving needs, the underlying principles remain the same: align with strategy, manage risk proactively, and deliver outcomes that create value. By mastering the concepts in this chapter, learners become better equipped to navigate diverse project environments and make informed decisions about the most suitable development approach. This understanding lays a strong foundation for advanced project management practice and prepares learners for the complexities they will encounter in real PMP-level scenarios.

Completing this chapter brings the reader to a clear understanding of how projects evolve from initiation phase to closure phase, and why different lifecycle approaches shape planning, delivery, and stakeholder engagement. The upcoming chapter builds directly on this foundation by exploring the core areas of performance that guide every lifecycle choice, such as team effectiveness, development approach, planning, and delivery. This transition helps the reader connect the structural project flow with the behavioral and performance-driven elements that make those structures work in practice, creating a seamless bridge between the Standard and the Guide.

References

1. Project Management Institute (PMI). The Standard for Project Management – Project Lifecycles. Project Management Institute, 2024. Primary source for all concepts related to project phases, development approaches, delivery cadence, and considerations for selecting an appropriate lifecycle. This chapter served as the exclusive reference for understanding predictive, adaptive, and hybrid approaches, as well as the variables influencing lifecycle selection.
2. Project Management Institute (PMI). A Guide to the Project management Body of Knowledge (PMBOK® Guide) – Eighth Edition. PMI, 2024. Consulted for supporting terminology and alignment with the broader project management framework, including integrated baselines, uncertainty management, and project management focus areas.
3. PMI Lexicon of Project Management Terms. Project Management Institute. Used to ensure consistency and accuracy in the use of project management terminology throughout the question bank, particularly terms such as lifecycle, phase gate, cadence, and development approach.

Answers

Q. No.	Answers	Q. No.	Answers	Q. No.	Answers	Q. No.	Answers
1	b	20	b	39	a, e	58	a, c
2	b	21	b	40	a, b	59	a, b
3	c	22	c	41	b, c	60	b, e
4	b	23	c	42	a, c	61	b, c
5	c	24	b	43	a, b	62	a, c
6	b	25	b	44	a, c	63	a, c
7	b	26	a	45	b, d	64	a, c
8	d	27	b	46	b, d	65	a, b
9	c	28	b	47	a, c	66	a
10	b	29	b	48	a, e	67	a
11	b	30	c	49	a, b	68	a
12	b	31	b	50	a, c	69	a
13	d	32	b	51	a, b	70	a
14	b	33	b	52	a, c	71	a
15	b	34	b	53	a, e	72	a
16	b	35	b	54	a, b	73	a
17	b	36	a, c	55	a, d	74	a
18	b	37	a, b	56	a, c	75	a
19	b	38	a, c	57	a, d	76	a

Q. No.	Answers
77	a
78	a
79	a
80	a
81	a
82	a
83	a
84	a
85	a
86	a
87	a
88	a
89	a
90	a
91	a
92	a
93	a
94	a
95	a

Q. No.	Answers
96	i - b ii - a iii - e iv - c v - d
97	i - e ii - b iii - c iv - a v - d
98	i – d ii - a iii - e iv - b v - c
99	i - e ii - d iii - c iv - b v - a

Q. No.	Answers
100	i - b ii - a iii - d iv - e v - c
101	i - c ii - d iii - e iv - a v - b
102	i - b ii - c iii - e iv - a v - d
103	i - b ii - d iii - e iv - c v - a

Q. No.	Answers
104	i - d ii - e iii - c iv - b v - a
105	i - c ii - e iii - a iv - b v - d
106	i - d ii - e iii - b iv - a v - c
107	i - d ii - e iii - b iv - a v - c

SECTION- II

Project Management Practices

Chapter 5
Project Management Performance Domain

Introduction

Each project brings its own set of circumstances, yet the foundation of project success often rests on a handful of key focus areas. These are known as project performance domains, seven essential pillars that offer structure and guidance from the earliest planning stages to final delivery. The domains of Governance, Scope, Schedule, Finance, Stakeholders, Resources, and Risk each contribute a unique perspective on what it takes to deliver meaningful results.

The real value of these domains emerges when considered as part of a cohesive system, rather than as isolated tasks. Actions or changes in one domain often influence outcomes in several others. For instance, an adjustment to the project's scope may have a direct effect on schedules, budgets, and even the risks involved. Recognizing these linkages enables project teams to anticipate challenges, make informed decisions, and maintain overall alignment with project goals.

This resource is intentionally structured as a question bank, distinct from a full-length instructional chapter. Instead of offering extensive explanations, it provides a wide variety of questions aimed at breaking down complex concepts into approachable, real-world scenarios. The design encourages active engagement, prompting readers to think critically, apply their knowledge, and reflect on practical situations that mirror those found in real project environments.

Whether at the beginning of a project management journey or looking to reinforce established skills, readers will find this question bank a practical companion. It is tailored to foster a deeper understanding of how the performance domains shape project outcomes and to support the development of confidence and problem-solving abilities. By working through these questions, readers can shift from passive learning to active mastery, ultimately gaining tools and insights to lead projects to success, regardless of industry or project type.

Objectives

This section is designed as a question bank to support your understanding of the key areas that drive project success, known as the project performance domains. Rather than providing lengthy explanations or theoretical discussions, this resource uses a variety of questions to encourage active learning and practical application. The goal is to help the readers think through common project scenarios, analyze how different domains interact, and sharpen their decision-making abilities.

By working through these questions, readers will be able to grasp the concepts of each domain, such as Scope, Schedule, Risk, or Resources. They will also gain insight into how these focus areas come together in real-world project environments. This question bank aims to prepare you for professional project management exams, as well as to boost readers' confidence in handling real project challenges.

Single select multiple choice questions

1. **Which of the following best explains why project management performance domains are described as "interactive, interrelated, and interdependent"?**
    a. They are each managed by different teams
    b. They are always sequential in each project phase
    c. They must work together as a system to enable successful project outcomes
    d. They are optional and can be excluded as needed

2. **What is the primary purpose of including both leading and lagging indicators in a project governance framework?**
    a. To provide redundant data for reporting
    b. To allow corrective action before issues arise and to assess results after the fact
    c. To measure resource utilization only
    d. To ensure compliance with agile methodologies

3. **Which process in the Governance domain establishes the official link between the project, its business case, and organizational goals?**
    a. Manage Project Knowledge
    b. Plan Sourcing Strategy
    c. Initiate Project or Phase
    d. Assess and Implement Changes

4. **In adaptive projects, how is the scope baseline typically managed?**
    a. Fixed at the start and only changed through formal change control
    b. Updated at each iteration and aligned with prioritized requirements
    c. Managed by the steering committee only
    d. Unchanged after project initiation

5. **Which artifact provides a hierarchical structure connecting project scope and intended value to product scope and is used to prioritize deliverables?**
    a. Work Breakdown Structure (WBS)
    b. Product backlog
    c. Value Breakdown Structure (VBS)
    d. Project charter

6. **What is the primary benefit of rolling wave planning in the Schedule domain?**
    a. It eliminates the need for detailed planning
    b. It allows for high-level planning initially and progressive elaboration as more information becomes available
    c. It fixes all milestones at project start
    d. It only applies to predictive lifecycles

7. **Which reserve types are recognized in the Finance domain and how do they differ from each other?**
    a. Contingency reserve (for known-unknowns, part of the baseline) and management reserve (for unknown-unknowns, not part of the baseline)
    b. Management reserve (for known-unknowns) and contingency reserve (for unknown-unknowns)
    c. Resource reserve and risk reserve
    d. Budget reserve and capital reserve

8. **Which of the following is described as a critical success factor for project outcomes in the Stakeholders domain?**
    a. Formal communication plans
    b. The number of team meetings
    c. An active and engaged project sponsor
    d. Fixed requirements

9. **In the Resources domain, what is one benefit of empowering self-organizing teams, especially in high-variability environments?**
    a. It reduces the need for any resource planning
    b. It allows for more effective adaptation and collaboration
    c. It ensures all decisions are made by the project manager
    d. It limits innovation and creativity

10. **According to the Risk domain, what is the difference between a risk and an issue?**
    a. A risk is a current event; an issue is a future possibility
    b. A risk is uncertain and may or may not occur; an issue has already occurred and requires immediate attention
    c. Both are interchangeable terms
    d. An issue is always positive

11. **Which of the following most accurately describes an effective use of the "Integrate and Align Project Plans" process within the Governance domain for a complex, multi-domain project?**
    a. Consolidating only the schedule and budget into the project plan
    b. Integrating all management plans and baselines from every relevant performance domain, and verifying their alignment with overall strategy and objectives
    c. Creating separate plans for each performance domain and keeping them independent
    d. Focusing only on stakeholder communications during planning

12. **During which process does the project manager gain the authority to allocate resources and make decisions for the project?**
    a. Manage quality assurance
    b. Initiate Project or Phase
    c. Develop Scope Structure
    d. Plan Communications Management

13. **Which of the following is a key risk of not using leading indicators in a project governance system?**
    a. Too much information is gathered
    b. Problems are only identified after they have already impacted the project, making prevention or early correction impossible
    c. Increased focus on value delivery
    d. Stakeholders are too proactive

14. **A project team in a highly regulated industry is tailoring the Scope domain. Which approach best balances regulatory compliance and adaptability?**
    a. Use only informal agreements for scope
    b. Develop a detailed WBS and scope baseline, but include iterative feedback mechanisms for requirements refinement
    c. Allow contractors to define and change the scope at will
    d. Ignore change control and focus only on deliverable count

15. **In a hybrid project, what is the primary challenge for the project manager when integrating predictive and adaptive scheduling components?**
    a. Deciding which tool to use
    b. Aligning high-level predictive milestones with adaptive, iteration-based task delivery, ensuring dependencies and priorities are maintained
    c. Using only backlog refinement
    d. Fixing all activities up front

16. **Which scenario best exemplifies value maximization within the Finance performance domain?**
    a. Achieving the lowest possible cost regardless of outcomes
    b. Balancing cost efficiency with strategic alignment, customer satisfaction, and innovation, even if some costs are higher
    c. Refusing to adjust budgets even for high-value opportunities
    d. Only tracking financial compliance

17. **What specific project risk management approach does the standard recommend for "unknown-unknown" risks?**
    a. List them in the risk register
    b. Allocate management reserves, managed at senior leadership discretion, and employ resilience planning
    c. Use only contingency reserves
    d. Ignore them until they materialize

18. **A project team is using a hybrid approach: the hardware stream is predictive, and the software stream is adaptive. What is the greatest risk if both streams are managed using the same schedule controls and reporting cadence?**
    a. The adaptive stream will become more efficient
    b. The predictive stream will be unable to meet milestones
    c. Misalignment between deliverables, dependencies, and stakeholder expectations due to a lack of tailored controls
    d. All streams will deliver at the same pace

19. **Which scenario best illustrates integrated performance domain interactions as described in PMBOK® v8?**
    a. Only the Scope domain is updated when requirements change
    b. Changes to schedule, scope, or finance are assessed for cascading impacts on resources, risk, and stakeholder engagement before approval
    c. The project manager delegates risk management to the finance team
    d. Stakeholders are never consulted on changes

20. **In a project with frequent regulatory updates, which process is most critical for ensuring compliance and maintaining value delivery?**
    a. Periodic stakeholder analysis
    b. Monitor and Control Project Performance with robust measurement and integrated change control
    c. Only initial risk identification
    d. Ignoring changes until the project closes

21. **Which tailoring consideration would be least relevant when selecting a scheduling approach for a global, distributed team?**
    a. Team experience
    b. Organizational culture
    c. Number of project phases
    d. Buy-in and trust among stakeholders

22. **A project's cost baseline excludes management reserves. What risk does this introduce if the project is exposed to unknown unknowns?**
    a. All risks will be mitigated
    b. There will be no funds available to address unforeseen work within scope
    c. Known risks will not be managed
    d. The cost baseline will automatically adjust

23. **According to the PMBOK® Guide, which of these would be considered a "vanity metric" in project measurement, and why should it be avoided?**
    a. Number of new users for a product
    b. Number of deliverables completed, regardless of value
    c. Cost variance to date
    d. Customer satisfaction score

24. **Which situation best demonstrates the influence of the Stakeholders domain on the Risk domain?**
    a. Stakeholders are surveyed only at project close
    b. Unidentified stakeholders create new risks as the project progresses
    c. Resource allocation is based only on the schedule
    d. Risk responses are planned before stakeholder analysis

25. **Which approach best supports team empowerment in the Resources domain, as described in PMBOK® v8?**
    a. Centralized decision making with strict reporting
    b. Team members making decisions about their work processes and deliverables within clear boundaries
    c. All work assigned only by the project manager
    d. No recognition or feedback

26. **How does the PMBOK® Guide recommend handling ambiguity and uncertainty that does not yet qualify as a risk?**
    a. Ignore it until it becomes a risk

b. Use collaborative problem-solving to clarify and resolve ambiguity before it escalates
c. Immediately escalate all ambiguous items to the sponsor
d. Apply risk responses

27. **In a project where the product backlog is managed by a product owner, which process is most directly responsible for ensuring scope aligns with stakeholder priorities at each iteration?**
    a. Validate Scope
    b. Elicit and Analyze Requirements
    c. Monitor and Control Scope
    d. Develop Scope Structure

28. **You are leading a project with a rapidly changing regulatory environment and multiple external vendors. Which of the following best supports ongoing compliance and alignment with project value delivery?**
    a. Schedule frequent meetings with the PMO
    b. Establish a governance framework that includes formal change control, stakeholder input, and iterative feedback loops for vendor integration
    c. Rely solely on each vendor's compliance protocols
    d. Fix the scope and schedule at project start and avoid changes

29. **A team is struggling with knowledge transfer in a virtual environment. Which solution best aligns with PMBOK® v8 guidance?**
    a. Schedule more status meetings
    b. Develop explicit knowledge repositories (manuals, databases) and facilitate tacit knowledge sharing through retrospectives and virtual mentoring
    c. Assign all knowledge management to the most experienced team member
    d. Ignore tacit knowledge as too difficult to transfer

30. **Your project's stakeholders become dissatisfied late in the project despite on-time, on-budget delivery. What is most likely the root cause?**
    a. Excessive schedule reporting
    b. Insufficient ongoing stakeholder engagement and feedback integration during execution
    c. Too many risk reviews
    d. Too much focus on explicit knowledge

31. **A project experiences repeated resource shortages despite robust planning and high team morale. Which domain is most likely being overlooked?**
    a. Stakeholders
    b. Resources, specifically, monitoring and control resourcing to track actual versus planned resource use and address shortages proactively
    c. Finance
    d. Quality

32. **In a project where scope, schedule, and finance are all tightly constrained, what is the strongest approach for managing risk?**
    a. Accept all risks and focus on execution
    b. Use robust, iterative risk identification and response planning, and maintain both contingency and management reserves
    c. Only perform qualitative risk analysis
    d. Relegate risk management to the end of the project

33. **Which governance approach is best for a rapidly innovating project team that values autonomy?**
    a. Strictly structured governance with centralized decision-making
    b. Lightweight, self-governing model with clear boundaries and iterative feedback
    c. Rigid process auditing
    d. Outsourcing all oversight

34. **Which artifact directly connects project deliverables to their expected value, enabling prioritization?**
    a. Issue log
    b. Work Breakdown Structure
    c. Value Breakdown Structure
    d. Schedule baseline

35. **What is the primary purpose of explicitly separating contingency and management reserves in project budgeting?**
    a. To make reporting easier
    b. To provide transparency and control over funds for known and unknown risks
    c. To avoid tracking reserves
    d. To reduce stakeholder questions

36. **What is the most critical success factor for positive project outcomes in stakeholder management?**
    a. Number of updates sent
    b. Project manager's technical credentials
    c. Active, empowered project sponsor
    d. Use of a single feedback tool

37. **Which resource management strategy best supports adaptability and high performance in a dynamic environment?**
    a. Centralized, fixed assignments
    b. Cross-functional, empowered teams with flexible agreements
    c. Outsourcing all project work
    d. No resource planning

38. **What is the recommended approach for managing "unknown-unknown" risks in a project?**
    a. Ignore them
    b. Allocate management reserves and develop resilience strategies
    c. Add more milestones
    d. Only use qualitative risk analysis

Multi-select multiple choice questions

39. **Which two elements are required for effective project governance metrics, according to the PMBOK® Guide?**
    a. Alignment with strategic goals
    b. Only lagging indicators
    c. Clear signaling mechanisms (e.g., leading indicators)
    d. Only compliance with standards
    e. Avoiding feedback mechanisms

40. **According to the Scope domain, which two structures help connect deliverables to intended value and facilitate prioritization?**
    a. Value Breakdown Structure (VBS)
    b. Stakeholder register
    c. Work Breakdown Structure (WBS)
    d. Product backlog
    e. Change log

41. **In the Schedule domain, which two actions are essential for maintaining a realistic project schedule?**
    a. Regularly updating the schedule based on performance
    b. Fixing all activities at project start
    c. Reanalyzing dependencies and resource allocations
    d. Ignoring stakeholder feedback
    e. Using the same schedule template for all projects

42. **In the Finance domain, which two are considered tangible metrics for project value?**
    a. Return on investment (ROI)
    b. Internal rate of return (IRR)
    c. Team satisfaction
    d. Daily standup attendance
    e. Kanban board progress

43. **In the Risk performance domain, which two strategies are valid for risk response?**
    a. Exploiting an opportunity
    b. Transferring a threat

c. Documenting only
d. Focusing only on the schedule
e. Ignoring all unknowns

44. **Which two actions are required to ensure effective change control in a predictive project, as outlined in the Governance domain?**
    a. Documenting all change requests in writing
    b. Assigning all changes to the product owner
    c. Routing changes through formal configuration management and integrated change control processes
    d. Allowing stakeholders to implement changes without documentation
    e. Approving or rejecting changes based on cost/schedule impact

45. **In the Scope domain, what two practices help prevent "scope creep" and ensure alignment with value delivery?**
    a. Maintaining a well-defined scope baseline or prioritized backlog
    b. Only defining scope at project close
    c. Employing ongoing scope monitoring and stakeholder feedback
    d. Fixing all deliverables up front and refusing any change
    e. Ignoring scope change requests

46. **Which two characteristics are most closely associated with high-performing project teams, as described in the Resources domain?**
    a. Shared ownership and trust
    b. Micromanagement
    c. Collaboration and adaptability
    d. Strict hierarchical control
    e. Resource hoarding

47. **According to the Risk domain, which two strategies are most appropriate for addressing threats and opportunities at both the project and overall level?**
    a. Threat mitigation and opportunity enhancement
    b. Ignoring threats
    c. Escalation to portfolio/program management
    d. Documenting but not acting
    e. Only using contingency reserves

48. **Which two tailoring considerations are especially important for stakeholder engagement in a global, virtual project team?**
    a. Inclusive, multilingual communication methods
    b. Frequent, informal stakeholder analysis
    c. Ignoring cultural differences
    d. Use of technology for real-time collaboration
    e. Mandating all stakeholders to attend in-person meetings

49. **In the context of project value, which two metrics would be most appropriate for measuring intangible value according to the Finance domain?**
    a. Customer satisfaction
    b. Internal rate of return (IRR)
    c. Innovation index
    d. Net Present Value (NPV)
    e. Cost performance index

50. **When tailoring stakeholder engagement for a highly dynamic project, which two practices are recommended?**
    a. Regularly updating stakeholder analysis and engagement strategies
    b. Only engaging stakeholders during project closure
    c. Using multiple feedback loops
    d. Relying on a single communication channel
    e. Ignoring stakeholder feedback

51. **Which two tailoring considerations are most relevant for resource management in a project involving new, untested technology?**
    a. Increased need for iterative scheduling
    b. Rigid, up-front resource allocation
    c. Flexibility and collaboration in team structures
    d. Ignoring supplier performance
    e. Focus on knowledge transfer and upskilling

52. **When planning risk responses, what are two critical elements for ensuring risk management remains effective throughout the project?**
    a. Iterative review and adaptation of risk responses
    b. Documenting all risks at project start and never revisiting
    c. Assigning clear risk owners
    d. Escalating every risk to portfolio management
    e. Ignoring stakeholder input on risks

53. **Which two conditions most often require a more formal, detailed schedule management approach?**
    a. High project criticality for strategic goals
    b. Low team experience
    c. High uncertainty and rapid change
    d. Projects with major regulatory/compliance requirements
    e. Fully agile teams

54. **In an adaptive project, which two practices are critical for aligning product backlog refinement with overall project value delivery?**
    a. Regular stakeholder feedback and prioritization
    b. Fixing the backlog at project start
    c. Iterative delivery and validation of increments
    d. Ignoring quality requirements
    e. Freezing releases after the first iteration

55. **Which two actions would best ensure that financial reserves are managed effectively to support project resilience?**
    a. Clearly separate contingency and management reserves
    b. Integrate reserves implicitly in the initial budget
    c. Regularly review and reallocate reserves based on emerging risks
    d. Use reserves only for procurement
    e. Never communicate reserve usage to stakeholders

56. **In a resource-constrained environment, which two resource management strategies help maintain the project schedule and quality?**
    a. Cross-training team members for flexibility
    b. Assigning all resources at project initiation
    c. Using just-in-time/lean techniques for physical resources
    d. Ignoring resource shortages
    e. Micromanaging all tasks

57. **When measuring project performance, which two metrics should be avoided as "vanity metrics," and why?**
    a. Number of team meetings
    b. Number of deliverables completed without a value context
    c. Cost performance index (CPI)
    d. Customer satisfaction score
    e. Number of emails sent

58. **Which two tailoring strategies are recommended for risk management in agile software projects?**
    a. Conducting risk reviews at the start of every iteration
    b. Waiting until the project closes to review risks
    c. Embedding risk items in the product backlog
    d. Using a fixed risk register from project start
    e. Ignoring stakeholder risk input

59. **For a project operating in a highly volatile market, which two practices best support adaptability and value delivery?**
    a. Frequent backlog refinement and reprioritization
    b. Freezing requirements after initial planning
    c. Regular use of rolling wave planning
    d. Minimizing stakeholder communications
    e. Single-phase delivery

60. **When tailoring resource management for a cross-functional team that includes both internal staff and external suppliers, which two actions are most effective?**
    a. Develop clear contracts and a shared team charter
    b. Assign all project management to the suppliers
    c. Use only informal agreements
    d. Foster open communication and regular performance feedback
    e. Rely only on resource allocation at project start

61. **In an agile project, which two governance tailoring strategies help ensure both autonomy and alignment with organizational goals?**
    a. Light, self-governing structure with clear boundaries and guardrails
    b. All decisions made by the PMO
    c. Iterative feedback loops and transparent status reporting
    d. Fixing all plans at project start
    e. Disallowing retrospectives

62. **Which two actions help minimize "scope creep" in complex, multi-stakeholder projects?**
    a. Ongoing validation of deliverables against acceptance criteria
    b. Allowing any stakeholder to add scope at any time
    c. Regular, formal scope change control reviews
    d. Ignoring stakeholder feedback
    e. Using only a static WBS

63. **For a project with distributed teams across different time zones, which two stakeholder engagement practices are most effective?**
    a. Asynchronous communication platforms
    b. Mandated synchronous meetings at all hours
    c. Multilingual and culturally aware communications
    d. Minimizing feedback opportunities
    e. Rotating time slots for key meetings

64. **Which two components are essential for effective project governance, regardless of structure?**
    a. Target metrics aligned to strategic goals
    b. Only after-action reviews
    c. Clear signaling (leading indicators)
    d. Isolated decision-making
    e. Ignoring lessons learned

65. **Which two practices in scope management best prevent scope creep?**
    a. Maintaining a clear baseline or prioritized backlog
    b. Allowing all stakeholders to add features anytime
    c. Continuous scope monitoring and feedback
    d. Ignoring change requests
    e. Avoiding customer reviews

66. **Which two are critical for maintaining realistic schedules in complex projects?**
    a. Regular updates based on performance data
    b. Ignoring stakeholder input
    c. Re-evaluating dependencies and resources
    d. Freezing the schedule at project start
    e. Using a generic template for all projects

67. **Which two financial metrics best capture intangible value?**
    a. Customer satisfaction
    b. Return on investment (ROI)
    c. Innovation index
    d. Cost variance
    e. Internal rate of return (IRR)

68. **Which two practices best enable stakeholder engagement in a distributed, multicultural project?**
    a. Multilingual, culturally aware communications
    b. One-size-fits-all updates
    c. Asynchronous collaboration platforms
    d. Limiting feedback to project close
    e. Ignoring virtual team needs

69. **Which two practices help mitigate the risk of resource shortages in a project?**
    a. Ongoing monitoring and control of actual vs. planned usage
    b. Assigning all resources at project start and never revisiting
    c. Cross-training and flexible team roles
    d. Limiting resource data collection
    e. Ignoring supply chain risk

70. **Which two strategies support effective risk management in adaptive projects?**
    a. Iterative risk reviews at each iteration
    b. Static risk register from project start
    c. Risk items embedded in the product backlog
    d. Ignore risk after planning
    e. Only escalate to PMO

Fill-in-the-blanks

71. **A __ is a group of related processes that are critical for the effective delivery of project value and work as an integrated system.**
    a. Performance domain
    b. Knowledge area
    c. Program
    d. Change log

72. **In adaptive lifecycles, the prioritized list of work items and features used to manage scope is called the __.**
    a. Product backlog
    b. WBS dictionary
    c. Issue log
    d. Schedule baseline

73. **The __ is the approved version of the time-phased project budget, excluding management reserves, and is used for comparison with actual results.**
    a. Cost baseline
    b. Change log
    c. Resource register
    d. Performance report

74. **In the Resources domain, __ refers to an individual with management authority over one or more resources.**
    a. Resource manager
    b. Project sponsor
    c. Product owner
    d. Team lead

75. **In the Risk domain, __ is an aggregate measure of the potential impact of all risks at any given point in the project.**
    a. Risk exposure
    b. Risk appetite
    c. Risk register
    d. Issue log

76. **In adaptive approaches, managing project changes typically involves __ management instead of formal change requests.**
    a. Backlog
    b. Resource
    c. Issue
    d. Schedule

77. **A __ is a hierarchical decomposition of the total scope of work to accomplish project objectives and create required deliverables.**
    a. Work Breakdown Structure (WBS)
    b. Change log
    c. Product backlog
    d. Schedule baseline

78. **In project finance, the __ is the approved version of the budget, excluding management reserves, and is used as the basis for comparison to actual results.**
    a. Cost baseline
    b. Value Breakdown Structure
    c. Funding strategy
    d. Issue log

79. **__ is the process of tracking, reviewing, and reporting overall project progress to meet defined objectives and ensure value delivery.**
    a. Monitor and Control Project Performance
    b. Rolling wave planning
    c. Plan Stakeholder Engagement
    d. Acquire Resources

80. **In the Stakeholders domain, an active __ is often cited as a critical success factor for positive project outcomes.**
    a. Project sponsorb
    b. Resource manager
    c. Procurement officer
    d. External vendor

81. **In PMBOK® v8, a __ is an action, planned or implemented, to address particular threats and opportunities in a project.**
    a. Risk response b. Scope baseline
    c. Issue log d. Work package

82. **In the Finance domain, __ is the process of aggregating estimated costs to establish an authorized cost baseline.**
    a. Develop Budget
    b. Estimate Costs
    c. Plan Financial Management
    d. Earned value analysis

83. **When using lean scheduling, deliverables are not assigned to the team; instead, work is "__" when there is capacity.**
    a. Pulled b. Fixed
    c. Deferred d. Outsourced

84. **The __ register is a project document that records all identified threats and opportunities.**
    a. Risk b. Issue
    c. Stakeholder d. Lessons learned

85. **In project governance, __ metrics provide early warning of potential deviations from goals, while lagging metrics assess past performance.**
    a. Leading b. Vanity
    c. Change control d. Earned value

86. **In the PMBOK® Guide, the document that provides a prioritized, value-driven list of work items in adaptive projects is the __.**
    a. Product backlog b. Quality report
    c. Schedule baseline d. Issue log

87. **The process of identifying, documenting, and assigning clear roles and responsibilities for project resources is known as __ management.**
    a. Resource b. Stakeholder
    c. Risk d. Financial

88. **In the Governance domain, effective __ mechanisms allow decision-makers to assess decisions, learn, and improve project outcomes.**
    a. Feedback b. Earned value
    c. Procurement d. Change log

89. **The process in which a project manager finalizes all activities, archives knowledge, and releases resources at the end of a project or phase is called __.**
    a. Close Project or Phase
    b. Monitor Risks
    c. Validate Scope
    d. Acquire Resources

90. **__ risk is the aggregate effect of uncertainty on the project as a whole, not just on individual events.**
    a. Overall b. Issue
    c. External d. Residual

91. **The process of consolidating and aligning all performance domain plans into a unified project management plan is known as __.**
    a. Integrate and Align Project Plans
    b. Rolling wave planning
    c. Plan Stakeholder Engagement
    d. Scope validation

92. **In PMBOK® v8, __ is a state of being unclear or not knowing what to expect, which can often be resolved through collaborative problem-solving before it escalates into risk.**
    a. Ambiguity b. Escalation
    c. Deliverable d. Trend analysis

93. **The __ is the process that completes all activities related to both successful and unsuccessful projects, phases, or contracts.**
    a. Close Project or Phase
    b. Validate Scope

c. Lead the Team
d. Plan Sourcing Strategy

94. **_ is a provision in the project management plan to mitigate schedule and/or cost risks, often subdivided into contingency and management types.**

a. Reserve b. Milestone
c. WBS d. Earned value

95. **In the Schedule domain, _ is the technique of planning future work at a high level while detailing near-term activities, supporting flexibility and adaptation.**

a. Rolling wave planning
b. Critical path method
c. Kanban
d. Baseline management

96. **In predictive environments, the process of escalating persistent obstacles to higher authority is called _.**

a. Escalation b. Decomposition
c. Mitigation d. Lead time

97. **In adaptive environments, the prioritized list of work items and features is called the _.**

a. Product backlog b. Procurement plan
c. Quality report d. Schedule variance

98. **The technique of detailing near-term work while planning later work at a higher level is called _.**

a. Rolling wave planning
b. Earned value
c. Quality assurance
d. Resource leveling

99. **The _ is the approved version of a time-phased project budget, excluding management reserves, and is used for performance comparison.**

a. Cost baseline b. Funding strategy
c. WBS d. Issue log

100. **The process of regularly updating how you will interact with stakeholders to meet their needs and ensure engagement is called _ management.**

a. Stakeholder engagement b. Risk
c. Resource d. Schedule

101. **The document that lists the type, quantity, and characteristics of resources needed for the project is the _ requirements.**

a. Resource b. Schedule
c. Stakeholder d. Scope

102. **The _ register records all identified threats, opportunities, and related responses.**

a. Risk b. Issue
c. Stakeholder d. Schedule

Match the following

103. **Match each performance domain to a key artifact or process:**

Table A	Table B
a. Governance	i. Rolling wave planning, critical path
b. Scope	ii. Cost baseline, estimate costs
c. Schedule	iii. Risk register, risk report
d. Finance	iv. Project charter, project management plan
e. Risk	v. WBS, product backlog

104. **Match each process to the performance domain where it is primarily found:**

Table A	Table B
a. Monitor and Control Finances	i. Resources
b. Acquire Resources	ii. Scope
c. Validate Scope	iii. Stakeholders
d. Plan Stakeholder Engagement	iv. Schedule
e. Develop Schedule	v. Finance

105. **Match each tailoring consideration to the performance domain where it is most strongly emphasized:**

Table A	Table B
a. Feedback mechanisms	i. Scope
b. Iterative scope refinement	ii. Governance
c. Rolling wave planning	iii. Schedule
d. Buffering for unknowns	iv. Resources
e. Resource empowerment	v. Finance

106. **Match each project document or tool to the domain in which it is most critical:**

Table A	Table B
a. Issue log	i. Governance
b. Lessons learned register	ii. Risk
c. Risk register	iii. Stakeholders
d. Product backlog	iv. Resources
e. Resource breakdown structure	v. Scope

107. **Match each key concept with the domain it is most associated with:**

Table A	Table B
a. Escalation	i. Schedule
b. Rolling wave	ii. Stakeholders
c. Empowerment	iii. Finance
d. Stakeholder map	iv. Governance
e. Contingency reserve	v. Resources

108. **Match each "check result" metric to the performance domain it best measures:**

Table A	Table B
a. Stakeholder satisfaction score	i. Scope
b. Scope definition accuracy	ii. Stakeholders
c. Schedule forecast versus baseline	iii. Resources
d. Cost variance (CV)	iv. Schedule
e. Resource downtime percentage	v. Finance

109. **Match each key tailoring consideration with the most relevant domain:**

Table A	Table B
a. Regional regulatory compliance	i. Scope
b. Iterative feedback loops	ii. Governance
c. Lean resource management	iii. Resources
d. Multilingual communication	iv. Risk
e. Frequent risk reviews	v. Stakeholders

110. **Match each scenario to the domain intervention that would most directly improve the outcome:**

Table A	Table B
a. Stakeholders unclear on benefits	i. Value-based scope mapping
b. Unplanned work frequently added	ii. Scope change control
c. Team disputes over roles and tasks	iii. Team charter/role clarity
d. Late deliverables due to underestimated effort	iv. Rolling wave planning
e. Budget consistently overruns due to risk events	v. Reserve analysis

111. **Match each advanced tailoring consideration to its primary performance domain:**

Table A	Table B
a. Regulatory escalation paths	i. Resources
b. Dynamic backlog reprioritization	ii. Governance
c. Kanban pull systems	iii. Scope
d. Multiphase funding release	iv. Finance
e. Iterative risk review	v. Risk

112. **Match each governance scenario to its description:**

Table A	Table B
a. Project initiation	i. Resources are expended to launch a project
b. Project replanning	ii. Project changes to preserve/capture value
c. Expansion/contraction	iii. Revisions require intentional review
d. Early termination (positive)	iv. Value can no longer be achieved
e. Early termination (negative)	v. Value achieved before schedule/budget

113. **Match the scope-related term to its definition:**

Table A	Table B
a. Scope baseline	i. Hierarchical decomposition of scope
b. WBS	ii. Hierarchical structure linking value
c. DoD (Definition)	iii. Features/functions of the end result
d. Product scope	iv. Criteria for considering work "done"
e. VBS	v. Approved version of scope documentation

114. **Match the schedule tool to its primary purpose:**

Table A	Table B
a. Critical path	i. Longest path determines project duration
b. Kanban	ii. Key events/achievements in the schedule
c. Gantt chart	iii. Visualizes schedule and dependencies
d. Burnup chart	iv. Visualizes workflow, limits work in progress
e. Milestone list	v. Tracks completed scope vs. plan

115. **Match each financial concept to its definition:**

Table A	Table B
a. CapEx	i. Funds for acquiring/maintaining assets (capital expenses)
b. OpEx	ii. Funds for daily operations (operational expenses)
c. Contingency	iii. Reserve for known-unknowns
d. Management	iv. Reserve for unknown-unknowns
e. EVM	v. Earned Value Management (performance measurement)

116. **Match each stakeholder tool to its primary function:**

Table A	Table B
a. Stakeholder map	i. Records info and engagement needs
b. Stakeholder register	ii. Mechanism for two-way communication
c. NPS	iii. Tracks stakeholder-related concerns
d. Feedback loop	iv. Visualizes interest, influence, impact
e. Issue log	v. Measures satisfaction/promoter status

117. **Match each resource management tool to its use:**

Table A	Table B
a. RACI matrix	i. Defines norms and ways of working
b. Team charter	ii. Clarifies roles/responsibilities
c. Resource histogram	iii. Assesses team/individual effectiveness
d. Lean scheduling	iv. Visualizes resource allocation
e. Performance review	v. Minimizes waste, limits WIP

118. **Match each risk response strategy to its primary purpose:**

Table A	Table B
a. Mitigation	i. Reduce threat probability/impact
b. Exploitation	ii. Ensure opportunity is realized
c. Transfer	iii. Move threat to third party (e.g., insurance)
d. Escalation	iv. Hand risk to higher authority
e. Acceptance	v. Acknowledge risk, no action unless triggered

Concept-based objective questions and answers

119. **Explain how tailoring the Scope performance domain differs in predictive versus adaptive projects, and why this distinction is important?**

    In predictive projects, scope is defined up front, managed with formal procedures, and changes are controlled. Adaptive projects manage scope through iterative refinement and frequent stakeholder feedback. Tailoring allows the approach to fit the environment and value goals, ensuring relevance and responsiveness.

120. **Describe the implications of choosing to include contingency and management reserves either explicitly or implicitly in the project budget.**

    Explicit reserves provide visibility and control over risk funds, while implicit reserves simplify budgets but reduce transparency. The choice impacts risk response, tracking, and budget management.

121. **Why must stakeholder engagement be reviewed and updated throughout a project's lifecycle?**

    Stakeholder interests, influence, and expectations shift as the project progresses. Continuous engagement ensures alignment, reduces uncertainty, and increases acceptance.

122. **Describe how the Monitor and Control Schedule process differs in predictive versus adaptive projects, and explain the impact of these differences on stakeholder engagement.**

    In predictive projects, schedule changes are managed through formal integrated change control, emphasizing baseline adherence. In adaptive projects, schedules are reviewed frequently, with progress measured by deliverables produced and accepted; velocity and backlog refinement are central. Adaptive methods enable more frequent stakeholder feedback and adjustment, increasing engagement and satisfaction.

123. **Explain the purpose of the "Plan Sourcing Strategy" process and discuss its influence on both the Governance and Resources domains.**

    Plan Sourcing Strategy determines whether work will be insourced, outsourced, or both, and sets criteria for vendor selection. This ensures governance decisions align sourcing with strategy, risk, and value, while also ensuring the right resources are acquired and managed for project success.

124. **A project manager is leading a distributed, multicultural team for a new digital product. What stakeholder engagement strategies, based on the PMBOK® Guide, should be prioritized and why?**

    The project manager should use inclusive, multilingual communications; leverage digital platforms for real-time collaboration; and tailor engagement approaches to cultural and time zone diversity. This reduces misunderstandings, increases buy-in, and ensures all voices are heard, supporting overall project value.

125. **How should project managers approach tailoring resource planning for a team with both high technical maturity and significant external procurement?**

    Resource planning should leverage the team's autonomy for internal tasks while integrating rigorous procurement strategies and clear contracts for external resources. This maximizes efficiency, reduces oversight costs, and ensures legal/commercial compliance.

126. **Explain how value is created in a project that is a component of a larger program, according to the Finance domain.**

    Some projects are enablers for broader program outcomes and may not deliver immediate direct value. Their value is realized as part of program-level benefits, so financial measures should account for future value, strategic alignment, and integration into the program's objectives.

127. **Discuss how "value maximization" is operationalized differently in the Finance and Scope domains, providing an example for each.**

    In Finance, value maximization expands beyond cost control to include strategic alignment, ROI, innovation, and customer satisfaction (e.g., approving extra features with high future payback). In Scope, value maximization means ensuring that every scope element directly contributes to the desired outcome, with unnecessary work eliminated (e.g., using a VBS to prioritize only high-value deliverables).

128. **Explain why it is essential to have both explicit and tacit knowledge management processes in a project, and give examples of each.**

Explicit knowledge (e.g., manuals, process documents) is easy to share and standardize but lacks context. Tacit knowledge (e.g., expert insights, team lessons) is difficult to codify but crucial for nuanced decision-making. Both are needed for full knowledge transfer: explicit for structure, tacit for adaptation and learning.

129. **In a scenario where a project team is distributed and includes contractors, what strategies from the Resources and Stakeholders domains should be combined to ensure optimal performance and engagement?**

Use clear contracts, explicit roles, and a shared team charter (Resources domain), combined with tailored, frequent, inclusive communication and feedback loops (Stakeholders domain). This aligns expectations, ensures buy-in, and fosters both accountability and motivation across organizational boundaries.

130. **You are assigned to a project where value delivery is consistently below stakeholder expectations. Using at least three performance domains, explain how you would diagnose and address the problem.**

Start with the Scope domain to assess whether requirements and deliverables match expected value; use Stakeholders to analyze gaps in engagement and feedback; leverage Governance to review integration and decision-making processes for alignment and adaptation. Cross-domain adjustments ensure that scope, engagement, and oversight are focused on meaningful outcomes.

131. **Explain why "rolling wave planning" is critical for projects with rapidly evolving requirements and how it integrates with risk and resource management.**

Rolling wave planning allows detailed planning for near-term tasks and high-level planning for future work. As requirements evolve, the plan is refined, risks are reassessed, and resources are allocated as needs emerge. This continuous process ensures flexibility and responsiveness in volatile environments.

132. **In a highly innovative project, how do Knowledge Management and Stakeholder domains work together to increase project success?**

Knowledge management captures and shares explicit and tacit insights, while stakeholder engagement ensures these insights are relevant and applied. Regular lessons-learned sessions and open communications support innovation and adaptation, driving higher value and satisfaction.

133. **Describe the process and benefits of using a Value Breakdown Structure (VBS) in scope management.**

A VBS links deliverables to value, allowing prioritization based on impact. It supports transparent decision-making, reduces scope creep, and ensures that project work is aligned with business objectives and stakeholder needs.

134. **How can "project resilience" be planned and measured within both the Risk and Finance domains?**

In Risk, resilience is planned by identifying potential disruptions and developing continuity and contingency plans; in Finance, it is measured by the availability and use of management reserves to address unknowns. Both require ongoing review and adjustment.

135. **Explain the significance of "shared team ownership" in project outcomes, referencing both the Resources and Stakeholders domains.**

Shared ownership increases accountability, motivation, and performance (Resources). It also enhances trust and aligns team actions with stakeholder expectations, improving project success and value delivery (Stakeholders).

136. **A project is behind schedule despite high team performance and efficient resource use. Which domains should be reviewed, and why might this occur?**

Review Schedule for planning and sequencing, Scope for unplanned work or requirements creep, and Stakeholders for misaligned priorities. This might occur due to unrealistic baselines, evolving scope, or lack of stakeholder alignment.

137. **How does project governance ensure integration with organizational strategy and continuous improvement throughout the lifecycle?**

Governance aligns project goals with strategy at initiation, oversees integration through planning and execution, incorporates feedback and lessons learned for adaptation, and ensures closure activities support value realization and knowledge transfer.

138. **In a complex project with rapid scope evolution, describe how the project manager should synchronize the activities of the Scope, Schedule, and Stakeholder domains for sustained value delivery.**

The project manager should use iterative planning (rolling wave) in Schedule, continuous backlog refinement in Scope, and frequent, tailored engagement in Stakeholders. Synchronizing these ensures that as requirements change, schedules adapt, and stakeholders remain aligned—maximizing value and minimizing rework.

139. **Explain the importance of integrating resource empowerment strategies with project governance in high-innovation environments.**

Empowering teams (Resources) increases adaptability and innovation. Governance must provide clear boundaries, strategic alignment, and feedback loops to balance autonomy with organizational objectives—enabling teams to innovate while maintaining control.

140. **Your project is at risk of missing crucial milestones due to underestimated effort and unplanned scope changes. Which domains are implicated, and what corrective measures should be implemented?**

Schedule (effort estimation and rolling wave planning), Scope (change control and alignment), and Stakeholders (expectation management) are implicated. Correction includes re-estimating, tighter scope control, and resetting stakeholder expectations.

141. **In a project using lean scheduling, how does the principle of "pull, don't push" impact team performance and value realization?**

Work is pulled by the team as capacity allows, reducing queues/waste and improving focus on high-value tasks. This increases throughput, team morale, and alignment with real project priorities and value.

142. **Describe how the Finance and Risk domains jointly support business continuity planning in a project subject to high-impact, low-probability events.**

Finance provides management reserves and funding for contingencies; Risk identifies and plans for disruptive events. Together, they ensure resources and plans are in place for continuity and rapid recovery.

143. **A major stakeholder is replaced mid-project. Using the Stakeholders and Governance domains, outline steps to realign the project.**

Identify and analyze the new stakeholders' needs, update engagement plans, and adjust governance processes (decision rights, reporting) to ensure the new stakeholder is integrated and aligned with project objectives.

144. **Explain the role and timing of "lessons learned" in project knowledge management and why ongoing capture is superior to post-project collection.**

Lessons learned should be captured throughout the project, not just at closure, to ensure real-time improvement and knowledge sharing. This supports adaptation and continuous improvement across all domains.

145. **In a project with shifting priorities and uncertain requirements, how does rolling wave planning connect with iterative risk management to sustain project value and control?**

Rolling wave planning provides flexibility in adapting to new requirements; iterative risk management ensures emerging risks are identified and addressed in each planning cycle. Together, they keep the project responsive and resilient, maintaining value and control despite uncertainty.

146. **Explain the importance of tailoring governance to project context, and give an example of how governance would differ between a small agile team and a multinational regulatory project.**

Tailoring ensures governance adds value without causing unnecessary overhead. Small agile teams need self-governance, minimal bureaucracy, and rapid feedback. Multinational projects require formal controls, regional adaptations, and integrated oversight to address compliance and complexity.

147. **Discuss the benefits and risks of iterative scope refinement in an environment of rapid external change.**

Iterative refinement ensures the scope stays relevant and aligned to value in dynamic conditions but can increase risk of misalignment if stakeholder feedback is not timely or if changes outpace team capacity.

148. **Explain how schedule management should be tailored for a global project team working across multiple time zones and cultures.**

Tailoring may require asynchronous communication, culturally sensitive milestone planning, and regular schedule updates to accommodate diverse working hours and expectations.

149. **Discuss how financial planning and risk management interact in a project subject to high-impact, low-probability events.**

Financial planning must include management reserves to fund unknowns; risk management identifies and plans for these events, ensuring business continuity through both proactive and reactive strategies.

150. **Explain why continuous stakeholder analysis and engagement is vital in projects with changing environments and priorities.**

Stakeholder needs and influence shift as projects evolve; ongoing analysis and engagement ensure alignment, reduce risk, and maximize value throughout the project lifecycle.

151. **Describe how resource management should be tailored for a highly virtual, multicultural team.**

Tailor by using digital collaboration tools, clear virtual norms, cross-cultural training, and explicit communication structures to ensure resource effectiveness and team cohesion.

152. **Explain how iterative risk management supports value delivery in agile and hybrid projects.**

Iterative risk reviews allow rapid identification and response to emerging threats and opportunities; frequent adaptation ensures continued alignment with project value and stakeholder priorities.

Conclusion

A comprehensive grasp of the project performance domains lays the groundwork for managing projects with clarity and purpose. These domains highlight the interconnected responsibilities that shape the journey from initial planning to successful delivery. Through the questions and scenarios presented in this section, the individual and collective importance of governance, scope, schedule, finance, stakeholders, resources, and risk has been illuminated. Each domain encourages a balanced focus, ensuring that project activities remain aligned, value-driven, and responsive to both challenges and opportunities.

However, simply knowing these domains is not enough in today's ever-changing project environments. Projects inevitably differ in their context, ranging from organizational culture and regulatory frameworks to industry specifics and stakeholder expectations. Approaches that are effective for one project may require adjustment for another. This reality emphasizes the importance of flexibility and the ability to adapt standard practices to better suit each unique project situation.

This concept of adaptation, commonly known as tailoring, enables project teams and leaders to make thoughtful adjustments to processes, methodologies, and tools based on the distinct needs of their projects. Being able to recognize when to modify standard approaches, combine techniques, or innovate new solutions is a hallmark of mature project management and often leads to greater efficiency and improved outcomes.

To build on the foundational knowledge of performance domains, the next chapter, presented as another set of targeted questions, will focus on the theme of *tailoring of project*. This upcoming section is structured as a question bank just like the current one, designed to prompt reflection and application of tailoring principles. The questions will guide readers through common scenarios where adaptation is necessary and will challenge them to think critically about how to choose, combine, or adjust practices to fit specific project environments.

By progressing from a strong understanding of performance domains to the thoughtful application of tailoring, this collection of questions aims to equip project professionals with both the depth and flexibility needed for real-world success. This structured, scenario-based approach not only supports exam readiness but also encourages the mindset and skills essential for effective management of any project, regardless of complexity or context.

References

1. A Guide to the Project Management Body of Knowledge , Seventh Edition. Project Management Institute. (Used as the foundational resource for the definition and explanation of project performance domains, including Governance, Scope, Schedule, Finance, Stakeholders, Resources, and Risk, as well as the concepts of tailoring and integration across domains.)

2. The Standard for Project Management. Project Management Institute. Referenced for principles, focus areas, and best practices that inform the performance domains and the need for adaptable project management.

3. Industry Best Practices and Case Studies. Supplementary scenarios and examples in the question bank were inspired by recognized best practices in contemporary project management literature and real-world applications.

Answers

Q. No.	Answers	Q. No.	Answers	Q. No.	Answers	Q. No.	Answers
1	c	17	b	33	b	49	a, c
2	b	18	c	34	c	50	a, c
3	c	19	b	35	b	51	c, e
4	b	20	b	36	c	52	a, c
5	c	21	c	37	b	53	a, d
6	b	22	b	38	b	54	a, c
7	a	23	b	39	a, c	55	a, c
8	c	24	b	40	a, c	56	a, c
9	b	25	b	41	a, c	57	b, e
10	b	26	b	42	a, b	58	a, c
11	b	27	c	43	a, b	59	a, c
12	b	28	b	44	a, c	60	a, d
13	b	29	b	45	a, c	61	a, c
14	b	30	b	46	a, c	62	a, c
15	b	31	b	47	a, c	63	a, c
16	b	32	b	48	a, d	64	a, c

Q. No.	Answers
65	a, c
66	a, c
67	a, c
68	a, c
69	a, c
70	a, c
71	a
72	a
73	a
74	a
75	a
76	a
77	a
78	a
79	a
80	a
81	a
82	a
83	a
84	a
85	a
86	a
87	a
88	a
89	a
90	a
91	a
92	a
93	a
94	a
95	a
96	a
97	a

Q. No.	Answers
98	a
99	a
100	a
101	a
102	a
103	a - iv b - v c - i d - ii e - iii
104	a - v b - i c - ii d - iii e - iv
105	a - ii b - i c - iii d - v e - iv
106	a - iii b - i c - ii d - v e - iv
107	a - iv b - i c - v d - ii e - iii

Q. No.	Answers
108	a - ii b - i c - iv d - v e - iii
109	a - ii b - i c - iii d - v e - iv
110	a - i b - ii c - iii d - iv e - v
111	a - ii b - iii c - i d - iv e - v
112	a - i b - iii c - ii d - v e - iv
113	a - v b - i c - iv d - iii e - ii

Q. No.	Answers
114	a - i b - iv c - iii d - v e - ii
115	a - i b - ii c - iii d - iv e - v
116	a - iv b - i c - v d - ii e - iii
117	a - ii b - i c - iv d - v e - iii
118	a - i b - ii c - iii d - iv e - v

Chapter 6
Tailoring

Introduction

Every project has its own unique environment, with its own specific goals, challenges, team members, and stakeholder expectations. It is because no single way of managing projects works for every situation. The concept of *tailoring* is all about making mindful adjustments to the way a project is run so that processes, tools, and team roles are a good fit for the project's needs, size, complexity, and the organization's goals.

This question bank is designed to help readers explore the practical aspects of tailoring in project management. Instead of providing a long instructional chapter, this resource uses a collection of carefully crafted questions to break down ideas about tailoring into manageable, real-world situations. The questions are intended to help readers think through how and why to adjust project planning, team engagement, governance, and delivery methods, rather than simply applying a fixed set of steps to every project.

By engaging with the questions in this bank, readers will see how tailoring helps project teams balance competing demands, such as delivering quickly, minimizing costs, maintaining quality, meeting stakeholder needs, and being ready for change. The aim is to make the topic of tailoring approachable and practical, giving readers the confidence to make informed choices and adapt their approach for the best possible results.

Objectives

The main purpose of this question bank is to make the idea of tailoring in project management clear and practical for all readers. Through a variety of question types and scenarios, this resource aims to show how tailoring can help projects achieve better alignment with their environment, team makeup, product needs, and organizational culture. Each question is crafted to encourage thoughtful consideration of when and how to adjust standard approaches, processes, or tools in response to specific project challenges or opportunities.

By working through this collection, readers will strengthen their ability to analyze a project's context, select and adapt suitable practices, and ensure that project management is neither too rigid nor too loose for the situation. The goal is not only to prepare for exams, but also to build real confidence in applying tailoring principles, so that every project, no matter how different, gets the approach it truly needs for success.

Single select multiple choice questions

1. **What is the main goal of tailoring in project management?**
   a. To follow industry best practices without exception
   b. To adjust the project approach, governance, and processes to fit a project's environment and objectives
   c. To use only predictive methods
   d. To always minimize project costs

2. **Which of the following is not considered a benefit of tailoring project management approaches?**
   a. Increased efficiency in using project resources
   b. Enhanced customer focus
   c. Strict adherence to only standard procedures
   d. Greater commitment from team members

3. **When selecting a lifecycle for a project, what is the primary consideration for tailoring?**
   a. The personal preference of the project manager
   b. The project's product, environment, and objectives
   c. A fixed industry template
   d. The number of stakeholders involved

4. **What does the term "suitability filter" refer to in the tailoring process?**
   a. A checklist for team training
   b. A decision-making tool to assess project context
   c. A software for resource allocation
   d. A budget approval form

5. **In what situation is tailoring for the organization especially important?**
   a. When there is no organizational policy
   b. When multiple projects must align with company standards
   c. When project teams are small
   d. When no documentation is needed

6. **What is one key reason to implement ongoing improvement as a part of tailoring?**
   a. To set a process and never change it
   b. To adjust methods based on lessons learned and review points
   c. To avoid involving the project team
   d. To focus only on budget tracking

7. **Which of the following best describes the tailoring process in a multi-organization project environment?**
   a. Only the primary organization's methods are used
   b. Each organization develops its own uncoordinated methods
   c. Tailored practices are harmonized across all participating organizations
   d. Only client requirements are considered

8. **What is a potential risk of failing to conduct diagnostics during the tailoring process?**
   a. Too much stakeholder involvement
   b. Missing opportunities for improvement
   c. Excessive project documentation
   d. Rigid use of agile tools

9. **When tailoring project engagement, which factor is most important to assess?**
   a. Team member hobbies
   b. Skills and capabilities of the project team
   c. The color of the office walls
   d. Number of vacation days taken

10. **What should be the first step in tailoring a project management approach?**
   a. Implementing lessons learned from previous projects
   b. Selecting the initial development approach
   c. Conducting a stakeholder meeting
   d. Writing a project charter

11. **Which of the following is a sign that further tailoring may be needed on a project?**
   a. Team members are highly motivated
   b. Stakeholders receive timely and relevant information
   c. There are frequent delays waiting for approvals
   d. The team has regular retrospectives

12. **A project is operating under strict regulatory standards, but the client requests frequent changes to requirements. Which tailored approach would best balance compliance and adaptability?**
    a. Use a purely predictive approach and reject all changes
    b. Adopt a hybrid approach, applying predictive rigor to compliance elements and adaptive methods to evolving requirements
    c. Only use adaptive methods for the entire project
    d. Ignore regulatory requirements to maximize flexibility

13. **In a multinational project, team members are spread across several time zones and cultural backgrounds. Which aspect of tailoring should receive the most attention to ensure project success?**
    a. Standardizing all communication tools without exceptions
    b. Tailoring engagement methods to accommodate cultural and geographic diversity, including flexible meeting times and customized communication strategies
    c. Only focusing on technical training
    d. Prioritizing only the senior management's preferences

14. **After a significant project setback, a team conducts a retrospective and identifies a gap in their risk management approach. What is the most effective next step, according to the tailoring process?**
    a. Continue without changes
    b. Tailor the risk management process by adding targeted risk identification and mitigation steps, then validate the effectiveness through ongoing review
    c. Outsource all risk management
    d. Eliminate all current risk controls

15. **A PMO wants to allow project managers more autonomy in tailoring their processes, but is concerned about losing organizational consistency. What strategy aligns with best tailoring practices?**
    a. Mandate the same approach for all projects
    b. Establish organizational guidelines and review mechanisms so tailored processes support both autonomy and alignment with company goals
    c. Remove all oversight
    d. Only allow tailoring on small projects

16. **When tailoring engagement in a project involving multiple external partners, what is a key risk if integration is not properly addressed?**
    a. Increased project transparency
    b. Enhanced innovation
    c. Fragmented teams leading to miscommunication, duplicated efforts, and reduced project outcomes
    d. Faster approvals

17. **A project team has tailored its approach for rapid delivery but is experiencing frequent quality issues. What is the most appropriate tailoring response?**
    a. Ignore quality problems to maintain speed
    b. Add targeted quality feedback and assurance measures, focusing on process improvements instead of just more verification steps
    c. Reduce team meetings to maximize delivery time
    d. Increase the number of stakeholders involved

18. **In a highly regulated industry, which tailoring strategy best ensures both compliance and efficiency?**
    a. Eliminate all adaptive practices
    b. Apply rigorous processes to regulated areas and adapt less regulated components as needed
    c. Use only the minimum required processes for all project aspects
    d. Prioritize speed over compliance

19. **A project's stakeholder group is dispersed globally with varying expectations. What is the most effective approach to tailoring communication?**
    a. Send the same report to all stakeholders regardless of role or location
    b. Customize communication methods and content to address specific stakeholder needs and cultural expectations
    c. Only communicate with local stakeholders
    d. Limit updates to project team members

20. **If a project team continually faces issues and risks they were unprepared for, what tailoring strategy is recommended?**
    a. Ignore the issues and hope for fewer problems
    b. Use diagnostics to explore root causes and identify gaps in processes, then tailor approaches to address those gaps
    c. Only add more documentation
    d. Reduce team size

21. **Which of the following best demonstrates tailoring for empowerment within a project team?**
    a. All decisions require executive approval
    b. Team members are supported and encouraged to own and develop their working environment and agreements
    c. External consultants make all decisions
    d. No feedback is solicited from the team

22. **A project team discovers that the chosen project management methodology is causing delays due to excessive approvals. What is the most effective tailoring solution?**
    a. Ignore the delays and proceed
    b. Streamline the approval process by delegating authority to appropriate team members for certain decisions
    c. Increase the number of approval steps
    d. Remove all approval requirements entirely

23. **In a project with both tangible and intangible deliverables, what tailoring approach best supports successful outcomes?**
    a. Use a single, rigid approach for both deliverable types
    b. Apply predictive approaches to tangible deliverables and adaptive approaches to intangible ones, forming a hybrid approach
    c. Disregard the differences and treat all deliverables the same
    d. Outsource only the intangible deliverables

24. **A project is experiencing waste due to too much work in progress. What is a recommended tailoring technique to address this?**
    a. Add more work streams
    b. Use value stream mapping and kanban boards to visualize work and identify bottlenecks
    c. Ignore the issue, expecting it to resolve itself
    d. Ban all multitasking

25. **The project team is composed of members from several partner organizations, each with its own processes. What tailoring step should be prioritized to ensure project cohesion?**
    a. Allow each group to use its own process with no coordination
    b. Harmonize tailored practices across all contributing organizations
    c. Prevent communication between teams
    d. Only follow the sponsor's procedures

26. **Which project scenario would most likely require frequent tailoring adjustments throughout the lifecycle?**
    a. A routine, repeatable project with stable requirements
    b. A highly innovative project in a volatile market with shifting stakeholder needs
    c. A small, internal audit project
    d. A project with only one stakeholder

27. **If a project's market is highly regulated and subject to frequent change, what is the most effective tailoring approach for compliance and adaptability?**
    a. Apply only predictive methods throughout
    b. Build in regular compliance reviews and allow for process adjustments as regulations evolve
    c. Ignore regulatory changes to avoid project delays
    d. Use only adaptive methods for all project components

28. **A project team is empowered to make decisions but lacks alignment with the organization's strategic goals. What tailoring response is most appropriate?**
    a. Remove all empowerment
    b. Align team decision-making with organizational policies and strategic direction
    c. Allow the team to set their own unrelated objectives
    d. Ignore the misalignment

29. **A project team, after conducting several retrospectives, identifies recurring issues with communication breakdown. Which tailoring action should be prioritized?**
    a. Continue with the same communication plan
    b. Tailor communication methods and channels, possibly including new tools or protocols, and validate their effectiveness in subsequent retrospectives
    c. Reduce the frequency of meetings
    d. Rely solely on written status reports

30. **In which scenario would tailoring for integration be most critical?**
    a. A solo project led by an individual contributor
    b. A project involving multiple contractors, suppliers, and internal teams with diverse processes
    c. A project using only one department's staff
    d. A project with no external dependencies

31. **A project's deliverables must comply with new international data protection laws that were introduced mid-way through execution. What is the most effective tailoring response?**
    a. Continue using the original approach
    b. Tailor project processes to include compliance checkpoints and data audits, and update stakeholder communication plans
    c. Ignore the new laws until project closure
    d. Only inform the sponsor of the changes

32. **After a merger, a project must now integrate teams with very different working cultures and processes. What should be the first tailoring step?**
    a. Mandate the larger team's existing process
    b. Facilitate integration planning sessions to harmonize governance, team norms, and communication practices
    c. Disband one of the teams
    d. Delay integration until after project delivery

Multi-select multiple choice questions

33. **Which two principles should guide the tailoring process for any project?**
    a. Rely on rigid, standardized processes
    b. Consider the unique project context and environment
    c. Use only tools approved by the PMO
    d. Balance competing demands such as speed and quality
    e. Avoid stakeholder input

34. **Which two factors should be considered when tailoring project management approaches for a project team?**
    a. Team size
    b. Project manager's favorite tool
    c. Team geography
    d. Ignoring customer feedback
    e. Standard meeting time

35. **Which two are examples of tailoring engagement in a project?**
    a. Empowering team members for local decisions
    b. Avoiding integration of external partners
    c. Assessing skills and capabilities of the team
    d. Ignoring organizational culture
    e. Only using external consultants

36. **When conducting diagnostics to assess tailoring effectiveness, which two methods are most commonly used?**
    a. Retrospectives
    b. Ignoring feedback
    c. Lessons learned
    d. Skipping meetings
    e. Random guesswork

37. **Which two aspects are important to evaluate when tailoring for product or deliverable?**
    a. Standards compliance
    b. Project manager's vacation schedule
    c. Type of product
    d. Number of unrelated stakeholders
    e. Team's lunch preferences

38. **Which two are possible outcomes of not tailoring project management approaches?**
    a. Ineffective project management
    b. Optimal process for every project
    c. Wasted resources
    d. Guaranteed customer satisfaction
    e. Always on-time delivery

39. **When tailoring for a product or deliverable, which two factors should be regularly reviewed throughout the project?**
    a. Technology stability
    b. Team's lunch schedule
    c. Industry market
    d. Project office location
    e. Holiday decorations

40. **Which two results are likely if a project team removes unnecessary or redundant processes during tailoring?**
    a. Increased project cost
    b. Reduced waste
    c. Streamlined work
    d. Loss of stakeholder trust
    e. Less clarity

41. **Which two actions support effective tailoring for engagement in a project environment?**
    a. Integrating diverse team members
    b. Ignoring communication needs
    c. Empowering local decision-making
    d. Avoiding collaboration
    e. Only following instructions

42. **When reviewing tailoring efforts, which two approaches help gather feedback for improvement?**
    a. Stakeholder feedback
    b. Ignoring issues
    c. Quality metrics
    d. Avoiding retrospectives
    e. Cancelling meetings

43. **Which two considerations are important when tailoring the performance domains for a specific project?**
    a. Project context
    b. Random selection of tools
    c. Organizational values
    d. Ignoring past experience
    e. Focus solely on speed

44. **In tailoring the performance domains for a highly complex, high-stakes project, which two actions are most critical?**
    a. Prioritizing only speed over quality
    b. Thoroughly analyzing the project context and aligning each performance domain with the project's risks and objectives
    c. Ignoring organizational culture
    d. Regularly reviewing and adjusting tailored practices as the project evolves
    e. Relying solely on external consultants

45. **Which two tailoring actions best address a project where stakeholder engagement is low and feedback is negative?**
    a. Ignore feedback and proceed as planned
    b. Tailor communication methods to be more timely and relevant
    c. Increase transparency and involve stakeholders in decision-making
    d. Reduce the number of status updates
    e. Limit stakeholder access to information

46. **When tailoring processes for a project dealing with highly sensitive information, which two considerations are most important?**
    a. Strengthening security and confidentiality controls
    b. Reducing documentation
    c. Ensuring compliance with relevant standards
    d. Ignoring technology changes
    e. Only focusing on cost savings

47. **When multiple organizations collaborate on a project, which two tailoring actions should be prioritized to achieve project cohesion?**
    a. Ignore differences in governance structures
    b. Harmonize tailored practices among organizations
    c. Align decision-making processes
    d. Only follow the lead organization's methods
    e. Keep all processes separate

48. **When tailoring for an innovative product in a fast-moving market, which two tailoring actions help maximize value delivery?**
    a. Incorporate iterative delivery with frequent stakeholder feedback
    b. Freeze requirements at project start
    c. Ignore competitor trends
    d. Build in mechanisms for rapid change and adaptation
    e. Prioritize only documentation

49. **Which two actions are central to tailoring for a project in a rapidly evolving technology sector?**
    a. Use only traditional project management methods
    b. Build in iterative feedback and regular adaptation cycles
    c. Ignore competitor advances
    d. Allow for incremental product releases
    e. Fix all requirements at project start

50. **When tailoring for large, sensitive projects, which two organizational supports are especially valuable?**
    a. PMO review and guidance
    b. Ignoring all organizational processes
    c. General project management methodology as a starting point
    d. No governance oversight
    e. Skipping lessons learned

51. **Which two diagnostic methods can reveal the need for further tailoring in ongoing projects?**
    a. Retrospectives
    b. Avoiding stakeholder feedback
    c. Quality metrics
    d. Ignoring lessons learned
    e. Random audits

52. **When working with multiple organizations, which two challenges does tailoring seek to address?**
    a. Harmonizing governance and delivery approaches
    b. Ensuring alignment across all organizations involved
    c. Increasing internal silos
    d. Eliminating all oversight
    e. Prioritizing only the largest organization's needs

53. **Which two factors are most important when tailoring for stakeholder engagement in volatile environments?**
    a. Timely, relevant communication
    b. Ignoring negative feedback

c. Balancing simplicity with deeper engagement when necessary

d. Avoiding transparency

e. Standardizing all messages

54. **Which two tailoring actions are necessary when working with a diverse, geographically dispersed project team?**

a. Customize engagement strategies to account for time zones

b. Ignore local customs and work hours

c. Use technology to facilitate collaboration

d. Require mandatory attendance at all meetings regardless of location

e. Disregard language barriers

55. **When a project's requirements are unstable and likely to change, which two tailoring techniques are most appropriate?**

a. Implement incremental and iterative delivery

b. Fix all requirements upfront

c. Increase process rigidity

d. Encourage frequent stakeholder feedback

e. Ignore requirement changes

56. **Which two factors should guide tailoring decisions when the organizational culture is highly empowering and values innovation?**

a. Delegate decision-making to the team

b. Increase external oversight

c. Encourage team ownership of processes

d. Require all decisions to be approved by executives

e. Ban experimentation

57. **For a project with frequent negative stakeholder feedback and low transparency, which two tailoring actions can improve the situation?**

a. Tailor communication for relevance and timeliness

b. Reduce stakeholder involvement

c. Increase transparency in reporting and meetings

d. Ignore feedback

e. Only hold private team meetings

58. **When tailoring project processes for a highly experienced team, which two approaches best support efficient delivery?**

a. Remove redundant processes

b. Add extra oversight

c. Empower the team to make local decisions

d. Limit opportunities for feedback

e. Require strict adherence to templates

59. **Which two tailoring activities help maintain project alignment when several external entities are involved?**

a. Coordinate integration planning among all partners

b. Ignore differences in organizational policies

c. Harmonize governance structures

d. Allow each entity to use its preferred reporting style

e. Exclude external partners from planning

60. **Which two outcomes are likely if the team regularly uses diagnostics such as retrospectives or quality metrics during tailoring?**

a. Early identification of improvement opportunities

b. Repeating the same mistakes

c. Stronger project performance

d. Increased confusion among team members

e. Reduced transparency

61. **When tailoring for a project with a very large and diverse team, which two actions are best for promoting effective engagement?**

a. Customize communication channels for different groups

b. Ignore time zone differences

c. Use standard reporting for all, regardless of audience

d. Schedule key meetings considering global availability

e. Limit input from junior team members

62. **Which two tailoring actions should a PMO take to ensure consistency and support across multiple projects?**
    a. Provide adaptable methodology templates
    b. Enforce a single process for all projects regardless of differences
    c. Share lessons learned and best practices
    d. Ignore feedback from project teams
    e. Avoid portfolio-level oversight

63. **Which two tailoring activities are essential for a project team working with technology that is both rapidly evolving and potentially obsolete?**
    a. Monitor technological trends and allow for mid-project process adaptation
    b. Ignore new advancements to avoid disruption
    c. Build in frequent checkpoints for technology reassessment
    d. Freeze all requirements at project start
    e. Rely solely on legacy systems

64. **When tailoring for team empowerment, which two features are most beneficial for complex, innovative projects?**
    a. Decentralized decision-making
    b. Strict top-down control
    c. Clear role definitions paired with autonomy
    d. No feedback mechanisms
    e. Complete process standardization

65. **A project's customer requests rapid delivery of each feature but also insists on high quality and thorough documentation. Which two tailoring actions can help the team respond?**
    a. Use incremental delivery with built-in quality reviews
    b. Ignore documentation to save time
    c. Develop documentation templates tailored for efficiency
    d. Deliver all features at once
    e. Reduce customer involvement

66. **The project is plagued by frequent misunderstandings between the client and the development team. Which two tailoring actions are most effective?**
    a. Introduce regular joint workshops or reviews
    b. Tailor communication to bridge technical and business language
    c. Stop client involvement
    d. Use only email for updates
    e. Freeze all requirements

Fill-in-the-blanks

67. **Tailoring involves the deliberate adaptation of the project management approach, governance, and __ to align with project objectives.**
    a. Stakeholders b. Cost baseline
    c. Processes d. Deliverables

68. **The process of adapting project management approaches based on project needs is called __.**
    a. Tailoring b. Standardization
    c. Delegation d. Forecasting

69. **A __ filter helps assess a project's characteristics and supports the selection of a suitable approach.**
    a. Suitability b. Financial
    c. Quality d. Schedule

70. **When tailoring for the organization, alignment with __ ensures consistency and compliance across projects.**
    a. Organizational policies
    b. Project manager's preferences
    c. External vendor rules
    d. Local office traditions

71. **The process of continuously evaluating and adjusting project management methods throughout the project lifecycle is known as __.**
    a. Ongoing improvement
    b. Static planning
    c. Documentation review
    d. Stakeholder mapping

72. **When tailoring project management approaches, key factors to consider include the project's environment, objectives, and __.**
    a. Stakeholder expectations
    b. Office color scheme
    c. Meeting frequency
    d. Data storage size

73. **In tailoring, the act of combining features from both predictive and adaptive approaches is called a __ approach.**
    a. Hybrid
    b. Sequential
    c. Waterfall
    d. Static

74. **Tailoring that involves changing communication and coordination methods to suit the team's distribution is called tailoring for __.**
    a. Project team geography
    b. Stakeholder location
    c. Office size
    d. Market reach

75. **The process of checking if tailored approaches are effective and aligned with outcomes is called __.**
    a. Verification and validation
    b. Cost analysis
    c. Simple review
    d. Status reporting

76. **The deliberate adaptation of project management processes to meet the unique needs of a project is known as __.**
    a. Tailoring
    b. Process mapping
    c. Benchmarking
    d. Standardization

77. **When integrating multiple organizations in a project, tailoring should focus on achieving __ among all parties.**
    a. Alignment and cohesion
    b. Independent strategies
    c. Rigid standardization
    d. Minimal documentation

78. **The act of periodically evaluating project processes to determine if further tailoring is needed is called __.**
    a. Diagnostics
    b. Resource allocation
    c. Estimation
    d. Budgeting

79. **When tailoring for the project team, an important question to ask is whether the team has the __, tools, and technology required for the project.**
    a. Skills
    b. Budget
    c. Lunch break
    d. Vacation plan

80. **A method that helps evaluate the best-fitting project approach by considering culture, dynamics, and project factors is called a __ filter.**
    a. Suitability
    b. Profitability
    c. Timeline
    d. Compliance

81. **__ allows project management practices to be adapted based on lessons learned during project execution.**
    a. Ongoing improvement
    b. Fixed methodology
    c. Static reporting
    d. Standardization

82. **In projects where project team members are not cooperative and work in silos, tailoring may involve conducting __ activities to strengthen collaboration.**
    a. Team-building
    b. Budget review
    c. Technical audits
    d. Customer surveys

83. **When the project team is unsure how to proceed, tailoring may involve providing appropriate __, mentorship, training, and knowledge-sharing practices.**
    a. Support mechanisms
    b. Vacation days
    c. Budget increases
    d. Penalties

84. **In tailoring for product delivery, evaluating the likelihood of changes to core requirements is referred to as assessing __.**
    a. Stability of requirements
    b. Cost fluctuation
    c. Market share
    d. Team mood

85. **The process of adapting the project management approach, governance, and processes to fit the project's environment and objectives is called __.**
    a. Tailoring b. Benchmarking
    c. Standardization d. Delegation

86. **When tailoring for organizational needs, a PMO may provide ideas and solutions from other projects as part of its __ role.**
    a. Support b. Silos
    c. Procurement d. Isolation

87. **Conducting periodic __, such as lessons learned or retrospectives, helps to assess and refine tailoring effectiveness.**
    a. Reviews b. Invoices
    c. Celebrations d. Sales pitches

88. **When tailoring projects with highly confidential products, an important attribute to assess is __.**
    a. Security b. Color scheme
    c. Office view d. Meeting snacks

89. **The process of combining predictive and adaptive approaches in a single project is referred to as a __ approach.**
    a. Hybrid b. Waterfall
    c. Sequential d. Repetitive

90. **Organizations that require strict oversight and structured practices typically have a low __ appetite.**
    a. Risk b. Budget
    c. Delivery d. Staffing

91. **A project team should evaluate the __ of requirements to decide how much adaptability to include in the project approach.**
    a. Stability b. Frequency
    c. Length d. Cost

92. **In tailoring, __ often provides initial methodologies and guidelines for project teams to adapt.**
    a. The Project Management Office (PMO)
    b. The client
    c. The marketing department
    d. The legal team

93. **When tailoring for the project, considering the __ of the product helps determine the level of process rigor required.**
    a. Type b. Revenue
    c. Customer loyalty d. Meeting frequency

94. **Tailoring decisions should always be made with the project's __ and constraints in mind.**
    a. Objectives b. Holidays
    c. Office layout d. Marketing slogan

95. **In tailoring, balancing potentially competing demands like speed, cost, and quality is necessary to create a __ operating environment for the project.**
    a. Practical b. Random
    c. Theoretical d. Uniform

96. **When multiple organizations participate in a project, tailoring must consider each entity's __ structures and delivery approaches.**
    a. Governance b. Color schemes
    c. Office parties d. Advertising

97. **When assessing whether to tailor for incremental and iterative delivery, a key question to ask is if the product can be __ and refined through repeated cycles.**
    a. Developed b. Ignored
    c. Priced d. Outsourced

98. **If the team is not receiving timely and relevant feedback from stakeholders, tailoring should focus on __ communication methods to improve engagement.**
    a. Adjusting
    b. Eliminating
    c. Standardizing
    d. Avoiding

99. **A project team working remotely across several countries is struggling with time zone conflicts. The team should tailor __ schedules to maximize participation and collaboration.**
    a. Meeting
    b. Resource allocation
    c. Budget review
    d. Office cleaning

100. **A project with a large number of external stakeholders is facing delays due to slow feedback cycles. Tailoring should focus on __ stakeholder engagement processes.**
    a. Accelerating
    b. Ignoring
    c. Eliminating
    d. Standardizing without review

Match the following

101. **Match each tailoring step with its main focus:**

Table A	Table B
a. Select initial approach	i. Ongoing process improvement
b. Tailor for organization	ii. Adjust processes for company policies
c. Tailor for project	iii. Choose method based on project characteristics
d. Implement improvement	iv. Adapt for project team and product needs
e. Diagnostics	v. Assess effectiveness through retrospectives

102. **Match each tailoring consideration with its description:**

Table A	Table B
a. Standards compliance	i. Regularly reviewing and refining project processes
b. Team diversity	ii. Tool for evaluating and selecting the right project approach
c. Stakeholder engagement	iii. Customizing communication and involvement for those impacted
d. Suitability filter	iv. Leveraging different backgrounds and skills within the project team
e. Ongoing improvement	v. Ensuring project practices fit the company's rules and requirements

103. **Match each tailoring step to the action it describes:**

Table A	Table B
a. Select initial approach	i. Decide on predictive, adaptive, or hybrid model
b. Tailor for organization	ii. Adjust for company policies and structures
c. Tailor for project	iii. Adapt based on project-specific needs
d. Implement improvement	iv. Make changes based on lessons learned
e. Diagnostics	v. Evaluate current practices for effectiveness

104. **Match each tailoring factor (Table A) with its corresponding tailoring approach/focus (Table B):**

Table A	Table B
a. Project team experience	i. Adjust process rigor to suit the product's complexity
b. Product type	ii. Consider skills and assign autonomy accordingly
c. Organizational culture	iii. Adapt methods to align with company values
d. Requirements stability	iv. Decide on the level of adaptability and feedback cycles
e. Stakeholder geography	v. Tailor communication and coordination tools

105. **Match each tailoring step (Table A) with the main benefit it delivers (Table B):**

Table A	Table B
a. Select initial approach	i. Enables continuous learning and adaptation
b. Tailor for organization	ii. Ensures approach fits company policy and structure
c. Tailor for project	iii. Provides the foundation for project methodology
d. Implement improvement	iv. Customizes approach for unique project needs
e. Diagnostics	v. Identifies areas for further tailoring

106. **Match each tailoring challenge (Table A) with a recommended solution (Table B):**

Table A	Table B
a. Delays waiting for approval	i. Team-building activities to promote collaboration
b. Team members work in silos	ii. Streamline approval by delegating authority
c. Unprepared for risks	iii. Use retrospectives to identify process gaps
d. Stakeholder disengagement	iv. Tailor communication for relevance and engagement
e. Poor quality deliverables	v. Focus on targeted quality improvements

107. **Match each project environment attribute (Table A) to a tailoring consideration (Table B):**

Table A	Table B
a. Regulatory strict	i. Increase rigor and oversight
b. Fast market	ii. Build in adaptability and rapid feedback
c. High diversity	iii. Customize engagement and communication
d. Large scale	iv. Use scalable processes and governance
e. High trust	v. Empower team for local decision-making

108. **Match each PMO function (Table A) with its benefit in the tailoring process (Table B):**

Table A	Table B
a. Methodology support	i. Shares proven ideas and solutions for tailoring
b. Policy alignment	ii. Ensures tailored methods comply with organization standards
c. Lessons learned	iii. Helps teams avoid repeating mistakes
d. Review/approval	iv. Maintains oversight for external impact tailoring
e. Portfolio context	v. Coordinates tailoring across related projects

109. **Match each tailoring principle (Table A) with its primary benefit (Table B):**

Table A	Table B
a. Empowerment	i. Enables rapid response to change
b. Alignment with policy	ii. Ensures compliance and consistency
c. Suitability filter	iii. Selects an approach that fits the context
d. Ongoing improvement	iv. Increases motivation and accountability
e. Integration planning	v. Prevents duplication and conflict

110. **Match each tailoring scenario (Table A) with the most suitable tailoring action (Table B):**

Table A	Table B
a. Team lacks required skills	i. Provide training and mentorship
b. Unclear stakeholder roles	ii. Clarify engagement and responsibility
c. High process waste	iii. Streamline and remove redundant steps
d. Changing regulatory landscape	iv. Increase compliance reviews
e. Global stakeholder group	v. Customize communication and timing

111. **Match each project tailoring decision (Table A) with the context or trigger (Table B)**

Table A	Table B
a. Add process steps	i. Diverse stakeholders or changing needs
b. Remove unnecessary processes	ii. Corporate culture or strategic change
c. Modify communication strategy	iii. Project involves both tangible and intangible work
d. Blend development approaches	iv. New risks or compliance needs emerge
e. Align with organizational values	v. To streamline work and reduce waste

112. **Match the tailoring benefit (Table A) with its result (Table B):**

Table A	Table B
a. Increased team empowerment	i. Greater innovation and initiative
b. Tailored customer engagement	ii. Improved satisfaction and feedback
c. Streamlined processes	iii. Higher efficiency and reduced costs
d. Ongoing improvement	iv. Sustained project relevance and quality
e. Harmonized governance	v. Smooth collaboration across organizations

113. **Match the tailoring consideration (Table A) to its desired project outcome (Table B):**

Table A	Table B
a. Regular diagnostics	i. ncreased efficiency and less waste
b. Team empowerment	ii. Regulatory compliance and audit readiness
c. Alignment with standards	iii. Higher satisfaction and project support
d. Stakeholder-tailored engagement	iv. Continuous process improvement
e. Streamlined reporting	v. Faster, more creative problem-solving

114. **Match each tailoring context (Table A) with the most appropriate action (Table B):**

Table A	Table B
a. High project complexity	i. Prioritize tailored engagement strategies
b. Frequent requirement changes	ii. Provide targeted training and mentorship
c. Multiorganizational projects	iii. Harmonize and integrate governance
d. Low team experience	iv. Increase feedback cycles and adaptability
e. Customer-driven projects	v. Use scalable frameworks and tools

115. **Match each scenario (Table A) with the most suitable tailoring action (Table B):**

Table A	Table B
a. Project in a highly regulated industry	i. Clarify team responsibilities and authority
b. Repeated project delays due to unclear roles	ii. Develop tailored engagement strategies
c. High turnover among team members	iii. Enhance compliance reviews and documentation
d. Rapidly expanding project scope	iv. Standardize onboarding and training
e. Lack of stakeholder interest	v. Implement scope control and review cycles

Concept-based objective questions and answers

116. **Explain why "tailoring" is considered essential in modern project management, using an example from a complex project environment.**

Tailoring is vital because no two projects are exactly the same. For example, a project to build a hospital will have different risks, stakeholder needs, and compliance requirements than a software development project. By tailoring processes—such as using more rigorous safety procedures and quality checks in construction, or more iterative feedback cycles in software—project teams can better align with their goals, resources, and constraints. This flexibility helps optimize value and improve project outcomes.

117. **Why is it important to consider the culture of an organization when tailoring project management practices? Provide an example.**

Culture shapes how teams communicate, make decisions, and approach challenges. For example, in an organization that values empowerment and local decision-making, a tailored approach might give teams more autonomy. In a more regulated environment, stricter oversight might be necessary. Tailoring for culture helps ensure practices are accepted and effective.

118. **Describe how ongoing improvement contributes to project success in the context of tailoring.**

Ongoing improvement encourages teams to reflect on what's working and what isn't throughout the project. By regularly reviewing processes, gathering feedback, and making adjustments, teams can respond quickly to issues and continuously enhance project performance, leading to better outcomes.

119. **Explain the role of the Project Management Office (PMO) in tailoring approaches for projects within an organization.**

The PMO often sets guidelines for tailoring, reviews and approves tailored approaches, and supports consistency across projects. It ensures that tailored methods align with organizational goals and helps teams access proven solutions from past projects.

120. **Explain how the suitability filter is used in tailoring project management approaches and give an example of its application.**

The suitability filter is a decision tool that helps project teams evaluate project characteristics—

such as culture, risk, complexity, and team dynamics—to determine whether a predictive, adaptive, or hybrid approach is best. For example, in a project with uncertain requirements and a fast-changing environment, the suitability filter would steer the team toward an adaptive or hybrid approach rather than a strict predictive one.

121. **Describe why ongoing improvement is essential in the tailoring process, especially in dynamic project environments.**

Ongoing improvement is critical because project environments often change as work progresses. By regularly reviewing processes, soliciting team feedback, and making adjustments, the team ensures that the tailored approach remains effective, relevant, and aligned with project goals—even in the face of new challenges or opportunities.

122. **How can tailoring support value delivery in a project where cost and speed are competing priorities?**

Tailoring allows the team to find the optimal balance between delivering quickly and minimizing costs by adjusting processes, resource use, and decision rights to fit the project's unique environment. For example, streamlining reporting can save time, while using iterative delivery can manage costs by enabling early feedback and course correction.

123. **Discuss how tailoring engagement can influence team empowerment and project outcomes, using an example.**

Tailoring engagement means giving teams the right level of autonomy based on their experience and the project's needs. For instance, in a creative design project, empowering the team to make key decisions and adjust processes can drive innovation and satisfaction, leading to better results. In contrast, more oversight might be needed in a regulated field.

124. **Why is it important to harmonize tailored practices when multiple organizations are involved in a project, and what risks arise if this is not done?**

Harmonizing tailored practices ensures all partners work towards common goals and processes, reducing misunderstandings and inefficiency. Without harmonization, teams may duplicate efforts, miss requirements, or even work at cross purposes—jeopardizing project success.

Conclusion

By working through the questions in this chapter, readers have learned how important it is to tailor project management practices to fit the unique needs of each project. The scenarios and explanations have shown that projects are not all the same, and that adjusting processes, tools, and ways of working is necessary for real success.

This question bank has helped readers build skills in making practical decisions, such as choosing the right project lifecycle, involving stakeholders in meaningful ways, and finding the best balance between speed, quality, and cost. It has also shown how to use project management techniques like diagnostics, integration planning, and team empowerment to solve problems and improve results as the project moves forward.

These lessons prepare readers for the next step, which is understanding Inputs & Outputs in project management. The next chapter, also in a question bank format, will help make sense of how information, documents, and deliverables move through a project. The knowledge gained from tailoring will help readers choose and use inputs and outputs more effectively, making their project management even stronger.

By connecting tailoring with the flow of inputs and outputs, readers will be ready to manage projects that are both flexible and well-organized, leading to better outcomes in any environment.

References

1. A Guide to the Project Management Body of Knowledge (PMBOK® Guide), Seventh and Eighth Edition. Project Management Institute

   This guide was used as the primary reference for concepts, terminology, and best practices related to tailoring project management processes, governance, lifecycles, stakeholder engagement, diagnostics, and continuous improvement.

2. The Standard for project management. Project Management Institute, 2021.

   Provided foundational principles and frameworks for project tailoring across different environments and project types.

3. PMI's Digital Platform for Standards.

   Accessed for up-to-date standards, definitions, and supplementary materials relevant to tailoring and other project management topics.

Answers

Q. No.	Answers
1	b
2	c
3	b
4	b
5	b
6	b
7	c
8	b
9	b
10	b
11	c
12	b
13	b
14	b
15	b
16	c
17	b
18	b
19	b
20	b
21	b
22	b
23	b

Q. No.	Answers
24	b
25	b
26	b
27	b
28	b
29	b
30	b
31	b
32	b
33	b, d
34	a, c
35	a, c
36	a, c
37	a, c
38	a, c
39	a, c
40	b, c
41	a, c
42	a, c
43	a, c
44	b, d
45	b, c
46	a, c

Q. No.	Answers
47	b, c
48	a, d
49	b, d
50	a, c
51	a, c
52	a, b
53	a, c
54	a, c
55	a, d
56	a, c
57	a, c
58	a, c
59	a, c
60	a, c
61	a, d
62	a, c
63	a, c
64	a, c
65	a, c
66	a, b
67	c
68	a
69	a

Q. No.	Answers
70	a
71	a
72	a
73	a
74	a
75	a
76	a
77	a
78	a
79	a
80	a
81	a
82	a
83	a
84	a
85	a
86	a
87	a
88	a
89	a
90	a
91	a
92	a

Q. No.	Answers
93	a
94	a
95	a
96	a
97	a
98	a
99	a
100	a
101	a - iii b - ii c - iv d - i e - v
102	a - v b - iv c - iii d - ii e - i
103	a - i b - ii c - iii d - iv e - v

Q. No.	Answers
104	a - ii b - i c - iii d - iv e - v
105	a - iii b - ii c - iv d - i e - v
106	a - ii b - i c - iii d - iv e - v
107	a - i b - ii c - iii d - iv e - v

Q. No.	Answers
108	a - i b - ii c - iii d - iv e - v
109	a - iv b - ii c - iii d - i e - v
110	a - i b - ii c - iii d - iv e - v
111	a - iv b - v c - i d - iii e - ii

Q. No.	Answers
112	a - i b - ii c - iii d - iv e - v
113	a - iv b - v c - ii d - iii e - i
114	a - v b - iv c - iii d - ii e - i
115	a - iii b - i c - iv d - v e - ii

CHAPTER 7
Inputs and Outputs

Introduction

Every project relies on a wide range of information, documents, and deliverables to move forward and achieve its goals. In project management, these are known as *inputs and outputs*. Inputs are the information, documents, or resources that a project begins with, while outputs are the results, deliverables, or updates produced by project activities. Understanding how these inputs and outputs connect and flow is essential for keeping a project organized, on track, and successful.

This chapter explores the key inputs and outputs used throughout a project. The reader will become familiar with how accepted deliverables are validated, how activity lists and backlogs help plan and organize work, and how documents like the assumption log, business case, and benefits management plan guide important decisions. The content also demonstrates how change requests, risk registers, and lessons learned registers play a role in adapting and improving the project as it progresses.

The questions in this chapter are designed not just to test recall, but to encourage the reader to think about how inputs and outputs work together in real project situations. Through these questions, the reader will practice recognizing which artifacts to use in different scenarios, how to track changes, document requirements, and ensure that everything produced by the project meets stakeholder needs.

Whether the reader is preparing for the PMP exam or aiming to strengthen project management skills, working through these questions will provide practical knowledge for managing information, making informed decisions, and delivering successful project outcomes.

Objectives

By engaging with the questions in this chapter, the reader will develop a comprehensive understanding of how inputs and outputs contribute to each stage of a project's lifecycle. The content is designed to help the reader recognize and distinguish between the various project artifacts, such as the project charter, requirements documentation, risk register, change log, and product backlog, and to grasp their significance in the overall project environment. As the reader practices with different scenarios, they will learn how outputs from one process often serve as critical inputs for another, reinforcing an integrated approach to project management.

The chapter challenges the reader to apply knowledge in practical situations, encouraging thoughtful analysis and selection of the most appropriate documents and deliverables to solve problems, support decision-making, and track project progress. It also highlights the importance of using inputs and outputs to maintain effective project governance and communication, ensuring that stakeholder needs are addressed, changes are properly controlled, and valuable lessons are captured for future projects.

Ultimately, by working through this question bank, the reader will not only build technical knowledge but also develop practical decision-making skills and confidence for both the PMP exam and real-world project management tasks. The aim is to empower the reader to skillfully manage and leverage project inputs and outputs, leading to more successful and well-governed project outcomes.

Single select multiple choice questions

1. **A deliverable is produced and verified by the project team. What must happen before this deliverable is considered "accepted deliverable" as an output?**
   a. It is added to the risk register
   b. It is validated by an authorized stakeholder against acceptance criteria
   c. It is automatically included in the final report
   d. It is listed in the activity attributes

2. **Which of the following is a dynamic, prioritized list that directly supports ongoing adaptation and value delivery in agile projects?**
   a. Scope baseline
   b. Product backlog
   c. Issue log
   d. Resource calendar

3. **When tailoring the change management process, which artifact is essential for tracking the status and outcome of every formal change request?**
   a. Change log
   b. WBS dictionary
   c. Quality management plan
   d. Status report

4. **Which project document is most critical for ensuring that evolving assumptions and constraints are tracked throughout the entire project lifecycle?**
   a. Issue log
   b. Assumption log
   c. Risk register
   d. Stakeholder register

5. **A project manager needs to justify a new funding request. Which document should be referenced to demonstrate how the proposed change supports strategic alignment and measurable benefits?**
   a. Project charter
   b. Benefits management plan
   c. Activity attributes
   d. Milestone list

6. **At what project stage is the business case most likely to influence go/no-go decisions, and what is its main function during execution?**
   a. During execution, to track deliverable quality
   b. Prior to project initiation, to establish project validity and objectives; during execution, as a reference for measuring project success
   c. After closure, to archive financial data
   d. Only during closing, to check stakeholder satisfaction

7. **Which of the following best describes the difference between the project charter and the project scope statement?**
   a. The charter provides only a high-level overview; the scope statement elaborates detailed deliverables and exclusions
   b. The scope statement is created before the charter
   c. The charter is updated at every phase; the scope statement is never updated
   d. They both serve as acceptance criteria for deliverables

8. **A project's schedule baseline is updated after a major change is approved. What is the most critical control that must be in place for this update to be valid?**
   a. The project manager's approval only
   b. Formal change control procedures
   c. Stakeholder consensus via email
   d. Only a verbal agreement with the sponsor

9. **Which planning document must specify how changes to requirements will be initiated, analyzed, and approved?**
   a. Project scope statement
   b. Requirements management plan
   c. Milestone list
   d. Activity list

10. **Why is the configuration management plan critical for project artifact integrity?**
    a. It tracks only team attendance
    b. It ensures artifacts are identified, tracked, and changes are recorded and reported, maintaining consistency
    c. It is only used in closing
    d. It replaces the quality management plan

11. **What is the significance of a requirements traceability matrix in a complex, multi-phase project?**
    a. It only lists completed requirements
    b. It provides a structure to track requirements from origin to deliverable and manage change throughout numerous phases
    c. It replaces the stakeholder register
    d. It is only used at project closure

12. **If a project's cost baseline excludes explicit contingency reserves, what risk does this present to financial management?**
    a. The project will always be under budget
    b. No funds will be available for identified risks, increasing the risk of overruns
    c. Earned value data will be more accurate
    d. There will be more management reserve

13. **In an adaptive project, which artifact is most likely to be used to prioritize work dynamically as new requirements emerge?**
    a. Change log
    b. Product backlog
    c. Benefits management plan
    d. Project calendar

14. **Which document directly supports the traceability of risk response actions to specific risk events?**
    a. Change log
    b. Risk register
    c. Performance measurement baseline
    d. Resource histogram

15. **What is the key advantage of using a lessons learned register throughout the project rather than only at closure?**
    a. It increases cost
    b. It enables immediate application of lessons and supports continuous improvement
    c. It is required by all standards
    d. It eliminates all risks

16. **A project is funded through periodic releases tied to milestone achievement. Which artifact documents these releases and total funding needs?**
    a. Cost baseline
    b. Project funding requirements
    c. Activity list
    d. Scope statement

17. **In a project with multiple vendors, which document is essential for specifying how external goods and services will be acquired and managed?**
    a. Risk management plan
    b. Procurement management plan
    c. Milestone list
    d. Issue log

18. **What is the primary function of quality control measurements as project outputs?**
    a. To track resource spending
    b. To document results of quality assurance activities and verify compliance with standards
    c. To list stakeholder complaints
    d. To replace the change log

19. **Which of the following best explains the purpose of project team assignments as an input and output?**
    a. To identify and record who is responsible for each role, supporting scheduling and accountability
    b. To track only who attends meetings
    c. To list all project risks
    d. To document financial reserves

20. **Which artifact is essential for defining the working days and shifts available for scheduled activities?**
    a. Project calendar
    b. Issue log
    c. Product backlog
    d. Resource breakdown structure

21. **A project manager needs to show the logical sequence and dependencies of all project activities. Which artifact is best suited for this?**
    a. Project schedule network diagram
    b. Milestone list
    c. Benefits management plan
    d. Quality management plan

22. **Which artifact should be referenced to determine if every requirement has been fulfilled by a deliverable?**
    a. Requirements traceability matrix
    b. Scope statement
    c. Cost baseline
    d. Change log

23. **Why is the skill matrix a valuable resource during resource planning?**
    a. It replaces the activity list
    b. It identifies skills available versus those required, highlighting gaps to be addressed
    c. It tracks only cost estimates
    d. It is used only in closing

24. **Which document is most useful for planning and tracking the acquisition of goods and services from outside the performing organization?**
    a. Procurement management plan
    b. Resource breakdown structure
    c. Quality test and evaluation documents
    d. Issue log

25. **What is the purpose of a resource breakdown structure (RBS)?**
    a. To visualize project milestones
    b. To organize resources by category and type for better planning and allocation
    c. To document only deliverable acceptance
    d. To provide a list of planned meetings

26. **Which artifact is most crucial for ensuring that the timing of funding aligns with the project's cost baseline and schedule?**
    a. Funding proposal
    b. Project funding requirements
    c. Issue log
    d. Change management plan

27. **What best describes the purpose of the requirements documentation?**
    a. To capture, analyze, and progressively elaborate requirements to ensure they are clear, complete, and acceptable
    b. To only list stakeholder names
    c. To act as the risk register
    d. To replace the project charter

28. **Which project output provides the most direct evidence that cost, schedule, and scope are being monitored in an integrated manner?**
    a. Benefits management plan
    b. Performance measurement baseline (PMB)
    c. Stakeholder register
    d. Activity list

29. **What is the main function of the project management plan as an input and output?**
    a. To document only the scope
    b. To describe how the project will be executed, monitored, and closed; and to serve as the central reference for all project activities
    c. To replace the benefits management plan
    d. To assign project team roles

30. **When an output is produced from a process and becomes an input to another process, what is this an example of?**
    a. Sequential process flow
    b. Integration of process outputs as inputs for project management continuity
    c. Isolated process mapping
    d. Closing phase

31. **A project experiences repeated scope creep because requested features were not traced to the original requirements or objectives. Which artifact, if properly maintained, would most effectively have prevented this issue?**
    a. Change log
    b. Requirements traceability matrix
    c. Milestone list
    d. Assumption log

32. **During an external audit, the project manager is asked to demonstrate that all deliverables comply with the originally agreed acceptance criteria and that stakeholder sign-off was obtained. Which sequence of outputs and approvals best provides this evidence?**
    a. Verified deliverables | Scope baseline | Risk register
    b. Accepted deliverables | Change log | Project schedule
    c. Verified deliverables | Accepted deliverables | Approval by authorized stakeholder
    d. Status report | Activity attributes | Milestone list

33. **If the cost baseline is frequently updated without corresponding updates to the funding requirements and schedule baseline, what is the most likely project risk?**
    a. Improved stakeholder satisfaction
    b. Inaccurate cash flow planning and potential funding shortfalls
    c. Increased team motivation
    d. Reduced need for change control

34. **A project manager discovers that the issue log contains several unresolved items that have stalled progress. Which document or artifact should the project manager consult to determine escalation protocols and responsibilities for resolving these issues?**
    a. Project schedule
    b. Communications management plan
    c. Benefits management plan
    d. Activity list

35. **In a hybrid project, the team delivers iterative increments of a product, while certain regulatory milestones must be achieved on a fixed schedule. Which combination of project management artifacts best supports planning, tracking, and compliance in this context?**
    a. Product backlog, milestone list, and schedule baseline
    b. Issue log, risk register, and lessons learned register
    c. Team charter, activity attributes, and skill matrix
    d. Change log, cost baseline, and stakeholder register

Multi-select multiple choice questions

36. **When revising the project cost baseline, which two actions are essential to maintain integrated project control?**
    a. Simultaneously update project funding requirements
    b. Ignore updates to the schedule baseline
    c. Communicate changes to all affected stakeholders
    d. Eliminate all contingency reserves
    e. Remove all change requests from the change log

37. **Which two documents are critical for providing traceability and control over requirements fulfillment throughout the project lifecycle?**
    a. Requirements traceability matrix
    b. Change management plan
    c. Resource calendar
    d. Requirements documentation
    e. Issue log

38. **A project manager is preparing for phase closure. Which two outputs should be emphasized to demonstrate that project objectives have been met and lessons are captured for future use?**
    a. Final report
    b. Assumption log
    c. Lessons learned register
    d. Change log
    e. Skill matrix

39. **In a complex, multi-vendor project, which two outputs are most critical for managing and controlling procurement activities?**
    a. Procurement management plan
    b. Procurement documentation
    c. Work performance information
    d. Skill matrix
    e. Milestone list

40. **When a change request is submitted, which two project artifacts must be updated to ensure transparent evaluation and recordkeeping?**
    a. Change log
    b. Risk register
    c. Stakeholder engagement plan
    d. Assumption log
    e. Project management plan

41. **During project planning, which two inputs are most crucial for developing a robust stakeholder engagement plan?**
    a. Stakeholder register
    b. Scope baseline
    c. Communications management plan
    d. Enterprise environmental factors (EEFs)
    e. Resource breakdown structure

42. **A team wants to streamline its reporting to focus on actionable project insights. Which two artifacts provide the most effective means for communicating project status and performance trends to stakeholders?**
    a. Work performance reports
    b. Quality management plan
    c. Status reports
    d. WBS dictionary
    e. Work performance information

43. **Which two artifacts are essential inputs for developing the project management plan to ensure alignment with organizational goals and value delivery?**
    a. Benefits management plan
    b. Business case
    c. Quality metrics
    d. Issue log
    e. Project schedule

44. **In an agile/adaptive project, which two types of backlogs are especially relevant for managing both high-level vision and near-term work cycles?**
    a. Product backlog
    b. Iteration backlog
    c. Lessons learned register
    d. Issue log
    e. Work performance data

45. **When managing a project with both internal and external resources, which two artifacts best support resource allocation and scheduling?**
    a. Resource breakdown structure
    b. Resource calendar
    c. Risk register
    d. Stakeholder register
    e. Quality control measurements

46. **When a risk is identified that affects both cost and schedule, which two artifacts must be updated to reflect the new risk and its potential impacts?**
    a. Risk register
    b. Cost baseline
    c. Quality management plan
    d. Schedule baseline
    e. Assumption log

47. **For a project under regulatory scrutiny, which two documents are essential for demonstrating compliance and traceability of requirements to deliverables?**
    a. Requirements traceability matrix
    b. Quality control measurements
    c. WBS dictionary
    d. Requirements documentation
    e. Milestone list

48. **When reviewing a project's financial health, which two outputs should be analyzed to forecast future budget performance and identify potential overruns?**
    a. Cost forecasts
    b. Work performance data
    c. Revenue forecasts
    d. Cost baseline
    e. Change log

49. **After a major team reorganization, which two artifacts must be updated to ensure accurate definition of roles and responsibilities?**
    a. Team charter
    b. Project team assignments
    c. Benefits management plan
    d. Product backlog
    e. Milestone list

50. **Which two project artifacts support effective transition and ongoing value after the final product is delivered to operations or the customer?**
    a. Final product, service, or result transition
    b. Benefits management plan
    c. Issue log
    d. Quality metrics
    e. Resource calendar

51. **During a quality review, which two outputs provide the most direct evidence of compliance with quality standards and process improvement recommendations?**
    a. Quality control measurements
    b. Quality reports
    c. Risk management plan
    d. Issue log
    e. Schedule baseline

52. **When integrating new regulatory requirements, which two artifacts are likely to be updated to reflect changes in project execution and compliance documentation?**
    a. Project management plan
    b. Configuration management plan
    c. Project funding requirements
    d. Requirements documentation
    e. Quality management plan

53. **In a project with a hybrid development approach, which two plans or documents are essential to successfully coordinate predictive and adaptive elements?**
    a. Development approach
    b. Schedule management plan
    c. Product backlog
    d. Risk register
    e. Stakeholder engagement plan

54. **To ensure all project risks are properly categorized and assessed, which two project artifacts are most relevant?**
    a. Risk register
    b. Risk breakdown structure (RBS)
    c. WBS dictionary
    d. Quality control measurements
    e. Change log

55. **When preparing a final report, which two types of information must be included to provide a comprehensive summary of project performance and benefits realization?**
    a. Summary of scope, quality, cost, and schedule objectives and variances
    b. Stakeholder register
    c. Degree to which business needs and benefits were achieved
    d. Product backlog
    e. Skill matrix

56. **When a project team is assessing overall performance and considering corrective action, which two types of work performance outputs are most useful for making data-driven decisions?**
    a. Work performance information
    b. Work performance reports
    c. Resource breakdown structure
    d. Schedule data
    e. Risk register

57. **For a project with frequent changes in resource availability, which two artifacts must be closely monitored and updated to maintain an achievable project schedule?**
    a. Resource calendar
    b. Project schedule
    c. Issue log
    d. Requirements traceability matrix
    e. Scope baseline

58. **When escalating unresolved issues, which two project plans or logs should provide guidance on escalation paths and responsible parties?**
    a. Issue log
    b. Communications management plan
    c. Cost baseline
    d. Team charter
    e. Final report

59. **When a project includes both physical and virtual assets, which two artifacts are essential for ensuring all required resources are documented and tracked for project execution?**
    a. Physical and virtual resource assignments
    b. Resource breakdown structure
    c. Quality test and evaluation documents
    d. Stakeholder register
    e. Schedule management plan

60. **Which two project management plans most directly guide the processes for identifying, evaluating, and responding to project risks?**
    a. Risk management plan
    b. Schedule management plan
    c. Quality management plan
    d. Resource management plan
    e. Configuration management plan

61. **In preparing for a major project release, which two outputs must be reviewed to confirm that all scope and quality requirements have been fulfilled and validated?**
    a. Verified deliverables
    b. Quality control measurements
    c. Product backlog
    d. Project calendar
    e. Team performance assessments

62. **When creating a sourcing strategy plan, which two considerations are most critical for aligning procurement decisions with project value and risk objectives?**
    a. Insourcing or outsourcing decisions
    b. Source selection criteria
    c. Project funding requirements
    d. Issue log
    e. Skill matrix

63. **Which two inputs are foundational for building a schedule model that reflects both time constraints and resource availability?**
    a. Activity attributes
    b. Project calendar
    c. Benefits management plan
    d. Work performance data
    e. Quality test and evaluation documents

64. **When integrating lessons from previous projects into current planning, which two organizational process assets should be referenced or updated?**
    a. Organizational knowledge repositories
    b. Lessons learned register
    c. Resource calendar
    d. Stakeholder engagement plan
    e. Change log

65. **For a project that will transition its deliverables to external operations, which two outputs are directly related to successful handover and sustained value realization?**
    a. Final product, service, or result transition
    b. Benefits management plan
    c. Issue log
    d. Schedule baseline
    e. Work performance data

66. **During project execution, which two documents are most critical for ensuring that all required team skills are present and that performance gaps are addressed?**
    a. Skill matrix
    b. Team performance assessments
    c. Issue log
    d. Risk register
    e. Activity list

67. **A team is struggling to track which requirements remain unfulfilled as the project nears completion. Which two artifacts should be reviewed to identify gaps?**
    a. Requirements traceability matrix
    b. Requirements documentation
    c. Work performance reports
    d. Quality reports
    e. Project schedule network diagram

68. **When a project involves strict regulatory requirements and multiple compliance checkpoints, which two plans or documents must be aligned to avoid noncompliance?**
    a. Quality management plan
    b. Requirements management plan
    c. Change management plan
    d. Milestone list
    e. Team charter

69. **In managing large-scale projects with many parallel work streams, which two artifacts are most useful for visualizing dependencies and avoiding scheduling conflicts?**
    a. Project schedule network diagram
    b. Activity list
    c. Quality reports
    d. Resource requirements
    e. Cost forecasts

70. **After making significant updates to the project management plan, which two additional artifacts are most likely to require immediate updates to maintain alignment and control?**
    a. Project document updates
    b. Change log
    c. Benefits management plan
    d. Communications management plan
    e. Issue log

Fill-in-the-blanks

71. **In project management, __ are the products, services, and capabilities created through the project and validated against established criteria before final approval.**
    a. Verified deliverables
    b. Accepted deliverables
    c. Quality metrics
    d. Lessons learned

72. **The __ is a project document that records all assumptions and constraints identified throughout the project lifecycle.**
    a. Issue log
    b. Assumption log
    c. Change log
    d. Benefit register

73. **A(n) __ is a formal proposal to modify any document, deliverable, or baseline within a project.**
    a. Risk response
    b. Change request
    c. Quality check
    d. User story

74. **The __ outlines the method used to create and evolve the product, such as adaptive, predictive, or hybrid.**
    a. Work breakdown structure
    b. Development approach
    c. Activity list
    d. Resource management plan

75. **__ is a living document that describes how the project will be executed, monitored and controlled, and closed.**
   a. Benefits management plan
   b. Project management plan
   c. Stakeholder register
   d. Team charter

76. **The __ provides a comprehensive list of all submitted changes along with their current status and disposition.**
   a. Change log b. Risk register
   c. Activity attributes d. Issue log

77. **A __ is any unique, verifiable product, result, or capability required to complete a process, phase, or project.**
   a. Work package b. Deliverable
   c. Baseline d. Schedule milestone

78. **The __ documents how, when, and by whom project information will be administered and disseminated.**
   a. Communications management plan
   b. Requirements management plan
   c. Quality management plan
   d. Issue log

79. **__ are quantitative assessments of the likely costs for resources required to complete an activity.**
   a. Budget forecasts
   b. Cost estimates
   c. Resource requirements
   d. Activity attributes

80. **A(n) __ is a hierarchical representation of project resources by category and type, such as labor, equipment, or materials.**
   a. Resource calendar
   b. Resource breakdown structure
   c. Skill matrix
   d. Project schedule

81. **The __ is a grid that links product requirements from their origin to the deliverables that satisfy them.**
   a. Requirements traceability matrix
   b. Milestone list
   c. Activity list
   d. Quality matrix

82. **__ are internal or external conditions that influence, constrain, or direct a project but are not under the immediate control of the team.**
   a. Organizational process assets
   b. Enterprise environmental factors
   c. Scope exclusions
   d. Quality standards

83. **The __ is a project document or repository used to record knowledge gained during a project, phase, or iteration for future use.**
   a. Benefits management plan
   b. Lessons learned register
   c. Risk register
   d. Stakeholder register

84. **__ is the approved version of the time-phased project budget, excluding management reserves, used as a basis for comparison to actual results.**
   a. Cost baseline
   b. Funding proposal
   c. Budget at completion
   d. Schedule baseline

85. **The __ identifies all project milestones and indicates whether they are mandatory or optional.**
   a. Project schedule
   b. Milestone list
   c. Quality test document
   d. Issue log

86. **__ are the approved version of formal scope documents, such as the scope statement and work breakdown structure, used as the basis for comparison to actual results.**
   a. Scope exclusions
   b. Scope baseline

c. Performance measurement baseline

d. Project management plan

87. **The __ describes how project resources will be acquired, allocated, monitored, and controlled throughout the project.**

a. Communications management plan

b. Resource management plan

c. Issue log

d. Skill matrix

88. **__ is a document that establishes the team's values, agreements, and operating guidelines.**

a. Team charter

b. Stakeholder engagement plan

c. Activity attributes

d. Quality report

89. **The __ is a component of the project management plan that describes how risks will be structured and managed.**

a. Issue log

b. Risk management plan

c. Change management plan

d. Quality management plan

90. **The __ is a dynamic list of work to be done, often written as user stories and prioritized to manage adaptive or agile project work.**

a. Milestone list

b. Product backlog

c. Project calendar

d. Stakeholder register

91. **__ is a calendar that identifies the working days and shifts available for scheduled activities in a project.**

a. Resource calendar

b. Project calendar

c. Activity list

d. Assumption log

92. **The __ is a document that formally authorizes the existence of a project and provides the project manager with authority to apply resources.**

a. Project scope statement

b. Project charter

c. Stakeholder register

d. Quality management plan

93. **__ are completed deliverables that have been checked for correctness through the Monitor and Control Scope process.**

a. Accepted deliverables

b. Verified deliverables

c. Approved changes

d. Project management plan updates

94. **The __ is a document that contains information about project stakeholders, including identification, assessment, and classification.**

a. Stakeholder engagement plan

b. Stakeholder register

c. Issue log

d. Team charter

95. **__ provides context to raw project data, allowing for analysis against the project management plan and informing decision-making.**

a. Work performance information

b. Status report

c. Change log

d. Project funding requirements

Match the following

96. **Match each artifact in Table A with its primary purpose or function in Table B:**

Table A	Table B
a. Change log	i. Lists all identified project milestones and their status
b. Milestone list	ii. Details the status and disposition of submitted changes
c. Resource breakdown structure	iii. Depicts hierarchical organization of resources
d. Lessons learned register	iv. Records knowledge gained for future use
e. Project charter	v. Formally authorizes the project and grants the manager authority

97. **Match the input or output in Table A with its best usage scenario in Table B:**

Table A	Table B
a. Schedule baseline	i. Baseline for measuring timing variance and slippage
b. Cost forecasts	ii. Predicting future budget performance
c. Quality management plan	iii. Planning how standards and improvements will be applied
d. Requirements documentation	iv. Defining and detailing stakeholder/business needs
e. Issue log	v. Tracking and resolving project problems as they arise

98. **Match each planning output (Table A) with the performance domain it most directly supports (Table B):**

Table A	Table B
a. Communications management plan	i. Resource performance domain
b. Schedule management plan	ii. Risk performance domain
c. Cost baseline	iii. Finance performance domain
d. Risk management plan	iv. Schedule performance domain
e. Resource management plan	v. Stakeholder performance domain

99. **4. Match each artifact (Table A) with what it primarily controls, enables, or tracks (Table B):**

Table A	Table B
a. Assumption log	i. Linking requirements to deliverables
b. Work performance reports	ii. Availability of resources for scheduling
c. Requirements traceability matrix	iii. Identified risks, owners, and response plans
d. Resource calendar	iv. Hypotheses and constraints throughout the project
e. Risk register	v. Communicating project status and decision data

100. **Match each document (Table A) to the process group it is most associated with (Table B):**

Table A	Table B
a. Project charter	i. Initiating
b. Requirements documentation	ii. Closing

Table A	Table B
c. Issue log	iii. Planning
d. Final report	iv. Monitoring and Controlling
e. Stakeholder register	v. Initiating

101. **Match each scenario (Table A) with the artifact that best resolves or manages it in Table B:**

Table A	Table B
a. Need to verify each requirement is fulfilled	i. Requirements traceability matrix
b. Unclear resource availability for next sprint	ii. Resource calendar
c. Frequent scope creep	iii. Scope baseline
d. Pending procurement decisions	iv. Procurement management plan
e. Identifying lessons for future projects	v. Lessons learned register

102. **Match each artifact (Table A) to the most closely related project process or output (Table B):**

Table A	Table B
a. Verified deliverables	i. Output of Develop Schedule
b. Approved change requests	ii. Output of Develop project charter
c. Change log	iii. Output of Perform Integrated Change Control
d. Project charter	iv. Input to Direct and Manage Project Work
e. Schedule baseline	v. Input to Validate Scope

103. **Match each aspect of project control (Table A) with the artifact that best enables it (Table B):**

Table A	Table B
a. Monitoring progress	i. Performance measurement baseline
b. Assessing future resource needs	ii. Work performance data
c. Identifying upcoming milestones	iii. Resource requirements
d. Ensuring process compliance	iv. Milestone list
e. Tracking actuals vs plan	v. Quality management plan

104. **Match each risk management activity (Table A) with its most appropriate supporting document (Table B):**

Table A	Table B
a. Categorizing sources of risk	i. Risk breakdown structure
b. Documenting risk responses	ii. Risk register
c. Tracking risk appetite	iii. Risk management plan
d. Summarizing risk exposure	iv. Risk report
e. Assigning risk owners	v. Risk register

105. **Match each output (Table A) with the project management plan component it most likely updates (Table B):**

Table A	Table B
a. Approved change requests	i. Financial management plan
b. Updated project funding requirements	ii. Change management plan
c. New knowledge in lessons learned	iii. Schedule management plan
d. Revised schedule baseline	iv. Organizational process assets
e. Revised stakeholder engagement approach	v. Stakeholder engagement plan

106. **Match each concept (Table A) with the artifact where it is most likely found or managed (Table B):**

Table A	Table B
a. Acceptance criteria	i. chedule management plan
b. Control thresholds	ii. Resource management plan
c. Roles and responsibilities	iii. Project scope statement
d. Strategic alignment	iv. Configuration management plan
e. Configuration control	v. Benefits management plan

107. **Match each project challenge (Table A) with the best artifact or approach to address it (Table B):**

Table A	Table B
a. Frequent misunderstandings with the client	i. Change log
b. Untracked changes causing confusion	ii. Resource calendar
c. Resources not available as planned	iii. Communications management plan
d. Project team unclear about deliverable scope	iv. Lessons learned register
e. No record of process improvement	v. Project scope statement

108. **Match each performance domain (Table A) with the artifact that most directly supports it (Table B):**

Table A	Table B
a. Stakeholder	i. Project schedule
b. Scope	ii. Stakeholder engagement plan
c. Schedule	iii. Requirements documentation
d. Quality	iv. Cost baseline
e. Finance	v. Quality management plan

109. **Match each scenario (Table A) with the most relevant artifact for proactive management (Table B):**

Table A	Table B
a. Need to confirm task dependencies	i. Resource requirements
b. Prepare for resource shortages	ii. Work performance information
c. Confirm project aligns with business case	iii. Project schedule network diagram
d. Track actual project spending	iv. Issue log
e. Monitor status of open issues	v. Benefits management plan

110. **Match each project output (Table A) with the phase or process group where it most influences project management (Table B):**

Table A	Table B
a. Project management plan	i. Initiating
b. Stakeholder register	ii. Monitoring and Controlling
c. Work performance data	iii. Closing
d. Change log	iv. Executing
e. Final report	v. Planning

111. **Match each artifact (Table A) with what it most commonly triggers or informs (Table B):**

Table A	Table B
a. Risk register	i. Project management plan updates
b. Activity attributes	ii. Risk response planning
c. Change log	iii. Project schedule development
d. Requirements documentation	iv. Resource scheduling
e. Resource calendar	v. Quality assurance/test planning

112. **Match each real-world need (Table A) with the artifact that addresses it (Table B):**

Table A	Table B
a. Review past errors and successes	i. Quality reports
b. Document contract payment terms	ii. Procurement documentation
c. Identify project exclusions	iii. Lessons learned register
d. Track regulatory compliance	iv. Project scope statement
e. Assign team responsibilities	v. Project team assignments

113. **Match each project update (Table A) with the artifact most likely to be revised (Table B):**

Table A	Table B
a. Change in stakeholder needs	i. Risk register
b. New risk identified	ii. Stakeholder engagement plan
c. Resource constraint encountered	iii. Verified deliverable
d. Adjustment to schedule	iv. Schedule baseline
e. Completed deliverable	v. Resource management plan

114. **Match each type of requirement (Table A) with its corresponding example (Table B):**

Table A	Table B
a. Business requirement	i. "Must be completed in 8 weeks"
b. Stakeholder requirement	ii. "System must support Spanish and English"
c. Functional requirement	iii. "User must be able to reset password via email"

Table A	Table B
d. Nonfunctional requirement	iv. "System response time must be under 2 seconds"
e. Project requirement	v. "Solution must align with organizational strategy"

115. **Match each artifact (Table A) with the type of project information it most directly contains (Table B):**

Table A	Table B
a. Quality management plan	i. Names, roles, and responsibilities
b. Status report	ii. Progress, forecasts, and status of the project
c. Project team assignments	iii. Standards, roles, improvement approaches
d. Final report	iv. Raw measurements and observations
e. Work performance data	v. Scope, objectives, milestones, benefits

116. **Match each resource management need (Table A) with the most relevant artifact (Table B):**

Table A	Table B
a. Document working days/shifts	i. Project team assignments
b. Identify skills vs needs	ii. Project calendar
c. Assign tasks by role	iii. Resource breakdown structure
d. Track material/equipment types	iv. Resource calendar
e. Monitor resource availability	v. Skill matrix

117. **Match each performance measurement (Table A) with the plan or baseline that serves as its reference (Table B):**

Table A	Table B
a. Cost variance	i. Schedule baseline
b. Schedule variance	ii. Scope baseline
c. Deliverable acceptance	iii. Cost baseline
d. Quality compliance	iv. Stakeholder engagement plan
e. Stakeholder satisfaction	v. Quality management plan

118. **Match each project artifact (Table A) with the type of update it most commonly requires (Table B):**

Table A	Table B
a. Project management plan	i. Plan updates
b. Risk register	ii. New risks/response actions
c. Lessons learned register	iii. New knowledge/experience entries
d. Stakeholder register	iv. Stakeholder changes
e. Change log	v. Status of change requests

119. **Match each project scenario (Table A) with the most relevant artifact for resolution (Table B):**

Table A	Table B
a. High defect rate discovered	i. Stakeholder engagement plan
b. Multiple stakeholders with conflicting needs	ii. Project team assignments
c. Project team confusion over task ownership	iii. Quality control measurements
d. Funding gaps during execution	iv. Project funding requirements
e. Need to analyze historical performance	v. Organizational process assets

120. **Match each process (Table A) with the artifact that is its primary output (Table B):**

Table A	Table B
a. Develop project charter	i. Risk management plan
b. Plan Risk Management	ii. Project scope statement
c. Define Scope	iii. Project charter
d. Control Schedule	iv. Quality reports
e. Manage Quality	v. Schedule baseline

Concept-based objective questions and answers

121. **A project team is halfway through executing a critical IT project when a client requests additional features. The project manager wants to ensure all new requirements are properly captured, linked to project objectives, and tracked until delivery. Describe the process and artifacts the project manager must use to ensure these new features are managed throughout the lifecycle, and explain why traceability is critical in this scenario.**

The project manager should update the requirements documentation and the requirements traceability matrix to capture, link, and track the new features. The requirements management plan should also be referenced or updated to ensure the process for requirements change is followed. The traceability matrix is critical because it links each requirement to business objectives and deliverables, enabling tracking from origin through validation and change management, preventing scope creep and missed deliverables.

122. **A construction project encounters unexpected site conditions, leading to changes in scope and schedule. The sponsor is concerned about the financial impact and wants real-time visibility into project spending and forecasts. Which project outputs should the project manager prioritize updating and sharing, and what is their role in managing cost performance?**

The project manager should update the cost baseline, cost forecasts, and work performance reports. The cost baseline captures approved changes, cost forecasts predict future spending, and work performance reports summarize actuals versus planned costs and provide actionable insights. These outputs enable the sponsor to clearly see the effect of site conditions on project finances and make informed decisions.

123. **In a multi-phase pharmaceutical development project, the regulatory environment changes midway, introducing new compliance standards. How should the project team integrate these changes to ensure ongoing compliance, and which documents must be updated?**

The project team should update the requirements documentation (to capture new compliance needs), the requirements traceability matrix (to link new requirements to deliverables), and the quality management plan (to ensure standards are met). The project management plan and schedule baseline may also require updates. This integration ensures all phases meet regulatory expectations, reducing the risk of rework or noncompliance penalties.

124. **A software development team using agile approaches is struggling to align sprint priorities with overall business objectives. What artifacts should be reviewed or updated to improve strategic alignment, and how do these ensure the project delivers intended value?**

The team should review and update the product backlog (to ensure the highest-value features are prioritized), the benefits management plan (which shows alignment with organizational strategy), and the business case (to reaffirm the project's intended value). Aligning the backlog with these documents ensures the team delivers what matters most to the business.

125. **A global project with teams in multiple countries suffers from repeated miscommunications, leading to delays and errors. Which plans and logs should be evaluated and adjusted to address these issues, and what best practices should be implemented?**

The communications management plan should be evaluated and tailored for time zones, language, frequency, and escalation. The stakeholder register should be updated to identify specific communication needs. Issue logs can track recurring problems so they can be addressed systematically. Best practices include regular reviews of communication effectiveness and adapting channels/methods as the team evolves.

126. **Midway through a government infrastructure project, new risks emerge that could affect both schedule and cost. What process should the project manager follow to ensure risks are properly documented, evaluated, and mitigated, and which artifacts are involved?**

The project manager should update the risk register (to document, categorize, and assign owners), revise the risk management plan if risk processes require changes, and potentially update the cost and schedule baselines if mitigation responses affect resources or timelines. Early and thorough documentation ensures risks are actively managed and communicated.

127. **A project team discovers that completed deliverables are rejected by stakeholders due to unclear acceptance criteria. How should the team remedy this issue to ensure future deliverables meet stakeholder expectations, and which project documents are involved?**

The team must update the project scope statement to include clear, measurable acceptance criteria for each deliverable. The requirements documentation and acceptance criteria in the requirements traceability matrix should also be clarified. This ensures deliverables are validated correctly before submission, minimizing rework and stakeholder dissatisfaction.

128. **During project execution, several team members express confusion about their individual roles and responsibilities, leading to duplicated efforts and missed tasks.**

Which project artifact is most effective for resolving this, and what steps should the project manager take?

The project manager should review and update the project team assignments to clearly define roles, responsibilities, and reporting lines. The team charter can also reinforce norms and expectations. Communicating these updates ensures everyone knows their duties, reducing overlap and gaps.

129. **A consumer product project is delayed due to the late delivery of critical parts from a supplier. What project management plan and documents should be reviewed or updated to address such procurement issues in the future?**

The procurement management plan should be reviewed to improve criteria for supplier selection, contract terms, and risk mitigation strategies. The procurement documentation should be updated with detailed records of performance and correspondence. These help prevent similar delays and support contractual remedies if necessary.

130. **An adaptive project is moving into a new release cycle, but the team is unsure which features are most important for the next iteration. Which artifacts and project management activities help clarify priorities and maintain alignment with business goals?**

The product backlog and iteration backlog should be reviewed and prioritized in collaboration with the product owner, referencing the benefits management plan and business case for strategic guidance. Regular backlog grooming and stakeholder input ensure focus on high-value work.

131. **A project manager is asked to present evidence that all quality standards have been met and that corrective measures were implemented where needed. Which outputs and supporting artifacts should be referenced, and how do they demonstrate quality assurance?**

Quality control measurements and quality reports provide evidence of compliance and document findings, recommendations, and corrective actions. The quality management plan should also be referenced to show that standards and procedures were followed.

132. **After several change requests are implemented, the project manager notices inconsistencies in scope and deliverables tracking. What should be done to restore alignment, and which documents must be reconciled?**

The project manager must ensure the change log is current, the requirements traceability matrix is updated for every approved change, and the project scope statement reflects the revised scope. These reconciliations maintain consistency and traceability.

133. **A project encounters frequent resource conflicts due to overlapping schedules and unclear availability. Which artifacts should be reviewed and updated to prevent such conflicts, and what processes can further improve resource utilization?**

The resource calendar and project schedule should be updated to reflect accurate availability. The resource management plan and project team assignments should be checked for clarity. Resource leveling and regular coordination meetings can further optimize usage.

134. **A senior executive asks for a summary of how the project's outcomes align with the original business case and strategic objectives at project closure. Which output best addresses this request, and what should it include?**

The final report should be presented, summarizing scope, cost, schedule, quality, benefits realization, and strategic alignment. It should reference the business case and benefits management plan to demonstrate fulfillment of organizational objectives.

135. **A project manager wants to ensure all lessons from the current project are available for future teams, including mistakes, successes, and recommendations.**

Which artifact is central to this knowledge transfer, and how should it be maintained and used?

The lessons learned register is key. It should be updated throughout the project and archived in the organization's knowledge repositories after closure. This enables future teams to avoid past mistakes and leverage best practices.

136. **Due to shifting stakeholder interests, project priorities have changed for a major deliverable. What steps should the project manager take to realign the project, and which documents should be updated?**

The project manager should update the stakeholder engagement plan, stakeholder register, and requirements documentation, and communicate changes to the project team. This ensures all stakeholders are informed, and project priorities are reflected in execution.

137. **The project team receives feedback that several requirements are ambiguous, leading to confusion during solution development. How can this issue be addressed to ensure requirements are clear and testable, and which documents are involved?**

Requirements documentation should be revised to be clear, measurable, and testable. The requirements management plan should stipulate the process for review and approval. The requirements traceability matrix also helps confirm completeness and clarity.

138. **A major risk has materialized, impacting both project timeline and cost. Which artifacts are updated as a result, and how do they help in managing the situation going forward?**

The risk register is updated to reflect the risk's occurrence and response actions. The cost baseline and schedule baseline are also adjusted if impacts are significant. These updates help manage stakeholder expectations and provide a new reference for future monitoring.

139. **A project sponsor requests a comparison of planned versus actual project performance to determine if corrective action is needed. Which outputs provide this information, and what analyses do they enable?**

Work performance information and work performance reports compare actuals to the baselines for scope, schedule, and cost. These enable variance analysis and trend evaluation, informing the need for corrective action.

140. **A team is utilizing both in-house and contracted third-party staff, leading to uncertainty about who is responsible for certain work packages. Which documents should be referenced to clarify roles and enforce accountability?**

Project team assignments and the resource management plan should be referenced for roles and responsibilities. The procurement management plan and procurement documentation also define external responsibilities.

141. **During a project audit, the auditor asks how the project ensured that every requirement was addressed and no requirements were missed. Which artifact(s) provide this assurance and how?**

The requirements traceability matrix provides assurance by documenting each requirement's origin, its link to business objectives, and its fulfillment through deliverables or tests.

142. **Project leadership notices a pattern of recurring issues that delay deliverables.**

What artifact and process should be leveraged to systematically address these issues and prevent recurrence?

The issue log should be used to document problems and track actions taken. Lessons learned register should capture root causes and solutions for future reference. Analyzing both enables continuous improvement.

143. **A project requires frequent reporting to an overseas client, with strict requirements for data accuracy and timeliness. Which project plan and supporting documents should be tailored to meet these requirements, and why is this important?**

The communications management plan should be tailored for frequency, data formats, and time zones. Work performance reports and status reports should be delivered as specified. This ensures data is accurate, timely, and meets client expectations, supporting trust and transparency.

144. **A new phase of a multi-year project is about to begin, and leadership wants to ensure that all prior knowledge is retained and transferred. Which processes and documents enable effective knowledge transition between phases?**

The lessons learned register and knowledge repositories are critical. A formal phase closure review should be conducted to capture and share lessons, ensuring new teams benefit from prior experience.

145. **A project with multiple deliverables is at risk of missing several contractual deadlines due to dependencies between teams. Which documents and analyses can the project manager use to identify bottlenecks and adjust plans?**

The project schedule, project schedule network diagram, and milestone list help identify dependencies and bottlenecks. Analyzing these enables adjustments to sequencing, resource allocation, and timelines.

146. **A company wants to track both direct and indirect benefits of a digital transformation program. What plan should be developed, and what should it include, to enable effective measurement and reporting of these benefits?**

A benefits management plan should be developed, including target benefits, metrics, timeframes, owners, and risks. It should specify how and when benefits will be measured and reported, and how alignment with organizational strategy will be maintained.

147. **After a project's completion, leadership wants to know why some benefits were not fully realized. What project documents should be reviewed, and how can this information be used to improve future projects?**

The final report, benefits management plan, and lessons learned register should be reviewed. These provide insights into actual versus planned benefits, root causes of shortfalls, and recommendations for future improvement.

148. **A project's funding is provided incrementally, tied to the achievement of specific milestones. Which documents and plans are critical for tracking, requesting, and justifying funding throughout the project?**

Project funding requirements, cost baseline, and milestone list are critical. They enable tracking of needed funds, justification for requests at each stage, and clear linkage to milestone achievement.

149. **A project is required to deliver a major software update during a short time window due to external, market-driven constraints. Which planning documents and scheduling tools are most important to ensure successful, timely delivery, and why?**

The schedule management plan, project schedule, and project calendar are essential. They define the scheduling methodology, control thresholds, and available working periods. The project schedule network diagram helps identify the critical path and necessary sequencing to meet the time constraints.

150. **A project manager is planning a complex project requiring tight integration between multiple teams and systems. Which artifacts and planning components are essential for ensuring effective configuration, change control, and integration management?**

The configuration management plan defines how artifacts are tracked and changed; the change management plan details change procedures; the project management plan integrates all subsidiary plans, and the requirements traceability matrix ensures changes are linked to requirements and deliverables.

151. **During an agile project, the team finds that the product backlog contains a mix of critical and outdated user stories, making sprint planning inefficient and misaligned with the product vision. How should the team address this issue using agile artifacts, and what is the role of backlog refinement in maintaining project alignment?**

The team should conduct regular backlog refinement (grooming) sessions to prioritize critical user stories, remove obsolete items, and clarify acceptance criteria. The product backlog should remain dynamic and reflect the current needs and vision, ensuring that each iteration delivers maximum value. This process is key to agile project alignment and efficient sprint planning.

152. **A scrum team is midway through a release and discovers that customer needs have shifted, requiring major changes in planned features. Which agile project documents and ceremonies facilitate adaptive change, and how are new requirements integrated into project delivery?**

The product backlog is updated to include new requirements, which are then prioritized by the product owner. Sprint planning meetings, along with backlog refinement sessions, allow for reprioritization and quick adaptation. This enables the team to integrate changing needs into upcoming sprints with minimal disruption.

153. **An agile project manager wants to demonstrate progress and value to stakeholders after every iteration, but stakeholders are confused about what to expect and when. What agile outputs should the team use for stakeholder communication, and how do these enhance transparency and feedback?**

The team should use iteration (sprint) reviews to present completed increments and update the product backlog. Work performance reports and regular status updates can be generated for stakeholders. These agile outputs ensure stakeholders see tangible progress and provide timely feedback, promoting engagement and transparency.

154. **A distributed agile team struggles with inconsistent collaboration and poorly communicated task ownership, leading to missed sprint commitments. Which agile artifacts and practices help clarify responsibilities and improve transparency in such a team?**

The team charter should establish working agreements and communication norms. The iteration backlog (or sprint backlog), along with Daily Stand-ups, clarifies task ownership and surfaces blockers. Agile boards (digital or physical) visually track assignments and progress.

155. **During a retrospective, the agile team finds that many defects are surfacing late in the release cycle, increasing rework and risk. Which project outputs and agile practices can help address this problem, and what process changes should be considered?**

Quality control measurements and a lessons learned register should be used to identify root causes. The team should implement continuous integration, automated testing, and frequent *definition of done* checks in each sprint. Documenting and acting on retrospective insights fosters continuous improvement in quality.

156. **A product owner is struggling to communicate shifting business priorities to the development team, resulting in misaligned deliverables. Which agile inputs and ceremonies help ensure the team is always working on the highest-priority requirements?**

The product backlog serves as the single source of truth for priorities. Regular backlog refinement and sprint planning meetings facilitate direct communication between the product owner and the team, ensuring that top-priority work is always selected for development.

157. **A regulator requests traceable evidence that each user story was implemented and validated according to requirements in an agile project. Which artifacts provide this traceability, and how should the team document the process?**

The requirements traceability matrix can be adapted for agile by linking user stories to acceptance criteria, test cases, and completed increments. The definition of done, sprint review outputs, and updated product backlog provide further documentation. This ensures each requirement is traceable from conception to validation.

158. **A cross-functional agile team must frequently update resource needs as team members shift between roles and projects. Which agile-friendly artifacts and practices can help manage dynamic resource allocation and support adaptive planning?**

The resource breakdown structure and skill matrix help visualize team capability and gaps. Regular agile ceremonies (like sprint planning and retrospectives) enable rapid reassignment of roles and responsibilities based on current needs and team strengths.

159. **In an agile project, stakeholders request more frequent updates on progress, risks, and impediments than the current reporting cadence allows. How can agile outputs and project management plans be adapted to meet these information needs without losing team focus?**

Work performance information and visual agile boards (e.g., burndown charts, Kanban boards) can be shared in real time. The communications management plan should be updated to specify more frequent review sessions or automated dashboard updates, balancing transparency with team productivity.

160. **A newly formed agile team is unsure how to define and measure "done" for each backlog item, resulting in inconsistent quality and stakeholder dissatisfaction.**

Which agile artifacts and outputs can help the team standardize completion criteria and ensure consistent value delivery?

The team should develop a clear *definition of done*, document acceptance criteria in the product backlog for each user story, and use quality control measurements to verify completion. The requirements documentation and quality management plan provide a framework for standardization.

Conclusion

As the reader completes this chapter, they will have developed a solid grasp of how inputs and outputs form the backbone of effective project management. Through varied scenarios and question formats, the reader has learned not just to recognize key documents and deliverables but also to understand their practical use and interconnectedness throughout the project lifecycle. This understanding is fundamental for ensuring that information moves fluidly across processes, stakeholders remain informed and engaged, and project objectives are consistently met.

The content has shown that successfully navigating inputs and outputs goes beyond documentation; it is about making informed choices, adapting to change, and supporting clear communication within the team and with stakeholders. By mastering these concepts, the reader is better equipped to maintain control over project direction, quality, and outcomes, as well as to respond thoughtfully to new challenges or opportunities as they arise.

With this foundation in place, the reader is now ready to explore the next chapter. Building on the knowledge of what information is needed and produced at each stage, the upcoming section will focus on how to use the right tools and methods to analyse data, solve problems, and deliver value throughout the project. This progression ensures the reader continues developing a well-rounded, practical skill set for successful project management in any setting.

References

1. A Guide to the Project Management Body of Knowledge (PMBOK® Guide), Seventh and Eighth Edition. Project Management Institute.

   This guide was used as the primary reference for concepts, terminology, and best practices related to tailoring project management processes, governance, lifecycles, stakeholder engagement, diagnostics, and continuous improvement.

2. The Standard for project management. Project Management Institute, 2021.

   Provided foundational principles and frameworks for project tailoring across different environments and project types.

3. PMI's Digital Platform for Standards.

   Accessed for up-to-date standards, definitions, and supplementary materials relevant to tailoring and other project management topics.

Answers

Q. No.	Answers
1	b
2	b
3	a
4	b
5	b
6	b
7	a
8	b
9	b
10	b
11	b

Q. No.	Answers
12	b
13	b
14	b
15	b
16	b
17	b
18	b
19	a
20	a
21	a
22	a

Q. No.	Answers
23	b
24	a
25	b
26	b
27	a
28	b
29	b
30	b
31	b
32	c
33	b

Q. No.	Answers
34	b
35	a
36	a, c
37	a, d
38	a, c
39	a, b
40	a, e
41	a, d
42	a, c
43	a, b
44	a, b

Q. No.	Answers
45	a, b
46	a, d
47	a, d
48	a, d
49	a, b
50	a, b
51	a, b
52	a, d
53	a, b
54	a, b
55	a, c
56	a, b
57	a, b
58	a, b
59	a, b
60	a, d
61	a, b
62	a, b
63	a, b
64	a, b
65	a, b
66	a, b
67	a, b
68	a, b
69	a, b
70	a, d
71	b
72	b
73	b
74	b
75	b
76	a
77	b
78	a
79	b
80	b
81	a

Q. No.	Answers
82	b
83	b
84	a
85	b
86	b
87	b
88	a
89	b
90	b
91	b
92	b
93	b
94	b
95	a
96	a - ii b - i c - iii d - iv e - v
97	a - i b - ii c - iii d - iv e - v
98	a - v b - iv c - iii d - ii e - i
99	a - iv b - v c - i d - ii e - iii

Q. No.	Answers
100	a - v b - iii c - iv d - ii e - i
101	a - i b - ii c - iii d - iv e - v
102	a - v b - iv c - iii d - ii e - i
103	a - ii b - iii c - iv d - v e - i
104	a - i b - ii c - iii d - iv e - v
105	a - ii b - i c - iv d - iii e - v

Q. No.	Answers
106	a - iii b - i c - ii d - v e - iv
107	a - iii b - i c - ii d - v e - iv
108	a - ii b - iii c - i d - v e - iv
109	a - iii b - i c - v d - ii e - iv
110	a - v b - i c - iv d - ii e - iii
111	a - ii b - iii c - i d - iv e - v

Q. No.	Answers
112	a - iii b - ii c - iv d - i e - v
113	a - ii b - i c - v d - iv e - iii
114	a - v b - ii c - iii d - iv e - i
115	a - iii b - ii c - i d - v e - iv
116	a - ii b - v c - i d - iii e - iv

Q. No.	Answers
117	a - iii b - i c - ii d - v e - iv
118	a - i b - ii c - iii d - iv e - v
119	a - iii b - i c - ii d - v e - iv
120	a - iii b - i c - ii d - v e - iv

CHAPTER 8
Tools and Techniques

Introduction

Project management is a dynamic field that requires the thoughtful application of various tools and techniques to plan, execute, monitor, and complete projects successfully. This chapter presents a wide range of tools and techniques, from communication methods and scheduling tools to quality improvement practices and team collaboration strategies. Whether managing risk through analysis, improving processes with visual aids, or facilitating stakeholder engagement, understanding how and when to apply these techniques is essential for effective project delivery.

In this question bank, the reader will encounter a variety of scenarios designed to reinforce the practical use of these tools and techniques. Each question goes beyond simple recall, encouraging the reader to think critically about real-world situations and choose the most appropriate approach for each context. By engaging with these questions, the reader will develop the confidence and insight needed to select and tailor the right tools for any project environment.

This interactive approach is intended to prepare the reader to build a strong foundation for day-to-day project management practice. Through careful study and application, the reader will be able to maximize the effectiveness of project teams, streamline communication, manage constraints, and drive projects toward successful outcomes.

Objectives

The primary aim of this chapter, presented in the form of different types of questions, is to help the reader become confident and agile in selecting and applying the wide range of tools and techniques that are essential to effective project management. By working through these carefully crafted questions, the reader will not only deepen their understanding of each tool or technique but will also develop the practical judgment needed to use them in real project scenarios.

After engaging with this chapter, the reader will be able to recognize when and how to use various tools, such as scheduling methods, communication models, risk analysis techniques, and process improvement frameworks, to address common project challenges. The questions are designed to encourage critical thinking, helping the reader connect theory to practice and make well-informed decisions in complex situations.

Additionally, the reader will learn how to tailor these tools and techniques to fit the unique needs of different projects and stakeholders, ensuring that their chosen approach is both effective and adaptable. This experience will strengthen the reader's readiness for the PMP exam, as well as enhance their ability to deliver value and lead teams in any project environment.

Ultimately, the objective is to equip the reader with not just technical knowledge, but also the confidence and flexibility to apply the right tool at the right time—resulting in more successful, well-managed projects.

Single select multiple choice questions

1. **What is the primary goal of active listening in project management communication?**
   a. To collect requirements
   b. To minimize the duration of meetings
   c. To reduce misunderstandings and miscommunications among stakeholders
   d. To ensure all stakeholders are copied on emails

2. **Which tool is best for visually organizing a large number of ideas into related groups to facilitate analysis?**
   a. Affinity diagram
   b. Burndown chart
   c. Flowchart
   d. Kanban board

3. **Are after-action reviews (AARs) most valuable for which of the following objectives?**
   a. Increasing project scope
   b. Reinforcing learning and improving future performance by reflecting on actions taken
   c. Replacing project documentation
   d. Avoiding stakeholder involvement

4. **Agile release planning is used to:**
   a. Assign resources to individual tasks
   b. Provide a high-level summary timeline for iterations and feature releases
   c. Develop the WBS
   d. Replace the sprint backlog

5. **What is the main advantage of alternative analysis in decision-making?**
   a. It guarantees stakeholder approval
   b. It provides a structured method to compare options and select the best approach
   c. It eliminates the need for a risk register
   d. It requires no data

6. **Analogous estimating is most appropriately used when:**
   a. There is detailed information about each activity
   b. Only limited information is available, and historical data from similar projects exists
   c. The project team prefers bottom-up techniques
   d. The project has no predecessors

7. **What is the key risk of relying solely on analogous estimating?**
   a. It is always more accurate than detailed estimating
   b. It can be less accurate due to differences between projects
   c. It eliminates the need for expert judgment
   d. It is preferred for all financial estimates

8. **What is the purpose of assumption and constraint analysis?**
   a. To limit stakeholder communication
   b. To identify risks from inaccurate or incomplete assumptions and constraints
   c. To determine project resource needs
   d. To avoid using historical information

9. **Which type of audit specifically reviews contract processes for completeness and accuracy?**
   a. Risk audit
   b. Quality audit
   c. Procurement audit
   d. Financial audit

10. **In adaptive (agile) projects, backlog management is mainly used to:**
    a. Freeze the project scope
    b. Maintain and prioritize the evolving list of work to be done
    c. Replace product roadmaps
    d. Assign resources to vendors

11. **What is the primary focus of backlog refinement?**
    a. Documenting lessons learned
    b. Reprioritizing and elaborating backlog items for upcoming iterations

c. Creating a detailed WBS
d. Managing the project budget

12. **Which estimating method involves aggregating estimates of the lowest-level components of the WBS?**
    a. Analogous estimating
    b. Bottom-up estimating
    c. Parametric estimating
    d. Relative size estimation

13. **What is a unique characteristic of branch and bound as a problem-solving technique?**
    a. It is used for team building
    b. It optimizes solutions by systematically eliminating non-optimal subproblems
    c. It is only applicable to cost estimation
    d. It provides qualitative results only

14. **What is the main use of a burndown chart in agile projects?**
    a. Showing completed work versus time left in a timebox
    b. Documenting project risks
    c. Analyzing project cost
    d. Detailing roles and responsibilities

15. **Which diagram is best for tracing an effect back to its root cause?**
    a. Kanban board
    b. Cause-and-effect (fishbone / Ishikawa) diagram
    c. Burnup chart
    d. RACI matrix

16. **What is the key difference between centralized and distributed management and leadership structures?**
    a. Centralized structures distribute authority among all team members
    b. Distributed structures empower individuals and decentralize decision-making
    c. Distributed structures require approval for every decision
    d. Centralized structures have no formal authority

17. **Which tool is best used to ensure specific steps in a process are completed or considered, often to avoid missing important items?**
    a. Checklist
    b. Kanban board
    c. Affinity diagram
    d. Mind mapping

18. **In agile environments, what is the main purpose of daily coordination meetings?**
    a. To review the risk register
    b. To align the team, declare intentions, and quickly surface obstacles
    c. To approve budgets
    d. To deliver stakeholder presentations

19. **What is one of the most critical factors when choosing communication technology for a project?**
    a. Project location only
    b. Urgency, availability, and compatibility for all stakeholders
    c. Number of emails sent
    d. The color scheme of the interface

20. **Which conflict resolution technique seeks a win-win solution by integrating multiple viewpoints?**
    a. Withdraw / avoid
    b. Compromise / reconcile
    c. Force / direct
    d. Collaborate / problem-solve

21. **What is the core purpose of a flowchart in project management?**
    a. To assign resources
    b. To visually represent process steps and decision points
    c. To estimate costs
    d. To document only project risks

22. **Which technique is best for comparing the strengths and weaknesses of alternatives, including their relative value or risk?**
    a. Parametric estimating
    b. Cost-benefit analysis
    c. SWOT analysis
    d. Decision tree analysis

23. **Which estimating technique uses statistical relationships between historical data and project parameters to forecast cost or duration?**
    a. Bottom-up estimating
    b. Analogous estimating
    c. Parametric estimating
    d. Multipoint estimating

24. **What is the primary purpose of a Kanban board in project management?**
    a. To visualize, track, and limit work in progress across stages
    b. To document the detailed project scope
    c. To record stakeholder contact information
    d. To assign project sponsorship

25. **What does a tornado diagram specifically visualize in project risk analysis?**
    a. Project team structure
    b. Task dependencies
    c. Sensitivity of outcomes to various risks or variables
    d. Stakeholder engagement levels

26. **Which technique is used to find the underlying cause of a problem to prevent recurrence?**
    a. Benchmarking
    b. Root cause analysis
    c. Burnup chart
    d. Affinity diagram

27. **What is the primary benefit of using rolling wave planning?**
    a. It fixes all project requirements at the start
    b. It allows detailed near-term planning while keeping future work at a higher level until more information is available
    c. It only applies to resource leveling
    d. It removes the need for a project schedule

28. **What is the focus of value stream mapping in process improvement?**
    a. Tracking the number of team meetings
    b. Identifying and eliminating waste in process steps
    c. Assigning extra resources to every activity
    d. Documenting project budgets

29. **The technique of resource leveling is best described as:**
    a. Assigning the most resources possible to each activity
    b. Adjusting start and finish dates to balance resource demand with supply, which may affect the critical path
    c. Ignoring dependencies between activities
    d. Assigning one resource per activity

30. **What is the main reason to use the RACI matrix in a project?**
    a. To document project costs
    b. To clarify roles and responsibilities for each activity or deliverable
    c. To visualize the project schedule
    d. To manage procurement contracts

Multi-select multiple choice questions

31. **Which two techniques are most effective for identifying root causes of defects in a process?**
    a. Affinity diagram
    b. Cause-and-effect diagram
    c. Root cause analysis
    d. Burndown chart
    e. RACI matrix

32. **When conducting a risk audit, which two areas are typically evaluated?**
    a. Contract compliance
    b. Effectiveness of the risk management process
    c. Project team structure
    d. Adequacy of risk responses
    e. Project cost estimates

33. **Which two characteristics best describe the purpose of rolling wave planning?**
    a. Locks the project plan at the start
    b. Enables detailed planning for immediate work
    c. Keeps future work at a high level until more information is available
    d. Replaces the need for a WBS
    e. Is used only for agile projects

34. **In an agile project, which two artifacts are most useful for tracking and communicating progress within an iteration?**
    a. Product backlog
    b. Burndown chart
    c. Kanban board
    d. Control chart
    e. RACI matrix

35. **Which two practices are most likely to improve knowledge transfer and learning in a project environment?**
    a. After-action reviews
    b. In-progress postmortems
    c. Resource smoothing
    d. Fast tracking
    e. Precedence diagramming

36. **When applying resource optimization, which two techniques are directly involved?**
    a. Resource leveling
    b. Critical chain method
    c. Resource smoothing
    d. Value stream mapping
    e. Benchmarking

37. **Which two types of communication methods are considered "interactive" according to the PMBOK® Guide?**
    a. Face-to-face meetings
    b. Project dashboards
    c. Instant messaging
    d. Pull communication
    e. Email newsletters

38. **In multipoint estimating, what are two key inputs required to calculate an expected duration?**
    a. Most likely estimate
    b. Risk register
    c. Optimistic estimate
    d. Project organization chart
    e. Stakeholder register

39. **Which two actions are important when using benchmarking to improve project performance?**
    a. Compare to similar organizations or projects
    b. Only use internal company data
    c. Identify good practices for improvement
    d. Ignore industry standards
    e. Avoid external sources

40. **Which two tools or techniques can be used to visualize and analyze process flow for improvement?**
    a. Flowchart
    b. Value stream mapping
    c. Kanban board
    d. RACI matrix
    e. Brainstorming

41. **Which two techniques are essential for engaging distributed or virtual teams effectively?**
    a. Colocation
    b. Communication technology
    c. Virtual collaboration tools
    d. Control charts
    e. Burnup charts

42. **When making a complex group decision, which two decision-making techniques can balance input and fairness?**
    a. Autocratic decision-making
    b. Multicriteria decision analysis
    c. Majority voting
    d. Withdraw/avoid
    e. Fast tracking

43. **Which two characteristics are most associated with the use of control charts in project management?**
    a. Measure process stability
    b. Visualize work in progress
    c. Identify points requiring corrective action
    d. Assign team responsibilities
    e. Track project funding

44. **For projects with high uncertainty and frequent changes, which two techniques help teams adapt quickly?**
    a. Rolling wave planning
    b. Backlog refinement
    c. Crashing
    d. Fast tracking
    e. Earned value analysis

45. **Which two tools are particularly effective for visualizing and communicating project status to stakeholders?**
    a. Project dashboards
    b. Project canvas
    c. Burnup chart
    d. Control chart
    e. Contract audit

46. **When conducting a stakeholder analysis, which two factors are most relevant for stakeholder classification?**
    a. Impact/influence grid
    b. Stakeholder cube
    c. Affinity diagram
    d. Fishbone diagram
    e. RACI matrix

47. **Which two approaches are recommended for managing conflict within project teams?**
    a. Collaborate/problem-solve
    b. Smooth/accommodate
    c. Avoid feedback
    d. Withdraw/avoid
    e. Assign more tasks

48. **Which two approaches are effective for prioritizing project requirements in a large project?**
    a. MoSCoW method
    b. 100-point method
    c. Burnup chart
    d. Fast tracking
    e. Control chart

49. **In process improvement, which two tools help identify areas of waste or inefficiency?**
    a. Value stream mapping
    b. Process analysis
    c. Backlog refinement
    d. Kanban board
    e. RACI matrix

50. **Which two estimation techniques can use historical data for forecasting project effort or cost?**
    a. Analogous estimating
    b. Parametric estimating
    c. Five-why analysis
    d. Mind mapping
    e. Project dashboard

Fill-in-the-blanks

51. **__ is a technique used to organize a large number of ideas or causes into groups for further review and analysis.**
    a. Burndown chart b. Affinity diagram
    c. Control chart d. Kanban board

52. **The process of __ involves reevaluating and updating items in the product backlog to ensure the most valuable work is prioritized for the next iteration.**
    a. Value stream mapping
    b. Backlog refinement
    c. Fast tracking
    d. Cost aggregation

53. **__ is a visual tool that tracks how much work remains versus the time left in a sprint or iteration.**
    a. Kanban board b. Burnup chart
    c. Burndown chart d. RACI matrix

54. **A __ is a structured, independent process to determine if project activities comply with policies, processes, and procedures.**
    a. Risk audit b. Inspection
    c. Audit d. Benchmarking

55. **__ estimating is an approach that calculates cost or duration based on statistical relationships using historical data and project parameters.**
    a. Bottom-up b. Analogous
    c. Parametric d. Multipoint

56. **The __ technique helps teams systematically find the underlying reason for a problem, ensuring that the problem does not recur.**
    a. Root cause analysis
    b. Burnup chart
    c. Mind mapping
    d. Five whys

57. **__ is used to visually represent the logical sequence and dependencies between project activities.**
    a. Precedence diagramming method
    b. Kanban board
    c. RACI matrix
    d. Stakeholder cube

58. **In an agile project, a __ is a prioritized list of work to be done, maintained, and updated throughout the project.**
    a. Product backlog b. Milestone list
    c. Earned value chart d. Project canvas

59. **The __ technique adjusts start and finish dates of activities to balance resource demand with supply, possibly affecting the project's critical path.**
    a. Resource leveling
    b. Crashing
    c. Rolling wave planning
    d. Value stream mapping

60. **__ is a structured meeting that focuses on analyzing what happened, why it happened, and how future performance can be improved.**
    a. Sprint review
    b. After-action review
    c. Benchmarking
    d. Preassignment

61. **The __ provides a visible, real-time display of information to the project team and stakeholders, often updated manually.**
    a. Work breakdown structure
    b. Information radiator
    c. Control chart
    d. Cost-benefit analysis

62. **The __ technique is an iterative method that repeatedly asks "why" to uncover the root cause of a problem.**
    a. Five whys
    b. SWOT analysis
    c. MoSCoW method
    d. Parametric estimating

63. **__ is an ongoing process focused on making incremental improvements to processes, products, or services over time.**
a. Fast tracking
b. Continuous improvement
c. Rolling wave planning
d. Resource smoothing

64. **A __ is a graphical representation that breaks down the causes of a problem into discrete branches, helping teams identify main or root causes.**
a. Fishbone diagram b. Burnup chart
c. Kanban board d. S-curve

65. **__ is a technique that breaks project scope down into smaller, manageable parts for better control and estimation.**
a. Parametric estimating
b. Decomposition
c. Resource optimization
d. MoSCoW method

66. **The __ model is used to assess and manage stakeholder engagement levels, comparing current with desired states.**
a. Responsibility assignment matrix
b. Stakeholder engagement assessment matrix
c. Control chart
d. Value breakdown structure

67. **__ is a technique for optimizing the allocation of resources without affecting the project's critical path, using float.**
a. Resource smoothing
b. Resource leveling
c. Preassignment
d. Control chart

68. **__ is an estimation technique that involves using expert knowledge from those with specialized skills or experience.**
a. Benchmarking b. Expert judgment
c. Fast tracking d. Cost-benefit analysis

69. **The __ method is used to estimate the minimum project duration and determine scheduling flexibility by identifying the sequence of activities with zero float.**
a. Critical path method
b. Kanban
c. Value stream mapping
d. Rolling wave planning

70. **__ is a graphical representation of the work completed toward a milestone, often used in agile projects.**
a. Burnup chart b. Control chart
c. Fishbone diagram d. Burndown chart

71. **__ is a technique that uses a decision matrix with weighted criteria to evaluate and rank multiple alternatives.**
a. Multicriteria decision analysis
b. SWOT analysis
c. Rolling wave planning
d. Five whys

72. **__ is a process of planning, coordinating, and facilitating effective group events to reach decisions or conclusions.**
a. Facilitation b. Negotiation
c. Observation d. Decomposition

73. **A __ provides a set of charts and graphs, often electronic, to show project metrics, status, and performance at a glance.**
a. Project dashboard b. Kanban board
c. Control chart d. Stakeholder cube

74. **__ is a decision-making method in which the largest group within a set decides, even if there is no majority.**
a. Unanimity b. Plurality
c. Compromise d. Fast tracking

75. **The __ technique is used to visually organize information, showing connections among ideas or concepts, often generated during brainstorming.**
a. Mind mapping
b. Control chart
c. Rolling wave planning
d. Value stream mapping

Match the following

76. **Match each tool or technique with its primary purpose:**

Table A	Table B
a. Affinity diagram	i. Diagnosing underlying reasons for problems
b. Root cause analysis	ii. Tracking remaining work versus time
c. Burndown chart	iii. Organizing large sets of ideas into groups
d. Kanban board	iv. Getting beyond symptoms to core issues
e. Five whys	v. Visualizing workflow and limiting WIP

77. **Match the tool or technique to the scenario where it is most useful:**

Table A	Table B
a. Stakeholder engagement assessment matrix	i. Monitoring process stability and variation
b. Control chart	ii. Identifying and eliminating process waste
c. Value stream mapping	iii. Comparing current and desired stakeholder engagement
d. MoSCoW method	iv. Learning from performance during the project
e. In-progress postmortem	v. Prioritizing requirements by must/should/could/will not

78. **Match each estimating technique with its key characteristic:**

Table A	Table B
a. Analogous	i. Uses statistical models and project parameters
b. Parametric	ii. Aggregates detailed activity estimates
c. Bottom-up	iii. Uses data from similar past projects
d. Multipoint	iv. Relies on specialized experience
e. Expert judgment	v. Uses optimistic, pessimistic, and most likely

79. **Match the quality or process tool to what it best visualizes or controls:**

Table A	Table B
a. Fishbone diagram	i. Process stability over time
b. Control chart	ii. Potential causes of a problem
c. Burnup chart	iii. Cumulative work completed
d. Checklist	iv. Sequence and decision points in a process
e. Flowchart	v. Ensuring all steps or items are addressed

80. **. Match each type of audit or review with its main focus:**

Table A	Table B
a. Risk audit	i. Compliance with quality standards
b. Quality audit	ii. Effectiveness of risk management process
c. Procurement audit	iii. Procurement process completeness
d. After-action review	iv. Improvement during project execution
e. In-progress postmortem	v. Learning from a project or milestone

81. **Match each agile artifact or tool with its direct benefit:**

Table A	Table B
a. Product backlog	i. Visualizing and managing workflow
b. Kanban board	ii. Dynamic prioritization of work
c. Daily coordination	iii. Quick team alignment and obstacle surfacing
d. Iteration burndown	iv. Stakeholder feedback on increments
e. Sprint review	v. Progress tracking for the sprint

82. **Match the communication concept with its best example:**

Table A	Table B
a. Interactive communication	i. Project collaboration platform
b. Push communication	ii. Company intranet portal
c. Pull communication	iii. Email broadcast
d. Communication model	iv. Real-time video call
e. Communication technology	v. Sender-receiver-feedback diagram

83. **Match each risk management activity (Table A) with its most appropriate supporting document (Table B):**

Table A	Table B
a. Multicriteria decision analysis	i. Ranked alternatives
b. Majority voting	ii. Most supported option
c. Autocratic decision-making	iii. Single leader's choice
d. Plurality	iv. Largest block decides
e. Consensus	v. Unanimous agreement

84. **Match each project management chart with its main use:**

Table A	Table B
a. Project dashboard	i. Visualizing work in progress
b. Control chart	ii. Cumulative progress towards goals
c. Burnup chart	iii. Process variation over time
d. S-curve	iv. High-level project status and metrics
e. Kanban board	v. Project performance trends over time

85. **Match each resource or team management technique with its focus:**

Table A	Table B
a. Resource leveling	i. Keeping resource use within limits (float only)
b. Resource smoothing	ii. Clarifying who does what
c. Responsibility assignment matrix	iii. Balancing resource use may affect the schedule
d. Preassignment	iv. Improving collaboration and trust
e. Team building	v. Assigning resources before planning

86. **Match each scenario with the most appropriate tool or technique:**

Table A	Table B
a. Identifying and ranking risks	i. Kanban board
b. Tracking work in progress	ii. Work breakdown structure (WBS)
c. Structuring project scope	iii. Probability and impact matrix
d. Comparing the project to the industry	iv. Trend analysis
e. Finding patterns in data	v. Benchmarking

87. **Match each technique with its main outcome/use:**

Table A	Table B
a. Brainstorming	i. Gathering stakeholder expectations
b. SWOT analysis	ii. Categorizing stakeholders
c. Stakeholder mapping	iii. Examining strengths/weaknesses/opportunities/threats
d. Mind mapping	iv. Generating a list of ideas quickly
e. Focus groups	v. Visualizing connections among ideas

88. **Match each estimation method with a suitable application:**

Table A	Table B
a. Analogous estimating	i. When specialist experience is available
b. Bottom-up estimating	ii. Projects with quantifiable parameters
c. Parametric estimating	iii. High-detail activity-level estimates
d. Multipoint estimating	iv. Early project phase with limited details
e. Expert judgment	v. Managing uncertainty in estimates

89. **Match each agile-related tool or ceremony with its main goal:**

Table A	Table B
a. Sprint review	i. Clarify and reprioritize upcoming work
b. Backlog refinement	ii. Demonstrate completed work to stakeholders
c. Velocity chart	iii. Measure team productivity over time
d. Daily standup	iv. Publicly display project status and progress
e. Information radiator	v. Share intentions and blockers

90. **Match each process management tool to what it primarily measures or supports:**

Table A	Table B
a. Control chart	i. Shortening project duration
b. Schedule compression	ii. Process variation/stability
c. Earned value analysis	iii. Integrated cost/schedule performance
d. Resource smoothing	iv. Resource use within available float
e. S-curve	v. Cumulative performance over time

91. **Match each risk response strategy with its definition:**

Table A	Table B
a. Accept	i. Remove the risk source or objective
b. Avoid	ii. Take no action except to monitor
c. Mitigate	iii. Reduce probability and/or impact
d. Transfer	iv. Ensure opportunity definitely happens
e. Exploit	v. Shift risk to a third party

92. **Match each communication skill or artifact with its most direct purpose:**

Table A	Table B
a. Active listening	i. Clarify meeting objectives
b. Meeting agenda	ii. Ensure understanding and reduce miscommunication
c. Visual controls	iii. Provide visible process status
d. Feedback	iv. Describe the sender-receiver process
e. Communication model	v. Support interactive communication

93. **Match each type of chart or diagram with the data or information it is best suited to display:**

Table A	Table B
a. Bar chart	i. Nominal data (categories)
b. Pie chart	ii. Ordinal data (ranked categories)
c. Histogram	iii. Discrete values (counts/frequencies)
d. Line graph	iv. Impact sensitivity of project variables
e. Tornado diagram	v. Continuous data (trends over time)

94. **Match each leadership or management trait with its impact on project teams:**

Table A	Table B
a. Emotional intelligence	i. Guides group to decisions/conclusions
b. Motivation	ii. Improves relationships and results
c. Conflict management	iii. Increases commitment and performance
d. Critical thinking	iv. Reduces tension/increases cooperation
e. Facilitation	v. Enables objective analysis and solutions

95. **Match each scheduling tool or technique with its most likely use:**

Table A	Table B
a. Precedence diagram	i. Balance the use of resources
b. Schedule network analysis	ii. Add resources to compress the schedule
c. Crashing	iii. Identify early/late dates, float
d. Fast tracking	iv. Show activity sequence and logic
e. Resource leveling	v. Parallelize activities for speed

96. **Match each knowledge management approach to its benefit:**

Table A	Table B
a. Lessons learned register	i. Capture and share project wisdom
b. Communities of practice	ii. Foster ongoing knowledge exchange
c. Storytelling	iii. Make lessons relatable/memorable
d. Information management	iv. Codify and provide access to info
e. Shadowing	v. Transfer tacit knowledge directly

97. **Match each analytical technique with its core function:**

Table A	Table B
a. Data analysis	i. Evaluate options under uncertainty
b. Decision tree analysis	ii. Discover insights from data
c. Regression analysis	iii. Find relationships between variables
d. Sensitivity analysis	iv. Evaluate the adequacy of contingency
e. Reserve analysis	v. Identify variables with the biggest impact

98. **Match each resource management technique to its application:**

Table A	Table B
a. Preassignment	i. Map team capabilities and gaps
b. Responsibility assignment matrix	ii. Maintain resource use within float limits
c. Resource smoothing	iii. Clarify roles and responsibilities
d. Resource leveling	iv. Assign resources before planning
e. Skill matrix	v. Balance resources, possibly change schedule

99. **Match each risk analysis tool with its primary output:**

Table A	Table B
a. Probability and impact matrix	i. Probability distribution of outcomes
b. Risk register	ii. Visualize risk relationships
c. Influence diagram	iii. Consolidated risk data and actions
d. Prompt list	iv. Risk prioritization
e. Monte Carlo simulation	v. Stimulate risk identification

100. **Match each leadership model or theory with its main focus:**

Table A	Table B
a. Servant leadership	i. Hands-on, directive management for unmotivated teams
b. Theory X	ii. Enable team performance through service
c. Theory Y	iii. Coaching, autonomy for motivated individuals
d. Herzberg's factors	iv. Stages of team development
e. Tuckman ladder	v. Motivators and hygiene in job satisfaction

Concept-based objective questions and answers

101. **A project team consistently finds that requirements are misunderstood, despite regular written updates. Which tools or techniques can address this issue, and how should they be applied?**

 Active listening, feedback loops, and interactive communication methods (e.g., face-to-face meetings) should be emphasized. Active listening ensures messages are understood, and feedback allows for clarification, reducing miscommunication.

102. **A software development project is running behind schedule, and the project manager needs to compress the timeline without reducing scope. Which schedule compression techniques could be considered, and what are their trade-offs?**

 Crashing (adding resources for critical path tasks) and fast tracking (performing tasks in parallel) are both viable. Crashing increases cost, while fast tracking increases risk of rework and coordination issues.

103. **A team wants to visualize the flow of work in progress, identify bottlenecks, and limit simultaneous tasks. Which tool is most appropriate, and what benefits does it offer?**

 A Kanban board is ideal. It makes workflow visible, highlights bottlenecks, and supports limiting work in progress, which increases focus and throughput.

104. **A project manager is tasked with selecting a supplier for a critical component among several options with different strengths. Which decision-making technique will provide a transparent, systematic selection process?**

 Multicriteria decision analysis allows for the comparison of alternatives using weighted criteria, providing a rational, auditable selection process.

105. **A recurring defect keeps appearing at a late stage in a product development project. Which combination of techniques should be used to identify and address the fundamental cause?**

 A cause-and-effect (fishbone) diagram, followed by root cause analysis and the five whys technique, will help uncover the underlying source and propose lasting solutions.

106. **A project team wants to ensure that lessons learned are captured and shared regularly, not just at the end of the project. What two practices best support this goal, and why are they valuable?**

 In-progress postmortems and after-action reviews (AARs) foster real-time knowledge capture, enabling teams to immediately adapt and improve rather than waiting until project closure.

107. **A project sponsor asks for a real-time, high-level summary of project progress, key risks, and outstanding issues. What tool best meets this need and how should it be implemented?**

 A project dashboard, updated regularly with key metrics, status indicators, and risk/issue summaries, provides concise, actionable insight for sponsors and stakeholders.

108. **During risk planning, a project manager wants to visualize which risks have the biggest potential impact on project outcomes. Which analytical tool is most effective for this purpose, and why?**

A tornado diagram is ideal; it ranks risks or variables by their relative impact, allowing prioritization of risk responses.

109. **A team working on a global project is struggling with time zone coordination and inconsistent communication habits. Which techniques should the project manager apply?**

Adopting virtual collaboration tools, updating the communications management plan to reflect time zone realities, and establishing clear meeting guidelines (potentially aided by virtual task boards and dashboards) will align the team.

110. **An organization wants to compare its project practices to those of industry leaders to improve performance. What is this process called, and how does it add value?**

Benchmarking systematically compares practices, metrics, and outcomes with peers or leaders, identifying gaps and opportunities for improvement.

111. **A construction project must allocate scarce resources across multiple simultaneous activities without changing the project end date. Which resource optimization technique should be used, and what is its limitation?**

Resource smoothing adjusts activities within their float so resource usage fits limits but cannot delay the project end date; not all resources may be optimized.

112. **A team is consistently missing critical deadlines because dependencies between tasks are poorly managed. Which scheduling tool or method can help address this?**

Precedence Diagramming Method (PDM) and schedule network analysis clarify logical relationships, dependencies, and float, allowing improved scheduling and risk management.

113. **A project manager is asked to justify a new project by showing that expected benefits outweigh the costs. Which tool or technique is most appropriate and what should be included in the analysis?**

Cost-benefit analysis compares the expected value of benefits to the total cost, highlighting strengths, weaknesses, and alternatives to support decision-making.

114. **When planning for stakeholder engagement, what models or tools can help prioritize outreach and communication strategies?**

Stakeholder mapping (impact/influence grid, stakeholder cube, salience model) visually categorizes stakeholders, aiding tailored engagement based on power, influence, and urgency.

115. **A project manager needs to estimate the time required to complete an activity that is highly uncertain. Which estimating technique provides the most realistic range, and why?**

Multipoint (e.g., three-point) estimating uses optimistic, pessimistic, and most likely values to reflect uncertainty and provide a probabilistic duration.

116. **A project team wants to structure deliverables and ensure that all work is covered with no overlap or gaps. What tool should they use, and what principle does it support?**

Work breakdown structure (WBS) uses decomposition to break scope into work packages, supporting the 100 percent rule (all work included, nothing extra).

117. **A team is deciding whether to build a new system from scratch or buy a commercial solution. Which technique should they use to support this decision, and what factors are considered?**

Make-or-buy analysis evaluates costs, resources, risks, and strategic fit for each option, supporting an informed decision.

118. **A product owner finds that the product backlog is growing quickly and becoming unfocused. Which process ensures the backlog remains relevant and prioritized?**

Backlog refinement involves constant review, reprioritization, and elaboration, helping the team focus on the highest value work for upcoming iterations.

119. **A project manager is confronted with a conflict between two team members over task ownership. What conflict management strategies are most likely to resolve the issue constructively?**

Collaborate/problem-solve (to integrate perspectives) or smooth/accommodate (to maintain relationships) are constructive; withdrawal or forcing are less desirable.

120. **A complex engineering project must monitor quality throughout execution, not just at delivery. Which tools should be used, and what do they measure?**

Quality control measurements (to verify compliance); control charts (to monitor process stability); and inspections (to check conformance to standards) are key.

121. **A team wants to motivate members to achieve challenging goals and maintain engagement throughout the project. Which motivation models or techniques can be applied?**

Incorporating intrinsic motivators (autonomy, mastery, purpose from Pink), recognizing achievement (Herzberg), and team empowerment all drive motivation and engagement.

122. **A project manager needs to ensure all project communications are appropriately tailored for the audience, urgency, and sensitivity. What factors should be considered when selecting communication technology?**

Urgency, availability, and reliability, ease of use, project environment (time zones, languages), and sensitivity/confidentiality inform appropriate technology choices.

123. **During a retrospective, a scrum team realizes that many stories are left incomplete each sprint. Which metrics or charts can help diagnose and improve sprint planning?**

Iteration burndown charts and velocity charts highlight trends in story completion, helping teams adjust how much work to commit to in the next iteration.

124. **A project team wants to identify which project variables have the greatest effect on the final outcome for risk planning. What analysis tool should they use, and what is its output?**

Sensitivity analysis (often displayed as a tornado diagram) ranks variables by their impact, informing risk prioritization.

125. **An organization wants to automate repetitive project tasks such as reminders and report generation. Which process improvement technique should be considered, and what are its benefits?**

Process automation (including robotic process automation) reduces manual work, increases accuracy, and frees up team capacity for higher-value tasks.

126. **A manager wishes to assess whether the project is on track for budget and schedule, using integrated metrics. Which technique should be applied?**

Earned Value Analysis (EVA) integrates scope, schedule, and cost data to measure performance and forecast outcomes.

127. **A project team wants to continuously improve its processes and products throughout the project. Which frameworks or methods support this?**

Continuous improvement frameworks such as plan-do-check-act (PDCA), Lean, Six Sigma, and retrospectives drive ongoing enhancement.

128. **A new project manager is unsure how to structure the team's first meeting to ensure participation and clarity of purpose. What technique should they apply?**

Facilitation ensures effective participation, mutual understanding, and buy-in to meeting outcomes.

129. **A project team needs to evaluate the effect of changes in one variable on the project's finish date, considering uncertainty. Which analysis should be conducted?**

What-if analysis simulates scenarios to assess the impact of changes or events on project objectives.

130. **An agile team wants to visualize the team's productivity rate and forecast how much work can be completed in future intervals. Which concept or tool should they use?**

Velocity (often tracked using burndown or burnup charts) provides a measure of productivity and informs future sprint planning.

131. **A project manager wants to ensure that the team's recommendations for process improvements are captured and acted upon immediately, rather than waiting until project closure. Which technique supports this goal, and how does it work?**

Retrospectives (commonly used in agile) are regular workshops held at the end of each iteration or major milestone. They enable teams to reflect on what worked, what didn't, and to assign actionable improvements. This ensures continuous learning and adaptation during the project lifecycle.

132. **A team is evaluating two alternative project approaches, each with different probabilistic outcomes and associated costs. What tool should be used to support this decision and what is the output?**

Decision tree analysis models each alternative as a set of branches, calculates Expected Monetary Value (EMV) for each possible path, and helps select the option with the optimal risk-adjusted outcome.

133. **A distributed team regularly encounters delays due to unclear assignment of accountability for key deliverables. Which tool can clarify roles and prevent overlap or gaps?**

A responsibility assignment matrix (such as a RACI matrix) maps deliverables/activities to individuals or groups, clarifying who is Responsible, Accountable, Consulted, and Informed, thus preventing confusion.

134. **A project manager needs to adjust the project schedule to optimize the use of resources, but cannot change the project's end date. Which specific technique should be used, and what limitations does it have?**

Resource smoothing optimizes resource allocation by moving activities within their available float without affecting the project's critical path or completion date. Its limitation is that it may not optimize all resources if the float is insufficient.

135. **A team is unsure how to best structure a complex brainstorming session to ensure everyone's ideas are included and organized for later analysis. Which technique can facilitate this, and how?**

Affinity diagramming enables teams to collect a large volume of ideas and then organize them into related groups, making it easier to identify themes and focus areas for action.

136. **An organization wants to monitor both the cost and schedule performance of a project in a single integrated view. Which method provides this capability, and what are its core metrics?**

Earned Value Management (EVM) integrates scope, schedule, and cost, providing metrics such as Cost Performance Index (CPI), Schedule Performance Index (SPI), and Variance at Completion (VAC).

137. **A project team needs to ensure that all steps of a complex process are completed each time, especially for regulatory compliance. What tool should be implemented, and how is it maintained?**

A checklist, developed from historical and best-practice data, ensures every required step is considered. It should be reviewed and updated regularly based on lessons learned and process changes.

138. **The project sponsor asks for a visualization of the sequence and logic of activities, including all dependencies, to identify high-risk points in the schedule. What tool provides this, and what is its advantage?**

A Precedence Diagramming Method (PDM) network diagram visually represents activities and dependencies, making it easier to spot critical paths, convergences, and potential bottlenecks.

139. **A team is asked to determine which project risks, if realized, would have the highest impact on objectives such as cost or schedule. Which tool supports this prioritization and how?**

A probability and impact matrix maps risks based on their likelihood and impact, allowing for the prioritization of responses to those risks that pose the greatest threat to objectives.

140. **After a phase of rapid change, a project manager wants to validate that all project communications are still effective for stakeholders' evolving needs. What technique should be applied, and what does it assess?**

Communication requirements analysis and communication styles assessment should be conducted, reviewing stakeholder needs, information channels, and the effectiveness of current communication methods to ensure alignment and understanding.

Conclusion

Completing this chapter marks a significant milestone in the reader's project management journey. By working through the wide array of tools and techniques explored here, the reader has not only strengthened their technical knowledge but also developed the practical skills needed to tackle the challenges of real-world projects with clarity and confidence.

Throughout this and previous chapters, the reader has learned to select and tailor the right tools, whether it is choosing the optimal scheduling method, applying a robust risk analysis, or facilitating transparent communication, to fit the needs of diverse teams, stakeholders, and project environments. These tools are more than just theory; they are the foundation for effective planning, decision-making, and delivery in any project.

As the reader moves forward, it is important to remember that success in project management is built on adaptability, teamwork, and a willingness to learn. The ability to analyze situations, choose the right technique, and continuously reflect and improve is what sets great project managers apart. With this toolkit in hand, the reader is now equipped to lead projects with confidence, foster collaboration, and deliver meaningful results for organizations and communities.

The journey does not end here. The next four practice sets will give the reader the chance to apply everything learned across all chapters, from foundational principles to advanced techniques, mirroring the complexity and variety of scenarios faced in both the PMP exam and professional practice. Embrace these sets as an opportunity to consolidate knowledge, test decision-making skills, and build the assurance needed for success.

With dedication and thoughtful preparation, the reader is now ready to approach any project challenge, confident in their ability to drive projects forward and deliver value at every stage. The tools and techniques mastered here are not just answers for an exam—they are the building blocks of a successful project management career.

References

1. A Guide to the Project Management Body of Knowledge (PMBOK® Guide), Seventh and Eighth Edition. Project Management Institute
2. The Standard for Project Management. Project Management Institute, 2021.
3. PMI's Digital Platform for Standards.

Answers

Q. No.	Answers
1	c
2	a
3	b
4	b
5	b
6	b
7	b
8	b
9	c
10	b
11	b
12	b
13	b
14	a
15	b
16	b
17	a
18	b
19	b
20	d
21	b
22	b
23	c
24	a
25	c
26	b
27	b
28	b
29	b
30	b
31	b, c
32	b, d
33	b, c
34	b, c
35	a, b

Q. No.	Answers
36	a, c
37	a, c
38	a, c
39	a, c
40	a, b
41	b, c
42	b, c
43	a, c
44	a, b
45	a, c
46	a, b
47	a, b
48	a, b
49	a, b
50	a, b
51	b
52	b
53	c
54	c
55	c
56	a
57	a
58	a
59	a
60	b
61	b
62	a
63	b
64	a
65	b
66	b
67	a
68	b
69	a
70	a

Q. No.	Answers
71	a
72	a
73	a
74	b
75	a
76	a - iii b - i c - ii d - v e - iv
77	a - iii b - i c - ii d - v e - iv
78	a - iii b - i c - ii d - v e - iv
79	a - ii b - i c - iii d - v e - iv
80	a - ii b - i c - iii d - v e - iv
81	a - ii b - i c - iii d - v e - iv

Q. No.	Answers
82	a - iv b - iii c - ii d - v e - i
83	a - i b - ii c - iiI d - iv e - v
84	a - iv b - iii c - ii d - v e - i
85	a - iii b - i c - ii d - v e - iv
86	a - iii b - i c - ii d - v e - iv
87	a - iv b - iii c - ii d - v e - i
88	a - iv b - iii c - ii d - v e - i

Q. No.	Answers
89	a - ii
	b - i
	c - iii
	d - v
	e - iv
90	a - ii
	b - i
	c - iii
	d - iv
	e - v
91	a - ii
	b - i
	c - iii
	d - v
	e - iv
92	a - ii
	b - i
	c - iii
	d - v
	e - iv

Q. No.	Answers
93	a - ii
	b - i
	c - iii
	d - v
	e - iv
94	a - iv
	b - iii
	c - ii
	d - v
	e - i
95	a - iv
	b - iii
	c - ii
	d - v
	e - i
96	a - ii
	b - i
	c - iii
	d - v
	e - iv

Q. No.	Answers
97	a - ii
	b - i
	c - iii
	d - v
	e - iv
98	a - iv
	b - iii
	c - ii
	d - v
	e - i
99	a - iv
	b - iii
	c - ii
	d - v
	e - i
100	a - ii
	b - i
	c - iii
	d - v
	e - iv

SECTION- III

Practice Sets

CHAPTER 9
Practice Set -1

Introduction

This chapter is designed as a comprehensive practice bank of unique question sets covering a wide range of project management themes, delivery contexts, and decision-making situations. It combines conceptual, scenario-based, case-study-driven, chart-based, matching, fill-in-the-blanks, and advanced integrated questions so that readers can test not only recall, but also judgment, interpretation, and strategic thinking. The questions vary intentionally in format, complexity, and difficulty level to reflect the broad demands of modern project management practice.

The chapter can be used both for individual preparation and for facilitated discussion, mentoring, or classroom-style review.

Objectives

The objective of this chapter is to strengthen the reader's ability to interpret project situations, apply the right tools and artifacts, analyze risks and value trade-offs, and respond effectively across predictive, adaptive, and hybrid environments. It aims to build confidence in handling practical project scenarios that involve governance, stakeholder engagement, sustainability, benefits realization, agile flow, procurement, quality, leadership, and uncertainty.

By working through these question sets, the reader should be able to develop sharper exam readiness, stronger analytical discipline, and a more integrated understanding of how project management principles operate in real decision contexts. The chapter is therefore intended not only to test knowledge but also to improve strategic judgment, adaptability, and professional reasoning across multiple question types and challenge levels.

Case study: Green Horizons

You are the Senior project manager for a global logistics firm, *LogiCore*, tasked with leading Project **Green Horizons**. The objective is to implement a Generative AI-driven routing system to reduce carbon emissions by 25% while maintaining current delivery speeds. The project is being managed using a **Hybrid** approach; the hardware infrastructure (server upgrades) follows a **Predictive** lifecycle, while the AI software development follows an **Adaptive (agile)** lifecycle. **Current Situation:** The project is six months into a twelve-month timeline. The hardware is 90% complete, but the AI development team is struggling with *Model Drift*; the AI's efficiency is dropping as it encounters real-world data variables it wasn't trained on. Simultaneously, a key stakeholder from the Compliance Department has raised concerns that the AI's data-gathering methods might violate new regional sustainability reporting laws that were passed after the project began.

The project sponsor is pressuring you to ignore the minor compliance ambiguity and focus on the *Value Delivery* of the carbon reduction targets to ensure the company hits its quarterly **Environmental, Social, and Governance (ESG)** goals.

1. **The Compliance Department stakeholder insists that the project be paused until a full audit of the AI data-gathering methods is conducted to ensure alignment with the new sustainability laws. However, the project sponsor argues that the cost of a pause would outweigh the "theoretical" risk of non-compliance. What is the best next step for the project manager acting as a Strategic Advisor?**
   a. Pause the AI development immediately to conduct the audit, as legal compliance is a non-negotiable project constraint.
   b. Facilitate a meeting between the sponsor and Compliance to perform a cost-benefit analysis of the non-compliance risk versus the value of hitting ESG goals.
   c. Continue development but create a contingency reserve specifically for potential legal fines, ensuring the project stays on schedule.
   d. Update the risk register with the new compliance law and request a formal decision from the Project steering committee regarding the project's direction.

2. **The AI development team reports that to fix the "Model Drift" issue, they need to pivot from the original scope to a more complex "reinforcement learning" model. This change will increase the software budget by 15% but is expected to increase long-term carbon savings by an additional 10%. As a Strategic Advisor, how should you evaluate this change?**
   a. Reject the change, as the Predictive Hardware component of the project is already near completion and cannot be altered.
   b. Use the "Value-Centric Thinking" framework to assess if the 10% increase in long-term carbon savings justifies the 15% budget increase.
   c. Submit a formal change request to the Change Control Board (CCB) specifically for the software scope, ignoring the hardware impact.
   d. Direct the team to stick to the original "Adaptive" backlog to ensure the Minimum Viable Product (MVP) is delivered on time.

3. **The technical challenges with the AI model, morale among the software developers is declining. They feel the Predictive Hardware team is "rigid" and doesn't understand the "fail-fast" nature of AI development. As a servant leader, which two actions should you take to improve cross-functional collaboration?**
   a. Implement "Experience Sharing" sessions where the hardware team explains their constraints and the software team explains the AI iterative process.
   b. Mandate that the hardware team adopts agile sprints to match the software team's cadence.
   c. Establish a shared "Value Dashboard" that shows how both teams' contributions are necessary to achieve the 25% carbon reduction goal.
   d. Move the software team to a separate location to reduce the friction caused by differing work styles.
   e. Increase the frequency of status reports to ensure both teams are being held accountable for their specific tasks.

4. **You are reviewing a Cumulative Flow Diagram (CFD) for the AI software development. The "work in progress" (WIP) band is widening significantly, while the "Done" band has plateaued over the last three sprints. At the same time, the hardware "burn-down chart" shows they are ahead of schedule. What is the most likely strategic risk to the project?**
   a. The project will finish under budget because the hardware team is so efficient.
   b. There is a bottleneck in the AI testing phase that will delay the realization of carbon-reduction value.
   c. The hardware team is over-allocating resources, causing the software team to lose focus.
   d. The AI team is "Gold Plating" the software, leading to a plateau in the "Done" category.

5. **The project is nearing completion, and the AI system is ready for hand-off to the operations team. However, the operations manager expresses fear that the AI will automate their staff's jobs and is subtly sabotaging the transition by delaying the final training sessions. What should the project manager do to ensure Sustainable Value Delivery?**
   a. Escalate the sabotage to the operations manager's supervisor and request a formal mandate for the training to begin.
   b. Highlight the "Sustainability Metrics" of the project to the staff, showing them how the AI makes their roles "Greener" and more strategically important.
   c. Offer a performance bonus to the operations team for completing the training on time to overcome their resistance.
   d. Document the delay as a "Risk Realized" in the final project report and transfer the ownership of the AI to the IT department instead.

Case study: Digital transformation and AI

You are the Lead project manager for *Apex Global,* a legacy manufacturing giant transitioning to a *Smart Factory* model. Project **Atlas** involves deploying an AI-driven predictive maintenance system across 12 international sites.

The Constraints:

- **Approach:** Hybrid. The physical sensor installation (Predictive) must be synchronized with the software's machine-learning iterations (Adaptive).
- **Stakeholders:** Regional managers are resistant, fearing that AI will lead to workforce reductions.
- **Governance:** The project must adhere to the new **2026 Sustainability and Ethics in AI (SEAI)** framework, which requires 100% transparency in algorithmic decision-making.

6. **The Regional Manager of the European plant refuses to grant the AI development team access to historical maintenance logs, citing data privacy concerns for his staff. This is causing a three-week delay in the software's training phase. As a Strategic Advisor, what is your best course of action?**
   a. Escalate the refusal to the Chief Operating Officer (COO) and request a formal directive to release the data.
   b. Organize a "Collaborative Governance" workshop with the Regional Manager and the Data Ethics officer to co-create a data anonymization protocol.
   c. Inform the AI team to use synthetic data instead of real logs to maintain the schedule while respecting the manager's concerns.
   d. Issue a formal warning to the Regional Manager that he is in violation of the project charter's resource allocation clause.

7. **During a mid-project review, the steering committee asks for a report on "Social Sustainability." They want to know how Project Atlas is impacting the long-term employability of the current maintenance staff. Which metric should you present to demonstrate Value Delivery?**
   a. The total number of maintenance hours reduced by the AI system.
   b. The "Upskilling Index," showing the percentage of staff trained to oversee and maintain the AI systems.
   c. The project's ROI based on reduced machinery downtime.
   d. A list of staff who have been reassigned to other non-AI-related departments.

8. **The AI model has identified a way to reduce energy consumption by 40%, but it requires the machines to run at a slower speed, which will decrease the monthly production volume by 5%. The original project charter prioritizes "Maximum Output." What should the project manager do?**
   a. Follow the Charter's directive and ignore the AI's energy-saving recommendation to ensure production targets are met.
   b. Adjust the machine speeds immediately to prioritize energy savings, as sustainability is a core 2026 project principle.
   c. Perform a "Value Trade-off Analysis" and present a business case to the sponsor comparing the cost of lost production vs. the savings and ESG brand value of the energy reduction.
   d. Ask the AI team to retrain the model to ignore energy consumption and focus exclusively on production speed.

9. **You are tailoring the project management approach for a new AI-integrated software module. Which three factors should most influence your choice between an Adaptive or Predictive lifecycle for this specific module?**
   a. The stability of the machine-learning requirements.
   b. The frequency of feedback needed from the end-users (factory workers).
   c. The fixed-price nature of the hardware procurement contract.
   d. The rate of change in regional AI compliance laws.
   e. The total number of internal project team members.
   f. The historical success of Waterfall projects in the organization.

10. **A senior executive expresses frustration during a sprint review, stating, "I don't see why we are 'wasting time' on iterative testing. Just build the software and show it to me when it's done." How should the project manager respond as a Strategic Advisor?**
    a. Explain that the agile Manifesto requires iterative testing and that the project must follow these rules.
    b. Use a "Value-to-Risk" diagram to show how iterative testing identifies critical AI flaws early, preventing costly large-scale failures later.
    c. Apologize for the delay and promise to move the project to a Waterfall model to satisfy the executive's preference for a single delivery.
    d. Invite the executive to a "Daily Stand-up" so they can see how hard the team is working every day.

11. **Halfway through Project Atlas, the government announces a new "Right to Repair" law that requires all AI-driven machinery to be user-serviceable without proprietary software locks. This contradicts your project's current "Closed-System" design. What is the best next step?**
    a. Continue with the "Closed-System" design, as the law will not take effect until after the project's launch date.
    b. Halt the project and wait for the final text of the law to be published before making any design changes.
    c. Conduct an impact assessment on the project's scope, budget, and long-term "Value at Risk," then present findings to the Change Control Board (CCB).
    d. Request the legal department to file for an exemption from the law, citing the project's contribution to national carbon reduction goals.

12. **A high-performing software engineer on the AI team has become "siloed," refusing to share her code with the rest of the team because she believes they "aren't technical enough" to understand it. This is creating a single point of failure. As a servant leader, what should you do?**
    a. Remove the engineer from the team to maintain a collaborative culture.
    b. Assign her a junior mentee and set a performance goal for "Knowledge Transfer" and "Team Capability Building."
    c. Offer her a promotion to a "Lead Architect" role so she doesn't have to work with the others.

d. Inform her that her behavior is a violation of the Team Charter and deduct from her quarterly bonus.

13. **To ensure the project remains sustainable, you are integrating a [A] into the procurement process. This tool allows you to evaluate vendors not just on price, but on their [B]:**

Options for [A]	Options for [B]
a. Triple Bottom Line Matrix	i. Carbon Footprint and Ethical Labor Standards
b. Fixed-price contract	ii. Delivery Speed
c. Work Breakdown Structure	iii. Historical Profit Margins

14. **Project Atlas is complete. The AI is running, and machine downtime has decreased by 30%. However, the expected 25% carbon reduction has only reached 5%. The sponsor wants to close the project and declare victory. What is your response as a Strategic Advisor?**

    a. Agree to close the project, as the primary technical goal (downtime reduction) has been met.

    b. Recommend a "Benefits realization Phase" to investigate the gap in carbon reduction and identify the necessary operational changes to reach the target.

    c. Close the project but note the carbon reduction failure in the "Lessons Learned" register.

    d. Re-open the software development phase immediately and spend the remaining contingency reserve to fix the AI.

15. **A factory floor worker suggests a small UI change to the maintenance tablet that would save them 10 minutes per shift. The IT lead rejects it, saying, "We don't have time for minor requests." As the PM, how do you handle this?**

    a. Side with the IT lead to ensure the project stays on schedule.

    b. Empower the worker by facilitating a quick "Value-Impact" assessment to see if the 10-minute saving across 500 workers justifies the UI change.

    c. Tell the worker to submit the request after the project has officially closed.

    d. Ignore the request and focus on the high-level AI model updates.

Case study: AI supply chain

You are the project manager for *Vanguard*, an initiative to automate a global supply chain using a **Hybrid** framework. The hardware installation in the warehouses is **Predictive**, while the AI routing software is **Adaptive**. **Current Data:** You are reviewing the **Velocity Chart** given in the following figure during the sprint 6 retrospective:

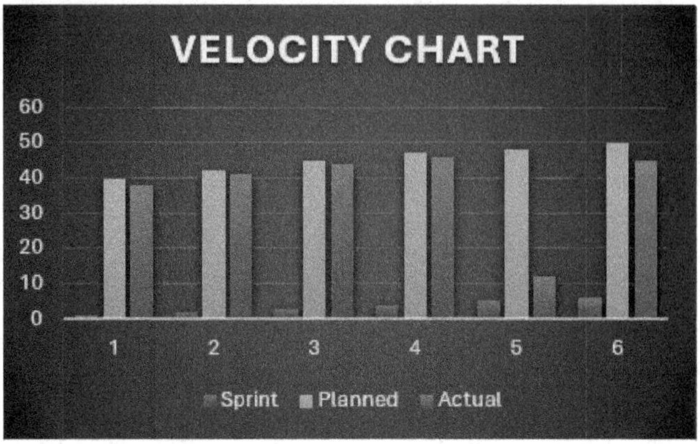

Figure 9.1: Velocity chart

16. **Referencing the preceeding Velocity Chart, the AI software team experienced a massive drop in "Actual" velocity during sprint 5. Upon investigation, you discover that the team spent 80% of their time fixing a "Data Poisoning" security flaw that was not in the original backlog. As a Strategic Advisor, what is the best way to address this with the project sponsor?**

    a. Present the chart and explain that the team's velocity dropped because they are "unproductive" and need more technical training.

    b. Reframe the sprint 5 dip as a "Value Protection" event, explaining how identifying and fixing the security flaw early prevented a total loss of strategic value and saved the company from potential legal liability.

    c. Adjust the chart to hide the "Actual" data for sprint 5 so the sponsor does not lose confidence in the agile methodology.

    d. Direct the team to work double shifts in sprint 7 to "make up" the lost story points shown in the chart.

17. **The "Vanguard" project must comply with the 2026 Circular economy Act, which mandates that all warehouse hardware must be 90% recyclable. Your current hardware vendor can only guarantee 75% recyclability. As a Strategic Advisor, what is your move?**

    a. Ignore the regulation for now, as the project is already in the execution phase and changing vendors would delay the launch by 3 months.

    b. Perform a "Triple Bottom Line" analysis to compare the cost of switching to a compliant vendor versus the potential fines and loss of "Green Brand Value."

    c. Ask the current vendor to provide a fake certificate of compliance to pass the initial audit.

    d. Cancel the hardware phase of the project and focus exclusively on the software, as software does not have recyclability constraints.

18. **You are evaluating four potential AI models for the "Vanguard" routing system. Based on the Value Matrix below, which model should you recommend as a Strategic Advisor?**

Model name	Accuracy	Energy consumption (Carbon cost)	Implementation time	Strategic value
Model A	98%	High	6 months	High
Model B	92%	Low	3 months	Very high
Model C	85%	Very low	2 months	Moderate
Model D	99%	Extreme	9 months	High

a. Model D, because it has the highest accuracy.

b. Model B, because it balances high strategic value with low environmental impact and faster time-to-market.

c. Model C, because it is the fastest to implement and has the lowest carbon cost.

d. Model A, because it meets the standard 6-month project window.

19. **A project manager is overseeing a global infrastructure project. Reviewing the Risk Heat Map Table (shown in the following table), they identify a specific risk in the "Critical" (Red) zone: a major supplier for specialized hardware is facing potential insolvency due to a local economic crisis.**

Risk ID	Probability (1 to 30)	Impact (1 to 30)	Severity Level	Color	Description / Notes
R1	30	30	**Critical**	● Red	Major system vulnerability (Data Poisoning), immediate mitigation required
R2	25	20	**High**	● Red	AI routing logic failure, potential disruption to global supply chain
R3	20	15	**High**	● Orange	Predictive Hardware calibration delays, moderate operational impact
R4	15	10	**Medium**	○ Yellow	Integration lag between adaptive and predictive modules
R5	10	25	**Medium**	○ Yellow	Vendor data latency affects real-time analytics
R6	10	10	**Low**	● Green	Minor UI bug, negligible business impact
R7	20	25	**High**	● Red	Cloud API throttling, affects AI model retraining
R8	15	20	**Medium**	● Orange	Warehouse sensor synchronization issue
R9	10	15	**Low**	○ Yellow	Documentation gap, training inefficiency
R10	5	10	**Low**	● Green	Cosmetic dashboard error, no operational risk

What is the most effective Strategic Advisor response to this risk?

a. Transfer the risk by purchasing an insurance policy that covers supplier failure.

b. Implement a "Multi-Sourcing" strategy immediately to distribute the procurement load across secondary vendors.

c. Accept the risk and set aside a 10% management reserve to cover the potential cost of finding a new supplier later.

d. Avoid the risk by changing the project scope to remove the requirement for that specific hardware.

20. **An organization is using a Fixed Price Incentive Fee (FPIF) contract for a high-stakes AI development project. The project reaches a "Point of Total Assumption" (PTA).**

Metric	Value
Target cost	500,000 USD
Target profit	50,000 USD
Price ceiling	600,000 USD
Share ratio	70/30 (Buyer/Seller)

Option	Contract type	Description
Option 1	**Firm-Fixed-Price (FFP)**	Set price regardless of effort.
Option 2	**Cost Plus Award Fee (CPAF)**	Reimbursable costs + fee based on performance satisfaction.

The actual costs have now reached 620,000 USD. How much will the Buyer pay the Seller?

a. 620,000 USD
b. 550,000 USD
c. 600,000 USD
d. 500,000 USD

21. **The project team is operating in a BANI (Brittle, Anxious, Non-linear, Incomprehensible) environment. The project manager notices that traditional risk identification methods (like SWOT analysis) are failing to capture rapidly emerging threats.**

Which technique should the project manager introduce to better manage these "Unknown-Unknowns"?

a. Increased Frequency of Status Meetings.
b. Monte Carlo Simulations with historical data from the 1990s.
c. Pre-mortems and scenario planning for extreme "Black Swan" events.
d. Strict adherence to the original risk management plan approved at the start of the year.

22. **A project requires a critical component from a vendor. The vendor offers two contract types. The project manager must choose the one that aligns with an Adaptive/agile delivery model where scope is expected to evolve.**

Option	Contract type	Description
Option 1	**Firm-Fixed-Price (FFP)**	Set price regardless of effort
Option 2	**Cost Plus Award Fee (CPAF)**	Reimbursable costs + fee based on performance satisfaction

Which should the project manager recommend?

a. Option 1, because it provides the highest budget certainty for the buyer.
b. Option 1, because it forces the vendor to be more efficient with their time.
c. Option 2, because it allows for flexibility in scope and incentivizes quality over rigid adherence to specs.
d. Neither; they should suggest a Time and Materials (T&M) contract with no ceiling.

23. **During a procurement audit, it is discovered that a sub-contractor has been violating local environmental regulations, which contradicts the project's Sustainability Backlog.**

As a Strategic Advisor, what is your first step?

a. Terminate the contract immediately and notify the press to show corporate responsibility.
b. Ignore the violation as long as the subcontractor delivers the components on time and within budget.

c. Meet with the subcontractor to develop a corrective action plan and verify compliance within a set timeframe.

d. Shift the responsibility to the legal department and wait for their official ruling before taking action.

24. **A multi-year digital transformation project is nearing completion. The project manager is following the Project Closure & Lessons Learned Cycle (see following figure). The "Financial & Administrative Closure" is complete, and the team is now in the "Value Validation" stage.**

***Figure 9.2:** Project closure phase*

What is the primary objective during "Value Validation"?

a. Ensuring all final invoices have been paid to the vendors.

b. Confirming that the project's delivered outcomes have achieved the intended business benefits and strategic value.

c. Archiving the project schedule and baseline documents in the PMO repository.

d. Releasing the project team members to their functional departments.

25. **During the "Knowledge Transfer" phase of a hybrid project, the project manager realizes that the most critical technical insights are held by a senior developer who is leaving the company in two days.**

What is the most effective way to ensure this knowledge becomes an OPA?

a. Request the developer write a 50-page technical manual before they leave.

b. Organize a "Knowledge Café" or "Lunch and Learn" session where the developer can share insights and answer questions from the remaining team.

c. Ask the developer to record a video of themselves coding and upload it to a shared drive.

d. Trust that the code documentation is sufficient for future teams to understand the logic.

26. **A project manager has successfully delivered a new AI-driven supply chain system. However, six months after project closure, the "Strategic Value" (Stage 2 in the closure cycle) is declining because the operations team has reverted to using manual spreadsheets.**

Which area of project management was likely neglected?

a. Quality management.

b. Procurement management.

c. Organizational change management and transition planning.

d. Financial closure.

27. **Match the following Closing Activities with their corresponding category in the Closure Cycle:**

Activity	Category
a. Releasing a 'Performance Bonus' to the team	i. Administrative closure
b. Updating the 'Risk Lessons Learned' database	ii. Value validation
c. Conducting a 'Benefits realization Audit'	iii. Knowledge transfer
d. Hosting a 'Project Post-Mortem' workshop	iv. Organizational asset update

28. **The project is officially closed. The project manager is updating the Lessons Learned Repository. They want to ensure the information is useful for future "Strategic Advisors" in the company.**

What is the best way to document a major failure that occurred during the project?

a. Omit the failure to protect the reputation of the project team and the sponsor.

b. Document the failure as a "Human Error" without providing specific details.

c. Describe the situation, the root cause of the failure, the impact, and the specific "Next Time" recommendations.

d. Record the failure in a private document that is only accessible to senior management.

29. **A project manager is reviewing the financial health of a hybrid infrastructure project. The following data is available:**

- **Budget at Completion (BAC)**: 1,000,000 USD
- **Earned Value (EV)**: 400,000 USD
- **Actual Cost (AC)**: 450,000 USD
- **Planned Value (PV)**: 380,000 USD

What is the Cost Performance Index (CPI), and what does it tell the project manager?

a. 0.89; The project is under budget.

b. 1.05; The project is ahead of schedule.

c. 0.89; The project is over budget, spending 1.12 USD for every 1.00 USD of value earned

d. 1.11; The project is performing efficiently.

30. **A team is struggling with a "Brittle" (BANI) project environment where small changes in user requirements cause massive technical failures. The project manager decides to increase the Technical Debt Transparency.**

What is the most effective way to do this?

a. Add a "Technical Debt" column to the Kanban board and track the age of these items.

b. Ignore the debt until the closing phase to ensure the launch date is met.

c. Hide the technical debt from the product owner to prevent anxiety during sprint reviews.

d. Delete old code and rewrite the entire system without informing stakeholders.

31. **An organization is launching a project that must comply with new 2026 Sustainability (ESG) mandates. The project manager is tasked with selecting a vendor.**

Which selection criterion should be weighted most heavily to align with the Strategic Advisor role?

a. The lowest bid price regardless of the vendor's carbon footprint.

b. The vendor's historical speed of delivery on previous non-ESG projects.

c. The vendor's "Sustainability Scorecard" and their plan for ethical resource sourcing.

d. The vendor's proximity to the project site is to reduce travel costs only.

32. **A project is using a Value-Based Prioritization approach. The product owner presents four features:**

Feature	Estimated value	Development cost	Risk level
A	100,000 USD	20,000 USD	Low
B	150,000 USD	80,000 USD	High
C	50,000 USD	10,000 USD	Low
D	200,000 USD	150,000 USD	Medium

Using the Value-to-Cost Ratio, which feature should be prioritized first?

a. Feature A (Ratio: 5.0)
b. Feature B (Ratio: 1.87)
c. Feature C (Ratio: 5.0)
d. Feature D (Ratio: 1.33)

Note: **If ratios are tied, consider the lower risk or higher total value.**

33. **The project sponsor is concerned about scope creep in an adaptive project. The project manager explains that in agile, scope is not "creeping" but "evolving."**

How does the project manager maintain control over this evolution?

a. By requiring a formal Change Request for every new User Story.
b. By maintaining a strictly prioritized Product Backlog and ensuring the "Definition of Ready" is met.
c. By telling the team to stop accepting feedback from users until the project is closed.
d. By increasing the budget every time a new feature is suggested.

34. **A project manager discovers that a team member is being excluded from technical discussions by other members due to their cultural background.**

As a leader focusing on psychological safety and D&I, what should the PM do?

a. Move the excluded member to a different project where they might "fit in" better.
b. Facilitate a team-building workshop focused on unconscious bias and establish clear ground rules for inclusion.
c. Do nothing, as technical discussions should be left to the "experts" in the group.
d. Discipline the team member for not speaking up louder during meetings.

35. **In a BANI environment, a project is considered "Non-linear," meaning small inputs can result in disproportionately large impacts.**

What is the best risk response for a "Non-linear" threat?

a. **Avoidance:** Trying to plan for every single possibility using a 2-year schedule.
b. **Resilience:** Building a "Modular Architecture" that allows parts of the project to fail without crashing the whole system.
c. **Acceptance:** Doing no planning and simply reacting when things break.
d. **Transference:** Buying a fixed-price contract to move all risk to a vendor.

36. **A project manager is closing a phase. They use a Knowledge Café to capture tacit knowledge. Which of the following is an example of Tacit Knowledge?**

a. The project's final budget spreadsheet.
b. A "How-To" guide for a software tool.
c. A senior engineer's "gut feeling" on how to handle a specific vendor conflict.
d. The signed project charter.

37. **Your project uses Monte Carlo Simulation to predict the finish date. The simulation shows a 90% probability of finishing by October 1st, but a 50% probability of finishing by August 15th. The sponsor demands an August 15th deadline.**

What is the most professional response?

a. Agree to the August 15th deadline and hope for the best.

b. Explain the risk levels and suggest a "Phased Release" to deliver high-value items by August 15th while managing expectations for the full scope.

c. Tell the sponsor that the simulation is wrong and August 15th is impossible.

d. Resign from the project to avoid a failure on your record.

38. **An AI project is using an Explainability Register. A stakeholder asks why a specific customer was denied a loan by the AI.**

Where should the project manager look to provide a transparent, ethical answer?

a. The project charter.

b. The Technical Specifications manual.

c. The Explainability Register's "Logic Traceability" section.

d. The Team Charter.

39. **A project manager is analyzing the Defect Density Chart (see the following figure) during the "Integration" phase of a software project. The chart shows that the defect density has spiked significantly above the established "Quality Threshold (VALUE = 1)."**

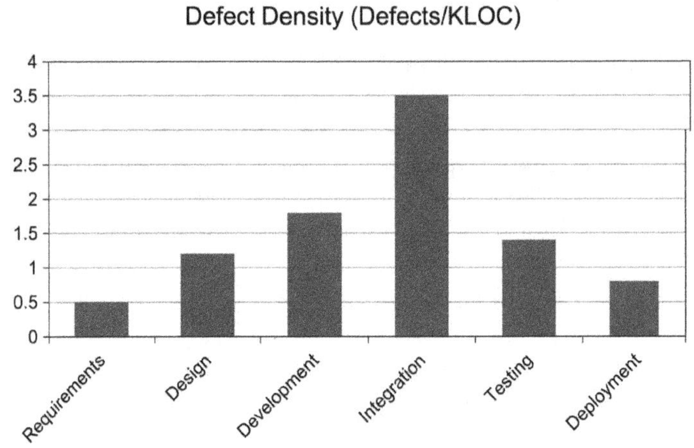

Figure 9.3: Defect density chart

What is the most appropriate first action for the project manager?

a. Request an immediate increase in the budget to hire more developers to fix the bugs.

b. Initiate a root cause analysis (RCA) to determine why the integration phase is producing a high volume of defects.

c. Lower the Quality Threshold line so that the project remains "in compliance" on paper.

d. Proceed to the next phase and plan to fix the defects during the project's closing stage.

40. **An organization is deciding between two global vendors for a critical AI module.**

- **Vendor A is located in a high-cost region but has a 95% "First-Time Right" quality record.**
- **Vendor B is 30% cheaper but has a 70% quality record and is located in a region with frequent power outages.**

As a Strategic Advisor, which concept should you use to justify selecting Vendor A?

a. Just-in-time (JIT) Manufacturing.

b. Total cost of quality (COQ), including the costs of internal and external failure.

c. Lowest Bid Procurement.

d. Maslow's Hierarchy of Needs.

41. **A project manager is performing a Quantitative Risk Analysis using a Decision Tree.**

Path	Probability	Impact (USD)
Path A: Build in-house	60% success / 40% failure	+200,000 / -50,000
Path B: Outsource	80% success / 20% failure	+150,000 / -20,000

What is the Expected Monetary Value (EMV) of Path A?

a. 150,000 USD

b. 100,000 USD

c. 120,000 USD

d. 80,000 USD

42. **A project team is spread across three countries: Japan, Brazil, and Germany. The project manager notices that the team members from Japan are very quiet during brainstorming sessions, while the Brazilian members are very vocal.**

Which skill must the project manager apply to ensure all voices are heard?

a. Technical Project Management.

b. Cultural Intelligence (CQ) and Facilitation.

c. Financial Auditing.

d. Software Development Lifecycle (SDLC) knowledge.

43. **A project manager is using Statistical Sampling to check the quality of hardware components. Out of a batch of 1,000, they test 50. This is an example of:**

a. Prevention.

b. Inspection.

c. Attribute sampling.

d. Variable sampling.

44. **During a quality audit, it is found that the project is using a process that is "In Control" but the results are consistently "Out of Specification" (meaning they don't meet customer requirements).**

What does this indicate?

a. The process is perfect and needs no change.

b. The process is stable but not capable of meeting the required standards.

c. The team is not working hard enough.

d. The quality audit was performed incorrectly.

45. **A project is facing a "Secondary Risk"—a risk that arises as a direct result of implementing a risk response. For example, installing a new backup generator (response to power failure) creates a new risk of fuel leakage.**

How should this be handled?

a. Ignore secondary risks; you can only solve one problem at a time.

b. Document and analyze the secondary risk in the risk register just like any other risk.

c. Remove the original risk response to avoid the secondary risk.

d. Blame the vendor who sold the backup generator.

46. **An organization is moving toward a Lean philosophy. The project manager is asked to identify "Muda" (Waste). Which of the following is an example of waste in a project environment?**

a. Frequent communication with stakeholders.

b. Partially completed work (work in progress) that sits idle for weeks.

c. Comprehensive testing before a product launch.

d. Training team members on new technologies.

47. **A project manager is managing a Matrix organization. A functional manager pulls a key resource off the project to work on a departmental emergency without consulting the PM.**

What should the project manager do first?

a. Fire the resource for leaving the project.

b. Complain to the CEO immediately.

c. Meet with the functional manager to discuss the impact on the project schedule and negotiate a resource-sharing plan.

d. Accept the situation and tell the team to work twice as hard.

48. **A project is using a Tornado Diagram. What is the primary purpose of this tool?**

a. To show the project's weather-related risks.

b. To identify which risks have the most significant impact on the project outcomes (Sensitivity Analysis).

c. To show the team's velocity over time.

d. To map out the project's communication channels.

49. **A project manager is comparing three potential projects for the company's 2026 portfolio.**

Project	Net Present Value (NPV)	Internal rate of return (IRR)	Payback Period
Project Alpha	250,000 USD	12%	18 Months
Project Beta	450,000 USD	10%	24 Months
Project Gamma	100,000 USD	18%	12 Months

If the organization's primary goal is to maximize total long-term value added to the company, which project should the project manager recommend?

a. Project Gamma, because it has the highest IRR.

b. Project Alpha, because it has a balanced NPV and Payback Period.

c. Project Beta, because it has the highest NPV.

d. Project Gamma, because it has the shortest Payback Period.

50. **In a multi-national procurement negotiation, a vendor uses a "Good Cop/Bad Cop" tactic. The lead negotiator is friendly, but their "manager" (who is not in the room) keeps rejecting every concession.**

As a Strategic Advisor, what is your best response?

a. Walk away from the negotiation immediately.

b. Identify the tactic and insist on speaking directly with the person who has the authority to make decisions.

c. Agree to the vendor's terms to avoid conflict and keep the project on schedule.

d. Use a similar tactic by pretending your sponsor is also rejecting the terms.

51. **A project has a Benefit Cost Ratio (BCR) of 1.7. What does this indicate?**

a. For every 1.00 USD spent, the project returns 1.70 USD in benefits.

b. The project is 70% over budget.

c. The project will take 1.7 years to pay back its initial investment.

d. The project's risks are 1.7 times higher than its rewards.

52. **During the procurement of a complex AI engine, the project manager includes a service level agreement (SLA) that requires "99.9% uptime." This is an example of:**

a. A Project Scope requirement.

b. A Quality Metric and a Non-functional Requirement.

c. A functional requirement.

d. A project constraint that should be avoided.

53. **A project manager is reviewing a Benefit management plan. They notice that a key "Intangible Benefit" is "Improved Brand Reputation."**

How should the PM measure this benefit after project closure?

a. By calculating the Net Present Value (NPV).

b. Through sentiment analysis of customer reviews and Net Promoter Scores (NPS).

c. By checking the project's final cost variance.

d. Intangible benefits cannot be measured and should be removed from the plan.

54. **You are managing a project with a total budget (BAC) of 500,000 USD. To date, you have spent 200,000 USD (AC) and earned 150,000 USD (EV) of work. Your sponsor asks for the Estimate to Complete (ETC), assuming the remaining work will be performed at the current budgeted rate.**

What is the ETC?

a. 350,000 USD   b. 300,000 USD

c. 150,000 USD   d. 250,000 USD

55. **A project manager is leading a global digital transformation project. During a monthly steering committee meeting, a key stakeholder expresses concern that the project's data center migration might violate new regional Environmental, Social, and Governance (ESG) carbon footprint regulations that were enacted after the project started. What should the project manager do first?**

a. Continue the migration as planned since the project was approved before the regulations.

b. Update the Issue Log and escalate the concern to the project sponsor immediately.

c. Perform an impact analysis to determine how the new regulations affect the project's compliance and objectives.

d. Revise the risk management plan to include regulatory non-compliance as a high-priority risk.

56. **Your agile team is experiencing "Quiet Quitting," where several high-performing members are doing the bare minimum and showing signs of burnout due to a BANI (Brittle, Anxious, Non-linear, Incomprehensible) work environment. As a servant leader, which action is most effective?**

a. Increase the frequency of Daily Stand-ups to monitor progress more closely.

b. Facilitate a retrospective specifically focused on psychological safety and team well-being.

c. Implement stricter WIP (work in progress) limits to reduce the team's cognitive load.

d. Offer financial bonuses for meeting upcoming sprint milestones to boost motivation.

57. **A project is nearing completion, and the organization is shifting toward a "Value-Led" delivery model. The Project Management Office (PMO) asks the project manager to demonstrate that the intended benefits are actually being realized. Which document should the project manager reference?**

a. The project charter.

b. The Work Performance Report.

c. The Benefits management plan.

d. The Project Schedule.

58. **During a complex negotiation with a vendor for an AI-based software module, the vendor demands a "Cost-Plus-Incentive-Fee" (CPIF) contract. The project manager is concerned about budget overruns. Which metric should the PM calculate to determine at what point the vendor begins to share the cost overruns?**

a. The Point of Total Assumption (PTA)

b. The Target Price

c. The Ceiling Price

d. The Benefit-Cost Ratio (BCR)

59. **An organization is using a Hybrid approach for a construction project with a high-tech smart-home component. The hardware is being built using Predictive methods, while the software is using scrum. The software team is blocked because the hardware prototype is delayed. What should the project manager do?**
    a. Tell the software team to stop working until the hardware is ready.
    b. Use a "Fishbone Diagram" to identify the root cause of the hardware delay.
    c. Ask the software team to work on features that do not require the hardware, such as the UI or cloud backend.
    d. Crash the hardware schedule by adding more resources to the assembly line.

60. **A project manager is overseeing a multi-national initiative to deploy AI-driven logistics. A new national privacy law is passed in one of the operating countries that restricts the use of facial recognition, a core feature of the project. The project is already in the execution phase. Which action should the project manager take to demonstrate Strategic Alignment?**
    a. Cancel the project in that specific country to avoid legal penalties.
    b. Consult with the legal department and the product owner to re-evaluate the project's Value Proposition in light of the new constraints.
    c. Instruct the technical team to find a way to bypass the software restriction using anonymized data.
    d. Update the risk register and continue development, assuming the law will have a grace period.

61. **Your organization has just adopted a "Circular economy" policy as part of its Environmental, Social, and Governance (ESG) goals. You are managing a project to build a new office complex. How should you integrate this policy into the project?**
    a. Hire an external consultant to handle all ESG reporting at the end of the project.
    b. Ensure the procurement plan prioritizes vendors with sustainable waste management and material recycling certifications.
    c. Add "ESG Compliance" as a low-priority item in the project charter.
    d. Focus solely on the budget and schedule, as ESG is a corporate-level responsibility, not a project-level one.

62. **A project manager is leading a distributed team using a Hybrid model. During a "Health Check," it is discovered that the "Non-linear" nature of the work is causing high anxiety among junior members. According to the Brittle, Anxious, Non-linear, Incomprehensible (BANI) framework, what is the best leadership response?**
    a. Implement a more rigid, predictive schedule to provide a sense of certainty.
    b. Foster Flexibility and Contextual Empathy by providing more frequent, transparent communication and "safe-to-fail" experiments.
    c. Replace the junior members with more experienced seniors who can handle high-stress environments.
    d. Ignore the anxiety, as it is a natural part of modern project management.

63. **Which of the following metrics is most important for a project manager to track in a 2026 Value-Driven delivery environment?**
    a. The number of tasks completed per week (Velocity).
    b. The variance between Planned Value (PV) and Actual Cost (AC).
    c. The Realized Benefit against the projected business case benchmarks.
    d. The number of hours worked by the team.

64. **A project manager is closing a project. The customer has signed off on all deliverables, but the PM realizes that the operational team (the users) has not been trained on the new system. What should the PM do?**
    a. Close the project immediately since the customer has signed off.
    b. Delay the project closure and facilitate a Knowledge Transfer session to ensure benefit sustainability.

c. Hand over the training manuals to the customer and consider the task complete.

d. Escalate the lack of training to the project sponsor as a failure of the customer.

65. **A project manager is leading an AI implementation project. During testing, it is discovered that the algorithm shows a significant demographic bias that could lead to unfair credit scoring for minority groups. The sponsor wants to release the product anyway to meet a critical market window. What should the PM do?**

a. Release the product as requested by the sponsor to ensure the project's financial success.

b. Refuse to release the product and report the sponsor to the PMO for an ethical violation.

c. Document the bias in the risk register and work with the technical team to implement a "Bias mitigation Plan" before release, even if it delays the project.

d. Launch the product but include a disclaimer that the results may be inaccurate for certain demographics.

66. **You are managing a project using a "Remote-First" strategy. You notice that "Virtual Fatigue" is decreasing team velocity and increasing the number of errors in the code. Which leadership intervention is most aligned with the 2026 People domain?**

a. Require all team members to turn on their cameras during all meetings to ensure engagement.

b. Implement "Asynchronous Communication" protocols and "No-Meeting Fridays" to respect cognitive load.

c. Increase the number of status reports to catch errors earlier.

d. Hire a "Remote Productivity Consultant" to monitor the team's screen time.

67. **A project is being executed in a highly volatile market. The project manager uses a Tornado Diagram during a quantitative risk analysis. What is the primary purpose of this tool?**

a. To show the relationship between two variables (Correlation).

b. To identify which individual risks have the greatest potential impact on the project outcome.

c. To track the project's progress against the baseline over time.

d. To visualize the sequence of steps in a complex process.

68. **An organization is moving from a project-based structure to a Value-Stream structure. As a project manager, your role is shifting toward managing the "Flow" of value. Which Lean metric should you prioritize to identify bottlenecks?**

a. Burnup Chart.

b. Cycle time.

c. Cost Performance Index (CPI).

d. Resource Histogram.

69. **Your project has a Net Present Value (NPV) of USD 50,000 and an internal rate of return (IRR) of 12%. The company's "hurdle rate" (minimum acceptable return) is 15%. Should the project have been approved?**

a. Yes, because the NPV is positive.

b. No, because the IRR is lower than the hurdle rate.

c. Yes, because an IRR of 12% is still a good return on investment.

d. It depends on the Payback Period.

70. **A project manager is overseeing a multi-billion-dollar infrastructure project. A major supplier has filed for bankruptcy due to a global economic shift. This supplier was providing a critical, long-lead-time component. What is the project manager's first action?**

a. Immediately invoke the force majeure clause in the contract.

b. Consult the risk register to see if a secondary supplier was previously identified and perform an impact analysis.

c. Request additional funding from the sponsor to expedite a replacement from a luxury vendor.

d. Terminate the project since the critical path is now permanently broken.

71. **In an effort to meet ESG goals, a PM discovers that a project subcontractor is using child labor in a remote region. The subcontractor is the only one capable of meeting the project's tight deadline. What should the PM do?**
    a. Continue with the subcontractor but monitor the situation closely to ensure safety.
    b. Immediately terminate the relationship with the subcontractor and report the finding to the organization's compliance officer, regardless of the schedule impact.
    c. Keep the information confidential until the project is delivered to protect the organization's reputation.
    d. Ask the subcontractor to hide the evidence before the next audit.

72. **An agile team is struggling with "Incomprehensibility" (the 'I' in BANI). The project requirements involve a cutting-edge quantum computing module that no one on the team fully understands. How should the PM/scrum master proceed?**
    a. Replace the team with quantum physics experts.
    b. Schedule a "Spike" (a time-boxed research period) to allow the team to build a prototype and gain knowledge.
    c. Revert to a Predictive/Waterfall model to enforce a strict design phase.
    d. Ask the product owner to remove the quantum module from the scope.

73. **During a final project review, it is determined that while the project met its "Iron Triangle" (Scope, Schedule, Budget) goals, the Net Present Value (NPV) has turned negative due to a shift in market interest rates. How should the PM document this in the final report?**
    a. Declare the project a total success because it met the internal baseline.
    b. Record the project as "Completed" but note the failure to meet the Value realization goals in the lessons learned.
    c. Omit the NPV data to ensure the team receives their bonuses.
    d. Change the project's baseline retroactively to make the NPV look positive.

74. **A project manager is managing a project with a Target Cost of USD 200,000, a Target Fee of USD 20,000, and a Share Ratio of 80/20 (80% buyer / 20% seller). If the Actual Cost comes in at USD 220,000, what is the final fee paid to the seller?**
    a. USD 20,000
    b. USD 16,000
    c. USD 24,000
    d. USD 22,000

75. **A project manager in a "Remote-First" organization is using AI-driven sentiment analysis to monitor team morale. The tool flags that the team is feeling "Anxious" (per the BANI framework) due to a sudden shift in corporate strategy. Which leadership style is required?**
    a. Transactional leadership (focus on rewards and punishments).
    b. Servant leadership with a focus on Sense-making (providing clarity and transparency).
    c. Laissez-faire leadership (letting the team figure it out on their own).
    d. Authoritative leadership (enforcing strict deadlines to distract from the anxiety).

76. **You are managing a project with a Target Cost of USD 500,000 and a Ceiling Price of USD 600,000. The Share Ratio is 60/40. If the Actual Cost is USD 650,000, what is the final price paid by the buyer?**
    a. USD 650,000
    b. USD 600,000
    c. USD 500,000
    d. USD 590,000

77. **Which document is used specifically to ensure that the project's output continues to provide value after the project team has disbanded?**
    a. The project charter.
    b. The Resource management plan.
    c. The Value Transition/Handoff Plan.
    d. The risk register.

78. **An agile team is working on a high-tech medical device. A regulatory body introduces a new audit requirement mid-sprint. What should the scrum master do?**
    a. Stop the sprint immediately and restart with the new requirement.

b. Ignore the requirement until the next release.

c. Invite the product owner to the next Daily Stand-up to discuss the impact on the Product Backlog.

d. Add the requirement to the current sprint Backlog and ask the team to work overtime.

79. **An organization is using AI to automate 40% of the project's technical tasks. The project team is worried about job security, leading to a significant drop in morale and productivity. As a project manager focusing on the People Domain, what is your most effective action?**

a. Explain that AI is mandatory for company efficiency and ignore the morale issues.

b. Facilitate a "Skills-Bridge" workshop to help the team learn how to manage and audit AI outputs, focusing on Augmented Intelligence.

c. Tell the team that no one will be fired until the project is over.

d. Increase the performance monitoring of the human staff to ensure they are keeping up with the AI.

80. **A major regional conflict has caused an immediate shutdown of your project's main manufacturing plant. The project is at a critical milestone. Which document should the PM consult first to determine the Resilience Strategy?**

a. The project charter.

b. The Business Continuity Plan and the risk management plan.

c. The Resource Histogram.

d. The Quality management plan.

81. **During the project closing, the PM realizes that the intended Environmental (E) goal of the project (reducing carbon emissions by 20%) was not met. However, the project was under budget and ahead of schedule. What should the PM do?**

a. Highlight the budget and schedule success and minimize the carbon footprint failure in the final report.

b. Document the failure to meet the ESG goal and conduct a root cause analysis to include in the Lessons Learned.

c. Change the project's original ESG goals to 10% so it looks like the project succeeded.

d. Refuse to sign off on the project closure until the goal is met.

82. **A project has a Benefit-Cost Ratio (BCR) of 2.5. A competing project has a BCR of 1.8. Based purely on the BCR, which project should the organization prioritize?**

a. The project with a BCR of 1.8.

b. The project with a BCR of 2.5.

c. Neither, as BCR is not a valid project selection metric.

d. The project that finishes sooner.

83. **A project manager is managing a hybrid project. The Predictive Hardware team and the agile software team have a major conflict regarding the timing of the integration phase. Which conflict resolution technique is most effective for a long-term professional relationship?**

a. Smoothing/Accommodating.

b. Forcing/Directing.

c. Collaborating/Problem Solving.

d. Compromising.

84. **You are calculating the Point of Total Assumption (PTA) for a Fixed Price Incentive Fee (FPIF) contract. The target cost is USD 1,000,000, the target fee is USD 100,000, the ceiling price is USD 1,200,000, and the buyer's share ratio is 80%. What is the PTA?**

a. USD 1,125,000 b. USD 1,200,000

c. USD 1,080,000 d. USD 1,150,000

85. **In the 2026 PMP context, "Value Velocity" refers to:**

a. How fast the team completes their tasks.

b. The speed at which the organization realizes actual business benefits from project outputs.

c. The frequency of the sprint retrospectives.

d. The rate at which the project budget is spent.

86. **Your project's To-Complete Performance Index (TCPI) is 1.2 based on the remaining Budget at Completion (BAC). This means:**
    a. The project is easier to complete than originally planned.
    b. The project must perform at 120% efficiency to finish within the original budget.
    c. The project is under budget.
    d. The project should be canceled immediately.

87. **A stakeholder insists on adding a new feature that does not align with the Strategic business case but will make the product more visually appealing. As a Strategic Advisor PM, what do you do?**
    a. Add the feature to please the stakeholder.
    b. Reject the feature and explain how it deviates from the project's **Value Proposition**.
    c. Ask the team to work on it in their spare time.
    d. Escalate the request to the CEO.

88. **What is the final step of a project closure in the 2026 standards?**
    a. Releasing the team.
    b. Archiving documents.
    c. Confirming the Value realization Handoff and documenting lessons learned.
    d. Having a celebration party.

Case study: Aurora Grid and AI Energy Transition

You are the Program project manager for *Aurora Grid*, a multinational project to modernize a utility company's energy distribution network through smart sensors, predictive maintenance, and an AI-based demand optimization platform. The project uses a *Hybrid* approach: physical grid hardware upgrades follow a predictive lifecycle, while the AI analytics and mobile field applications follow adaptive delivery. The board approved the project largely because of its expected strategic benefits: a 22% reduction in outage time, 18% lower maintenance cost, and a measurable reduction in carbon emissions. Eight months into execution, the hardware work is on schedule, but the AI model has begun producing optimization decisions that disproportionately deprioritize low-income neighborhoods during peak demand. At the same time, a new regional energy fairness regulation requires utilities to demonstrate transparent, non-discriminatory decision logic. A major vendor supplying recyclable sensor units has also notified the team of a probable production shortfall due to rare-material sourcing restrictions. The sponsor wants the next steering review to focus on schedule confidence and board messaging, while the compliance lead insists the AI ethics issue is now the most urgent threat to strategic value.

89. **The sponsor asks you to avoid highlighting the fairness issue in the upcoming steering review because it may trigger concern from the board and delay funding for the next tranche. What is the best response as a Strategic Advisor?**
    a. Focus the review on schedule and cost because ethics concerns belong to operations after go-live.
    b. Present the issue as a strategic value-at-risk item, including regulatory, reputational, and benefits-realization implications.
    c. Remove the fairness issue from the dashboard and keep it in a private team register.
    d. Escalate directly to the board without informing the sponsor.

90. **The AI team proposes temporarily disabling the fairness constraints in the model to recover optimization performance and preserve the deployment date. Which decision is most appropriate?**
    a. Approve the change because value delivery takes priority over emerging compliance interpretation.
    b. Reject the proposal unless the team can demonstrate compliance, explainability, and risk-mitigated benefit impact.
    c. Let the product owner decide independently because the software workstream is adaptive.
    d. Freeze all AI development until the hardware workstream is complete.

91. **The recyclable sensor vendor's shortfall may delay installation in two regions. Which procurement response best protects both strategic and ESG objectives?**
    a. Switch immediately to the cheapest alternative supplier, even if recyclability falls below policy thresholds.
    b. Conduct a risk-adjusted sourcing analysis that compares alternate suppliers on continuity, ESG compliance, and total long-term value.
    c. Delay procurement decisions until the next quarterly governance review because hardware is still nominally on plan.
    d. Remove the recyclability requirement because the project's main KPI is outage reduction.

92. **During an integrated review, the hardware team argues that the software team is causing unnecessary delay through repeated fairness testing. The software team argues that rushing integration could lock bias into the solution at scale. What should you do first?**
    a. Force the software team to align with the hardware milestone because predictive work has less flexibility.
    b. Facilitate a joint dependency and value-risk review to align both teams on shared outcomes, constraints, and release criteria.
    c. Separate the teams' governance forums so each can optimize independently.
    d. Transfer software testing ownership to the compliance department.

93. **The PMO asks you what single indicator would best show whether Aurora Grid is truly succeeding in a value-driven environment. Which metric is strongest?**
    a. Percentage of hardware packages installed against baseline.
    b. Sprint velocity of the AI analytics team.
    c. Realized benefit trend combining outage reduction, compliant service equity, and carbon improvement against the business case.
    d. Number of risks closed per month.

Case study: Meridian Nexus

You are leading *Meridian Nexus*, a complex initiative to redesign a global pharmaceutical cold-chain network using IoT monitoring, AI-driven route optimization, and a digital command center. The organization operates in more than 20 countries and must comply with emerging cross-border data rules, medical logistics regulations, and stricter sustainability reporting. The physical retrofit of refrigerated warehouses and smart packaging is being managed predictively. The AI command center, exception management workflows, and partner dashboards are being delivered adaptively. The business case promises faster delivery, lower spoilage, reduced carbon emissions, and improved equitable access to temperature-sensitive medicines in underserved regions. Ten months into the program, the pilot has reduced spoilage in urban markets but has underperformed in remote areas because the AI model optimizes toward stable infrastructure and deprioritizes low-volume regions. A civil society advisory group alleges the solution is reinforcing geographic inequity. At the same time, a cybersecurity review finds that one third-party logistics provider stores telemetry data in a jurisdiction now considered high risk under a newly updated data sovereignty rule. The executive committee is debating whether to launch on time in major markets and fix fairness later, or delay the rollout for re-architecture and governance redesign.

94. **The executive committee prefers launching in the largest markets first and deferring the remote-access problem to a later release. What is the strongest PM recommendation?**

a. Approve the phased launch because the realized value in major markets justifies later social benefit adjustments.

b. Recommend a launch decision only after evaluating whether phased deployment materially violates the project's equitable-access value case and governance commitments.

c. Reject any phased rollout because adaptive delivery never allows staged value realization.

d. Let the AI product lead decide because this is a software prioritization matter.

95. **A cybersecurity review shows one logistics partner stores sensitive telemetry in a jurisdiction now classified as high risk. What should you do first?**

a. Continue operations quietly while the legal team studies the update.

b. Initiate an immediate integrated impact assessment on compliance, operational continuity, partner obligations, and release readiness.

c. Terminate the logistics provider immediately without transition planning.

d. Reclassify the risk as operational only because the data is not customer-facing.

96. **In a retrospective, the adaptive team says the predictive infrastructure milestones are forcing them into premature release commitments. The infrastructure team says the adaptive team keeps changing operational assumptions. Which action best addresses the root issue?**

a. Replace hybrid governance with one single predictive schedule for all teams.

b. Create integrated release criteria, shared dependency mapping, and decision triggers for changes that affect both lifecycles.

c. Move all design decisions to the command center product owner.

d. Separate reporting lines so each team can optimize within its own methodology.

97. **The sponsor asks for a single KPI to reassure investors before launch. Which KPI is most credible in a strategic value context?**

a. Number of command center user stories accepted.

b. Percentage of warehouses retrofitted.

c. Composite benefit realization showing spoilage reduction, equitable service coverage, compliant data handling, and carbon performance.

d. Average sprint burndown accuracy.

98. **The operations leadership fears the digital command center will reduce local autonomy, causing passive resistance to training and adoption. What is the best PM response to protect long-term value delivery?**

a. Escalate resistance as non-compliance and require mandatory adoption immediately.

b. Launch a change enablement plan that reframes the system as decision support, includes local feedback loops, and builds role transition capability.

c. Delay all training until the system is fully stable to avoid confusion.

d. Transfer ownership to IT because adoption issues begin after project delivery.

Burn-down chart-based multiple choice questions

Use the sprint Burn-down chart for Project *Orion* to answer the following questions:

The actual line remains above the ideal line for most of the sprint, shows flat sections around Days 3 to 4 and Days 5 to 6, drops sharply on Day 7, and ends above zero on Day 10.

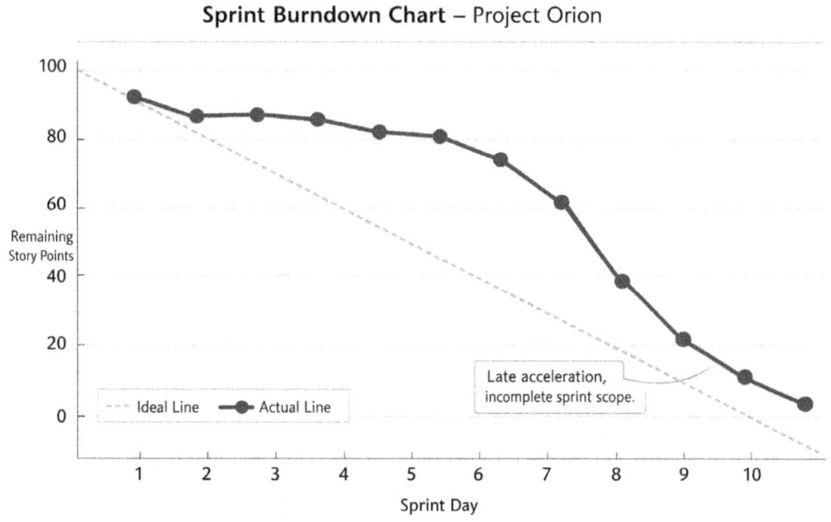

***Figure 9.4:** Sprint Burn-down chart*

99. **The burndown chart shows nearly flat progress around Days 3–4 and Days 5–6. What is the strongest interpretation of this pattern?**
    a. The team intentionally reduced velocity to improve morale.
    b. A workflow bottleneck or blocked work prevented items from reaching the done status.
    c. The product owner removed significant scope mid-sprint.
    d. The team completed most stories early and then slowed down intentionally.

100. **The chart shows a sharp burn on Day 7 after several slower days. Which explanation is most conceptually sound?**
    a. Multiple items were likely completed together after a bottleneck was cleared.
    b. The team added more story points and accelerated progress automatically.
    c. The burndown chart is invalid because progress should always be linear.
    d. The scrum master changed the ideal line to match the actual line.

101. **The actual line ends above zero on Day 10. What does this most directly indicate?**
    a. The sprint was completed successfully with extra capacity remaining.
    b. The team underreported completed work.
    c. Some committed sprint scope remained unfinished at the sprint end.
    d. The team exceeded the ideal forecast and therefore outperformed expectations.

102. **If the actual burndown remains above the ideal line for most of the sprint, what should the PM or scrum master focus on first?**
    a. Pressuring the team to work longer hours in the next sprint.
    b. Investigating flow constraints, estimation quality, and sprint planning realism.
    c. Eliminating retrospectives to save time.
    d. Increasing the team size immediately without root cause analysis.

103. **If this late-burn and incomplete-scope pattern repeats across multiple sprints, what is the most significant conceptual risk?**

 a. The team will become too dependent on burndown charts.

 b. Stakeholders may lose confidence because delivery predictability and forecasting credibility decline.

 c. Velocity will automatically increase due to repetitive learning.

 d. The backlog will become unnecessary because the chart already reflects scope.

104. **The actual burndown remains above the ideal line, but the team reports that several large stories were almost complete by Day 8. What is the most important conceptual weakness in using only this burndown chart to assess sprint health?**

 a. Burndown charts cannot be used in scrum projects.

 b. The chart does not reveal work aging or how much effort is trapped in partially completed items.

 c. The chart always exaggerates the amount of remaining work.

 d. The chart proves the team estimated incorrectly in every case.

105. **If the product owner had added 12 story points on Day 6 and the chart was not annotated, what analytical error is most likely when interpreting the late-sprint pattern?**

 a. Assuming all late variance is caused only by delivery underperformance rather than a scope change.

 b. Concluding the team improved because the ideal line remained straight.

 c. Believing a burn-down cannot include backlog changes.

 d. Assuming scope additions always reduce stakeholder value.

106. **A PM notices that this sprint's burndown pattern repeats a prior trend: slow burn early, steep burn late, incomplete finish. Which systemic improvement is most likely to improve predictability without encouraging unhealthy speed pressure?**

 a. Increase story size so fewer items need to be tracked.

 b. Reduce work in progress and tighten the definition of done to encourage earlier completion flow.

 c. Raise the sprint commitment to motivate stronger output.

 d. Remove review checkpoints so the team can burn points faster.

107. **The team argues that the sharp Day 7 drop proves the sprint recovered successfully. Which is the strongest coaching response?**

 a. Agree, because any late catch-up means the sprint process is healthy.

 b. Emphasize that batch completion may hide unstable flow and late discovery risk even if some progress was recovered.

 c. Conclude the team should skip retrospectives since the chart self-corrected.

 d. Focus only on total points burned because timing inside the sprint is irrelevant.

108. **If leadership wants one companion metric to pair with this Burn-down chart for a more reliable view of flow performance, which would be most useful?**

 a. Team attendance percentage.

 b. Cumulative flow or cycle time data to expose queue buildup and completion delays.

 c. Number of emails sent during the sprint.

 d. Budget variance for the entire quarter.

Case study: Orion

You are the scrum master for *Project Orion*, a digital operations platform being delivered in two-week sprints. The latest sprint Burn-down chart shows the team stayed above the ideal line for most of the sprint, flattened around Days 3–4 and Days 5–6, then burned sharply on Day 7 before ending with work still remaining on Day 10. During the sprint review, the team explained that several stories were nearly complete by Day 8 but were delayed in testing because two senior testers were diverted to support a production incident in another product line. On Day 6, the product owner also added a high-priority compliance story after a legal clarification from the audit team. Senior leadership is worried because this is the second sprint in a row with late acceleration and incomplete delivery. The Release Manager argues that the sharp Day 7 drop proves the team recovered well enough, while the product owner believes the real issue is poor adaptability to urgent scope shifts. The engineering lead warns that too much work is being started in parallel and not completed early enough to create a stable flow.

109. **What is the strongest interpretation of the sharp Day 7 drop in the context of this case?**
    a. It proves the sprint fully recovered and no systemic issue remains.
    b. It likely reflects batch completion after delayed testing, which may hide unstable flow rather than demonstrate healthy recovery.
    c. It confirms the product owner should add more urgent stories mid-sprint in the future.
    d. It means the team's estimates were perfect, but the burndown chart was misdrawn.

110. **Which factor most weakens the reliability of using this burndown chart alone to judge team performance?**
    a. Burndown charts cannot represent agile work accurately.
    b. The chart does not clearly show the effect of mid-sprint scope addition and delayed testing queues on remaining work.
    c. The ideal line should always change whenever a tester is absent.
    d. The chart becomes invalid whenever a compliance story is added.

111. **If leadership wants to improve predictability in the next sprint without creating pressure-driven behavior, what is the best immediate improvement?**
    a. Increase the sprint commitment to force faster completion.
    b. Reduce work in progress, surface blocked items earlier, and rebalance test capacity before items accumulate late in the sprint.
    c. Remove testing from the definition of done so points burn sooner.
    d. Ask developers to self-approve completed stories when testers are unavailable.

112. **The product owner argues that poor adaptability to urgent scope shifts is the main problem. What is the most balanced PM/scrum master response?**
    a. Agree fully, because urgent scope changes are the only cause of missed sprint commitments.
    b. Reject the point because scope should never evolve once a sprint begins.
    c. Recognize that urgent scope shifts matter, but emphasize that weak flow and overloaded testing amplified the disruption.
    d. Escalate the product owner for changing scope without asking the engineering lead first.

113. **Which companion metric would best help confirm whether the real issue is too much parallel work and late-stage queue buildup?**
    a. Team attendance percentage.
    b. Cumulative flow or cycle time analysis showing work item aging and testing queue expansion.
    c. Budget variance for the release train.
    d. Number of meetings held during the sprint.

Case study: Helios

You are the Delivery Lead for *Project Helios*, a hybrid initiative to launch a smart-building optimization platform. The hardware deployment is progressing predictively, while the analytics engine and tenant portal are delivered adaptively. During the last four sprints, the **Cumulative Flow Diagram (CFD)** has shown a widening work in progress band, a growing Testing band, and a nearly flat Done band. The product owner argues that the output is acceptable because developers are continuously starting work. The QA lead says the system is becoming unstable due to late integration and rising defect discovery. A sponsor wants to accelerate launch because one pilot customer is ready, while the operations team warns that incomplete quality validation could damage credibility if the first deployment fails. The engineering manager believes too many partially completed stories are masking the real delivery risk. Refer to CFD *Figure 9.5* related to the unhealthy and improved flow and answer the questions:

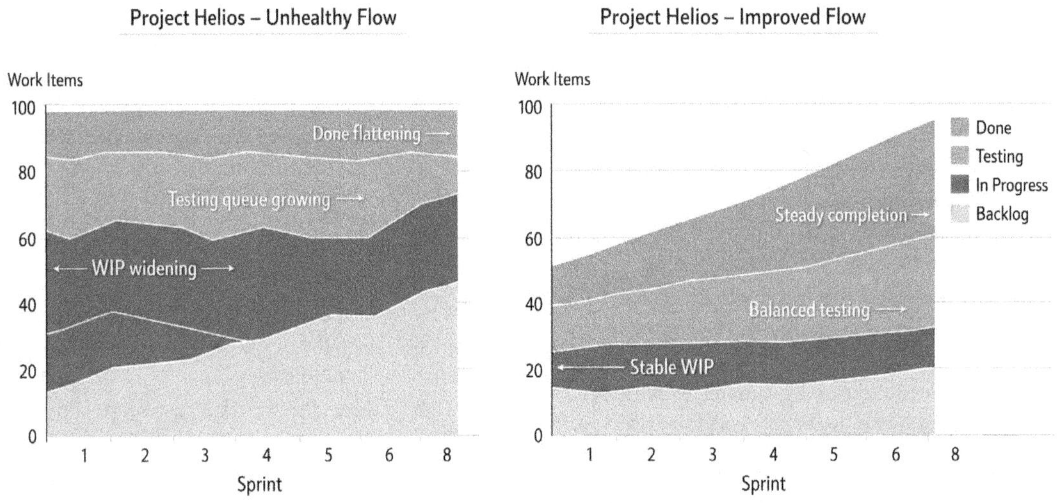

***Figure 9.5:** Cumulative Flow Diagram*

114. **What is the strongest interpretation of a widening work in progress band and a flat Done band on the CFD?**
    a. The team is maximizing flexibility by keeping more options open.
    b. Flow is degrading because work is accumulating faster than it is being completed.
    c. The backlog is becoming more strategic.
    d. The team has achieved an ideal balance between development and testing.

115. **If the Testing band is steadily expanding while Done remains nearly flat, what is the most likely systemic issue?**
    a. The product owner is under-prioritizing defects.
    b. A downstream validation bottleneck is limiting the completion flow.
    c. Developers are finishing too few user stories by design.
    d. The project needs a larger backlog.

116. **The sponsor wants to launch early because one pilot customer is ready. What is the best PM recommendation based on the CFD pattern?**
    a. Launch immediately because early market entry is always worth quality trade-offs.
    b. Delay the launch decision until completion flow and quality stability improve enough to support reliable release confidence.
    c. Remove testing criteria so more items can reach Done quickly.
    d. Approve a partial launch without examining operational readiness.

117. **Which improvement would most directly address the CFD pattern without encouraging superficial output?**
    a. Increase WIP limits so the team can start more stories in parallel.
    b. Reduce WIP, strengthen pull discipline, and rebalance test capacity to finish work earlier.
    c. Replace retrospectives with executive audits.
    d. Measure developers only on the number of items started.

118. **What is the most significant risk if this CFD pattern continues for several more sprints?**
    a. The team will become too specialized in analytics work.
    b. Delivery predictability and release credibility will decline as queue aging and hidden quality risk increase.
    c. The backlog will automatically shrink.
    d. Sprint goals will become irrelevant to stakeholders.

Case study: Polaris

You are the agile delivery manager for *Project Polaris*, a cloud migration and intelligent workflow automation program. The team's *Velocity Chart* shows the following delivered story points over six sprints: 42, 44, 40, 19, 46, and 28. The planned velocity was 40 per sprint. Investigation shows sprint 4 was heavily consumed by remediating an urgent security weakness, while sprint 6 absorbed multiple support requests from an early release in another business unit. Senior leadership is concerned that the erratic trend means the team is unreliable. The product owner argues that the chart does not reflect value protection work. A release train engineer warns that if these interruptions continue, future forecasting will become misleading. The sponsor wants to know whether to reduce scope, increase team size, or keep the current plan.

119. **What is the strongest interpretation of the sprint 4 velocity collapse from 40 planned to 19 delivered?**
    a. The team became fundamentally less capable during that sprint.
    b. The sprint absorbed unplanned protective work that reduced visible feature throughput but may have preserved future value.
    c. Velocity charts always prove underperformance when output falls below plan.
    d. The team should no longer use velocity as a planning input.

120. **Why is sprint 6 an important warning sign even though its velocity is higher than sprint 4?**
    a. It shows the team is becoming more productive under pressure.
    b. It suggests that support demand from external releases is consuming delivery capacity and may distort future forecasting.
    c. It proves the security work in sprint 4 was unnecessary.
    d. It means scope no longer matters in sprint planning.

121. **What is the best PM response when leadership labels the team "unreliable" based only on the velocity chart?**
    a. Agree and recommend replacing several team members to stabilize output.
    b. Reframe the discussion to distinguish planned feature throughput from interruption-driven work and value protection activities.
    c. Stop reporting velocity entirely and report only sprint burndown instead.
    d. Increase sprint commitments to restore confidence.

122. **If interruptions from security and support work are becoming normal, what planning adjustment is most appropriate?**
    a. Keep using 40 as the full commitment because it is the aspirational target.
    b. Introduce capacity allocation or a reservable buffer for unplanned but expected operational work.

c. Remove all support work from the team so the chart looks cleaner.

d. Double the team size immediately to absorb all uncertainty.

123. **Which conclusion about future forecasting is most justified from this velocity pattern?**

a. Forecasts should use the highest recent sprint because it proves peak potential.

b. Forecasts should rely on the original plan because interruptions are temporary by definition.

c. Forecasts should be probabilistic or range-based because recurring interruptions make a single-point velocity assumption fragile.

d. Forecasting is impossible whenever velocity varies across sprints.

124. **In the side-by-side CFD comparison, what is the strongest reason the improved-flow panel is more trustworthy for release forecasting than the unhealthy-flow panel?**

a. It shows more total work entering the system, which guarantees faster delivery.

b. Its narrower and more stable bands suggest lower flow variability and more predictable completion behavior.

c. It proves the team size increased, which automatically improves throughput.

d. It removes the need for release criteria because the Done band is rising.

125. **Comparing the two CFDs, which signal most strongly suggests that the unhealthy-flow system is carrying hidden quality risk?**

a. The backlog band declines over time.

b. The Testing band expands while Done grows slowly, implying delayed validation and risk accumulation.

c. The improved-flow panel has a green Done band.

d. The improved-flow panel has less work in progress than backlog.

126. **If a sponsor asks what single leadership mistake most likely contributed to the unhealthy CFD pattern, what is the best answer?**

a. Allowing the team to finish too many items too early.

b. Rewarding work started more than work completed, which encouraged excessive parallelism.

c. Using a Cumulative Flow Diagram instead of a burndown chart.

d. Setting strict quality criteria before release.

127. **In the improved-flow panel, which conclusion is the most defensible regarding system capacity?**

a. Capacity appears more balanced across stages because queue growth is controlled and completion is steadier.

b. Capacity must have doubled because Done rises faster.

c. Testing is no longer necessary because the Testing band is smaller.

d. Work in progress was eliminated entirely.

128. **If the unhealthy CFD panel were observed in a project with a critical launch milestone, what would be the most strategically sound next step?**

a. Preserve the launch date and defer all unresolved testing work to post-release support.

b. Use the comparison to justify immediate flow stabilization actions before making a confident launch commitment.

c. Stop measuring flow because the CFD may discourage the team.

d. Focus only on backlog reduction because that is the clearest sign of progress.

Use the side-by-side velocity comparison image for Project Polaris to answer the following questions.

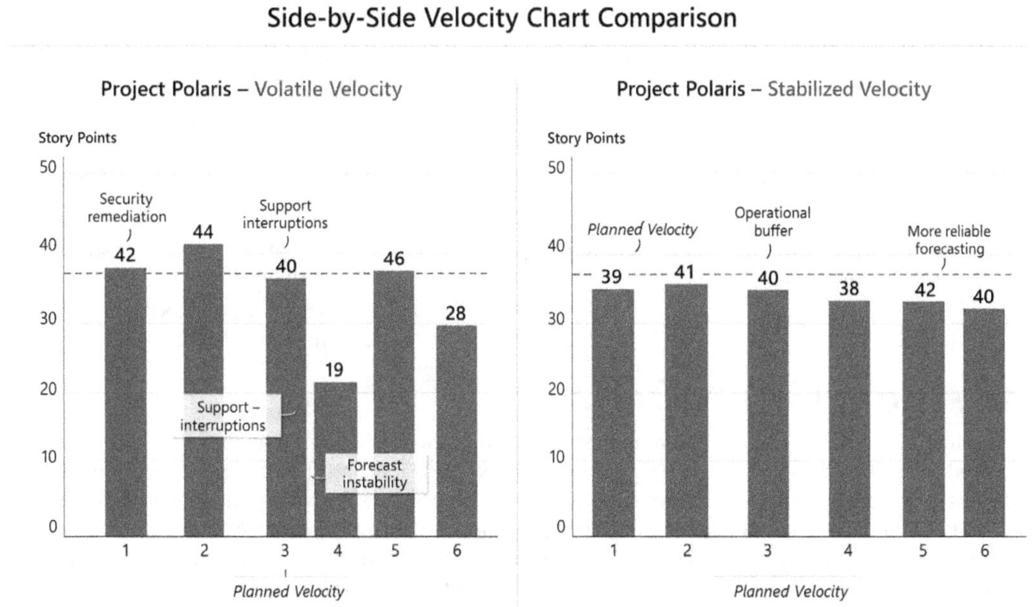

Figure 9.6: *Velocity chart*

129. **In the comparison image, what most strongly explains why the stabilized panel is more reliable for forecasting than the volatile panel?**
    a. It contains one sprint above plan, which guarantees future overperformance.
    b. It shows lower variation around planned capacity, which supports a more credible release prediction.
    c. It proves the team is larger than before.
    d. It eliminates the need for backlog prioritization.

130. **Looking at the volatile panel, what is the strongest reason sprint 4 should not be read simply as team underperformance?**
    a. A sharp drop always means the team intentionally slowed down.
    b. The drop may reflect interruption-driven protective work that preserved system integrity but reduced visible feature throughput.
    c. Velocity charts cannot be used when security issues exist.
    d. Sprint 4 should be ignored completely because it is an outlier.

131. **If leadership wants to move from the volatile pattern to the stabilized pattern, what planning shift is most appropriate?**
    a. Increase sprint commitments so the team is forced to normalize around the target.
    b. Introduce explicit capacity protection and buffers for security, support, and operational interruption demand.
    c. Stop tracking interruptions to protect morale.
    d. Average the volatile sprints and keep planning against the original target only.

132. **What is the most defensible interpretation of the stabilized panel's closeness to the planned line?**
    a. The team has eliminated all uncertainty from delivery.
    b. The system appears to be handling expected interruption demand with more disciplined capacity management.
    c. The team no longer needs retrospectives.
    d. Scope can now expand freely without affecting commitments.

133. **If a sponsor sees both panels and asks which one better supports confident portfolio decisions, what is the strongest answer?**
    a. The volatile panel, because it shows peak potential in some sprints.
    b. The stabilized panel, because more consistent throughput improves dependency planning and commitment credibility.
    c. Both are equally useful because averages always matter more than spread.
    d. Neither, because velocity should never be used in management conversations.

Case study: Orion Delta

You are leading *Project Orion Delta*, a digital platform transformation using iterative delivery. Recent performance data is mixed. The *burndown chart* shows progress staying above ideal for most of the sprint, flattening twice, then dropping sharply before ending with unfinished work. The cumulative flow diagram shows widening work in progress and Testing bands over several sprints, although the latest sprint shows slight improvement. Meanwhile, the velocity chart is volatile, with one major collapse linked to urgent security work and another weak sprint linked to support demand from an early release. The sponsor believes the latest sprint's late recovery proves the team is back on track. The product owner says the issue is too much urgent work entering the system. The engineering lead argues the real problem is unstable flow: too much work is being started, too much is waiting in testing, and throughput is being distorted by interruption demand.

134. **Considering all three charts together, what is the strongest overall diagnosis?**
    a. The team is healthy because late sprint recovery offsets earlier instability.
    b. The delivery system is experiencing structural flow instability amplified by interruption demand and late-stage validation queues.
    c. The charts are contradictory and therefore unusable for decision making.
    d. The only meaningful issue is that velocity is below the target line.

135. **Which action would most likely improve all three signals over time?**
    a. Raise sprint commitments so the team burns more work earlier.
    b. Lower WIP, protect test capacity, and reserve explicit capacity for urgent security and support work.
    c. Replace the burndown with a single executive progress percentage.
    d. Ignore velocity until the next release.

136. **If the sponsor asks which chart most clearly reveals hidden queue buildup, what is the best answer?**
    a. The burndown chart, because it shows all unfinished work directly.
    b. The cumulative flow diagram, because widening bands reveal where work is accumulating in the system.
    c. The velocity chart, because bar height always reveals testing load.
    d. All three charts reveal queue buildup equally well.

137. **If the product owner argues that urgent work is the main driver and the engineering lead argues that system design is the deeper issue, what is the most balanced conclusion?**
    a. Urgent work is irrelevant because adaptive teams should handle all change automatically.
    b. Both are partially correct: urgent work is the trigger, but weak flow design and insufficient capacity protection magnify its effect.

c. The engineering lead is wrong because queue buildup is normal in agile systems.

d. The product owner is wrong because interruption work should never be accepted.

138. **If leadership wants one message that best summarizes what these charts imply for release planning, which is strongest?**

a. Release confidence should be based on peak sprint output because it reflects team potential.

b. Release confidence should depend on stable completion flow and protected capacity, not late recoveries or isolated high-velocity sprints.

c. The burndown chart alone is enough to set release dates.

d. If one sprint improves, the entire trend can be considered corrected.

139. **In a Hybrid project, the hardware work may follow a ______ lifecycle while the software work follows an ______ lifecycle.**

a. adaptive; predictive

b. predictive; adaptive

c. incremental; waterfall

d. agile; plan-driven only

140. **A widening Testing band on a CFD usually indicates a downstream ______ that is reducing completion ______.**

a. milestone; budgets

b. bottleneck; flow

c. resource pool; morale

d. strategy; quality threshold

141. **If a burndown chart ends above zero at sprint close, some committed ______ remains unfinished, reducing delivery ______.**

a. scope; predictability

b. backlog; cost baseline

c. testing; ethics

d. value; governance

142. **In a value-led environment, success is best measured by realized ______ against the approved business ______.**

a. tasks; process

b. defects; workflow

c. benefits; case

d. velocity; assumption

143. **In a BANI context, the best response to team ______ is more transparency, shorter feedback loops, and psychological ______.**

a. efficiency; scoring

b. anxiety; safety

c. specialization; resilience

d. conflict; authority

144. **When a velocity chart becomes erratic because of recurring support and security work, forecasting should become more ______ and capacity should be more explicitly ______.**

a. optimistic; expanded

b. fixed; hidden

c. probabilistic; reserved

d. linear; compressed

145. **A Strategic Advisor should treat an emerging AI fairness issue as value-at-______ because it can affect compliance, reputation, and benefit ______.**

a. handoff; dashboards

b. risk; realization

c. closure; planning

d. backlog; velocity

146. **In sustainable procurement, the lowest bid should be balanced against total long-term ______ and ESG-related ______.**

a. value; risk

b. burn rate; staffing

c. training; compliance logs

d. reporting; process debt

147. **When too much work is started and little is finished, lowering ______ and strengthening pull discipline usually improves delivery ______.**
   a. velocity; costs
   b. WIP; flow
   c. risk; governance
   d. quality; independence

148. **During project closure, sustainable value is strengthened by a formal value ______ and operational knowledge ______.**
   a. transition; transfer
   b. audit; cancellation
   c. baseline; approval
   d. estimate; compression

149. **Which definition best matches the risk register?**
   a. A document that formally authorizes the project and gives the project manager authority to apply organizational resources.
   b. A living repository of identified risks, their analysis, owners, responses, and status.
   c. A chart that shows the amount of remaining work over time during a sprint.
   d. A plan that defines how project benefits will be measured after delivery.

150. **Which definition best matches the project charter?**
   a. A document that describes how vendor proposals will be evaluated during procurement.
   b. A formal document that authorizes the project, states high-level objectives, and assigns the project manager authority.
   c. A work management board is used to visualize flow and limit work in progress.
   d. A report that compares actual cost against earned value.

151. **Which definition best matches the Benefits management plan?**
   a. A document that defines how expected benefits will be realized, measured, sustained, and transitioned.
   b. A list of all assumptions and constraints used to estimate the schedule.
   c. A log used to track issues, owners, due dates, and resolution status.
   d. A matrix that assigns team responsibilities to project tasks.

152. **Which definition best matches the Cumulative Flow Diagram (CFD)?**
   a. A diagram that maps communication paths between stakeholders.
   b. A chart that shows the distribution of defects by root cause category.
   c. A visual flow chart showing work items across states over time to reveal bottlenecks, queue growth, and throughput trends.
   d. A financial chart that displays cumulative project spending against budget baseline.

153. **Which definition best matches the Explainability Register?**
   a. A register that documents the rationale, traceability, and decision logic behind AI-driven outputs to support transparency and compliance.
   b. A list of all approved vendors and contract award dates.
   c. A repository of meeting notes captured during sprint retrospectives.
   d. A log of all user-reported defects after production launch.

154. **A project manager reviews a Gantt Chart for a regulatory transformation program and notices that one activity on the critical path has zero float, while several non-critical activities have five to seven days of float. A key architect proposes reassigning two shared specialists from a non-critical workstream to the critical activity for one week. What is the strongest interpretation of this move?**
   a. It is strategically sound because protecting a zero float activity can reduce schedule risk if the reassigned work remains within available float.
   b. It is always unsafe because any resource reassignment automatically creates a new critical path.

c. It is unnecessary because float on non-critical work should never be consumed.

d. It is equivalent to crashing the entire project and therefore requires immediate executive approval.

155. **A quality lead presents a Pareto Chart of customer defects showing that two defect categories account for roughly 78% of all reported issues, while six other categories make up the remaining 22%. The engineering manager wants to launch eight parallel improvement initiatives so every category is addressed at once. What should the PM recommend?**

a. Focus first on the vital few categories with the greatest cumulative impact, then reassess before expanding effort.

b. Split resources equally across all defect categories to ensure fairness.

c. Ignore the largest categories because they are already well understood.

d. Replace the Pareto Chart with a burnup chart because quality defects are time-based.

156. **A manufacturing workstream uses a Control Chart to monitor a calibration process. The latest sample points remain within the upper and lower control limits, but eight consecutive points fall on the same side of the mean and trend upward. What is the most defensible conclusion?**

a. The process is unquestionably stable because no point exceeded a control limit.

b. The process may be showing a non-random shift or emerging special-cause variation even though it has not yet crossed control limits.

c. The process is out of specification, which proves customer requirements are not being met.

d. The control chart should be ignored unless the average also changes.

157. **A PM reviews a Histogram of cycle times for user stories and sees a long right tail with a small number of items taking far longer than the rest. What is the strongest interpretation?**

a. The process is uniformly stable because most items finish near the average.

b. A subset of work is experiencing unusually long delays, suggesting special-case complexity or flow blockage.

c. The team should increase WIP to smooth out the tail.

d. The histogram proves the backlog is correctly prioritized.

158. **A quality engineer creates a Scatter Diagram comparing test environment response time with defect escape rate across releases. The points show a clear upward trend. What is the most defensible conclusion?**

a. Slower test environments may be associated with higher defect escape, but further analysis is needed before claiming causation.

b. The slower environment definitively causes all escaped defects.

c. The scatter diagram should be replaced by a Gantt chart to confirm the relationship.

d. Correlation means the release schedule can be shortened safely.

159. **A Run Chart of daily incident volume stays flat for two weeks and then rises steadily for seven consecutive days after a platform migration. All values remain within historical operating range. What should the PM infer first?**

a. There is no concern because the values are still within historical limits.

b. The upward run suggests a meaningful trend shift that may reflect a migration-related change in system behavior.

c. The migration has succeeded because the trend is visible.

d. Run charts cannot be used for operational monitoring.

160. **A PM reviews a Resource Histogram showing team allocation by week and notices that specialist demand exceeds available capacity in Weeks 3, 4, and 6, while other weeks remain below the capacity line. What is the most strategic interpretation?**

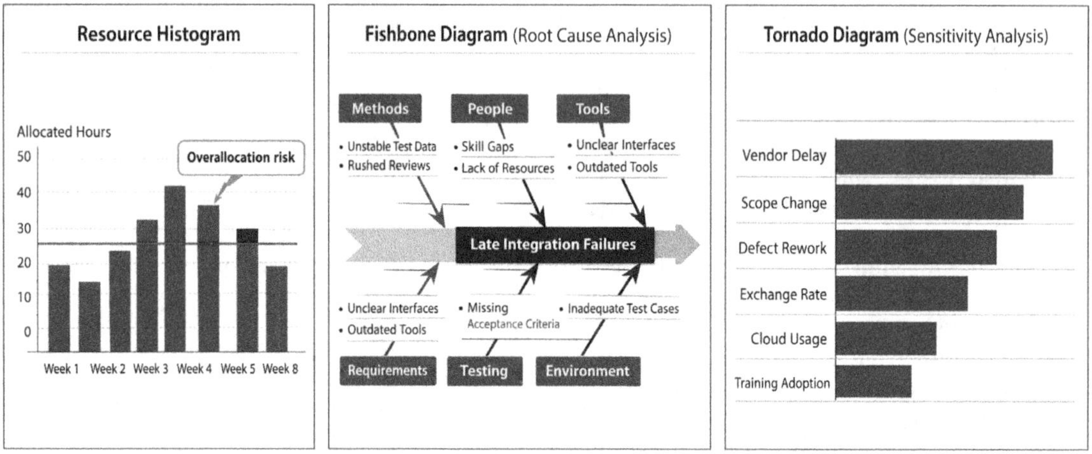

***Figure 9.7:** Resource histogram chart*

a. The team is highly efficient because utilization peaks above capacity.

b. The schedule contains resource overallocation risk that may require leveling, smoothing, or replanning to prevent delay and burnout.

c. Capacity lines are only informational and do not affect schedule performance.

d. The PM should increase all future assignments to keep utilization consistently above the line.

161. **A quality workshop uses a Fishbone Diagram to analyze repeated late integration failures. The major branches include Methods, People, Tools, Requirements, testing, and Environment. What is the primary value of using this chart at this stage?**

a. It proves which single cause is correct so the team can stop further analysis.

b. It structures possible causes systematically so the team can explore root-cause patterns rather than treating symptoms in isolation.

c. It replaces the need for defective data because brainstorming is more reliable than evidence.

d. It quantifies schedule variance directly across all work packages.

162. **A steering committee reviews a Tornado Diagram for project cost sensitivity. The longest bars are Vendor Delay and Scope Change, while Cloud Usage and Training Adoption show smaller bars. What is the strongest management implication?**

a. Management attention should focus first on the factors with the largest sensitivity because they have the greatest influence on cost outcomes.

b. The smallest bars should be addressed first because they are easiest to control.

c. Tornado diagrams are only useful after the project has closed and cannot influence planning.

d. The PM should average all bars and treat every variable as equally important.

163. **A PM evaluates two implementation strategies using a Decision Tree. Strategy A has a 60% chance of yielding a benefit of ₹18,00,000 and a 40% chance of causing a loss of ₹4,00,000. Strategy B has an 80% chance of yielding a benefit of ₹12,00,000 and a 20% chance of causing a loss of ₹1,00,000. Which interpretation is strongest?**

a. Strategy A is stronger because its maximum payoff is higher, regardless of probability.

b. Strategy B is stronger because its expected monetary value is higher and downside exposure is lower.

c. Both strategies are equal because they both involve uncertainty.

d. Decision trees should not be used unless outcomes are deterministic.

164. **A process dashboard shows values staying within Control Limits, but two recent points are very close to the upper control limit after a long stable period. What is the most defensible PM interpretation?**

a. No action is ever needed unless a point crosses the limit.

b. The process is still in control, but the pattern may justify closer observation for an emerging special-cause shift.

c. The process is automatically out of specification.

d. Control limits should be tightened immediately to force compliance.

165. **A Burnup Chart shows completed scope rising steadily, but the total scope line also rises throughout the release. What is the strongest conclusion?**

a. The team is definitely underperforming because the total scope line changed.

b. Delivery is progressing, but scope growth is affecting release predictability and should be actively managed.

c. Burnup charts cannot represent adaptive delivery accurately.

d. The release is complete as long as completed scope is increasing.

Case study: Nexus Forge

You are the project manager for *Project Nexus Forge,* a hybrid transformation to deploy a digitally integrated manufacturing platform across four plants. The predictive workstream includes facility retrofits and network infrastructure, while adaptive teams deliver analytics, scheduling automation, and operator interfaces. Over the last month, executives reviewed multiple charts. The *Gantt Chart* shows one integration milestone with zero float. *A Pareto Chart* of recent defects reveals that two root categories account for most escaped issues. A *Control Chart* of calibration quality remains within limits but trends upward. A *Histogram* of cycle times shows a long right tail. A *Scatter Diagram* suggests a positive relationship between test-environment latency and escaped defects. A *Run Chart* of incident volume rises after the most recent deployment. At the same time, a *Resource Histogram* shows specialist over-allocation, a *Fishbone Diagram* highlights requirements, methods, and environment causes for late integration failures, and a *Tornado Diagram* ranks vendor delay and scope change as the strongest cost sensitivities. leadership wants a confident launch date, but the delivery data is mixed.

166. **Considering all charts together, what is the strongest overall diagnosis?**

a. The program is healthy because no single chart proves failure on its own.

b. The program is facing compounded flow, quality, and capacity risks that threaten launch credibility unless managed as a system.

c. The only meaningful issue is that the calibration process remains within control limits.

d. The data is too varied to support any practical decision.

167. **Which action is most likely to improve both schedule confidence and defect performance?**

a. Focus only on the zero-float milestone and ignore the defect data until after launch.

b. Reduce specialist overallocation, address the dominant Pareto categories first, and stabilize test-environment latency before forcing dates.

c. Add more work in parallel so the Gantt chart looks busier and more productive.

d. Replace all charts with a single executive summary percentage.

168. **Which chart gives the clearest evidence that a small number of defect causes deserve first attention?**
    a. Gantt Chart
    b. Pareto Chart
    c. Histogram
    d. Run Chart

169. **Which pair of charts most directly supports the argument that environment instability is contributing to escaped defects?**
    a. Scatter Diagram and Fishbone Diagram
    b. Gantt Chart and Tornado Diagram
    c. Control Chart and Resource Histogram
    d. Run Chart and Burnup Chart

170. **If executives demand a launch date despite mixed signals, what is the strongest PM response?**
    a. Commit to the earliest date because the Gantt critical path is the only governing signal.
    b. Provide a range-based launch forecast tied to flow, defect concentration, capacity constraints, and the top tornado sensitivities.
    c. Refuse to provide any date because charts are inherently unreliable.
    d. Use the average of all charts as a compromise date.

171. **Which conclusion best fits the long right tail in the cycle-time histogram?**
    a. All work items are flowing at the same pace.
    b. A small subset of items is aging significantly longer, which may be masking systemic blockers or exceptional complexity.
    c. Scope is fully stabilized.
    d. The team should raise WIP limits.

172. **A project sponsor is currently neutral toward a transformation initiative, but the stakeholder engagement assessment matrix shows the desired level is leading. The sponsor controls budget releases and influences several senior stakeholders. What is the best PM action?**
    a. Leave the sponsor at neutral because active support is not essential once funding is approved.
    b. Create a targeted engagement strategy that aligns the sponsor to strategic outcomes, decision visibility, and visible advocacy behaviors.
    c. Reduce sponsor involvement to avoid interference with the team.
    d. Escalate the sponsor's neutral stance as a governance breach.

173. **The SEAM shows one highly influential regulator as resistant and one high-interest user group as supportive. What is the strongest interpretation for engagement planning?**
    a. Focus first on the supportive user group because resistance cannot be changed.
    b. Prioritize converting or managing the resistant regulator because influence and current engagement gap create strategic risk.
    c. Treat both stakeholders the same because SEAM does not guide prioritization.
    d. Remove the regulator from the matrix until compliance is formally requested.

174. **A PM updates the SEAM monthly, but stakeholder behaviors are not changing. Which action best improves the usefulness of the matrix?**
    a. Replace the matrix with a communications calendar only.
    b. Link each engagement gap to specific influence tactics, measurable behavior indicators, and named ownership.
    c. Stop measuring desired engagement levels because they are subjective.
    d. Increase meeting frequency for all stakeholders equally.

175. **A risk response to reduce cybersecurity exposure requires a major architecture change. This will likely delay one milestone but substantially reduce the probability of a catastrophic breach. Which principle should guide the PM?**
    a. Accept the original architecture because milestone movement always destroys value.

b. Evaluate the trade-off through risk-adjusted value, not schedule optics alone.

c. Ignore the risk until it triggers because redesign introduces certainty loss.

d. Transfer the decision entirely to the technical team.

176. **A response to a supply chain threat creates a new environmental compliance exposure with an alternate vendor. What is the most appropriate treatment of this new risk?**

a. Ignore it because secondary risks are unavoidable side effects of good decisions.

b. Record and analyze it explicitly as a secondary risk and integrate it into response planning.

c. Delete the original risk from the register once a workaround exists.

d. Move it to lessons learned because it came from a response action.

177. **In a highly uncertain environment, the PM has several plausible but low-frequency, high-impact threats with weak historical data. Which approach is strongest?**

a. Use only historical probability tables because expert judgment is subjective.

b. Combine scenario planning, premortems, and resilience-oriented response design to address uncertainty beyond conventional estimates.

c. Exclude the threats from the register until they become more measurable.

d. Convert all such threats into assumptions so the schedule can be finalized.

178. **You are leading a nationwide digital health transformation for a hospital network that is deploying an AI-assisted patient triage platform, replacing fragmented intake workflows across 40 facilities. The project uses a hybrid approach: predictive infrastructure and cybersecurity hardening, adaptive software configuration and clinical workflow design. Six months before launch, a pilot shows promising reductions in wait time and improved clinician utilization; however, three interconnected issues now emerge simultaneously. First, the ethics review board finds that triage recommendations for non-native language speakers are materially less accurate because training data underrepresents them. Second, a critical cloud subcontractor announces a pricing model change that would increase long-term operating costs by 22% after implementation. Third, several hospital directors who were previously supportive are becoming resistant because they fear that aggressive rollout will damage patient trust if clinical edge cases are mishandled publicly. The sponsor insists that the strategic imperative is speed because competitor hospitals are already marketing AI-enabled care pathways. What is the strongest next move for the project manager acting in a value-led, strategic capacity?**

a. Preserve the rollout date, treat language bias as a post-launch enhancement, renegotiate cloud pricing later, and ask communications to manage public concern so first-mover advantage is not lost.

b. Escalate the language-bias finding only, because ethical risk outweighs procurement and stakeholder resistance until fairness is fully resolved.

c. Facilitate an integrated decision review that reframes the situation around value-at-risk, incorporating clinical safety, equity, long-term operating economics, stakeholder trust, and release options such as phased scope or controlled deployment.

d. Pause the entire program indefinitely and request a complete redesign of both the platform and the business case before any further decision is made.

179. **A pharmaceutical company is running a global cold-chain modernization program that includes IoT sensors, predictive maintenance, advanced analytics, and regional compliance automation. You inherit the program midway through execution. Earned value metrics appear healthy, sprint demonstrations are frequent, and the steering committee is praising the team for visible output. Yet during a deeper review, you discover the following: operational teams are bypassing the new workflows in two regions; cumulative flow data shows rising queue aging in validation; the benefits management plan has not been updated since initiation despite regulatory shifts in two markets; and the procurement team has selected a low-cost hardware supplier whose environmental practices now conflict with the company's public sustainability commitments. Several leaders want you to reassure the board that delivery remains "green, compliant, and on track" because formal baselines still look acceptable. Which response best reflects advanced PMBOK v8 judgment?**

a. Confirm the program is on track because baselines, demos, and earned value still indicate acceptable performance, and resolve adoption and ESG issues after transition.

b. Reassess the program through a benefits, adoption, compliance, and sustainability lens, update decision data, and present the board with a more complete picture of realized versus merely reported progress.

c. Replace agile metrics with predictive control metrics only so the steering committee receives a simpler and more disciplined governance model.

d. Remove the sustainability concern from the program dashboard because procurement savings contribute positively to total business value.

180. **You are managing the final integration phase of a genomics-enabled precision medicine platform across public and private hospitals. The technical teams are high performing, but the environment has become deeply BANI: a small change in one country's data-consent interpretation has triggered cascading architecture reviews elsewhere; clinicians are anxious that AI recommendations may reduce professional autonomy; a senior engineer who owns the explainability layer is about to resign; and a key government stakeholder who was once supportive is now neutral after media scrutiny of algorithmic accountability. The sponsor asks for a "simple success narrative" for the ministry briefing, focused on schedule adherence and innovation prestige. At the same time, the implementation teams need immediate direction on risk ownership, stakeholder engagement, and knowledge retention. What should the project manager do first?**

a. Prepare a concise success narrative for the ministry first, then address team risks afterward so external confidence is protected before internal complexity is discussed.

b. Launch a coordinated response that combines transparent stakeholder reframing, explicit retention and transfer of critical explainability knowledge, and rapid re-evaluation of cross-border consent impacts before reinforcing any success narrative.

c. Delegate stakeholder concerns to the communications team, technical knowledge retention to engineering, and consent interpretation to legal, so each function can optimize within its expertise.

d. Freeze all integration work until every stakeholder is returned to a fully supportive state and every compliance interpretation is harmonized.

Conclusion

This chapter has been structured to provide a broad, practice-oriented journey across modern project management thinking through multiple question types, contexts, and challenge levels. By working through conceptual items, case studies, chart-based interpretation, matching exercises, fill-in-the-blanks, and high-difficulty integrated scenarios, the reader is encouraged to move beyond memorization and develop stronger analytical reasoning, situational judgment, and strategic decision-making capability. The intentional separation of answers from many of the question flows supports reflection before validation and makes the chapter suitable for self-study, mentoring, discussion, and advanced exam preparation. Taken together, these question sets are meant to reinforce not only knowledge of project management principles, tools, and artifacts, but also the professional ability to apply them with confidence across uncertain, value-driven, and evolving delivery environments.On a similar lines, readers are encouraged to practice the question set in next chapter. This will further strengthen the concepts across all the dominas of project management.

References

1. A Guide to the Project Management Body of Knowledge (PMBOK® Guide), Seventh Edition.
2. A Guide to the Project Management Body of Knowledge (PMBOK® Guide), Eighth Edition.
3. Project Management Institute (PMI) Examination Content Outline (ECO) for the PMP® examination.
4. Project management standards, principles, and good practices relating to predictive, adaptive, and hybrid delivery.
5. Frameworks and concepts associated with value delivery, benefits realization, governance, and stakeholder engagement.
6. Quality, risk, procurement, and closure practices commonly applied in complex project environments.
7. Agile, Lean, flow-based, and chart interpretation methods used for burndown, burnup, cumulative flow, velocity, resource, and sensitivity analysis.
8. Contemporary perspectives on ESG, sustainability, AI ethics, explainability, and strategic value-led project delivery.
9. Organizational learning, knowledge transfer, change enablement, and transition practices supporting long-term value realization.

Answers

Q. No.	Answers
1	d
2	b
3	a, c
4	b
5	b
6	b
7	b
8	c
9	a, b, d
10	b

Q. No.	Answers
11	c
12	b
13	a - i b – ii c - iii
14	b
15	b
16	b
17	b
18	b

Q. No.	Answers
19	b
20	c
21	c
22	c
23	c
24	b
25	b
26	c

Q. No.	Answers
27	a-i b-iv c-ii d-iii
28	c
29	c
30	a
31	c
32	a

Q. No.	Answers
33	b
34	b
35	b
36	c
37	b
38	c
39	b
40	b
41	b
42	b
43	b
44	b
45	b
46	b
47	c
48	b
49	c
50	b
51	a
52	b
53	b
54	a
55	c
56	b
57	c
58	a
59	c
60	b
61	b
62	b
63	c
64	b
65	c
66	b
67	b
68	b
69	b

Q. No.	Answers
70	b
71	b
72	b
73	b
74	b
75	b
76	b
77	c
78	c
79	b
80	b
81	b
82	b
83	c
84	a
85	b
86	b
87	b
88	c
89	b
90	b
91	b
92	b
93	c
94	b
95	b
96	b
97	c
98	b
99	b
100	a
101	c
102	b
103	b
104	b
105	a
106	b

Q. No.	Answers
107	b
108	b
109	b
110	b
111	b
112	c
113	b
114	b
115	b
116	b
117	b
118	b
119	b
120	b
121	b
122	b
123	c
124	b
125	b
126	b
127	a
128	b
129	b
130	b
131	b
132	b
133	b
134	b
135	b
136	b
137	b
138	b
139	b
140	b
141	a
142	c
143	b

Q. No.	Answers
144	c
145	b
146	a
147	b
148	a
149	b
150	b
151	a
152	c
153	a
154	a
155	a
156	b
157	b
158	a
159	b
160	b
161	b
162	a
163	a
164	b
165	b
166	b
167	b
168	b
169	a
170	b
171	b
172	b
173	b
174	b
175	b
176	b
177	b
178	c
179	b
180	b

CHAPTER 10
Practice Set -2

Introduction

This practice set has been designed to strengthen students' understanding of contemporary project management through a practical, application-oriented approach. Rather than focusing solely on theoretical recall, the questions are framed around realistic situations that reflect the complexity of today's project environments. The set covers a broad range of relevant themes, including agile and Hybrid delivery approaches, AI governance, **Environmental, Social, and Governance (ESG)** considerations, risk management, value delivery, ethics, and strategic decision-making. Overall, it aims to encourage careful interpretation, critical thinking, and confident application of project management principles in both examination and professional contexts.

Objectives

The primary objective of this question set is to help students develop the ability to interpret situational questions accurately, think from a project manager's perspective, and select responses based on sound project management principles. It also seeks to reinforce key PMP-style concepts by connecting them with practical and decision-based scenarios. In addition, the set is intended to build confidence in addressing questions related to compliance, stakeholder expectations, ethics, sustainability, uncertainty, and value-focused delivery. By working through these questions, students can strengthen both their exam readiness and their broader understanding of modern project management practice.

Multiple choice questions

1. **A project manager is leading a global initiative to implement a decentralized finance (DeFi) platform. A sudden change in international banking regulations makes the current architecture potentially non-compliant. The project sponsor, fearing a loss of first-mover advantage, insists on proceeding as planned. What is the PM's most appropriate action?**
    a. Follow the sponsor's directive to ensure the project meets its strategic deadline.
    b. Perform a detailed regulatory impact analysis and present the findings, including the risk of legal non-compliance, to the steering committee.
    c. Immediately halt all development work until a new legal framework is provided.
    d. Update the risk register and continue work, but add a disclaimer to the project status report.

2. **Your agile team is using an AI-assisted coding tool that has significantly increased velocity. However, the quality assurance (QA) team reports a spike in "Logic Fragility" where the AI-generated code passes unit tests but fails in complex integration. How should the PM/scrum master address this in a BANI environment?**
    a. Disable the AI tool and return to 100% manual coding to ensure stability.
    b. Implement "human-in-the-loop" (HITL) mandatory code reviews specifically focused on architectural logic.

c. Reprimand the developers for relying too heavily on automated tools.

d. Increase the length of the sprints to allow more time for manual QA.

3. **A project is being executed using a Hybrid approach. The hardware components (Predictive) are delayed by three weeks due to a logistics strike. The software team (agile) has finished their current backlog. To maintain Value Velocity, what should the project manager do?**

a. Place the software team on administrative leave to save costs until the hardware arrives.

b. Facilitate a session with the product owner to re-prioritize the backlog to include cloud-based simulations or features that do not require physical hardware.

c. Ask the software team to assist the hardware team with logistics planning.

d. Crash the hardware schedule by paying a premium for air freight, regardless of the budget impact.

4. **Your organization has committed to a Net-Zero 2030 goal. You are managing a project to build a new data center. During procurement, the lowest-cost vendor has a poor carbon footprint rating, while a more expensive vendor is carbon-neutral. Which metric should you use to justify selecting the more expensive vendor?**

a. Return on investment (ROI).

b. Total cost of quality (COQ), including the "Failure Cost" of non-compliance with corporate ESG goals.

c. Net present value (NPV).

d. Benefit-Cost Ratio (BCR) based strictly on initial capital expenditure.

5. **A project manager is managing a project with a Budget at Completion (BAC) of USD 800,000. Currently, the Earned Value (EV) is USD 200,000 and the Actual Cost (AC) is USD 250,000. If the current cost variance is expected to continue for the remainder of the project, what is the Estimate at Completion (EAC)?**

a. USD 800,000 b. USD 850,000

c. USD 1,000,000 d. USD 750,000

6. **A project manager is leading a mission-critical infrastructure project using a Hybrid approach. A third-party AI service used for predictive maintenance undergoes a major "Model Drift," leading to a 15% increase in false positive alerts that disrupt the hardware team's schedule. What should the project manager do first?**

a. Immediately switch to a different AI provider to maintain schedule integrity.

b. Update the Issue Log and perform a root cause analysis to determine if the drift is due to data quality or the model's internal logic.

c. Instruct the hardware team to ignore the AI alerts and follow the original predictive maintenance schedule.

d. Escalate the issue to the Chief Technology Officer (CTO) as a critical failure of the AI strategy.

7. **Your organization has just implemented a "Social Equity" clause in its ESG policy, requiring all projects to ensure that at least 20% of the project budget is spent with local, minority-owned businesses. You are managing a software development project and realize that your current primary vendor does not meet these criteria. What is your most strategic move?**

a. Request a waiver from the sponsor, arguing that software development is too specialized for local sourcing.

b. Review the procurement plan to identify non-critical modules that can be carved out and awarded to local, minority-owned firms.

c. Terminate the current vendor contract immediately to ensure 100% compliance.

d. Ignore the policy for this project cycle since the contract was signed before the policy was enacted.

8. **An agile team is working in a BANI (Brittle, Anxious, Non-linear, Incomprehensible) environment. The product owner frequently changes the priority of the backlog based on "gut feelings" about market volatility, causing the team to feel "Anxious" and lose focus. As the scrum master, how should you intervene?**

   a. Tell the product owner to stop changing priorities until the end of the project.

   b. Facilitate a "Data-Driven Transparency" session where the product owner must justify priority shifts using real-time market data or customer feedback.

   c. Increase the length of the Daily Stand-up to 30 minutes to discuss the changes in detail.

   d. Allow the team to choose their own tasks regardless of the product owner's priorities.

9. **A project manager is managing a complex merger. The project has a Budget at Completion (BAC) of USD 2,000,000. Currently, the project is 40% complete. The Actual Cost (AC) is USD 900,000. The organization's leadership has issued a mandate that the project *must* finish within the original budget. What is the required To-Complete Performance Index (TCPI)?**

   a. 1.09 b. 0.89

   c. 1.20 d. 1.00

10. **Durin a project audit, it is discovered that the project's internal rate of return (IRR) has dropped from 18% to 11% because of increased labor costs. The company's minimum acceptable return (hurdle rate) is 12%. As a Strategic Advisor, what recommendation should the PM make to the steering committee?**

    a. Close the project immediately as it no longer meets the financial hurdle.

    b. Perform a "Value Engineering" exercise to see if costs can be reduced or benefits increased to bring the IRR back above 12%.

    c. Continue the project anyway, as 11% is still a positive return.

    d. Hide the new IRR data until the project is completed.

11. **A project manager is leading a digital transformation project that involves deploying a generative AI tool for customer service. During a risk review, a stakeholder raises concerns about "algorithmic bias" that could lead to discriminatory outcomes. How should the project manager proceed to ensure AI governance?**

    a. Ignore the concern as it falls under the operational phase, not the project phase.

    b. Update the risk register and schedule a specialized audit to validate the AI training datasets for diversity and representativeness.

    c. Transfer the risk to the software vendor by adding a liability clause to the contract.

    d. Implement a "human-in-the-loop" (HITL) process and consider the risk mitigated.

12. **Your organization has committed to a "Net-Zero 2030" initiative. You are managing a construction project, and the primary supplier informs you that switching to carbon-neutral steel will increase costs by 15% and delay the schedule by three weeks. What is the BEST course of action?**

    a. Stick to the original plan to ensure the project remains on budget and on schedule.

    b. Use the project's management reserve to cover the cost increase and update the schedule.

    c. Perform a cost-benefit analysis comparing the late-delivery penalties against the long-term strategic value of ESG compliance.

    d. Request the Change Control Board (CCB) to approve the change based on the organization's strategic sustainability goals.

13. **A project uses a hybrid approach: hardware development follows a predictive lifecycle, while software features are developed using scrum. The hardware team reports a delay in the prototype. How should the project manager coordinate the software team?**
    a. Ask the software team to stop working until the hardware prototype is ready.
    b. Direct the software team to use a simulated environment or "stubs" to continue development and testing iteratively.
    c. Switch the hardware team to an agile framework to match the software team's velocity.
    d. Inform the sponsor that the project's hybrid nature is failing and recommend moving to a fully predictive model.

14. **During a project to implement an AI-driven predictive maintenance system, the legal department informs you of a new data privacy regulation (similar to GDPR) that goes into effect in three months. What should the project manager do first?**
    a. Immediately stop all data processing activities to avoid potential fines.
    b. Conduct an impact analysis to determine which project deliverables are affected by the new regulation.
    c. Submit a change request to the CCB to extend the project timeline.
    d. Ask the legal department to handle the compliance requirements so the team can focus on technical tasks.

15. **You are managing a global project with a virtual team. You notice that team members from a specific region are consistently silent during "Retrospectives" and "Daily Stand-ups." What should you do to improve engagement?**
    a. Mandate that every team member must speak for at least two minutes during meetings.
    b. Switch to asynchronous communication tools and provide "anonymous" feedback channels to respect different cultural communication styles.
    c. Replace the silent team members with more vocal individuals to ensure transparency.
    d. Report the lack of participation to the functional managers of those team members.

16. **A company is undergoing a strategic pivot toward "value-based project management." As a project manager, you are asked to justify the continuation of a project that is 50% complete but has a declining Benefit-Cost Ratio (BCR) due to market shifts. What should be your primary focus?**
    a. The amount of "Sunk Costs" already invested in the project.
    b. The project's alignment with the new strategic objectives and the "Expected Monetary Value" (EMV) of remaining work.
    c. Finishing the project as planned to ensure the team remains occupied.
    d. Reducing the scope to match the original BCR.

17. **In a complex hybrid project, the "Point of Total Assumption" (PTA) is a critical metric for a Fixed Price Incentive Fee (FPI) contract. If the Ceiling Price is USD 200,000, the Target Price is USD 170,000, the Target Cost is USD 150,000, and the Buyer's Share Ratio is 60%, what is the PTA?**
    a. USD 175,000
    b. USD 180,000
    c. USD 183,333
    d. USD 200,000

18. **You are managing a project to develop an AI-powered medical diagnostic tool. A key stakeholder insists on adding a feature that was not in the original scope but would significantly improve patient outcomes. The project is already over budget. What is the most ethical decision?**
    a. Refuse the request because the project is over budget and it constitutes "scope creep."
    b. Evaluate the feature's impact on the project's "Social Value" and present a business case to the CCB.
    c. Add the feature secretly by reallocating funds from the quality assurance budget.
    d. Ask the stakeholder to find external funding for the additional feature.

19. **Your project team is struggling with "Anxiety" and "Non-linearity" as described in the BANI framework. The project environment is highly volatile due to rapid AI advancements. How should you adapt your leadership style?**
    a. Implement stricter controls and detailed micro-management to reduce uncertainty.
    b. Foster a culture of "Resilience" and "Empathy," and focus on short, iterative cycles to allow for rapid pivoting.
    c. Stick to the original project management plan to provide a sense of stability.
    d. Increase the frequency of status reports to the executive team.

20. **A project manager is using a Kanban board to manage software defects. The "work in progress" (WIP) limit for the "testing" column is 5, but there are currently 8 items in that column. What is the immediate consequence?**
    a. The team is working at maximum efficiency.
    b. There is a bottleneck in the testing phase, and the team should stop taking new tasks and "Swarm" to clear the backlog.
    c. The project manager should increase the WIP limit to 10 to accommodate the items.
    d. This is a normal occurrence in agile and does not require action.

21. **Which of the following best describes "Value realization"?**
    a. Ensuring the project is delivered on time and under budget.
    b. The process of verifying that the project's outputs actually result in the benefits defined in the business case after handover.
    c. The final payment received from the client upon project completion.
    d. The internal rate of return (IRR) calculated during the initiation phase.

22. **You are leading a project that requires a high degree of innovation. You want to encourage "psychological safety" within the team. Which action is most effective?**
    a. Rewarding the team only when they achieve perfect results.
    b. Publicly identifying the person responsible for a mistake so others can learn.
    c. Encouraging team members to take calculated risks and treating failures as "Learning Experiments."
    d. Limiting communication between team members to avoid conflicts.

23. **A project manager is evaluating two projects. Project A has an NPV of USD 100,000 and will take 3 years. Project B has an NPV of USD 120,000 and will take 5 years. Based on NPV, which project should be selected?**
    a. Project A, because it is shorter.
    b. Project B, because it has a higher NPV.
    c. Both projects, as they both have positive NPVs.
    d. Neither project, as NPV does not account for the time value of money.

24. **During a project, a stakeholder who has high power but low interest suddenly becomes very vocal and critical of the project's environmental impact. How should the project manager update the stakeholder engagement assessment matrix?**
    a. Keep the stakeholder in the "Monitor" quadrant.
    b. Move the stakeholder to the "Keep Satisfied" quadrant and increase the frequency of ESG-related reporting to them.
    c. Move the stakeholder to "Manage Closely" and involve them in sustainability reviews.
    d. Ignore the stakeholder as their interest level was initially recorded as low.

25. **You are managing a project using an "Iterative" lifecycle. During the third iteration, the customer realizes that the market has shifted, and the product needs a major feature change. How do you handle this?**
    a. Refuse the change, as the scope was locked during the first iteration.
    b. Accept the change and incorporate it into the backlog for the next iteration.
    c. File a formal change request and stop all work until it is approved by the CCB.
    d. Charge the customer a penalty for changing their mind mid-project.

26. **In the context of AI governance, what is "Explainability"?**
    a. The ability to explain the project schedule to stakeholders.
    b. The requirement that AI decision-making processes can be understood and traced by humans.
    c. The process of translating code into a different programming language.
    d. The project manager's ability to justify the project's budget.

27. **A team is using "Planning Poker" to estimate user stories. One team member consistently picks much higher numbers than everyone else. What should the scrum master do?**
    a. Average the numbers and move on to the next story.
    b. Ask the team member to explain their perspective to see if they have identified hidden risks or complexities.
    c. Tell the team member to align their estimates with the rest of the group.
    d. Disregard that team member's estimate as an outlier.

28. **A project to install solar panels across multiple corporate sites is facing resistance from local facility managers who are concerned about maintenance costs. This is an example of a conflict in which domain?**
    a. Process
    b. People
    c. Business environment
    d. Technical

29. **You are managing a project with a "Negative Risk" that has a 20% probability and a USD 50,000 impact. You decide to purchase insurance for USD 5,000 that covers the full impact. What risk response strategy is this?**
    a. Mitigate   b. Avoid
    c. Transfer   d. Accept

30. **A project manager is calculating the "Estimate to Complete" (ETC) for a project where the original budget (BAC) was USD 500,000. Currently, the AC is USD 200,000 and the EV is USD 150,000. The project manager believes the remaining work will be performed at the budgeted rate. What is the ETC?**
    a. USD 300,000   b. USD 350,000
    c. USD 400,000   d. USD 450,000

31. **A project manager is leading a global AI implementation. The team is highly decentralized, and the project is using a "Follow-the-Sun" development model. Communication is breaking down due to time zone overlaps of only one hour. What is the BEST strategy to ensure project continuity?**
    a. Require one region to work night shifts to increase overlap to four hours.
    b. Implement a robust "Asynchronous Documentation" policy where every task handoff is accompanied by a recorded video brief and an updated Kanban card.
    c. Move the project to a single location to eliminate time zone issues.
    d. Reduce the project scope so that handoffs are not required daily.

32. **You are managing a multi-year infrastructure project. The contract is Fixed-Price with Economic Price Adjustment (FP-EPA). Significant inflation in the price of raw materials has triggered the EPA clause. How should you handle the budget update?**
    a. Use the management reserve to cover the inflation costs.
    b. Update the cost baseline and communicate the new funding requirements to the sponsor based on the predefined price index in the contract.
    c. Negotiate with the vendor to absorb the inflation costs to protect the project budget.
    d. Cancel the project as it is no longer financially viable.

33. **An agile team is using a "Self-Correcting" mechanism where they use AI to analyze their past velocity and predict future sprint capacity. The AI suggests a 20% reduction in velocity due to upcoming "Technical Debt" spikes. What should the scrum master do?**
    a. Ignore the AI and push the team to maintain their current velocity.
    b. Present the AI's findings to the team during sprint Planning and facilitate a discussion on whether to reduce the sprint commitment.
    c. Hard-code the 20% reduction into the next three sprints without consulting the team.
    d. Ask the AI to find a way to eliminate the technical debt without reducing velocity.

34. **A project manager is overseeing a "Green Energy" initiative. A local community group is protesting the project due to concerns about the impact on local wildlife, despite the project meeting all legal environmental standards. What is the most proactive response?**
    a. Ignore the protests since the project is legally compliant.
    b. Hire a security firm to ensure project work is not disrupted.
    c. Engage in "Social Dialogue" by holding town hall meetings to understand concerns and explore "Co-creation" of mitigation strategies.
    d. Sue the community group for delaying the project.

35. **In a hybrid project, the hardware team (Predictive) and software team (agile) have different definitions of "Done." This is causing integration failures. What should the project manager do?**
    a. Force the software team to adopt the hardware team's detailed specification requirements.
    b. Create a "Common Definition of Done" (CDoD) specifically for integration points that both teams must satisfy.
    c. Allow each team to keep their own definitions and fix integration issues during the closing phase.
    d. Replace the leads of both teams to reset the culture.

36. **Your organization is moving from a "Project-Centric" to a "Product-Centric" delivery model. You are now a Product project manager. What is your primary shift in focus?**
    a. Focusing on meeting the triple constraint (Scope, Time, Cost).
    b. Focusing on the "long-term lifecycle value" and continuous delivery of features based on customer feedback.
    c. Focusing on closing the project as quickly as possible to move to the next one.
    d. Focusing solely on the technical excellence of the product.

37. **During a high-stakes negotiation with a vendor for a "cloud computing" contract, the vendor offers you a personal "referral bonus" if you sign by the end of the week. What should you do?**
    a. Accept the bonus but do not let it influence your decision.
    b. Decline the bonus and report the offer to your organization's legal or ethics department.
    c. Use the bonus amount to negotiate a lower price for the company.
    d. Accept the bonus and share it with your project team.

38. **A project team is experiencing "Storming." Two senior developers are clashing over the architecture of a new AI module. The conflict is stalling progress. What is the best conflict resolution technique to use here?**
    a. **Forcing:** Tell them which architecture to use so the project can move on.
    b. **Smoothing:** Tell them that their friendship is more important than the technical details.
    c. **Collaborating:** Facilitate a session where both developers present their logic and work together to find a "win-win" hybrid solution.
    d. **Withdrawal:** Let them figure it out on their own.

39. **You are using the "Three-Point Estimating" (PERT) technique. For a critical task, the Optimistic time is 10 days, the Most Likely is 20 days, and the Pessimistic is 42 days. What is the Beta Distribution (PERT) estimate?**

a. 20 days b. 22 days
c. 24 days d. 26 days

40. **A project manager is leading a "Digital Inclusion" project in a developing region. The project is falling behind because the local infrastructure is "Brittle" (per the BANI framework). How should the PM respond?**

a. Increase the project's complexity to overcome the brittle infrastructure.
b. Build in "Redundancy" and "Slack" into the project plan to account for frequent infrastructure failures.
c. Request a transfer to a more stable project.
d. Demand that the local government fix the infrastructure immediately.

41. **You are managing a project where the "Cost Performance Index" (CPI) is 0.8 and the "Schedule Performance Index" (SPI) is 1.2. Which of the following is true?**

a. The project is under budget and ahead of schedule.
b. The project is over budget and ahead of schedule.
c. The project is over budget and behind schedule.
d. The project is under budget and behind schedule.

42. **In the 2026 ECO, "Strategic Alignment" is paramount. A project no longer aligns with the company's updated 5-year strategy. What is the project manager's responsibility?**

a. Continue the project anyway to avoid wasting the budget.
b. Proactively recommend a "Project Pivot" or termination to the sponsor to preserve organizational resources.
c. Hide the misalignment from the stakeholders until the project is finished.
d. Change the company's strategy to match the project.

43. **An agile team is using "Relative Sizing" for stories. They use a "Reference Story" that is 5 Story Points. A new story is estimated to be twice as complex. What should its point value be in a Fibonacci sequence?**

a. 8 b. 10
c. 13 d. 15

44. **A project manager is conducting a "Lessons Learned" session. A team member is hesitant to share a mistake that cost the project two weeks. How can the PM encourage honesty?**

a. Promise that no one will be fired for what they say in the room.
b. Frame the session as a "Blame-Free Post-Mortem" focused on systemic improvements rather than individual failures.
c. Record the session and send it to the CEO.
d. Offer a cash prize for the biggest mistake shared.

45. **A "Risk Report" shows that a project has a high "residual risk" even after all planned responses are implemented. What should the PM do?**

a. Ignore the residual risk as it is already been addressed once.
b. Communicate the level of residual risk to the stakeholders and ensure it is within the organization's "Risk Appetite."
c. Cancel the project because the risk is too high.
d. Take out more insurance.

46. **Your project is using "Value Stream Mapping" to identify waste. You find that the "Hand-off" between the design team and the development team takes 5 days of waiting time. What is this waiting time called?**

a. Lead Time
b. Cycle time
c. Non-Value-Added Time
d. Throughput

47. **A project manager is leading a merger of two companies' IT systems. The cultures are very different—one is "Hierarchical," and the other is "Adhocracy." What is the PM's biggest challenge?**
    a. Technical compatibility
    b. Change management and cultural integration
    c. Budgetary constraints
    d. Legal compliance

48. **Which document defines how the project's "Benefits" will be measured and who is responsible for monitoring them?**
    a. Project charter
    b. Benefits management plan
    c. Business case
    d. Stakeholder engagement plan

49. **A project manager is using "MoSCoW" prioritization. A stakeholder insists that a "Could-Have" feature be treated as a "Must-Have." The project is near its deadline. What should the PM do?**
    a. Change it to "Must-Have" to please the stakeholder.
    b. Use the "Change Control Process" to evaluate the impact of this change on the "Must-Haves."
    c. Tell the stakeholder it is too late for changes.
    d. Add the feature but do not tell the other stakeholders.

50. **In an AI project, the team identifies a "Black Swan" event—a highly improbable but high-impact risk. Since it was not in the risk register, how should it be funded if it occurs?**
    a. Contingency Reserve
    b. Management Reserve
    c. Operational Budget
    d. Personal funds of the PM

51. **A project manager is leading a "Circular economy" initiative for a consumer electronics company. The goal is to design a product that is 100% recyclable. During the design phase, the engineering team reports that a non-recyclable adhesive is required to meet safety standards. What should the project manager do first?**
    a. Direct the team to use the non-recyclable adhesive to ensure safety compliance.
    b. Research alternative "Bio-based" or "Reversible" adhesives that meet both safety and circularity requirements.
    c. Update the project charter to reflect that 100% recyclability is no longer possible.
    d. Ask the marketing department to change the project's environmental claims.

52. **You are managing an AI-driven credit scoring project. A regulator requests an explanation of why a specific loan application was rejected by the algorithm. The current AI model is a "Black Box" neural network. How should the project manager address this?**
    a. Tell the regulator that AI decisions are proprietary and cannot be explained.
    b. Implement "Explainable AI" (XAI) techniques, such as LIME or SHAP, to provide a human-understandable rationale for the algorithm's outputs.
    c. Manually review the rejected application and create a justification after the fact.
    d. Switch the entire project to a simple linear regression model to ensure transparency.

53. **A project is 60% complete. The "To-Complete Performance Index" (TCPI) based on the "Budget at Completion" (BAC) is 1.4. The "Cost Performance Index" (CPI) is 0.7. What does this indicate?**
    a. The project is performing well and will likely finish under budget.
    b. The project is significantly over budget, and achieving the original BAC is now highly unrealistic.
    c. The team needs to work 40% faster to meet the schedule.
    d. The project should be cancelled immediately.

54. **In a hybrid project, the "Value Stream Map" reveals that the software team's "cycle time" is increasing because they are waiting for "Definition of Ready" (DoR) approval from a predictive-leaning PMO. How should the PM resolve this?**
    a. Tell the software team to work faster to compensate for the wait time.
    b. Negotiate with the PMO to "Delegate authority" and streamline the DoR process for agile work packages.
    c. Move the entire project to a predictive model to align with PMO standards.
    d. Ignore the delay as it is a standard part of organizational governance.

55. **Your organization is adopting "Sustainable Procurement" practices. You are evaluating two vendors for a data center project. Vendor A is 10% cheaper. Vendor B uses 100% renewable energy and has a "Take-Back" program for old hardware. How should you proceed?**
    a. Select Vendor A to save costs for the project.
    b. Select Vendor B, as their "Lifecycle Cost" and "Strategic ESG Value" outweigh the initial price difference.
    c. Ask Vendor A if they can match Vendor B's environmental standards for the same price.
    d. Flip a coin, as both vendors meet the technical requirements.

56. **During an AI project, the team identifies that the "data drift" is causing the model's accuracy to drop in a production-like environment. What is the most appropriate project management response?**
    a. Close the project, as the model is no longer working.
    b. Schedule a "re-training sprint" and establish a continuous monitoring plan for data quality.
    c. Blame the data scientists for using poor-quality data.
    d. Lower the accuracy requirements in the project scope statement.

57. **A project manager is using "agile Earned Value Management." If the team's "Velocity" is 20 points per sprint and the total backlog is 200 points, how many sprints are remaining?**
    a. 5 sprints
    b. 10 sprints
    c. 20 sprints
    d. It cannot be determined without knowing the budget.

58. **You are managing a project in a "Non-linear" environment (BANI framework). A sudden geopolitical event has made your primary supply route unavailable. What is the best leadership approach?**
    a. Wait for the situation to stabilize before making a move.
    b. Use "scenario planning" to identify three alternative routes and immediately pivot to the most resilient one.
    c. Stick to the original logistics plan and hope for the best.
    d. Ask the project sponsor to take over the logistics decisions.

59. **An organization wants to ensure "Value realization" for a new AI tool. Who is primarily responsible for ensuring the value is achieved *after* the project is closed and transitioned to operations?**
    a. The project manager
    b. The project sponsor and the business owner
    c. The AI Developer
    d. The scrum master

60. **You are leading a diverse team. One team member's cultural background values "high power distance," and they are hesitant to disagree with you in meetings. How can you ensure their expertise is heard?**
    a. Force them to speak first in every meeting.
    b. Use "1-on-1" check-ins and "Delphi Technique" style anonymous surveys for decision-making.
    c. Assume they agree with everything you say.
    d. Publicly challenge their ideas to see if they will defend them.

61. **Which of the following is a key component of "digital governance"?**
    a. Ensuring everyone has a laptop.
    b. Managing the ethical, legal, and security implications of data and AI algorithms.
    c. Moving all project files to the cloud.
    d. Using a digital Kanban board instead of a physical one.

62. **A project's "Estimate at Completion" (EAC) is USD 250,000, and the BAC is USD 200,000. The project is 50% complete. What is the "Variance at Completion" (VAC)?**
    a. USD 50,000 b. -USD 50,000
    c. USD 25,000 d. -USD 25,000

63. **In a "scrum of scrums," what is the primary purpose?**
    a. For the product owners to argue about priorities.
    b. To coordinate dependencies between multiple agile teams working on the same product.
    c. For the CEO to get a status update from all teams.
    d. To replace individual team retrospectives.

64. **A project manager is managing a "Net-Zero" building project. They realize that the chosen insulation material, while highly efficient, is produced in a factory with poor labor practices. What should the PM do?**
    a. Use the material because it helps meet the project's environmental goal.
    b. Flag the "Social Sustainability" risk and seek an alternative supplier with ethical labor certifications.
    c. Ignore the issue as the PM is only responsible for the project's direct outputs.
    d. Report the factory to the media.

65. **What does the term "psychological safety" mean for a high-performing project team?**
    a. Everyone feels safe from physical harm.
    b. Team members feel safe to take risks, admit mistakes, and voice concerns without fear of punishment.
    c. The team has a high level of job security.
    d. The office has a relaxed and quiet environment.

66. **An AI project is using "reinforcement learning." The team is worried the AI might develop "Unintended Behaviors." What governance tool should be used?**
    a. A standard risk register.
    b. An "AI Ethics Framework" with predefined "Guardrails" and a "Kill Switch" mechanism.
    c. A Gantt Chart.
    d. A fixed-price contract.

67. **A project manager is calculating "Total Float." A task has an Early Start (ES) of Day 5 and a Late Start (LS) of Day 12. What is the Float?**
    a. 5 days b. 7 days
    c. 12 days d. 17 days

68. **In the "BANI" framework, what does "Incomprehensible" mean for a project manager?**
    a. The project manager does not understand the technology.
    b. Cause-and-effect relationships are so complex that they are impossible to trace in real-time.
    c. The stakeholders are speaking a different language.
    d. The project documentation is poorly written.

69. **A "Minimum Viable Product" (MVP) is being developed. What is the main goal of an MVP?**
    a. To release a cheap version of the product to save money.
    b. To test business hypotheses and gather "validated learning" from early users with the least effort.
    c. To finish the project early.
    d. To provide a version of the product with no bugs.

70. **A project manager is using "Continuous Integration/Continuous Deployment" (CI/CD) in a software project. This is an example of which agile principle?**
    a. Welcoming changing requirements.
    b. Delivering working software frequently.
    c. Sustainable development.
    d. Simplicity is essential.

Case study: AI-driven supply chain overhaul

You are the project manager for *Project Nexus*, a multi-national initiative to integrate AI into a predictive supply chain system. The project is hybrid. The core AI engine is developed in sprints, while the global warehouse hardware retrofitting follows a Waterfall schedule.

71. **(Case Study Part A) Two months into the project, the AI team discovers that the historical data provided by the regional warehouses contains significant "hidden biases" regarding supplier lead times. If left unaddressed, the AI will prioritize suppliers with poor labor records. What should the project manager do first?**
    a. Continue with the data as-is to avoid a 4-week schedule delay.
    b. Initiate a "Data Ethics Audit" and work with the product owner to reprioritize the backlog to include a data-cleansing epic.
    c. Inform the hardware team to stop work until the AI data issue is resolved.
    d. Delete the biased data and use industry averages instead.

72. **(Case Study Part B) The hardware team reports that a critical sensor component is stuck in customs due to a new environmental regulation. The "To-Complete Performance Index" (TCPI) to meet the original budget is now 1.25, while your current CPI is 0.85. How should you communicate this to the steering committee?**
    a. Report that the project is on track and the sensor delay will be absorbed.
    b. Present a "Recovery Plan" that includes a request for additional funding or a scope reduction, as the current budget is no longer feasible.
    c. Tell the committee that the hardware team is responsible for the delay.
    d. Stop the AI development until the sensors arrive.

73. **(Case Study Part C) At the end of the project, the AI system is functional, but the warehouse managers refuse to use it because they do not understand how it makes "Priority 1" shipping decisions. Which 2026 ECO concept was missed?**
    a. Value realization
    b. AI Explainability (XAI) and change management
    c. Total cost of quality (COQ)
    d. Risk mitigation

74. **Match the project management framework/concept to its primary focus:**

a. BANI	i. Focuses on the "Triple Bottom Line" and waste elimination
b. Circular economy	ii. Describes an environment that is Brittle, Anxious, Non-linear, and Incomprehensible
c. Value realization	iii. The process of ensuring outputs translate into actual business benefits
d. XAI	iv. Ensuring AI decision-making is transparent to human users

75. **A project team is using "Self-Correction" AI to manage their Kanban board. The AI automatically flags a "Bottleneck" in the QA column. What is the most "agile" response from the project manager?**
    a. Ignore the AI and trust the QA lead's manual reports.
    b. Facilitate a "Swarming" session where developers help the QA team clear the backlog.
    c. Discipline the QA team for falling behind.
    d. Increase the WIP (work in progress) limit to hide the bottleneck.

76. **You are managing a project to build a carbon-neutral data center. A key stakeholder insists on using a cheaper, non-sustainable cooling system to save USD 500,000. This directly contradicts the "ESG Guardrails" in the project charter. What is your best course of action?**
    a. Accept the change to show stakeholder flexibility.
    b. Refer the stakeholder to the "Strategic ESG Objectives" and the Charter, then escalate to the sponsor if they persist.
    c. Implement the change but hide the environmental impact in the final report.
    d. Quit the project on ethical grounds immediately.

77. **In a "Non-linear" project environment, you realize that a small change in a software API has caused a massive, unexpected failure in a hardware component. This is a characteristic of:**
    a. A simple cause-and-effect relationship.
    b. The "Non-linear" aspect of the BANI framework.
    c. Poor project planning.
    d. A "Known-Unknown" risk.

78. **Your project is using "Sustainable Procurement." You have two bids:**
    - **Bid A: USD 1.2M, 2-year lifespan, 50% recyclable.**
    - **Bid B: USD 1.5M, 5-year lifespan, 95% recyclable.**

    Which should you recommend based on "total cost of ownership" (TCO) and "Circular economy" principles?
    a. Bid A, because the initial cost is lower.
    b. Bid B, because the annual cost is lower and it aligns better with sustainability goals.
    c. Neither, both are too expensive.
    d. Bid A, and then upgrade it later.

79. **A project manager is calculating the "internal rate of return" (IRR) for a green energy project. If the IRR is 12% and the company's "hurdle rate" is 15%, what should the recommendation be?**
    a. Accept the project because 12% is a high return.
    b. Reject the project because it does not meet the minimum required return (hurdle rate).
    c. Accept the project only if the NPV is zero.
    d. It depends on the project's "Social Value" score.

80. **An agile team is struggling with "Anxiety" (from BANI) due to rapid shifts in AI technology. As a servant Leader, how do you support them?**
    a. Demand higher productivity to keep their minds off the stress.
    b. Create a "Safe-to-Fail" environment and provide training time for new AI tools.
    c. Cancel all meetings to give them more time to work.
    d. Micromanage their daily tasks to provide structure.

81. **On a "Burndown Chart," the "Remaining Work" line is consistently above the "Ideal Trend" line. What does this indicate?**
    a. The team is ahead of schedule.
    b. The team is behind schedule and may need to re-scope the iteration.
    c. The project is under budget.
    d. The velocity is higher than planned.

82. **Which amongst the following domain focus is most concerned with "Ensuring the project complies with sustainability and ethical labor standards"?**
    a. People
    b. Process
    c. Business environment
    d. Technical excellence

83. **A project manager is using "generative AI" to draft a project management plan. Who is ultimately responsible for the accuracy and ethical compliance of that plan?**
    a. The AI software vendor.
    b. The IT department.
    c. The project manager.
    d. The project sponsor.

84. **In a hybrid project, the "Critical Path" is delayed by 10 days. However, the agile software team is 2 weeks ahead of schedule. Can the software team's progress offset the critical path delay?**
    a. Yes, because they are part of the same project.
    b. No, the Critical Path is determined by the longest sequence of dependent tasks; agile "float" does not automatically reduce it.
    c. Only if the software is on the Critical Path.
    d. Yes, if you move the software developers to the hardware team.

85. **A project is at the "Closing" phase. To ensure "Value realization," what is the most important final activity?**
    a. Handing over the technical documentation.
    b. Releasing the project team.
    c. Conducting a "Benefits realization Handoff" with the operational managers.
    d. Throwing a project completion party.

86. **What is "Digital Twin" technology often used for in modern project management?**
    a. To create a duplicate project manager.
    b. To create a virtual simulation of a physical asset to test scenarios and risks before implementation.
    c. To backup project files.
    d. To manage two projects at once.

87. **A project manager is evaluating "Social Value." This includes:**
    a. Only the profit made by the company.
    b. The positive impact the project has on the community, diversity, and employee well-being.
    c. The number of social media followers the project has.
    d. The cost of the project's launch party.

88. **In an AI project, "human-in-the-loop" (HITL) refers to:**
    a. A project manager who is always in meetings.
    b. A governance requirement where a human must review and approve critical AI-generated decisions.
    c. The process of hiring more humans for the team.
    d. A type of computer hardware.

89. **A team's "Lead Time" is 15 days, and their "cycle time" is 3 days. What is the "Queue Time"?**
    a. 18 days b. 5 days
    c. 12 days d. 45 days

90. **You are managing a project to implement an AI-based recruitment tool. You discover the tool is excluding candidates from certain zip codes. This is an example of:**
    a. Geographic optimization.
    b. Algorithmic bias and an ethical risk.
    c. Efficient resource filtering.
    d. A "Technical Debt" issue.

91. **Your project is transitioning from a "linear supply chain" to a "circular supply chain" model. A supplier provides a component that is cheaper but non-recyclable, while another provides a "Cradle-to-Cradle" certified component at a 20% premium. As a project manager, focus on Lifecycle Value, what is your best course of action?**
    a. Select the cheaper component to protect the project's short-term CPI.
    b. Perform a Lifecycle Cost (LCC) analysis that includes disposal costs and carbon taxes to justify the 20% premium for the circular component.
    c. Ask the sponsor to decide, as this is a financial trade-off.
    d. Use the cheaper component but donate the savings to an environmental charity.

92. **A project manager is leading an AI-driven logistics project. The team identifies "Data Decay, where the AI's predictive accuracy drops because the underlying market data has changed fundamentally. Which process should be triggered?**
    a. Perform integrated change control.
    b. Implement continuous monitoring and model re-calibration.
    c. Close project or phase.
    d. Update the risk register and wait for the next steering committee.

93. **In the 2026 ECO, "Strategic Value" is a core performance metric. You are managing a project with an NPV of USD 500,000, but it will increase the company's carbon footprint by 15%. A second project has an NPV of USD 300,000 but reduces the footprint by 10%. If the company has a "Net-Zero" strategic mandate, which project has higher "Strategic Value"?**
    a. Project 1, because the NPV is USD 200,000 higher.
    b. Project 2, because it aligns with the strategic mandate despite the lower NPV.
    c. Neither, as they both have flaws.
    d. Both, the PM should combine them into one program.

94. **A project manager is using "Value Stream Mapping" (VSM) and identifies a "Motion Waste" where developers must manually port AI training results between two incompatible systems. What is the most effective lean response?**
    a. Hire more developers to speed up the manual porting.
    b. Automate the data transfer process using a CI/CD pipeline to eliminate the non-value-added motion.
    c. Tell the developers to be more careful to avoid errors.
    d. Document the manual process as a "Standard Operating Procedure."

95. **You are managing a hybrid project where the software team uses "Mob Programming" for complex AI logic. The PMO, which is used to individual task tracking, demands to know why three developers are working on one task. How should you respond?**
    a. Tell the developers to work separately to satisfy the PMO.
    b. Explain that Mob Programming reduces "Rework" and "Knowledge Silos," leading to higher quality and faster overall throughput for complex tasks.
    c. Create fake tasks in the system to hide the fact that they are working together.
    d. Ask the PMO to attend a Mob Programming session.

96. **In an AI project, "Technical Debt" is accumulating because the team is using "Quick-and-Dirty" data scraping methods to meet a deadline. What is the long-term risk to Value realization?**
    a. There is no risk; the project will finish early.
    b. The model will become "Fragile" and expensive to maintain, eventually eroding the business value it was meant to create.
    c. The team will get faster at scraping data.
    d. The project budget will increase.

97. **A project manager is calculating the "To-Complete Performance Index" (TCPI) to meet a revised "Estimate at Completion" (EAC) of USD 400,000. The current AC is USD 250,000 and the remaining work value (BAC - EV) is USD 180,000. What is the TCPI?**

a. 1.0 b. 1.2

c. 0.83 d. 1.5

98. **Your organization's culture is shifting toward "Adhocracy" (flexible and entrepreneurial). As a project manager, how should your leadership style change?**

a. Increase the number of formal reports and approval gates.

b. Empower the team to make decentralized decisions and focus on "Outcome-Based" rather than "Activity-Based" tracking.

c. Implement stricter time-tracking for all employees.

d. Focus solely on hierarchical communication with senior management.

99. **A "Social Value" audit reveals that your project's new automated kiosk system is difficult for elderly users to navigate. This is a failure in which 2026 ECO domain?**

a. Process

b. Business environment (ESG/Social Impact)

c. Technical excellence

d. Schedule management

100. **During a "Retrospective," an agile team realizes they have been over-committing in every sprint. What should the scrum master suggest?**

a. Work overtime to meet the commitment.

b. Use "Historical Velocity" as a guardrail for the next sprint's commitment to ensure a sustainable pace.

c. Lower the quality standards to finish tasks faster.

d. Ask the product owner to stop adding stories to the backlog.

101. **A project manager is managing a "Digital Twin" project for a smart city. A major "Black Swan" event (a sudden global chip shortage) occurs. How should the PM lead the team through this "Incomprehensible" (BANI) situation?**

a. Demand that the vendors deliver the chips as contracted.

b. Facilitate "Cross-Functional Brainstorming" to find alternative technologies or software-based workarounds.

c. Suspend the project indefinitely.

d. Reprimand the procurement lead for not anticipating the shortage.

102. **You are leading a national SmartGrid Predictive Analytics Program involving multiple utilities, a cybersecurity authority, and an international funding agency. Midexecution, the regulatory commission issues a new directive requiring all AIdriven outageprediction models to undergo an additional "explainability validation" step before deployment. This requirement was not part of the original scope and will affect vendor contracts, testing timelines, and integration workflows.**

The sponsor insists that the public launch date must not slip, citing political commitments. Meanwhile, the engineering team is already overloaded, and the vendor warns that incorporating the new validation step will require additional effort and may introduce delays unless priorities are adjusted.

You review the situation and realize that the new directive affects compliance, scope, schedule, vendor obligations, and value delivery sequencing

What are the two most appropriate actions the project manager should take next?

a. Immediately escalate to the sponsor and request approval to ignore the new directive until after launch, since the deadline is politically sensitive.

b. Conduct a structured impact analysis with regulatory, technical, legal, and vendor teams to understand implications across the delivery system.

c. Rebaseline the schedule internally without formal approval to absorb the new validation step and avoid alarming stakeholders.

d. Facilitate a valueprioritization discussion with the sponsor and key stakeholders to explore scope tradeoffs or phased delivery options.

e. Direct the engineering team to work overtime temporarily to maintain the launch date while incorporating the new validation requirement.

103. **You are leading a project to develop an AI for medical triage. The AI's "False Negative" rate is higher for certain ethnic groups. What is the most important "Governance Guardrail" to implement?**

a. Increase the project's marketing budget.

b. Implement "Algorithmic Fairness" testing and bias mitigation protocols before any production release.

c. Accept the error rate as a "residual risk."

d. Hire more doctors to manually check every decision.

104. **A project manager is using "Monte Carlo Simulation" to predict the project's finish date. The simulation shows a 90% probability of finishing by October 1st and a 50% probability by September 1st. What date should the PM communicate to the stakeholders to manage expectations effectively?**

a. September 1st

b. October 1st

c. August 1st

d. Somewhere in between

105. **What is "Continuous Value Delivery"?**

a. Delivering the entire project scope on the very last day.

b. Breaking the project into small, functional increments that provide value to the customer as soon as they are released.

c. Paying the project team on a continuous basis.

d. Providing a 24/7 help desk for the project.

106. **A project is using a "Fixed-Price" Contract for the hardware and "Time and Materials" (T&M) for the AI software development. What type of contract is this?**

a. Cost-plus

b. Hybrid contract

c. Unit price

d. Fixed-price incentive fee

107. **A project team is experiencing "Communication Overload" from too many Slack channels and emails. Which "Lean" principle should the PM apply?**

a. Eliminate waste (Over-processing of information).

b. Build quality in.

c. Deliver fast.

d. Optimize the whole.

108. **You are managing a project in a "Brittle" (BANI) environment. The project's success depends on a single specialized cloud provider. What is the best risk response?**

a. Stick with the provider and hope they do not fail.

b. Implement a "Multi-Cloud" strategy or a local failover to build "Resilience."

c. Sue the provider if they have an outage.

d. Cancel the project.

109. **A project manager is conducting a "Benefit-Cost Analysis." The total benefits are USD 200,000 and the total costs are USD 150,000. What is the BCR?**

a. 0.75 b. 1.33

c. 1.5 d. 0.5

110. **Which 2026 PMP concept refers to the ethical requirement that AI systems must have a "Kill Switch" or a way for humans to override autonomous decisions?**

a. Value realization

b. Human-in-the-loop (HITL) and human agency

c. Technical debt

d. Data drift

111. **You are the project manager for "Project Prometheus," an initiative to implement an AI-driven credit scoring system for a global bank. During the Execution phase, a local regulatory body introduces new AI Explainability (XAI) requirements. Your lead data scientist informs you that meeting these requirements will decrease the model's predictive accuracy by 12%, potentially impacting the projected Return on Investment (ROI). Meanwhile, the Chief Risk Officer (CRO) insists on "human-in-the-loop" (HITL) oversight, while the product owner wants a fully autonomous system to minimize operational costs.**

What should be the project manager's first course of action to address the conflicting requirements?

a. Update the risk register and escalate the ROI impact to the project sponsor.

b. Facilitate a multi-criteria decision analysis (MCDA) workshop with the CRO, product owner, and data science team.

c. Prioritize the regulatory requirements and update the project management plan to reflect a predictive-adaptive hybrid approach.

d. Request a change through the Formal Change Control Board (CCB) to adjust the project's success metrics.

112. **Your project involves the construction of a high-tech manufacturing facility. The organization has recently committed to ESG (Environmental, Social, and Governance) targets. You are evaluating two primary suppliers for the cooling systems.**

Factor	Supplier A (Traditional)	Supplier B (Circular)
Initial Purchase Cost	USD 450,000	USD 580,000
Operational Efficiency	Standard	20% higher than standard
End-of-Life Policy	None (Landfill)	Buy-back & refurbishment program
Carbon Footprint	120 Tons CO_2/year	85 Tons CO_2/year

Applying total cost of ownership (TCO) and Circular economy principles, how should the project manager justify the selection of Supplier B to the Finance Department, which is focused on the "hurdle rate"?

a. Highlight that Supplier B's initial cost is a sunk cost and will be recovered via operational efficiency.

b. Present a lifecycle cost analysis showing that the buy-back value and energy savings result in a lower NPV over 10 years.

c. Argue that the ESG reputation risk of choosing Supplier A outweighs any financial savings.

d. Use a weighted scoring model where "environmental impact" is given the highest weight regardless of cost.

Refer to the S-curve (in the figure) dashboard based on the following data and answer the questions from 113 to 116:

Week	PV	EV	AC
1	10	8	12
2	22	16	28
3	35	25	42
4	50	32	60

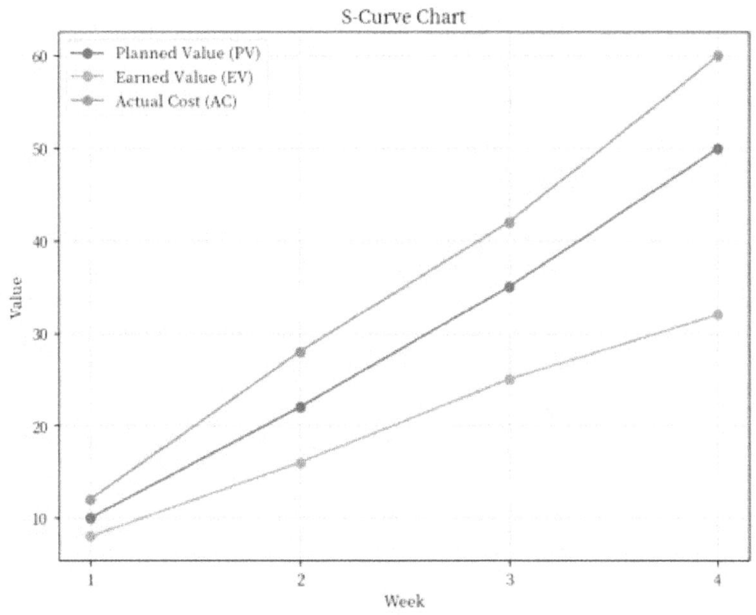

Figure 10.1: *S-curve chart*

You are the project manager for a national smartgrid modernization initiative. The project involves upgrading substations, deploying IoTenabled smart meters, and integrating a cloudbased gridanalytics platform. The work is being executed through multiple subcontractors and internal engineering teams.

During the Week4 governance review, you present the S-curve. The dashboard shows:

- Actual Cost (AC) is significantly higher than both PV and EV
- Earned Value (EV) is lagging behind the planned progress
- Subcontractor overtime has increased due to unexpected rework
- A key stakeholder from the regulatory authority has raised concerns about delays
- The sponsor insists that "the project must not slip further because the public launch date is fixed"

Your team appears stressed, and several engineers privately mention that requirements are still evolving because the regulatory body keeps issuing clarifications.

113. **The regulatory authority keeps issuing new clarifications, causing rework and overtime. What should you do first to stabilize the situation?**
    a. Ask the sponsor to intervene and stop the regulatory authority from sending changes
    b. Establish a structured changeclarification cadence with the regulatory authority
    c. Reject all new clarifications until the next phase
    d. Escalate the issue to the PMO for guidance

114. **The S-curve shows AC rising faster than PV and EV. What is the most appropriate interpretation?**
    a. The project team is performing more work than planned
    b. The project is overspending without achieving equivalent progress
    c. The project is on track but frontloading costs
    d. The project is under budget but behind schedule

115. **You discover that subcontractor overtime is the primary driver of cost overrun. What should you do next?**

a. Immediately stop overtime and freeze all subcontractor work

b. Conduct a rootcause workshop with the subcontractor and internal team

c. Issue a change request to increase the cost baseline

d. Replace the subcontractor with a new vendor

116. **The sponsor insists the public launch date cannot slip. Based on the S-curve and team stress indicators, what should you do?**

a. Recommend scope tradeoffs to protect the fixed launch date

b. Push the team to work additional overtime to recover the schedulee

c. Rebaseline the schedule without formal approval

d. Inform the sponsor that the date must slip due to performance issues

Case study: SmartGrid Resilience

You are the project manager for a multiyear national *SmartGrid Resilience Program* funded jointly by the *Ministry of Power*, a consortium of regional utilities, and an international energyinnovation grant. The program aims to modernize substations, deploy IoTenabled predictivemaintenance sensors, and integrate an AIdriven outageresponse platform. Work is distributed across multiple vendors, internal engineering teams, cybersecurity authorities, and regulatory bodies.

Recent developments include:

- The regulatory commission has issued new compliance directives requiring additional validation steps for AIbased decisionmaking.
- The cybersecurity authority has flagged datasovereignty concerns related to cloudbased analytics.
- A major subcontractor is experiencing resource attrition, slowing field deployment.
- The sponsor insists that the public launch date cannot slip, citing political commitments.
- The PMO has mandated quarterly benefits realization reporting, even though benefits will materialize only after full rollout.
- Several team members report burnout, citing unclear priorities and constant requirement shifts.
- A senior stakeholder from one of the utilities is bypassing the changecontrol process and directly influencing the engineering team.
- A crossfunctional integration workshop revealed that teams are working in silos, with inconsistent interpretations of requirements.

You must navigate governance, compliance, team performance, vendor management, benefits realization, and stakeholder alignment, all under schedule pressure.

117. **A senior utility stakeholder continues to bypass the changecontrol process and directly instructs engineers to modify configurations, claiming urgency due to regulatory pressure. The engineers feel obligated to comply. What should you do first to restore governance discipline without escalating conflict?**

a. Escalate the stakeholder's behavior to the sponsor and request intervention

b. Reinforce the governance model, clarify decisionmaking boundaries, and redirect all changes through the formal process

c. Allow the changes temporarily to avoid delays and document them later

d. Ask the engineers to ignore the stakeholder's instructions until further notice

118. **New compliance directives require additional validation steps for AIbased decisionmaking. These directives were issued midexecution and may affect design, testing, and vendor contracts. What is the most appropriate next step?**
   a. Freeze all work until compliance is fully understood
   b. Conduct a structured impact assessment with regulatory, legal, and technical teams
   c. Reject the directives because they were not part of the baseline
   d. Immediately update the design documents to reflect the new directives

119. **Team members report burnout due to shifting priorities and unclear expectations. Productivity is dropping, and quality issues are increasing. What should you do first?**
   a. Request additional resources from the PMO
   b. Facilitate a prioritization and alignment workshop to clarify workload and expectations
   c. Approve compensatory time off for the team
   d. Reassign tasks to the subcontractor to reduce workload

120. **A subcontractor responsible for field deployment is experiencing resource attrition, causing delays. They request schedule relief. What is the BEST action?**
   a. Terminate the subcontractor and onboard a new one
   b. Conduct a joint risk review and agree on mitigation strategies
   c. Penalize the subcontractor for nonperformance
   d. Absorb the work into the internal team to maintain the schedule

121. **The PMO requires quarterly benefits reporting, but benefits will only materialize after full rollout. What should you do?**
   a. Push back and request exemption
   b. Report leading indicators, interim proxies, and early signals of value
   c. Delay reporting until benefits are measurable
   d. Provide estimates without validation to meet the requirement

122. **The cybersecurity authority raises concerns about data sovereignty in the cloudbased AI platform. This may require architectural changes. What should you do first?**
   a. Escalate the issue to the sponsor
   b. Facilitate a technical deepdive with cybersecurity experts and the vendor
   c. Pause all AI integration work
   d. Document the concern and continue execution

123. **The sponsor insists the public launch date cannot slip due to political commitments. Based on current delays, what is the most appropriate response?**
   a. Recommend scope tradeoffs or phased delivery to protect the fixed date
   b. Push the team to work overtime to recover schedule
   c. Rebaseline the schedule without formal approval
   d. Inform the sponsor that the date must slip

124. **A crossfunctional workshop reveals that IT, field operations, cybersecurity, and regulatory teams are working in silos with inconsistent interpretations of requirements. What should you do?**
   a. Create an integrated crossfunctional working group with shared objectives and synchronized workflows
   b. Ask each team to submit weekly status reports
   c. Escalate the issue to the steering committee
   d. Increase meeting frequency across teams

125. **Frequent requirement clarifications from the regulatory body are causing rework and confusion. What is the BEST preventive action?**
   a. Establish a structured clarification cadence and formal intake mechanism
   b. Reject all new clarifications
   c. Ask the sponsor to intervene
   d. Proceed with work and incorporate clarifications later

126. **You discover that a team lead is underreporting issues to avoid negative visibility. This behavior is creating blind spots in risk management. What should you do?**
   a. Escalate immediately to HR
   b. Coach the team lead on transparency, reinforce ethical expectations, and create a safe environment for reporting
   c. Ignore it to maintain morale
   d. Replace the team lead with someone more transparent

127. **You are leading a transformation project to implement an AI-driven predictive maintenance system for a global logistics firm. The AI model has flagged a critical failure risk in the main distribution hub, suggesting a complete shutdown for 48 hours. The Chief Operating Officer (COO) is skeptical and refuses to halt operations without understanding why the AI made this recommendation, as the current manual sensors show no issues. Which action should the project manager take to resolve this conflict and maintain project integrity?**
   a. Request the data science team to provide the raw neural network weights to the COO to prove the model's complexity.
   b. Utilize Explainable AI (XAI) techniques, such as SHAP or LIME values, to provide a visual breakdown of the specific variables (e.g., vibration frequency vs. heat) driving the recommendation.
   c. Override the AI recommendation and trust the manual sensors to avoid a high-impact operational shutdown.
   d. Escalate the issue to the project sponsor, citing that the AI is the "single source of truth" according to the project charter.

128. **Your project relies on a "just-in-time" delivery of specialized quantum sensors. A sudden geopolitical shift has rendered your primary supplier's region "Brittle," resulting in an immediate 400% increase in lead times. Your Project Management Office (PMO) suggests sticking to the original procurement plan to avoid "sunk cost" penalties with the current vendor. Applying the principles of a BANI environment, what is the most effective leadership response?**
   a. Perform a total cost of ownership (TCO) analysis to justify sticking with the current vendor despite the delays.
   b. Implement a parallel path strategy by immediately qualifying an alternative supplier, even if it incurs higher upfront costs.
   c. Update the risk register and notify stakeholders that the project finish date is now indefinitely delayed.
   d. Invoke the Force Majeure clause to cancel the contract and wait for the geopolitical situation to stabilize.

129. **During a mid-project review of a software-as-a-service (SaaS) rollout, you notice that while the development team is completing "Stories" ahead of schedule, the deployment lead time has increased. A Value Stream Map reveals that the security compliance check (DevSecOps gate) is taking 10 days, while coding takes only 3 days. As the project manager, how should you optimize the Value Stream?**
   a. Increase the development velocity to "push" more features through the security gate.
   b. Reassign developers to the security team to help manually process the backlog.
   c. Implement Automated Security Scanning within the CI/CD pipeline to move toward a "Shift-Left" security posture.
   d. Shorten the sprint duration from 2 weeks to 1 week to increase the frequency of security reviews.

130. **You are managing a 10-year infrastructure project involving sensitive citizen data. A risk specialist identifies a "Harvest Now, Decrypt Later" threat, where malicious actors steal encrypted data today to decrypt it once quantum computing becomes commercially viable. How should this risk be handled in the risk management plan?**

    a. Dismiss the risk as it is outside the current project's 10-year window of "active" relevance.

    b. Budget for and implement quantum-safe encryption (post-quantum cryptography) standards immediately for all data at rest.

    c. Transfer the risk by purchasing a high-premium cyber insurance policy.

    d. Accept the risk, noting that encryption technology will likely evolve naturally by the time a threat materializes.

2026 case study: EverGreen infrastructure project

You are the lead project manager for *EverGreen*, a USD 500 million initiative to convert an aging industrial zone into a carbon-neutral *Smart District*. The project uses AI for energy grid optimization and requires strict adherence to the new *2026 Sustainability Disclosure Standards*.

131. **The project sponsor is concerned that while the project is "on time and on budget" according to traditional Earned Value Management (EVM), the public perception is negative because the promised "Carbon Neutrality" has not been quantified yet. According to the 2026 focus on Value over Outputs, what is your best course of action?**

    a. Stick to CPI and SPI reporting, as these are the objective measures defined in the project management plan.

    b. Implement a Benefit realization Dashboard that tracks real-time carbon offset data alongside traditional financial metrics.

    c. Reallocate the contingency reserve to a marketing campaign to improve public perception.

    d. Wait until the project is closed to measure sustainability, as "value" can only be determined post-launch.

132. **The AI model used to allocate affordable housing within the "EverGreen" district is found to be inadvertently prioritizing applicants from specific zip codes, creating an ethical risk. As the project manager, how do you handle this technical and ethical bottleneck?**

    a. Ignore the bias if the model meets the technical "Accuracy" threshold of 95%.

    b. Conduct an Algorithmic Audit and implement a "human-in-the-loop" (HITL) review process to ensure equitable distribution.

    c. Delete the data related to zip codes so the AI cannot see it, assuming this will fix the bias.

    d. Terminate the AI contract and return to manual processing to avoid legal liability.

133. **Your primary concrete supplier has just reported that their logistics chain has a higher carbon footprint than initially disclosed, potentially threatening your "Net Zero" certification. How do you manage this secondary risk?**

    a. Accept the risk, as the supplier's emissions (Scope 3) are outside of your direct project control (Scope 1).

    b. Collaborate with the supplier to optimize their Value Stream or switch to a Circular economy provider who uses recycled materials.

    c. File a breach of contract claim against the supplier to recover the "Net Zero" certification costs.

    d. Update the project scope to remove the "Net Zero" requirement to maintain the current schedule.

134. **The city council is debating between two types of solar glass for the district. Option A is cheaper to install (lower CapEx) but degrades in 10 years. Option B is 30% more expensive but lasts 25 years and is 100% recyclable (lower OPEX and Salvage cost). Which financial model should you present to the council to support the most sustainable choice?**

a. A net present value (NPV) calculation focused only on the first 5 years of operation.

b. A Lifecycle Costing (LCC) model that demonstrates the lower total cost of ownership for Option B over 25 years.

c. A simple payback period model to show how quickly Option A returns the initial investment.

d. An internal rate of return (IRR) report that ignores decommissioning costs.

135. **You are the project manager for a financial services firm. The software development team is using scrum (agile), while the regulatory compliance and hardware teams are using Waterfall (Predictive). The "Definition of Done" for the software team does not include the 4-week mandatory security audit required by the Waterfall compliance team, leading to a major bottleneck. As the project manager, what is the most effective way to integrate these two disparate workflows?**

a. Force the software team to adopt Waterfall approach for the entire project to ensure compliance alignment.

b. Create a Hybrid Transition Layer where the agile team's "Definition of Done" is updated to include a "Security Ready" status, triggering the Waterfall audit.

c. Instruct the software team to continue their sprints and handle the security audit as a "post-project" activity.

d. Remove the security audit requirement, citing the need for "agile speed" and "Value Delivery."

136. **You lead a globally distributed team across three time zones. During a sprint retrospective, team members in Asia express that they feel "invisible" and "excluded" from decision-making, which usually happens during the London and New York office hours. Applying servant leadership principles, what should you do to improve team cohesion?**

a. Record all meetings and send the transcripts to the Asian team so they can read what was decided.

b. Implement a "Follow the Sun" Meeting Rotation, where the meeting times rotate weekly to ensure the burden of "out of hours" work is shared equally.

c. Designate the New York office as the "Headquarters" and mandate that all critical decisions happen during its window for consistency.

d. Replace the Asian team members with contractors in a closer time zone to simplify project logistics.

137. **Your project sponsor is used to seeing Gantt charts and percent complete metrics. However, your development team is providing Velocity and Burndown Charts. The sponsor is confused and believes the project is failing because they do not see "milestone dates" for software features. How should the project manager bridge this reporting gap?**

a. Convert the team's Story Points into "Hours" to create a traditional Gantt chart for the sponsor.

b. Develop a Hybrid Dashboard that maps agile Story Points to Predictive Milestones, showing "Feature Completion" as a percentage of the total Value Stream.

c. Ignore the sponsor's request and insist that they learn how to read agile charts.

d. Ask the team to stop using agile and switch to Waterfall reporting to satisfy the sponsor.

138. **You are managing a massive aerospace project. Ten different agile teams are working on sub-components of a single navigation system. You notice that while individual teams are "Green," the integrated system is failing during assembly. What is the most appropriate scaling technique to resolve this?**
   a. Increase the number of developers in each team.
   b. Establish a scrum of scrums (SoS) or a Scaled Agile Framework (SAFe) "Sync" to focus specifically on cross-team dependencies and integration.
   c. Appoint a single "Super-Manager" to make all decisions for the ten teams.
   d. Cancel the agile approach and move all teams back to a single, large Waterfall structure.

139. **You are transitioning a traditionally "Predictive" organization to a "Hybrid" model. Which of the following are considered Systemic Impediments to agile adoption? (Select three.)**
   a. Rigid annual budgeting cycles.
   b. The use of Kanban boards for task tracking.
   c. Functional "Silos" that prevent cross-departmental collaboration.
   d. A "Command and Control" leadership culture.
   e. Having a dedicated Project Room (War Room) for the team.

140. **Your organization is hiring an external vendor to develop a custom AI module. The Scope is not fully defined, but the CFO insists on a "Fixed Price" contract to minimize financial risk. You know that a standard Fixed Price contract will lead to constant "Change Requests" and friction. Which contract type should you propose to balance the CFO's need for cost certainty with the team's need for agile flexibility?**
   a. **Firm Fixed Price (FFP)**: Lock in the price and scope immediately to protect the budget.
   b. **Graduated Fixed Price**: A contract where both parties agree on an hourly rate, but if the vendor finishes early, they get a higher rate; if they finish late, they get a lower rate.
   c. **Capped Time and Materials (T&M)**: Pay for actual hours worked, but with a "Not-to-Exceed" (NTE) ceiling to protect the budget.
   d. **Cost Plus Incentive Fee (CPIF)**: The buyer pays all costs plus a fee based on the vendor achieving specific performance goals.

141. **You are managing a hybrid project. The product owner wants to prioritize high-value features for the next two sprints. However, the tech lead identifies a major architectural risk that could cause a system-wide crash if not addressed now. Using the concept of a Risk-Adjusted Backlog, how should the project manager advise the product owner?**
   a. Prioritize only the high-value features to ensure the "Value Delivery" metric is met for the quarter.
   b. Place the "Risk mitigation" task at the very bottom of the backlog, as it provides no immediate "Value" to the customer.
   c. Re-prioritize the backlog to include the Risk mitigation task near the top, balancing "Business Value" with "Risk Reduction."
   d. Cancel the next sprint and move the entire team to Waterfall to handle the technical risk.

142. **At the start of a hybrid project, your stakeholders are demanding a "precise" date and cost for the final delivery. The project involves a high degree of R&D in the agile software component. Which concept should you use to manage stakeholder expectations regarding the accuracy of your estimates?**
   a. **The S-Curve**: To show how costs will accumulate over time.
   b. **The Cone of Uncertainty**: To explain that estimates will become significantly more accurate as the team completes early iterations and more "Unknowns" become "Knowns."
   c. **Monte Carlo Simulation**: To provide a single, 100% certain date for completion.
   d. **Critical Path Method (CPM)**: To show that the software R&D cannot be estimated because it is not on the critical path.

143. **Your hybrid project is 6 months in. The Waterfall teams are frustrated by the constant "changing requirements" from the agile side, and the agile team is exhausted by the "excessive documentation" required by the Waterfall governance. Team velocity is dropping, and morale is low. What is the best servant leadership action to take?**

   a. Increase the frequency of status meetings to "push" the teams to work harder.

   b. Conduct a Joint Retrospective specifically to identify "Friction Points" between the two methodologies and collaboratively simplify the reporting requirements.

   c. Tell the Waterfall team to stop complaining and the agile team to just write the documents.

   d. Replace the project leadership, as the current friction is a sign of management failure.

144. **You are managing a 35-person hybrid team split between Austin and Bangalore. Two senior developers are in a heated conflict over the priority of the "GPU Cloud Cluster," a limited resource needed for training the project's AI models. One developer is working on a high-value customer feature, while the other is working on a critical "Security Patch." Both claim their task is the top priority. As the project manager, what is the most effective conflict resolution technique to use?**

   a. **Force/Direct**: Order the developers to stop arguing and assign the resource to the customer feature to protect revenue.

   b. **Smooth/Accommodate**: Tell both developers that they are doing a great job and ask them to work it out themselves by next week.

   c. **Collaborate/Problem solve**: Conduct a joint session to review the Project Value Map and the risk register, determining which task has the higher "Cost of Delay" (CoD).

   d. **Compromise/Reconcile**: Split the GPU cluster 50/50 between both developers, even if it makes both training models take twice as long.

145. **During a virtual stand-up, you notice that a usually high-performing team member has become withdrawn, rarely speaks, and has missed their last two "Story" deadlines. You suspect burnout due to the intense "Crunch Mode" the project has entered. Which action demonstrates the highest level of emotional intelligence?**

   a. Publicly ask the team member during the stand-up why their velocity has dropped to encourage accountability.

   b. Schedule a private One-on-One session to practice "active listening," offering support and discussing potential workload adjustments or time off.

   c. Send an official warning email citing the missed deadlines as a performance issue.

   d. Wait for the next sprint retrospective to see if the team brings it up as a group problem.

146. **Your PMO has introduced an AI tool that automatically assigns tasks to developers based on their "Historical Velocity" and "Skill Tags." The team complains that the AI is assigning them repetitive, boring tasks and not allowing them to work on "Stretch Goals" that would help their career growth. How should the project manager handle this conflict between AI efficiency and human development?**

   a. Trust the AI's assignments, as it is data-driven and removes human bias from resource allocation.

   b. Override the AI's assignments and allow for a self-organizing team model where members can pick at least 20% of their own tasks (innovation time).

   c. Tell the team that efficiency is the priority and they can work on stretch goals on their own time.

   d. Delete the "Skill Tags" in the AI so it starts assigning tasks randomly.

147. **You are the project manager in a matrix organization. A functional manager pulls a key developer off your project to handle an "internal department emergency" without consulting you. This will cause your current sprint to fail. Task: What is your first step to resolve this conflict of authority?**

a. Escalate the issue to the project sponsor immediately to get the developer back.

b. Meet with the Functional Manager to understand the "Emergency" and negotiate a Resource Sharing Agreement or a temporary replacement.

c. Tell the developer to ignore their functional manager and stay on the project.

d. Accept the loss and tell the team to work double shifts to make up the lost time.

148. **To accelerate the project schedule, a senior developer uses an unapproved, third-party AI coding assistant to generate a complex security module. The AI-generated code works perfectly in testing, but the developer did not disclose its use, fearing that the Project Management Office (PMO) would reject it due to data privacy concerns. As the project manager, once you discover this, what is your most ethical course of action?**

a. Keep the information confidential since the code works and the project is back on schedule.

b. Immediately remove the code, conduct a Security and Bias Audit, and update the stakeholder transparency report regarding the use of AI tools.

c. Reward the developer for their "innovative" thinking and encourage other team members to do the same.

d. Wait until the final project audit to see if the external auditors catch the AI-generated code.

149. **Your project is part of a corporate initiative to reduce the company's carbon footprint. Your team is currently working 60-hour weeks to meet a "Green" certification deadline. While the project is hitting its environmental targets, the "Social" (S) pillar of ESG is failing because team turnover has reached 25% due to exhaustion. How should you re-balance the project to ensure sustainable team performance?**

a. Hire more contractors to keep the 60-hour pace without burning out the permanent staff.

b. Negotiate a deadline extension with the sponsor, explaining that the project's "Sustainability" value is undermined by the unsustainable "Social" cost to the team.

c. Cancel the Green certification and focus only on the financial ROI to simplify the project.

d. Implement a "Wellness App" for the team to track their stress levels while maintaining the current schedule.

150. **Your project uses an AI "sentiment analysis" tool that monitors team communications (Slack/ Teams) to provide a "Team Health Score." The team feels the tool is "Big Brother" and has stopped communicating openly, leading to a breakdown in collaboration. How should the project manager restore psychological safety?**

a. Explain that the AI is for their own good and they should trust the data.

b. Discontinue the automated sentiment monitoring and replace it with human-centered feedback loops, such as anonymous retrospectives and 1-on-1s.

c. Punish team members who are not communicating enough to force the AI score back up.

d. Ask the AI to ignore the "negative" sentiment to make the reports look better for the sponsor.

151. **A supplier offers a critical project component at a 30% discount, but they cannot provide documentation regarding their "end-of-life" recycling process. A second supplier is more expensive but provides a full Circular economy Certification. Which choice aligns with the focus on Value Delivery?**

a. Choose the cheaper supplier to maximize the project's initial budget performance (CPI).

b. Choose the more expensive supplier, documenting the Lifecycle Value and ESG compliance as a key project benefit.

c. Buy from the cheaper supplier and use the 30% savings to plant trees to "offset" the lack of recycling.

d. Split the order between both suppliers to "hedge" the risk.

152. **Which of the following are considered violations of the PMI Code of Ethics in a 2026 project environment? (Select three.)**
   a. Using a vendor because they are a personal friend, without a competitive bidding process.
   b. Disclosing a "Quantum Risk" to stakeholders even if it might cause the project to be cancelled.
   c. Falsifying an AI "Accuracy Report" to meet a project milestone.
   d. Prioritizing a high-performing developer for a promotion.
   e. Accepting a "Consulting Fee" from a software vendor your project just hired.

153. **You are the Senior project manager for "Sentinella," a USD 1.2 billion digital transformation for a Tier-1 global bank. The project has three pillars:**
   - **Migrating core banking to a quantum-safe Cloud.**
   - **Implementing AI Hyper-personalization to provide real-time financial advice to 50 million customers.**
   - **Ensuring 100% compliance with the 2026 DORA Supervisory Actions, which require proof of "Digital Operational Resilience" against systemic cyber threats.**

   Six months before the launch, a "Stress Simulation" (Digital Twin) reveals that a third-party cloud provider's failover mechanism takes 15 minutes—exceeding the DORA-mandated 5-minute maximum for critical financial functions. The vendor claims a fix will cost an additional USD 5 million and take 3 months.

   As the project manager, what is the most appropriate action to maintain compliance?
   a. Accept the 15-minute window and update the risk register, as USD 5 million is outside the current budget.
   b. Invoke the DORA Third-Party Risk Clause in the contract, requiring the vendor to meet the regulatory standard at their own expense or face termination.
   c. Change the project scope to classify the affected function as "non-critical" to bypass the 5-minute requirement.
   d. Request an immediate emergency fund from the sponsor to pay the vendor and stay on schedule.

154. **You are reviewing the Critical Path for the AI hyper-personalization module. The following are the tasks and their dependencies:**
   - **Data Privacy Audit (4 weeks)**
   - **AI Model Training (6 weeks) - Depends on A**
   - **Customer UI Beta (3 weeks) - Depends on B**
   - **Regulatory Filing for AI Transparency (XAI) (5 weeks) - Depends on B**

   If Task B (AI Model Training) is delayed by 2 weeks due to a "GPU Scarcity" risk, what is the impact on the project finish date?
   a. No impact, as Task D has enough "Float."
   b. The project finish date will shift by exactly 2 weeks because Task B is on the Critical Path.
   c. Only the UI Beta (Task C) is delayed; the regulatory filing (Task D) can start early.
   d. The project is delayed by 4 weeks because of the "risk ripple effect."

155. **The "Sentinella" AI starts rejecting loan applications from a specific minority demographic at a rate 40% higher than the national average. The AI "Black Box" cannot explain why. The business team wants to launch anyway to hit their "Market Share" KPI. Task: What is your responsibility as the project manager according to the 2026 Ethics in Finance standards?**
   a. Approve the launch; the AI is likely identifying "hidden risks" that humans cannot see.
   b. Halt the rollout of the lending module and mandate a "Bias Audit" to ensure the AI follows the Fair Lending Acts.
   c. Launch the module but add a disclaimer that "AI decisions are final."

d. Adjust the AI settings manually to approve everyone from that demographic to "balance the numbers" without fixing the underlying model.

156. **Which of the following are considered "High-Impact" risks specific to a 2026 BFSI Digital Transformation? (Select three.)**

a. **Quantum decryption**: Legacy data is being intercepted and stored for future decryption.

b. **Regulatory drift**: Changes in **Central Bank Digital Currency (CBDC)** standards mid-project.

c. **Flash volatility**: AI trading algorithms react to a project milestone in a way that affects the bank's stock.

d. **Talent attrition**: A team member leaves the project for a competitor.

e. **Operational cost**: The cost of office stationery is increasing by 5%.

157. **Project "Sentinella" has officially gone live. The technical migration to the quantum-safe cloud is complete, and the AI hyper-personalization engine is active. However, the initial data shows that only 10% of customers are using the new AI financial advisor, far below the 40% target defined in the business case. As the project manager, what is your responsibility during the "Closing" phase regarding this shortfall?**

a. Close the project immediately since all "scope" items (the software) have been delivered.

b. Work with the sponsor and Business Owner to conduct a "Benefits Gap Analysis" and transition the project to an "Operational Improvement" phase.

c. Update the business case to lower the target to 10% so the project can be marked as a "Success."

d. Blame the marketing department for the low adoption rate in the Final Project Report.

158. **Two weeks after launch, the bank's core system suffers a "Black Swan" event—a non-linear system failure that neither the AI nor the engineers can explain. The system is fluctuating between "Normal" and "Critical Failure" every 10 minutes. Stakeholders are anxious and demanding immediate "Certainty." In this BANI environment, which leadership style should the project manager adopt?**

a. **Directive/Autocratic**: Tell stakeholders exactly when the system will be fixed, even if you do not know, to calm their anxiety.

b. **Transparent/Adaptive**: Admit the situation is "Incomprehensible" in the short term, but establish a Command Center for real-time experimentation and transparent, hourly status updates.

c. **Avoidant**: Wait for the AI to fix itself since the logic is too complex for human intervention.

d. **Defensive**: Review the contract to see which vendor can be held legally liable for the downtime.

159. **At the very end of the project, you are performing a final audit. Here is the data:**

- **Total Budget (BAC): USD 1.2 Billion**
- **Actual Cost (AC): USD 1.3 Billion**
- **Earned Value (EV): USD 1.2 Billion**
- **Planned Value (PV): USD 1.2 Billion**

Based on this data, what is the final status of project "sentinella"?

a. The project finished on schedule and under budget.

b. The project finished behind schedule and over budget.

c. The project finished on schedule but over budget with a Variance at Completion (VAC) of -USD 100 Million.

d. The project finished ahead of schedule but under budget.

160. **You are the lead program manager for "apex-quantum," a project spanning 12 countries. The goal is to move the global supply chain from a "project-based" model to a "product-led" model using a proprietary AI that predicts geopolitical instability.**

In the middle of the transition, the "project" team is hitting all milestones, but the "product" metrics (customer lifetime value and churn) are declining. The executive board is frustrated and wants to revert to a traditional Project Management Office (PMO) structure to "regain control." As the project manager, what is the most strategic response?

a. Agree with the board and revert to traditional Waterfall reporting to ensure stability.

b. Implement a Value Stream Mapping audit to identify where the "Silos" are preventing the flow of value, and advocate for shifting the budget from "Output-based" to "Outcome-based" funding.

c. Increase the frequency of status meetings to daily to show the board you have "control."

d. Resign, citing that the organization is not ready for a product-led transition.

161. **A sudden trade embargo is placed on a specific rare-earth mineral essential for your project's AI hardware. Your geopolitical risk model (AI) failed to predict this "Black Swan." Stakeholders are accusing the project of gross negligence. How do you handle this crisis according to BANI leadership principles?**

a. Blame the AI developer for the model's failure and demand a refund.

b. Practice Radical Transparency: Acknowledge the "Incomprehensible" nature of the event, activate a Parallel Procurement Path for synthetic alternatives, and update the risk model with the new data.

c. Hide the impact of the embargo from the stakeholders until a solution is found to avoid panic.

d. Cancel the project, as the rare-earth shortage makes it impossible to finish under the original charter.

162. **Your project uses a "Tier-1" AI vendor. However, an audit reveals that the "Tier-3" data-labeling firm they use in a developing nation is violating the project's Social Sustainability (ESG) standards. The Tier-1 vendor claims they are not responsible for Tier-3 actions. What is your ethical and professional obligation?**

a. Accept the Tier-1 vendor's explanation to maintain the project schedule.

b. Demand that the Tier-1 vendor perform a supply chain Remediation or switch to a certified "Ethical AI" provider, even if it causes a 6-month delay.

c. Rewrite the ESG policy to exclude Tier-3 vendors to simplify compliance.

d. Report the Tier-3 vendor to the local authorities and continue using them in the meantime.

163. **Match the BANI challenge to the PM leadership capability required to overcome it.**

BANI challenge	PM capability
a. Brittle: The project's funding source is tied to a volatile cryptocurrency	i. Empathy and psychological safety
b. Anxious: The team is terrified that the AI they are building will replace their jobs	ii. Resilience and redundancy
c. Non-linear: A minor bug in the code causes a total global system outage	iii. Context and XAI (Explainability)
d. Incomprehensible: The AI makes a decision that saves USD 10 million, but no one can explain how	iv. Adaptability and systems thinking

Case study: The BFSI project-to-product

You are the lead program manager for *Project Phoenix*, a multi-year initiative for a global Tier-1 bank. The goal is to migrate from legacy monolithic banking systems to a real-time, AI-driven, CBDC-compatible product ecosystem. The environment is **Brittle, Anxious, Non-linear, Incomprehensible (BANI)** and governed by strict **Digital Operational Resilience Act (DORA)** and ESG regulations.

164. **During the migration of the AI Hyper-personalization engine to a quantum-safe cloud, a new DORA-related regulatory update requires an immediate audit of all third-party sub-processors. This audit was not in the original scope. The product is 85% complete and nearing a critical market-entry window. What should the project manager do first?**

   a. Request a budget increase and schedule extension from the project sponsor.

   b. Update the risk register and perform a qualitative risk analysis on the regulatory change.

   c. Meet with the Compliance Officer to determine the specific "Definition of Done" for the new audit requirements.

   d. Direct the development team to prioritize the audit tasks over remaining feature development.

165. **A Tier-2 hardware vendor for the bank's new CBDC hardware security modules (HSMs) reports a 4-month delay due to geopolitical conflict in the semiconductor region. This delay will impact the integration phase but not the immediate software sprints. How should the project manager handle this?**

   a. Execute the fallback plan by sourcing alternative, lower-spec modules to maintain the schedule.

   b. Conduct a "What-If" scenario analysis to determine the impact on the overall product roadmap and benefits realization.

   c. Inform the stakeholders that the project will be delayed by 4 months due to force majeure.

   d. Crash the software development schedule to make up for the time lost in hardware procurement.

166. **The bank is transitioning from a "project" mindset to a "product" mindset. The steering committee is frustrated because the "Project Phoenix" budget is being consumed, but they are not seeing the traditional "Project Closure" report. What is the best way to explain this to them?**

   a. Explain that in a product-centric model, value is delivered incrementally and the "project" never truly ends until the product is retired.

   b. Create a final project report based on the current milestones achieved to satisfy the committee.

   c. Advise the committee that "Project Closure" has been replaced by "Benefit realization" tracking and continuous discovery.

   d. Request the PMO to redefine the project as a series of smaller projects with clear start and end dates.

167. **The AI hyper-personalization model is found to be inadvertently flagging a specific demographic as "high risk" for CBDC loans, violating ESG and fair-lending policies. The model is already in production. What is the project manager's most urgent action?**

   a. Immediately roll back the model to the previous version and notify the ethics committee.

   b. Start a new sprint to fix the bias while keeping the current model active to avoid revenue loss.

   c. Instruct the data science team to mask the demographic data so the model cannot "see" it.

   d. Consult the legal department to see if the bias falls within "acceptable regulatory margins."

168. **To meet the DORA deadline, the lead architect suggests bypassing the "chaos engineering" testing phase for the CBDC ledger, arguing that the code is "mathematically sound." This would save three weeks. What should the project manager do?**
    a. Accept the suggestion as the DORA deadline is a non-negotiable regulatory constraint.
    b. Reject the suggestion, explaining that DORA requires proven operational resilience, which requires stress testing.
    c. Allow the bypass but document it as high-priority technical debt in the Product Backlog.
    d. Escalate to the Chief Information Security Officer (CISO) for a final decision.

169. **A high-ranking stakeholder from the Retail Banking division demands a feature that directly contradicts the CBDC's privacy-by-design architecture. The stakeholder is known for being "anxious" and demanding. How should the project manager respond?**
    a. Include the feature in the backlog to appease the stakeholder and deprioritize it later.
    b. Facilitate a meeting between the stakeholder and the Chief Privacy Officer to align on regulatory constraints.
    c. Refuse the request immediately, citing the project charter and the BANI nature of the project.
    d. Request the project sponsor to intervene and remove the stakeholder from the steering committee.

170. **During the transition to quantum-safe encryption, it is discovered that 20% of legacy mobile banking apps will no longer be supported. This will alienate a significant customer segment. What is the best strategic move?**
    a. Proceed with the migration; security takes precedence over customer retention in BFSI.
    b. Propose a "Legacy Support" bridge project while developing a phased migration plan for affected customers.
    c. Delay the quantum-safe migration until the marketing team can convince customers to upgrade their devices.
    d. Use a less secure encryption method for the legacy apps to maintain compatibility.

171. **Three key developers on the CBDC team are headhunted by a competitor. The team's velocity drops significantly during a critical sprint. What should the scrum master/project manager do?**
    a. Ask the remaining team members to work overtime to maintain the velocity.
    b. Inform the product owner that the sprint goal is at risk and re-negotiate the scope of the current sprint.
    c. Immediately hire contractors at a higher rate to replace the lost developers.
    d. Cancel the current sprint and restart once new resources are onboarded.

172. **The procurement department selects a cloud vendor that is 20% cheaper but has a poor carbon footprint rating, which conflicts with the Bank's new ESG-focused project charter. How should the project manager proceed?**
    a. Approve the vendor to stay under budget; ESG is a "soft" requirement.
    b. Recommend the more expensive, green-certified vendor, highlighting the "benefit-to-risk" ratio regarding the bank's reputation.
    c. Ask the cheaper vendor to provide a plan to improve their carbon footprint over the next 5 years.
    d. Split the workload between both vendors to balance cost and ESG requirements.

173. **The development team is using scrum, but the regulatory reporting team requires a detailed Gantt chart and 6-month predictive milestones for DORA audits. How can the project manager bridge this gap?**
    a. Force the dev team to switch to Waterfall to ensure compliance.
    b. Implement a "hybrid" reporting layer where scrum outputs (velocity/burndown) are mapped to high-level predictive milestones.

c. Tell the regulatory team that agile does not support Gantt charts and they must adapt to the new way of working.

d. Hire a dedicated "Project Coordinator" to manually create fake milestones for the auditors.

174. The CBDC pilot is technically successful, but user adoption is 40% lower than projected in the business case. The project sponsor wants to close the project as a "technical success." What should the project manager do?

a. Agree and close the project; the PM's job is technical delivery.

b. Advocate for an "Extended Discovery" phase to identify and solve the barriers to user adoption.

c. Update the benefits realization plan to reflect the lower adoption rates and close the project.

d. Suggest a massive marketing campaign to "force" adoption before closing the project.

175. The bank's primary data center is located in a region where political tensions are rising. The project manager has a contingency plan to move to a secondary site, but it will increase latency for AI hyper-personalization. What is the best action?

a. Wait for an actual disruption before acting to avoid unnecessary costs.

b. Perform a "Pre-mortem" with the team to refine the transition plan and assess "Latency vs. Resilience" trade-offs.

c. Move to the secondary site immediately to ensure 100% uptime, regardless of latency.

d. Buy insurance to cover the potential losses from a data center outage.

176. A complex AI model fails in production, causing incorrect CBDC ledger entries. The cause is a "black box" interaction that the developers cannot explain. Under BANI, how should the project manager lead the recovery?

a. Pressure the developers until they find the exact root cause.

b. Implement a "Safe-to-Fail" circuit breaker that reverts to human-validated ledger entries while the AI is investigated.

c. Blame the vendor who provided the AI library and seek legal damages.

d. Delete the AI model and return to the previous manual system permanently.

177. The Central Bank suddenly changes the technical specifications for CBDC interoperability. The product owner wants to incorporate this immediately, but it will rewrite 30% of the existing code. How should the project manager handle this?

a. Reject the change as "scope creep" and stick to the original charter.

b. Facilitate a "Pivot vs. Persevere" session with the steering committee to evaluate the strategic necessity of the change.

c. Update the project plan and tell the team to start over.

d. Accept the change but do not tell the stakeholders about the 30% rework to avoid panic.

178. In a high-pressure DORA audit, a junior developer admits they missed a critical security patch 2 months ago. The project manager knows the CISO will be furious. What should the project manager do?

a. Reprimand the developer publicly to show the CISO that errors are not tolerated.

b. Protect the developer's anonymity while focusing the team on an immediate "Search and Remediate" mission.

c. Report the developer to HR for negligence.

d. Hide the error and hope the audit does not find it.

179. The Project Phoenix team is spread across 4 time zones (New York, London, Singapore, and Mumbai). Communication is breaking down, and the Mumbai team feels "left out" of key decisions made in London. What is the best intervention?

a. Require everyone to work "London hours" for three months.

b. Implement a "Follow-the-Sun" documentation policy where every decision is recorded in a shared, asynchronous workspace.

c. Move all key decision-makers to a single location.

d. Stop the Singapore and Mumbai teams from making decisions; they should only execute.

180. **The bank is heavily reliant on a single AI cloud provider. The project manager realizes this is a "Brittle" dependency under the BANI framework. What is the recommended strategy?**

a. Immediately migrate 50% of the workload to a second provider, even if it doubles the cost.

b. Develop a "containerization" and "multi-cloud" strategy to ensure the product can be ported to another provider within 48 hours.

c. Negotiate a 10-year contract with the current provider to ensure they cannot "drop" the bank.

d. Do nothing; the current provider is too big to fail.

181. **The team reports that the "AI training" phase is taking 5 times longer than estimated due to unexpected data complexity. This is a non-linear delay. How should the project manager adjust?**

a. Add more GPUs to the training cluster to force a linear speed-up.

b. Work with the product owner to re-prioritize the "AI-driven" features and focus on "rule-based" features for the MVP.

c. Request a 500% increase in the timeline for this phase.

d. Tell the team to use a smaller, less accurate dataset to finish on time.

Conclusion

This chapter is designed to take readers on a practical journey through contemporary project management concepts, using a variety of question types, contexts, and difficulty levels. By engaging with conceptual questions, case studies, chart interpretations, matching exercises, fill-in-the-blank activities, and complex integrated scenarios, readers can go beyond simple memorization. This approach fosters the development of analytical reasoning, situational judgment, and strategic decision-making skills.

The deliberate separation of answers from many question sets encourages reflection prior to verification, making this chapter ideal for self-study, mentoring, discussions, and advanced exam preparation. Collectively, these question sets aim to enhance not only the understanding of project management principles, tools, and artifacts but also the confidence to apply them effectively in uncertain, value-driven, and dynamic delivery environments.

Similarly, readers are encouraged to tackle the question set in the next chapter, which will further solidify their grasp of concepts across all areas of project management.

References

1. A Guide to the Project Management Body of Knowledge (PMBOK® Guide), Seventh Edition.
2. A Guide to the Project Management Body of Knowledge (PMBOK® Guide), Eighth Edition.
3. Project Management Institute (PMI) Examination Content Outline (ECO) for the PMP® examination.
4. Project management standards, principles, and good practices relating to predictive, adaptive, and hybrid delivery.

Answers

Q. No.	Answers
1	b
2	b
3	b
4	b
5	c
6	b
7	b
8	b
9	a
10	b
11	b
12	d
13	b
14	b
15	b
16	b
17	c
18	b
19	b
20	b
21	b
22	c
23	b
24	c
25	b
26	b
27	b
28	c
29	c
30	b
31	b
32	b
33	b
34	c
35	b

Q. No.	Answers
36	b
37	b
38	c
39	c
40	b
41	b
42	b
43	c
44	b
45	b
46	c
47	b
48	b
49	b
50	b
51	b
52	b
53	b
54	b
55	b
56	b
57	b
58	b
59	b
60	b
61	b
62	b
63	b
64	b
65	b
66	b
67	b
68	b
69	b
70	b

Q. No.	Answers
71	b
72	b
73	b
74	a- ii b- i c- iii d- iv
75	b
76	b
77	b
78	b
79	b
80	b
81	b
82	c
83	c
84	b
85	c
86	b
87	b
88	b
89	c
90	b
91	b
92	b
93	b
94	b
95	b
96	b
97	b
98	b
99	b
100	b
101	b
102	b, d

Q. No.	Answers
103	b
104	b
105	b
106	b
107	a
108	b
109	b
110	b
111	b
112	b
113	b
114	b
115	b
116	a
117	b
118	b
119	b
120	b
121	b
122	b
123	a
124	a
125	a
126	b
127	b
128	b
129	c
130	b
131	b
132	b
133	b
134	b
135	b
136	b
137	b

Q. No.	Answers
138	b
139	a, c, d
140	c
141	c
142	b
143	b
144	c
145	b
146	b
147	b
148	b
149	b
150	b
151	b
152	a, c, e
153	b
154	b
155	b
156	a, b, c
157	b
158	b
159	c
160	b
161	b

Q. No.	Answers
162	b
163	a - ii b - i c - iv d - iii
164	c
165	b
166	a
167	a
168	b
169	b
170	b
171	b
172	b
173	b
174	b
175	b
176	b
177	b
178	b
179	b
180	b
181	b

CHAPTER 11
Practice Set -3

Introduction

This chapter presents a comprehensive set of practice scenarios designed to strengthen conceptual understanding and application-based thinking. It covers a wide range of project management situations across different industries, helping readers interpret realistic case studies, analyze stakeholder concerns, evaluate risks, and choose the most appropriate project manager response in line with PMI principles. Each case is structured to encourage deeper reasoning and practical decision-making, enabling aspirants to connect theory with real-world project environments.

Objectives

By working through this chapter, aspirants will gain an in-depth understanding of the topics covered and develop stronger judgment in applying project management concepts to complex project situations. The objective is to build both confidence and competence, so learners are well prepared to approach the PMP exam with clarity, accuracy, and readiness.

Case study 1: Sustainability transformation

A global fashion brand is transitioning to sustainable materials across its supply chain. Suppliers operate in multiple countries with different regulatory standards and varying maturity in environmental reporting. Marketing wants to announce sustainability progress early to support a highvisibility campaign, while operations warns that supplier readiness is uneven and audit evidence is incomplete. The project uses a hybrid approach: supplier onboarding is managed predictively, while reporting dashboards and stakeholder messaging are iterated in short cycles. The project manager must balance compliance, brand risk, supplier collaboration, and value delivery without creating commitments the organization cannot yet support.

1. **Several suppliers say they will miss the first sustainability milestone because they do not fully understand the new evidence requirements. What should the project manager do first?**
    a. Escalate the issue to the sponsor and request approval to revise the milestone
    b. Work with operations and the suppliers to clarify the requirements and identify the specific capability gaps
    c. Extend the milestone for all suppliers so the program remains fair across regions
    d. Ask the audit team to decide which suppliers should remain in scope

2. **Marketing wants to announce that the brand has achieved full sustainable sourcing, but supplier audits are still incomplete in several regions. What should the project manager do next?**
    a. Approve a limited campaign that highlights the long-term vision rather than current readiness
    b. Ask operations to accelerate audit closure so marketing can keep the original message
    c. Present the current readiness level and recommend messaging that is accurate and supportable

d. Defer the decision to the legal team because reputational statements are outside the project scope

3. **Suppliers in different countries are interpreting the sustainability criteria differently, creating conflicting data submissions. What should the project manager do?**

a. Conduct a cross-supplier clarification workshop and publish a common interpretation guide

b. Ask each regional lead to decide the best interpretation for their suppliers

c. Reduce the reporting detail so suppliers can comply more easily

d. Escalate to the steering committee because the requirement baseline is no longer stable

4. **External environmental auditors request additional evidence for supplier traceability, and the request may affect the reporting sprint currently in progress. What should the project manager do?**

a. Defer the request until the next sprint because the current commitment is already in progress

b. Work with the team to provide the required compliance evidence and replan the sprint if needed

c. Ask the suppliers to respond directly to the auditors so the project team can stay focused on delivery

d. Tell the auditors that the project cannot absorb scope growth during audit season

5. **One strategic supplier requests a two-week extension to complete certification. The delay may affect the launch message but not the pilot rollout. What should the project manager do first?**

a. Approve the extension because the supplier is strategically important

b. Reject the request to protect the original communications plan

c. Assess the impact on commitments, dependencies, and stakeholder expectations before deciding

d. Ask procurement to decide because certification timing is a supplier issue

6. **Operations warns that two suppliers may withdraw because the new requirements exceed their current capabilities. What should the project manager do next?**

a. Immediately begin supplier replacement to protect the program timeline

b. Update the risk register, analyze response options, and prepare contingencies with operations and procurement

c. Remove those suppliers from the current release and continue with the remaining network

d. Ask the sponsor whether supplier retention is more important than sustainability targets

7. **Cultural differences are causing repeated misunderstandings in supplier meetings, even though the project schedule is still on track. What should the project manager do?**

a. Tailor the communication approach and meeting format to the needs of the supplier groups involved

b. Increase the number of status meetings so issues surface more quickly

c. Route all communication through written minutes to avoid interpretation issues

d. Ask regional managers to handle supplier conversations without the core project team

8. **A supplier proposes an alternative eco-material that could reduce cost, but the long-term durability data is limited. What should the project manager do?**

a. Approve the material for the pilot because pilots are designed for experimentation

b. Reject the proposal because uncertain durability could damage the brand

c. Evaluate the option against sustainability goals, quality requirements, and risk tolerance before deciding

d. Ask marketing to decide because the material affects customer perception more than delivery

9. **Marketing asks the project manager to accelerate the supplier rollout so the campaign can launch before a competitor's announcement. What should the project manager do?**
   a. Reprioritize the highest-value regions and negotiate trade-offs based on constraints and readiness
   b. Agree to the acceleration and ask operations to absorb the delivery pressure
   c. Defer the campaign request until all suppliers reach full maturity
   d. Request a formal change only after the accelerated launch is completed successfully

10. **Supplier audits show inconsistent reporting definitions for recycled content, making cross-region dashboards unreliable. What should the project manager do next?**
   a. Pause all reporting until every supplier can produce identical data sets
   b. Implement a standardized reporting template and data dictionary, then rebaseline the dashboard logic if needed
   c. Ask each region to publish its own dashboard to preserve progress while standards mature
   d. Escalate the issue to executive leadership because supplier data quality is outside project control

Case study 2: National railway ticketing modernization

A national railway authority is modernizing its ticketing platform for web, kiosk, and mobile channels while maintaining uninterrupted daily operations. The program involves migrating legacy reservation logic, integrating fare engines across regions, and improving accessibility for passengers with diverse needs. Government oversight is strict, and public trust is sensitive because even small disruptions affect millions of travelers. The delivery approach is hybrid: core migration and compliance work are managed predictively, while customer-facing features are released incrementally. The project manager must balance reliability, transparency, stakeholder expectations, regulatory obligations, and incremental value delivery.

11. **During integration testing, the legacy fare engine crashes intermittently when regional discount rules are applied together. What should the project manager do first?**
   a. Escalate to the transport minister because public systems require executive attention
   b. Work with the technical team to isolate the failure conditions and identify the underlying cause
   c. Suspend all regional discount features so testing can proceed on the base fare logic
   d. Replace the legacy module because intermittent failures indicate it is no longer viable

12. **Government regulators request additional transparency reports on fare-calculation changes that were not originally planned for this release. What should the project manager do?**
   a. Add the reports to the backlog and defer them to a later release because the current scope is committed
   b. Work with the team to provide the required compliance information and adjust plans if needed
   c. Ask the sponsor to negotiate a reduced reporting expectation with the regulators
   d. Continue with the release as planned and submit the reports after go-live

13. **Passenger advocacy groups request mobile-first accessibility features that were not part of the current release scope. What should the project manager do next?**
    a. Reject the request because the scope is already baselined, and accessibility improvements can wait
    b. Evaluate the impact on value, compliance, release timing, and dependencies before deciding
    c. Ask the development team to add the features quietly so passenger trust is protected
    d. Tell the advocacy groups that the product owner will revisit the request after full rollout

14. **Developers are unclear about a newly issued security control for payment-token handling, and work on the mobile release is already underway. What should the project manager do?**
    a. Ask the developers to continue with their best interpretation so that velocity is preserved
    b. Reduce the control to fit the current release schedule and document the gap later
    c. Facilitate immediate clarification with security specialists and align implementation before proceeding further
    d. Stop all mobile work until the sponsor approves a revised delivery plan

15. **The transport minister wants a live demo next week, but the team says the end-to-end booking flow is still unstable. What should the project manager do?**
    a. Agree to the demo and instruct the team to stabilize only the visible screens
    b. Provide a realistic readiness update and propose a safer demo scope aligned to what is stable
    c. Cancel the demo because incomplete demonstrations damage credibility
    d. Ask the minister's office to decide whether the risk is acceptable

16. **Ticketing data from different regions shows inconsistent passenger-category mapping, which is causing inaccurate reports. What should the project manager do next?**
    a. Standardize the mapping rules and data definitions, then update the reporting logic as needed
    b. Ask each region to publish its own report so that progress is not delayed by central alignment
    c. Remove low-volume passenger categories to simplify the data model
    d. Escalate to executive leadership because regional data ownership is outside project control

17. **A vendor requests early payment, stating that delayed cash flow may affect kiosk hardware delivery. What should the project manager do first?**
    a. Approve the request because delivery continuity is more important than contract formality
    b. Review the contract terms and the vendor's performance status before making a decision
    c. Reject the request so other vendors do not expect similar treatment
    d. Ask finance to decide because payment is not a project-management matter

18. **Public complaints increase during beta testing because passengers find the mobile booking flow confusing. What should the project manager do?**
    a. Continue the beta unchanged because real users always resist new interfaces at first
    b. Work with the team to analyze usability feedback and incorporate the highest-value improvements
    c. Pause the beta so dissatisfaction does not become public criticism
    d. Remove advanced features so the booking flow becomes simpler immediately

19. **The team is overwhelmed by parallel modules, and defects are increasing as work in progress expands. What should the project manager do next?**
    a. Add more developers immediately so each module has dedicated coverage
    b. Reprioritize work based on capacity and criticality, and reduce concurrent commitments
    c. Extend the overall schedule before changing team focus so expectations remain realistic
    d. Ask each module lead to decide what can be delayed within their area

20. **A new cybersecurity regulation is announced two months before release. What should the project manager do first?**
    a. Ask the developers to implement stricter controls immediately so the deadline is protected
    b. Conduct a regulatory impact assessment to determine required changes to scope, design, and timing
    c. Pause the project until the legal team confirms the exact obligations
    d. Submit the current release and plan a compliance patch afterward

Case study 3: Agricultural drone deployment program

A government agriculture department is deploying drones for crop monitoring, irrigation analysis, and pest detection across multiple farming regions. Adoption is uneven because some farmers see the drones as intrusive, while others want faster access to actionable insights. Drone pilots are limited, flight permissions vary by district, and weather conditions create operational uncertainty. The project uses a hybrid approach: regulatory approvals and deployment planning are managed predictively, while farmer reports and dashboard improvements are delivered iteratively. The project manager must balance safety, adoption, data quality, and seasonal value delivery.

21. **Farmers in one district are resisting drone flights because they believe the images may be used for tax enforcement rather than crop support. What should the project manager do first?**
    a. Continue flights because delaying would reinforce resistance behavior
    b. Engage the affected stakeholders, clarify the program purpose, and address trust concerns directly
    c. Reduce image resolution so the farmers become more comfortable with drone use
    d. Ask the district administration to mandate participation, so the rollout stays on schedule

22. **Drone pilots report that updated flight-safety protocols are ambiguous, and different teams are interpreting them differently. What should the project manager do?**
    a. Ask the pilots to follow their local judgment because field conditions vary by district
    b. Clarify the procedures with the relevant experts and publish a common operating guide
    c. Suspend all flights until the sponsor approves a revised safety policy
    d. Reduce the number of protocols so pilots can work more quickly

23. **Repeated weather disruptions are delaying field validation of crop-health models, and the planting season is approaching. What should the project manager do next?**
    a. Update the weather-related risk responses and adjust the validation plan to protect the highest-value work
    b. Cancel the field validation because seasonal constraints make complete testing unrealistic
    c. Replace the pilots with teams from less affected regions
    d. Continue the original schedule and accept that some areas will be tested later

24. **Farmers request additional training because they do not understand how to interpret the pest-detection heat maps. What should the project manager do?**
    a. Provide tailored training and examples so farmers can apply the information correctly
    b. Simplify the heat maps by removing secondary indicators and deliver the training later
    c. Delay the rollout until every district can attend the same in-person workshop
    d. Ask local officials to interpret the maps on behalf of the farmers

25. **The drone vendor proposes a new sensor upgrade that could improve pest detection, but it may delay the current release by two weeks. What should the project manager do first?**
    a. Approve the upgrade because improved accuracy is more important than the schedule
    b. Reject the upgrade because seasonal deployment deadlines matter more than technical enhancement
    c. Evaluate the impact on value, timing, testing, and farmer outcomes before deciding
    d. Ask the pilots to decide because they will use the new sensors in the field

26. **Drone imagery from two regions shows inconsistent moisture analysis, making the dashboard unreliable. What should the project manager do next?**
    a. Ask each region to publish separate moisture metrics to avoid delaying the rollout
    b. Investigate the data-quality issue and determine whether calibration, processing, or environmental factors are causing the inconsistency
    c. Reduce the moisture indicators shown on the dashboard until the next release
    d. Replace the drones in the affected regions because hardware inconsistency is the most likely cause

27. **The sponsor wants a faster rollout to show results before the next budget review. What should the project manager do?**
    a. Agree to accelerate and ask the field teams to absorb the pressure
    b. Reprioritize the highest-value districts and negotiate trade-offs based on capacity and seasonal constraints
    c. Delay the rollout until every district can receive the complete solution at once
    d. Request a formal change after the accelerated deployment proves successful

28. **Farmers in low-connectivity areas ask for printed summaries in addition to digital dashboards. What should the project manager do?**
    a. Reject the request because the program is intended to modernize reporting, not preserve paper methods
    b. Tailor the communication format to stakeholder needs while maintaining the digital product strategy
    c. Delay the rollout until connectivity conditions improve across all districts
    d. Remove dashboard enhancements so the team can focus on printed outputs instead

29. **Drone pilots request additional safety equipment after near-miss incidents during windy conditions. What should the project manager do?**
    a. Approve the equipment immediately because safety concerns should never wait
    b. Evaluate the safety need, feasibility, and cost impact, then act based on the findings
    c. Reject the request because training should be enough to manage field risk
    d. Ask the farmers to fund the equipment since they benefit from the drone results

30. **A drone crashes during testing with no injuries, but the incident raises concern among pilots and local officials. What should the project manager do first?**
    a. Pause the entire program until a new drone model is selected
    b. Initiate an incident investigation and determine corrective actions before resuming similar tests
    c. Replace the pilot because public confidence depends on visible accountability
    d. Continue testing because no injuries occurred and the schedule is already tight

Case study 4: Hospital pharmacy automation

A hospital is automating pharmacy operations using robotic dispensing, barcode verification, and medication workflow integration across inpatient units. Patient safety is the highest priority, but pharmacists are concerned about role changes, and nurses worry that any disruption could delay treatment. The vendor has strong robotics experience but limited healthcare implementation history. The delivery approach is hybrid: regulatory readiness, validation, and safety protocols are predictive, while interface improvements and workflow refinements are tested iteratively. The project manager must balance safety, adoption, training, vendor coordination, and compliance in a high-risk clinical environment.

31. **Pharmacists fear that automation will reduce their professional role and lead to staffing cuts. What should the project manager do first?**
    a. Tell the pharmacists that staffing decisions are outside the project and should not affect implementation
    b. Conduct a change-impact assessment and engage the pharmacists on how roles and workflows will evolve
    c. Reduce the automation scope so the current staffing model is preserved
    d. Ask hospital leadership to communicate that resistance will not alter the project direction

32. **Nurses report delays in medication dispensing during pilot use of the robotic system, but the source of the delay is unclear. What should the project manager do?**
    a. Ask the nurses to adapt temporarily because pilot periods always involve slower workflows
    b. Facilitate a root cause analysis with nursing, pharmacy, and vendor representatives
    c. Reduce the robot's workload by routing more medications back to manual dispensing immediately
    d. Escalate to the hospital board because clinical delays cannot be tolerated in pilot mode

33. **The vendor requests an extra week for calibration, saying it will reduce dispensing defects but affect the pilot timeline. What should the project manager do first?**
    a. Approve the request because safety-related quality always outweighs schedule
    b. Reject the request because pilot momentum is critical for adoption
    c. Assess the impact on patient safety, schedule, validation, and stakeholder expectations before deciding
    d. Ask the nursing leadership to decide because they experience the downstream impact

34. **The hospital board requests additional safety checks before wider rollout, and the change may affect the validation timeline. What should the project manager do?**
    a. Integrate the safety checks into the plan and rework the rollout timeline if needed
    b. Push back because the pilot already included sufficient validation for operational use
    c. Ask the vendor to perform the checks after go-live, so that schedule slippage is minimized
    d. Reduce other testing activities so the new safety checks can fit without changing dates

35. **Pharmacists request a manual override for urgent medication situations, but the vendor warns that improper use could bypass safety logic. What should the project manager do next?**
   a. Approve the override because clinical urgency should always come before automation controls
   b. Reject the request because any bypass undermines the value of automation
   c. Evaluate the safety, workflow, and governance implications before deciding on the design
   d. Ask the vendor to decide because they understand the technical risk better than the users

36. **During testing, the robot mislabels medication bins in a small number of cases. What should the project manager do first?**
   a. Stop the affected testing path, address the defect immediately, and verify the fix before continuing
   b. Continue testing because a low error rate is acceptable during early validation
   c. Reduce robot speed so mislabeling has less operational impact while testing continues
   d. Delay all testing until the vendor submits a formal corrective-action plan

37. **Nurses want more hands-on practice before the new pharmacy workflow expands to additional wards. What should the project manager do?**
   a. Provide targeted training and simulation time so nurses can build confidence before broader rollout
   b. Delay expansion until every nurse completes the same full training program
   c. Reduce the complexity of the ward workflow so that less training is required
   d. Ask charge nurses to train staff informally while the rollout continues

38. **The vendor wants to postpone documentation updates until after rollout so the team can focus on build stabilization. What should the project manager do?**
   a. Approve the delay because working software is more important than documentation in pilot mode
   b. Reinforce the documentation requirements and integrate them into the delivery plan
   c. Ask the pharmacists to maintain the missing documentation after go-live
   d. Reduce documentation detail so the vendor can comply with minimal effort

39. **Hospital leadership wants weekly dashboards on safety incidents, adoption, and dispensing turnaround times. What should the project manager do?**
   a. Tailor the reporting to leadership needs while ensuring the team can sustain the reporting cadence
   b. Reject the request because weekly reporting creates unnecessary overhead during rollout
   c. Ask the vendor to provide the dashboards since most system metrics come from the automation platform
   d. Reduce the dashboard scope to only schedule and budget so reporting stays simple

40. **Pharmacists disagree on the future-state workflow for exception handling, and the conflict is slowing decisions. What should the project manager do?**
   a. Select the workflow personally so the team can move forward without more debate
   b. Escalate the disagreement to hospital leadership because pharmacists own the process outcome
   c. Facilitate a structured discussion focused on patient safety, workflow needs, and decision criteria
   d. Ask the vendor to recommend the workflow that best matches the software design

Case study 5: Renewable energy battery storage project

A renewable energy company is building a large-scale battery storage facility to support grid stability and peak-load balancing. Environmental approvals are strict, the safety profile is complex, and the technology stack is new to much of the team. The project includes civil works, battery module installation, cooling systems, monitoring software, and grid integration. The delivery model is hybrid: regulatory, safety, and construction controls are managed predictively, while dashboards, analytics, and some commissioning activities are refined iteratively. The project manager must balance safety, technical reliability, regulatory compliance, stakeholder confidence, and schedule pressure tied to market incentives.

41. **Environmental approval for a cooling-system component is delayed, and construction sequencing may be affected. What should the project manager do first?**
    a. Assess the impact on schedule, dependencies, and alternative work paths before deciding on corrective action
    b. Replace the environmental consultant because approvals should have been anticipated earlier
    c. Reduce the environmental scope to preserve the construction sequence
    d. Continue with the original plan and absorb the delay later in commissioning

42. **Battery modules overheat during commissioning tests, and engineers disagree on whether the issue is software tuning or hardware configuration. What should the project manager do?**
    a. Facilitate a technical investigation to identify the cause before deciding on corrective action
    b. Continue testing because the issue may stabilize as the modules are conditioned
    c. Replace the battery vendor because overheating is unacceptable in any form
    d. Delay the entire project until the sponsor approves a recovery strategy

43. **Civil and electrical engineers disagree on cooling-system design trade-offs, and the conflict is slowing the final design review. What should the project manager do?**
    a. Select the preferred design personally, so procurement is not delayed
    b. Escalate the disagreement to the sponsor because the issue is affecting the schedule
    c. Facilitate a structured discussion using safety, reliability, and lifecycle criteria
    d. Ask the vendor to choose the design that is easiest to support after handover

44. **The sponsor asks whether testing can be shortened to qualify for an expiring market incentive. What should the project manager do?**
    a. Approve a shorter test cycle because market timing is critical to project value
    b. Present the safety and reliability risks, then explore other options for meeting incentive goals
    c. Ask the engineering lead to decide whether reduced testing is acceptable
    d. Delay the incentive discussion until commissioning is complete

45. **A new battery-safety regulation is announced during construction, and its applicability to the current design is not yet clear. What should the project manager do first?**
    a. Ask the engineers to implement stricter controls immediately so that rework is minimized
    b. Conduct a compliance impact assessment to determine required design and schedule changes
    c. Pause all construction until the legal team provides the final interpretation
    d. Reduce the project scope so the regulation affects fewer systems

46. **A major equipment vendor requests early payment, claiming that delayed cash flow could affect the delivery of the thermal monitoring system. What should the project manager do first?**
    a. Review the contract terms and the vendor's delivery status before deciding
    b. Approve the request because monitoring-system delays would create project-wide risk
    c. Reject the request so that payment governance remains consistent across suppliers
    d. Ask finance to decide because payment timing is outside the project scope

47. **Test data from installed battery strings show inconsistent discharge performance across identical configurations. What should the project manager do next?**
    a. Accept the variation because commissioning data often stabilizes over time
    b. Reduce the test scope so commissioning can proceed on schedule
    c. Facilitate a root cause analysis of the performance inconsistency
    d. Replace the battery strings in the lowest-performing section immediately

48. **Local community groups raise concerns about fire risk and emergency preparedness near the battery site. What should the project manager do?**
    a. Share the validated safety approach, listen to concerns, and engage stakeholders in the response plan
    b. Explain that safety concerns are already covered by the environmental approval process
    c. Reduce the facility capacity so the community sees that the company is responsive
    d. Delay construction until the community fully supports the project

49. **The sponsor requests weekly demonstrations of monitoring dashboards and commissioning progress, but the team says that preparing demos is taking time away from defect resolution. What should the project manager do?**
    a. Reject the request because defect resolution is more important than sponsor visibility during commissioning
    b. Tailor the demo cadence and scope so stakeholder needs are met without overwhelming the team
    c. Ask engineers to rotate demo preparation on top of their existing workload
    d. Stop demonstrations until all critical defects are closed

50. **Engineers request an additional thermal-simulation tool that could improve commissioning decisions but would require extra cost and onboarding time. What should the project manager do first?**
    a. Approve the tool because better modeling is critical in a high-risk energy project
    b. Reject the request because new tools introduced late usually reduce delivery efficiency
    c. Evaluate the expected value, cost, implementation effort, and timing before deciding
    d. Ask the sponsor to decide because the request affects the project budget

Case study 6: Airline reservation system moderization

A major international airline is modernizing its reservation ecosystem to support dynamic pricing, partner-airline interoperability, loyalty integration, and high-volume digital booking across regions. The program replaces parts of a 20-year-old architecture with cloud-based services while preserving mission-critical booking continuity. Teams are distributed across time zones, and integration with partner carriers is uneven because standards and readiness vary. Marketing wants a global campaign tied to the launch, but legal and architecture teams warn that some markets have unresolved data-residency and performance concerns. The project uses a hybrid delivery model: migration controls and regulatory readiness are managed predictively, while customer-facing capabilities are iterated in shorter cycles. The project manager must balance operational stability, partner coordination, legal compliance, customer experience, and schedule pressure without creating commitments the delivery teams cannot yet support.

51. **Multi-city itineraries fail intermittently during end-to-end testing, but single-leg bookings remain stable. What should the project manager do first?**
    a. Delay the launch until every booking path has zero defects
    b. Work with the team to isolate the failure pattern and determine the underlying cause
    c. Remove multi-city booking from the release so the remaining scope stays on schedule
    d. Ask partner airlines to validate their interfaces before the internal team continues testing

52. **Partner airlines request changes to the shared API specifications after integration work has already started. What should the project manager do next?**
    a. Approve the changes to protect partner relationships and avoid future disputes
    b. Evaluate the impact on scope, testing, partner dependencies, and release timing before deciding
    c. Reject the changes because integration standards should not move once the build begins
    d. Ask marketing to decide because partner interoperability affects the launch campaign

53. **Marketing wants to keep the aggressive launch date even though architects warn that stability risk remains high in peak-load scenarios. What should the project manager do?**
    a. Commit to the date and ask the technical team to focus only on the most visible issues
    b. Present the risks clearly and explore trade-offs such as phased scope, pilot markets, or revised timing
    c. Cancel the launch campaign because technology constraints should drive all business decisions
    d. Ask the sponsor to decide whether the team should accept the technical risk

54. **Legal raises concerns that some customer data may violate regional data-residency rules in the proposed cloud design. What should the project manager do first?**
    a. Ask engineers to implement stricter controls immediately so that rework is minimized
    b. Conduct a compliance impact assessment to determine what design and release changes are required
    c. Pause the migration program until legal confirms the final interpretation for every country
    d. Move all customer data to one region to simplify governance

55. **Integration issues with partner airlines appear to come from different interpretations of the same API standard. What should the project manager do?**
    a. Facilitate a joint technical workshop and publish clarified interface rules for all partners
    b. Ask each partner to continue with their own interpretation so the release can keep moving

c. Remove interoperability features from the first release and revisit them later

d. Replace the integration team because a shared standard should not produce inconsistency

56. **Distributed teams in three regions are making local decisions that later conflict during integration. What should the project manager do next?**

a. Increase the amount of documentation and require all decisions to be made in writing

b. Establish a clearer coordination cadence, decision path, and integration review rhythm across teams

c. Reduce the number of participating regions so coordination becomes simpler

d. Ask each regional lead to decide independently and reconcile conflicts during final testing

57. **The sponsor pressures the project manager to accelerate delivery so the airline can announce modernization progress before a competitor. What should the project manager do?**

a. Reprioritize the highest-value capabilities and negotiate trade-offs based on constraints and risk

b. Agree to the acceleration and ask the teams to absorb the extra pressure

c. Defer all launch communication until the full program is complete

d. Submit a formal change only after the accelerated release succeeds

58. **Cloud migration testing reveals latency spikes during price recalculation under load. What should the project manager do first?**

a. Reduce cloud usage and move critical services back to the legacy platform

b. Facilitate a technical performance analysis to identify the source of the bottleneck

c. Delay all remaining testing until the cloud architecture is redesigned

d. Accept the latency temporarily because it may normalize in production

59. **QA teams in different regions are using inconsistent test data, which is creating conflicting defect results. What should the project manager do next?**

a. Standardize the test data strategy and align teams on common definitions and scenarios

b. Allow each region to keep its own data because local realism is more important than comparability

c. Reduce the number of end-to-end tests so data inconsistency affects fewer results

d. Replace the QA lead in the region generating the highest number of defects

60. **Developers request an additional performance-testing tool that could improve bottleneck detection but would require extra budget and onboarding time. What should the project manager do first?**

a. Reject the request because adding tools late usually slows delivery

b. Approve the request because performance assurance is critical in airline systems

c. Evaluate the expected value, cost, implementation effort, and timing before deciding

d. Ask QA to decide because they will use the tool most often

Case study 7: Renewable energy wind farm construction

A renewable energy developer is constructing a coastal wind farm that includes turbine foundations, access roads, grid interconnection, environmental monitoring, and remote operations capability. The project is under strong public scrutiny because local communities are concerned about noise, visual impact, and the effect on protected bird habitats. Supply delays for imported blades are threatening the construction sequence, while early commissioning tests show vibration anomalies in several turbines. The project uses a hybrid approach: civil works, approvals, and safety controls are managed predictively, while monitoring dashboards and some commissioning refinements are delivered iteratively. The sponsor wants to accelerate commissioning to qualify for expiring incentives, but environmental auditors and engineers warn that unresolved technical and compliance risks remain. The project manager must balance safety, environmental compliance, community trust, technical reliability, and market-timing pressure.

61. **Imported turbine blade shipments are delayed, and the civil contractor asks whether installation crews should be reassigned. What should the project manager do first?**
    a. Reassign the crews immediately so no site labor remains idle
    b. Assess the schedule impact, dependency chain, and alternative work paths before deciding
    c. Cancel near-term installation activities until the supplier confirms a fixed date
    d. Ask the contractor to absorb the delay because blade logistics are a procurement issue

62. **Community leaders demand additional consultation sessions because residents are concerned about turbine noise at night. What should the project manager do?**
    a. Decline the request because the project already completed the required public meetings
    b. Plan additional stakeholder engagement focused on concerns, data, and response options
    c. Ask the sponsor to handle community relations so the project team can stay focused on construction
    d. Reduce turbine operating hours immediately to demonstrate goodwill

63. **Environmental auditors request additional documentation on bird-migration monitoring that was not included in the original plan. What should the project manager do?**
    a. Integrate the required documentation work into the plan and adjust activities if needed
    b. Push back on the request because late documentation changes will disrupt commissioning
    c. Ask the environmental consultant to respond independently so the core team can protect the schedule
    d. Delay all construction until the auditors complete their review

64. **Engineers disagree on turbine placement trade-offs between wind capture and environmental exposure. What should the project manager do?**
    a. Choose the design personally so permitting is not delayed
    b. Facilitate a structured discussion using agreed technical and environmental criteria
    c. Escalate the disagreement to the sponsor because schedule pressure is increasing
    d. Ask the contractor to choose the easiest placement for construction

65. **Early commissioning tests show vibration anomalies in several turbines. What should the project manager do first?**
   a. Continue commissioning because minor anomalies are common in new equipment
   b. Facilitate a root-cause investigation before deciding on corrective action or rollout impact
   c. Replace the turbine vendor because vibration indicates unacceptable quality
   d. Stop the entire program until the sponsor approves a recovery strategy

66. **The sponsor wants to accelerate commissioning to qualify for expiring incentives. What should the project manager do?**
   a. Approve the acceleration and ask the teams to absorb the pressure
   b. Present the constraints and risks, then explore trade-offs such as phased commissioning or revised scope
   c. Reject the request because incentive-driven dates are outside project control
   d. Submit a formal change only after the faster commissioning succeeds

67. **Unpredictable coastal weather is causing repeated schedule slips in foundation work. What should the project manager do next?**
   a. Update the risk responses and resequence work to protect the most critical milestones
   b. Accept the delay because weather risk cannot be influenced
   c. Replace the contractor because the schedule performance is slipping
   d. Reduce the number of turbines in the first phase

68. **Residents raise concerns about night-time turbine noise after construction begins. What should the project manager do?**
   a. Explain that noise is already covered by the approval process and continue as planned
   b. Engage stakeholders, review the evidence, and discuss response options based on actual impact
   c. Commit immediately to redesigning turbine placement so concerns are resolved quickly
   d. Pause all turbine work until the community withdraws its objections

69. **Engineers request an advanced simulation tool that could improve turbine-placement decisions but would require extra budget and onboarding time. What should the project manager do first?**
   a. Approve the tool because better modeling is always worth the cost in large infrastructure projects
   b. Reject the request because introducing tools late usually slows execution
   c. Evaluate the expected value, cost, timing, and adoption effort before deciding
   d. Ask the sponsor to decide because the request affects the budget

70. **Environmental approval for one turbine cluster is delayed, and the contractor asks whether work should continue elsewhere. What should the project manager do first?**
   a. Continue all work as planned because one cluster should not affect the full site
   b. Assess the impact on dependencies, permits, and sequencing before deciding on alternative work
   c. Replace the environmental consultant because the delay threatens incentives
   d. Reduce the environmental scope so the approval can be simplified

Case study 8: Luxury hotel chain renovation program

A luxury hotel chain is renovating flagship properties across Asia and Europe while keeping each hotel partially operational. The program includes lobby redesigns, room upgrades, **Heating, Ventilation, and Air Conditioning (HVAC)** modernization, and smart-room automation. Guest experience is highly sensitive because renovations directly affect paying customers and brand reputation. Contractors vary in maturity, premium materials are delayed, and local regulations differ across countries. Hotel managers want strict work-hour controls to reduce guest disruption, while the sponsor keeps proposing additional wellness and premium-service features. A new fire-safety regulation in one market adds inspection demands, and quality checks reveal finish inconsistencies across properties. The project uses a hybrid approach: construction controls and regulatory work are managed predictively, while customer-facing design refinements and smart-room features are iterated in shorter cycles. The project manager must balance guest experience, design consistency, compliance, contractor performance, and schedule pressure across multiple locations.

71. **Guests are complaining about noise during daytime room renovations at an active property. What should the project manager do?**
    a. Stop all renovation work until occupancy decreases
    b. Adjust work schedules and sequencing to reduce disruption while preserving progress where possible
    c. Continue the work unchanged because renovation inconvenience is unavoidable
    d. Offer discounts to guests instead of changing the work plan

72. **A contractor requests early payment, claiming that delayed cash flow will affect premium-fixture procurement for two properties. What should the project manager do first?**
    a. Approve the payment so material continuity is protected across all properties
    b. Review the contract terms, contractor performance status, and governance rules before deciding
    c. Reject the request so that other contractors do not expect similar treatment
    d. Ask finance to decide because payment timing is outside the project scope

73. **The sponsor proposes adding wellness-center features to two hotels after design packages are already approved. What should the project manager do next?**
    a. Approve the features because premium amenities are central to the hotel brand
    b. Reject the idea because design changes always create a delay late in construction
    c. Evaluate the impact on scope, procurement, guest areas, and schedule before deciding
    d. Ask the design team to include the features quietly so the sponsor remains satisfied

74. **Supply delays for premium materials are threatening lobby completion dates in multiple properties. What should the project manager do first?**
    a. Assess the schedule impact, dependencies, and alternative sourcing or sequencing options before deciding
    b. Replace all delayed suppliers immediately so a stronger message is sent to the market
    c. Accept lower-grade materials so opening dates remain unchanged
    d. Pause renovation work across all properties until shipments are confirmed

75. **A new fire-safety regulation in one country requires additional inspections before room floors can reopen. What should the project manager do?**
    a. Integrate the required inspections into the plan and adjust reopening activities if needed
    b. Delay the inspections until the current renovation wave is complete so the contractor can stay productive
    c. Ask the contractor to proceed and document the inspections after guest areas reopen

d. Reduce the renovation scope in that country so compliance becomes easier

76. **Quality reviews show visible finish differences between renovated rooms in different flagship hotels. What should the project manager do next?**
    a. Accept the variation because local contractors naturally apply finishes differently
    b. Implement targeted quality audits and clarify finish standards across properties
    c. Replace the contractors at the properties with the most visible defects
    d. Reduce the design specification detail so future differences attract less attention

77. **The design team remains split between two lobby concepts, and the disagreement is delaying procurement packages. What should the project manager do?**
    a. Select the concept personally so procurement can proceed without further delay
    b. Escalate the disagreement to the sponsor because design disputes are outside PM authority
    c. Facilitate alignment using agreed brand, guest-experience, and operational criteria
    d. Ask the contractor to choose the concept that is easiest to construct

78. **Hotel managers demand stricter work-hour controls after complaints from high-paying guests increase. What should the project manager do?**
    a. Reject the request because schedule pressure is already too high across properties
    b. Tailor the work-hour policy and sequencing to reduce disruption while protecting critical milestones
    c. Reduce the renovation scope so that less daytime work is needed
    d. Ask contractors to decide their own work hours based on local convenience

79. **The sponsor requests weekly dashboards comparing guest disruption, budget, and completion status across properties. What should the project manager do?**
    a. Reject the request because weekly reporting will create too much administrative effort
    b. Tailor the reporting to sponsor needs while ensuring the team can sustain the cadence
    c. Reduce the dashboard to only schedule data so preparation remains simple
    d. Ask contractors to provide the dashboards directly to the sponsor

80. **Contractors in different countries are working from inconsistent installation instructions for smart-room components. What should the project manager do?**
    a. Replace the contractors using the least consistent interpretation of the instructions
    b. Reduce design complexity so different instructions matter less in practice
    c. Standardize instructions and documentation, then confirm alignment across all properties
    d. Continue work and reconcile differences during final snagging

Case study 9: Logistics fleet automation program

A logistics company is automating its fleet with telematics devices, route-optimization software, predictive maintenance triggers, and real-time driver-behavior monitoring. The goal is to reduce fuel cost, improve delivery reliability, and increase asset visibility across regions. Drivers worry that the system may be used for disciplinary action rather than operational improvement, while fleet managers request more analytics and dispatchers want more flexibility in route changes. During pilot testing, some telematics devices fail intermittently, creating inaccurate location data, and the optimization engine produces inconsistent route recommendations in congested areas. Legal warns that driver-consent and privacy requirements vary by country. The vendor wants to defer some documentation work to maintain rollout speed, while the sponsor wants to accelerate deployment to capture fuel savings this quarter. The project manager must balance adoption, privacy, technical reliability, operational value, and schedule pressure in a hybrid delivery environment.

81. **Drivers say the new monitoring system feels intrusive and may be used against them. What should the project manager do first?**
    a. Tell the drivers that adoption is mandatory because the company has already invested in the platform
    b. Conduct a change-impact assessment and clarify how the data will be used and governed
    c. Reduce the monitoring features so drivers become more comfortable with the rollout
    d. Ask regional managers to enforce compliance individually in their depots

82. **Several telematics devices fail intermittently during pilot runs, creating inaccurate location tracking. What should the project manager do?**
    a. Continue the pilot because early device instability is normal and can be corrected after rollout
    b. Facilitate a root cause analysis to determine whether the issue is hardware, installation, or network-related
    c. Replace all telematics devices with a different model immediately
    d. Reduce the pilot scope so the remaining devices can be monitored more closely

83. **The sponsor wants to accelerate rollout to capture fuel savings this quarter, but the route-optimization engine is still inconsistent in congested urban routes. What should the project manager do?**
    a. Approve the acceleration and ask dispatch teams to work around engine inconsistencies manually
    b. Review constraints and negotiate trade-offs such as phased rollout, route exclusions, or revised timing
    c. Delay the program until every route type performs equally well under all traffic conditions
    d. Ask the drivers to decide which rollout pace is acceptable

84. **Drivers request additional training because they do not understand how behavior scores affect coaching and dispatch decisions. What should the project manager do?**
    a. Provide targeted training with practical examples so drivers can understand and use the system effectively
    b. Reject the request because the rollout schedule cannot absorb more training time
    c. Delay the rollout until every driver completes the same extended training program
    d. Remove behavior scoring from the first release so training becomes unnecessary

85. **The route-optimization engine gives inconsistent recommendations for similar delivery patterns in urban areas. What should the project manager do?**
    a. Facilitate a technical deep-dive to determine whether the issue is data quality, constraints, or model logic
    b. Simplify the algorithm immediately so dispatchers can work with more predictable outputs
    c. Replace the vendor because route inconsistency undermines trust in the program
    d. Ignore the issue until more routes have been added to the pilot

86. **Legal warns that driver-consent and privacy obligations vary by country and may affect how monitoring data is stored and used. What should the project manager do first?**
    a. Ask the vendor to implement stricter controls immediately so the program stays on schedule
    b. Conduct a privacy impact assessment to determine what changes are required by the jurisdiction
    c. Pause the rollout in every country until a universal policy is approved
    d. Reduce data collection globally so the legal issue is avoided altogether

87. **Regional managers request customized dashboards for fuel use, driver behavior, and maintenance trends. What should the project manager do?**
    a. Approve the dashboards because local managers understand their own regions best
    b. Reject the request because customization creates unnecessary complexity in enterprise systems
    c. Evaluate the impact on value, consistency, and implementation effort before deciding
    d. Ask the vendor to choose which dashboard variations should be supported

88. **The vendor wants to postpone documentation updates until after rollout so the team can focus on stabilization. What should the project manager do?**
    a. Approve the deferral because operational software matters more than documentation during pilot delivery
    b. Reinforce the documentation requirements and integrate them into the delivery plan
    c. Ask dispatchers to maintain the missing documentation after go-live
    d. Reduce the documentation scope so the vendor can comply with less effort

89. **Driver resistance remains high in one region even after initial communication sessions. What should the project manager do next?**
    a. Replace the drivers who continue to resist the new system
    b. Address the specific concerns through tailored engagement, local champions, and targeted support
    c. Reduce the rollout scope in that region so the rest of the program can proceed faster
    d. Ignore the resistance because adoption usually improves once the system is mandatory

90. **Fleet managers want additional predictive analytics on maintenance and fuel trends, but the current release is already tightly planned. What should the project manager do?**
    a. Approve the analytics because leadership visibility is central to the program's value
    b. Reject the request because the current plan cannot absorb more work
    c. Evaluate the impact on value, capacity, and release objectives before deciding
    d. Ask the sponsor to decide which analytics matter most

Case study 10: Insurance claims automation system

A large insurance company is automating claims intake, triage, fraud detection, and workflow routing using AI-assisted classification and business-rule orchestration. The program aims to shorten claim cycle time, reduce operating costs, and improve customer visibility. Claims processors worry that automation will reduce their role to exception handling, while customer-service teams want real-time claim status updates and clearer messages for policyholders. During testing, the AI model misclassifies certain claim types and produces inconsistent fraud-risk scores for similar cases. Compliance warns that regulators require explainability for automated decisions, and IT security raises concerns about sensitive customer data being used in training sets. The sponsor wants to accelerate rollout to capture cost savings this fiscal year, while data migration reveals missing and duplicate claim records in the target platform. The project manager must balance regulatory compliance, trust in AI outputs, data quality, customer experience, and delivery pressure in a high-scrutiny insurance environment.

91. **Claims processors fear that automation will reduce their role and limit career growth. What should the project manager do first?**
    a. Tell the processors that role decisions are outside the project and should not affect adoption
    b. Conduct a change-impact assessment and engage them on future workflows and responsibilities
    c. Reduce the automation scope so current roles remain mostly unchanged
    d. Ask HR to announce that staffing decisions are not under discussion

92. **The AI model misclassifies several claim types during testing, causing incorrect routing. What should the project manager do?**
    a. Continue the rollout because a small error rate is expected in early model training
    b. Facilitate a technical analysis to determine whether the issue is data quality, labeling, or model logic
    c. Reduce the number of claim categories so the model has fewer routing decisions to make
    d. Replace the vendor because classification accuracy is already undermining trust

93. **Compliance states that regulators require explainability for automated claim decisions. What should the project manager do first?**
    a. Ask the vendor to add more explanation fields immediately so the rollout date is protected
    b. Conduct a compliance impact assessment to determine what design and process changes are required
    c. Pause all AI-related work until regulators publish more detailed examples
    d. Replace automated decisions with manual routing in every case

94. **Customer-service teams request real-time claim status updates for policyholders. What should the project manager do?**
    a. Approve the feature because customer transparency is central to the transformation strategy
    b. Reject the request because the current release is already tightly planned
    c. Evaluate the impact on value, dependencies, and release objectives before deciding
    d. Ask the sponsor to decide because customer experience is a business issue

95. **IT security warns that sensitive customer data in the model-training set may create privacy and governance risk. What should the project manager do first?**
    a. Reduce the training data immediately so the model can continue improving with less risk
    b. Conduct a privacy impact assessment to determine what controls or changes are required
    c. Ask the vendor to take ownership because training-set management is their technical responsibility
    d. Delay the project until the security team provides a final approval memo

96. **The sponsor wants to accelerate rollout this fiscal year to capture operating-cost savings. What should the project manager do?**
    a. Approve the acceleration and ask the claims teams to absorb the operational risk temporarily
    b. Review constraints and negotiate trade-offs such as phased rollout, limited claim categories, or revised timing
    c. Delay the rollout until every automation component performs perfectly across all claim types
    d. Ignore the request because cost pressure should not influence project decisions

97. **The AI model produces inconsistent fraud-risk scores for similar claim patterns. What should the project manager do?**
    a. Continue rollout because fraud scoring will improve after more production data is collected
    b. Facilitate a technical analysis to determine whether the inconsistency comes from data, feature selection, or model behavior
    c. Reduce the fraud-detection model to a simpler rule set immediately
    d. Replace the AI vendor because trust in the scoring model is already damaged

98. **Customer-service teams request clearer claim-status messages because policyholders do not understand what the current updates mean. What should the project manager do?**
    a. Reject the request because messaging improvements are outside the automation scope
    b. Tailor the communication design to user needs and assess the implementation effort

c. Reduce the number of claim states shown to customers so the issue disappears

d. Ask the vendor to decide which messages are easiest to support technically

99. **The IT security team warns that historical training data may include sensitive personal information that was not approved for model use. What should the project manager do?**

a. Ignore the warning because the model has already been trained on the data set

b. Conduct a privacy impact assessment and determine the required remediation actions

c. Reduce the training data volume and continue model tuning without further review

d. Delay the project indefinitely until all old data is revalidated manually

100. **Data migration reveals both missing and duplicate claim records in the new platform. What should the project manager do first?**

a. Continue the migration because the remaining records can be corrected after go-live

b. Replace the migration team because data defects should not occur at this stage

c. Facilitate a data-quality analysis to identify the source and scope of the migration issue

d. Reduce the migrated data fields so the record set becomes easier to reconcile

Case study 11: Smart port digitalization program

A major coastal port authority is implementing a digital transformation program to automate cargo handling, vessel scheduling, customs clearance, and yard management. The port handles millions of containers annually, and recurring congestion has increased vessel delays, demurrage costs, and public pressure for modernization. The program includes IoT sensors on cranes, AI-assisted berth allocation, and a blockchain-enabled customs documentation flow that must integrate with legacy crane-control systems and agency databases.

Stakeholders include shipping lines, customs officials, freight forwarders, crane operators, environmental regulators, and multiple vendors. Crane operators fear automation will reduce their role, while customs teams worry about transparency, data access, and auditability. During testing, the berth-allocation engine gives conflicting recommendations during peak periods, and sensor data from similar cranes does not align consistently across terminals.

Meanwhile, a vendor requests early payment due to cash-flow issues, the sponsor wants to accelerate rollout before the next fiscal review, and regulators request additional environmental documentation related to new digital infrastructure. The project uses a hybrid approach: compliance, procurement, and infrastructure controls are managed predictively, while dashboards and some operational workflows are refined iteratively. The project manager must balance adoption, integration risk, compliance, operational continuity, and schedule pressure.

101. **Crane operators fear that automation will reduce their role and influence in terminal operations. What should the project manager do first?**

a. Tell the operators that modernization decisions are already final and should not affect rollout

b. Conduct a change-impact assessment and engage the operators on future workflows and responsibilities

c. Reduce the automation scope so manual crane control remains the dominant process

d. Ask terminal leadership to communicate that resistance will not change the program direction

102. **Customs officials are concerned that the blockchain documentation flow may expose data in ways that conflict with existing oversight rules. What should the project manager do first?**

a. Remove the blockchain component so customs can continue using current methods

b. Conduct a compliance impact assessment to determine what controls or design changes are required

c. Ask the vendor to reassure customs that blockchain records are inherently secure

d. Delay the customs integration until after the rest of the port platform is live

103. **IoT modules are failing to integrate consistently with legacy crane-control systems across terminals. What should the project manager do?**

a. Replace the legacy crane systems so the new digital stack can proceed without constraint

b. Facilitate a joint technical workshop to align integration assumptions and identify the source of the mismatch

c. Reduce the IoT rollout to a single terminal until legacy systems are retired

d. Ask the vendor to own all integration issues because the modules are part of its solution

104. **The berth-allocation engine gives conflicting recommendations during peak traffic periods. What should the project manager do first?**

a. Continue with the rollout because the engine will improve after more operational data is collected

b. Reduce the AI logic to a simpler rule set immediately, so outputs become more predictable

c. Facilitate a technical deep-dive to determine whether the inconsistency is caused by data, constraints, or model behavior

d. Delay the entire port program until the berth-allocation engine is fully redesigned

105. **Environmental regulators request additional documentation about the new digital infrastructure's energy use and site impact. What should the project manager do?**

a. Integrate the documentation work into the plan and adjust activities if needed

b. Push back because the program's main objective is operational efficiency, not environmental reporting

c. Ask the infrastructure vendor to respond independently so rollout dates are protected

d. Delay the digital rollout until the regulators approve every subsystem in advance

106. **A vendor requests early payment, claiming that delayed cash flow could affect the deployment of key terminal equipment. What should the project manager do first?**

a. Approve the payment because equipment delays would threaten the entire program timeline

b. Review the contract terms, current delivery status, and governance rules before deciding

c. Reject the request so other suppliers do not expect the same treatment

d. Ask finance to decide because vendor payments are outside project scope

107. **The sponsor wants to accelerate rollout to improve port competitiveness before the next fiscal review. What should the project manager do?**

a. Approve the acceleration and ask terminal teams to absorb the delivery pressure

b. Review constraints and negotiate trade-offs such as phased rollout, reduced scope, or revised timing

c. Delay all communication until the full program is complete and stable

d. Submit a formal change only after the faster rollout succeeds

108. **Freight forwarders request additional dashboard features for shipment visibility and queue forecasting. What should the project manager do?**

a. Approve the request because better visibility is central to the port modernization strategy

b. Reject the request because the current release is already committed

c. Evaluate the impact on value, capacity, dependencies, and release objectives before deciding

d. Ask the vendor to decide which features are easiest to support technically

109. **IoT sensor data from similar cranes is inconsistent across terminals, making utilization analytics unreliable. What should the project manager do?**
   a. Ignore the inconsistency because trends will stabilize once more data is collected
   b. Replace all sensors in the least reliable terminal first
   c. Facilitate a data-quality and root cause analysis to identify calibration, configuration, or environmental issues
   d. Reduce the analytics scope so fewer sensor inputs affect the dashboard

110. **Customs officials ask for weekly progress reviews on integration, auditability, and adoption readiness. What should the project manager do?**
   a. Reject the request because weekly reporting would create too much overhead for the team
   b. Tailor the communication cadence and content to customers' needs while ensuring the team can sustain it
   c. Reduce the updates to monthly summaries so reporting remains simple
   d. Ask the sponsor to handle customs communication directly

Case study 12: University research management system

A large university is implementing a centralized research-management system to streamline grant applications, ethics approvals, publication tracking, budget monitoring, and collaboration workflows. Researchers currently rely on fragmented local tools, which creates duplicated effort, inconsistent data, and compliance gaps across departments. The new platform must integrate with grant agencies, internal finance, departmental repositories, and identity systems while remaining easy to use for both faculty and research administrators.

Senior professors resist adoption because they believe the system increases administrative burden, while junior researchers want mobile-friendly workflows and simpler collaboration features. The ethics committee requires stricter access controls for sensitive studies, and finance reports repeated mismatches between budget codes and research records during testing. The vendor requests more time to stabilize the grant-agency APIs, but the sponsor wants to announce the launch at a major academic conference.

The project uses a hybrid approach: compliance, data migration, and integration controls are managed predictively, while dashboards, mobile workflows, and some user-facing capabilities are refined iteratively. The project manager must balance academic culture, compliance, technical stability, and schedule pressure.

111. **Senior professors resist adopting the system because they believe it adds unnecessary administration. What should the project manager do first?**
   a. Tell the professors that the transformation has already been approved and adoption is expected
   b. Conduct a change-impact assessment and engage them on workflow concerns and future benefits
   c. Reduce the system scope so manual grant administration remains the dominant method
   d. Ask department heads to enforce compliance without further discussion

112. **Finance reports repeated mismatches between budget codes and research records during integration testing. What should the project manager do?**
   a. Facilitate a root cause analysis with finance, data, and integration teams
   b. Replace the finance interface because repeated mismatches indicate an incompatible design
   c. Remove low-value budget fields so data mapping becomes easier
   d. Continue testing and correct the mismatches after launch

113. **The ethics committee demands stricter access controls for sensitive studies. What should the project manager do first?**
   a. Delay the full rollout until every access-control scenario is redesigned
   b. Conduct a compliance impact assessment to determine required design and process changes
   c. Ask the vendor to add stricter permissions immediately, so the launch date is protected
   d. Remove access to sensitive-study workflows from the first release entirely

114. **The vendor requests two additional weeks to stabilize the grant-agency APIs. What should the project manager do first?**
   a. Approve the request because external-agency integration is too important to challenge
   b. Reject the request because the conference date cannot be moved
   c. Assess the impact on schedule, dependencies, and launch commitments before deciding
   d. Ask the sponsor to decide whether the delay is acceptable

115. **The sponsor wants to announce the launch at an academic conference, but the pilot dashboard shows Week 6 increases in API defects, finance mismatches, and ethics access issues. What should the project manager do?**
   a. Approve the announcement because adoption has improved from 48% to 57%
   b. Present the readiness trend transparently and recommend messaging that matches the actual pilot status
   c. Ask the vendor to accelerate fixes so the original conference message remains accurate
   d. Delay all conference communication until the entire system is fully deployed across campus

116. **Junior researchers request mobile-friendly collaboration features that were not in the current release plan. What should the project manager do?**
   a. Approve the request because junior researchers are the most frequent daily users
   b. Reject the request because the current release is already committed
   c. Evaluate the impact on value, dependencies, and release objectives before deciding
   d. Ask senior professors to decide whether the feature is necessary

117. **External grant-agency integration is delayed, and the team is unsure whether to continue building dependent workflows. What should the project manager do first?**
   a. Continue all dependent work unchanged so the team does not lose momentum
   b. Assess the impact on sequencing, dependencies, and alternative work paths before deciding
   c. Replace the integration team because the dependency is now threatening the launch
   d. Remove the dependent workflows from the release immediately

118. **Researchers say the new workflows are confusing and slow them down. What should the project manager do?**
   a. Ask users to adapt because every new platform creates temporary discomfort
   b. Conduct workflow clarification sessions and gather targeted usability feedback
   c. Reduce the number of workflow steps immediately so the issue disappears
   d. Delay rollout until every department agrees on the same preferred process

119. **The sponsor requests weekly demos for deans and grant administrators, but the team says demo preparation is affecting defect resolution. What should the project manager do?**
   a. Reject the demos because fixing quality issues is more important than stakeholder visibility
   b. Tailor the demo cadence and scope so stakeholder needs are met without overwhelming the team
   c. Ask the vendor to run the demos so the project team can stay focused on delivery
   d. Stop demos until all critical defects are closed

120. **Data migration reveals missing publication and grant records in the new platform. What should the project manager do first?**
   a. Continue migration because the remaining records can be corrected after go-live
   b. Replace the migration team because records should not be missing at this stage
   c. Facilitate a data-quality analysis to identify the source and scope of the migration issue
   d. Reduce the number of migrated fields so reconciliation becomes simpler

Case study 13: National emergency response platform

A national disaster-management agency is building an emergency-response platform that integrates real-time weather feeds, **Geographic Information System (GIS)** mapping, resource allocation, medical triage coordination, and citizen alerts. The platform must support millions of concurrent users during crises and enable police, fire, medical, meteorology, and local government agencies to coordinate through a shared operational view.

During integration, GIS layers load inconsistently across regions, the alert-broadcast module shows performance risk under load, and cybersecurity auditors flag vulnerabilities in citizen-notification controls. Medical teams request additional triage features, while meteorology officials demand higher-frequency weather updates. The sponsor wants to accelerate rollout before monsoon season, but local governments say the training materials are too technical for field teams.

The vendor also requests early payment due to cash-flow pressure. The project manager must balance life-critical reliability, compliance, multi-agency coordination, and schedule pressure.

121. **GIS layers load inconsistently across regions during integration. What should the project manager do first?**
   a. Facilitate a technical root cause analysis with GIS, infrastructure, and regional teams
   b. Replace the GIS vendor because mapping inconsistency is unacceptable in an emergency platform
   c. Reduce GIS features so the system becomes simpler to stabilize
   d. Continue testing and correct the issue after launch

122. **Cybersecurity auditors flag vulnerabilities in the citizen-alert controls. What should the project manager do first?**
   a. Conduct a security impact assessment to determine what fixes are required before release
   b. Ignore the issue temporarily because monsoon readiness is more important than security perfection
   c. Reduce the alert features so the vulnerabilities affect fewer workflows
   d. Delay the program indefinitely until every security concern is closed

123. **Medical teams request additional triage features that are not part of the current release. What should the project manager do?**
    a. Approve the features because medical users are critical stakeholders in emergency response
    b. Reject the request because the release scope is already committed
    c. Evaluate the impact on value, dependencies, and release objectives before deciding
    d. Ask the sponsor to decide because triage is operational rather than technical

124. **Local governments say the training materials are too technical for field teams. What should the project manager do?**
    a. Ask field teams to adapt because operational systems are naturally complex
    b. Tailor and simplify the training materials to the needs of field responders and local staff
    c. Delay rollout until every region can attend the same advanced training program
    d. Reduce platform features so the training burden is lower

125. **A vendor requests early payment, claiming that delayed cash flow could affect infrastructure support for the alert-broadcast module. What should the project manager do first?**
    a. Approve the request because alerting reliability is too important to risk
    b. Review the contract terms, delivery status, and governance rules before deciding
    c. Reject the request so other suppliers do not expect the same treatment
    d. Ask finance to decide because payment timing is outside the project scope

126. **The sponsor wants to accelerate rollout before the monsoon season. What should the project manager do?**
    a. Approve the acceleration and ask agencies to absorb the delivery pressure
    b. Review constraints and negotiate trade-offs such as phased rollout, narrowed scope, or revised timing
    c. Delay communication until the full platform is ready nationwide
    d. Reduce testing so the launch date can still be achieved

127. **Based on the load-test table, which issue should the project manager prioritize first before a broader rollout?**
    a. Weather-feed latency, because it is 18 seconds above target
    b. GIS refresh time, because it is almost three times the target
    c. Field-team training completion is below 70%
    d. Alert delivery success, because failing to meet 99.5% reliability directly threatens citizen notification during crises

128. **Agencies complain that the end-to-end workflows are unclear across jurisdictions. What should the project manager do?**
    a. Ask agencies to adapt because emergency procedures are always complex
    b. Conduct cross-agency workflow clarification workshops and align decision points
    c. Reduce the number of workflow steps immediately so the issue disappears
    d. Delay rollout until every agency agrees on one identical process

129. **The alert-broadcast module performs poorly under load. What should the project manager do first?**
    a. Approve the rollout because most non-peak test results are acceptable
    b. Reduce the number of alerting scenarios in the first release
    c. Facilitate a performance analysis to identify the bottleneck before selecting a mitigation
    d. Replace the alerting vendor because emergency systems cannot tolerate weak performance

130. **Multiple agencies demand different dashboard layouts. What should the project manager do?**
   a. Approve all requests so each agency gets exactly what it wants
   b. Reject all requests because standardization is always more efficient
   c. Evaluate the impact on value, consistency, and implementation effort before prioritizing
   d. Ask the vendor to decide which dashboard variations should be supported

131. **A key stakeholder becomes unresponsive during planning, and several decisions now lack input. What should the project manager do?**
   a. Escalate immediately because silent stakeholders create project risk
   b. Remove the stakeholder from the register because they are no longer participating
   c. Tailor the engagement strategy and re-establish a communication path suited to the stakeholder
   d. Continue planning without the input, and correct decisions later if needed

132. **A low-probability risk has an extremely high impact if it occurs. What should the project manager do?**
   a. Ignore it because the probability is low and the team already has many risks
   b. Add it to the risk register and plan an appropriate response or contingency
   c. Convert it to an issue so leadership takes it more seriously
   d. Remove lower-impact risks and focus only on this one

133. **A team member consistently misses deadlines, and morale is starting to decline. What should the project manager do first?**
   a. Replace the team member before the behavior affects more work
   b. Escalate to functional management immediately
   c. Discuss the issue directly, understand the cause, and coach on expectations and support needed
   d. Reassign the most important tasks to stronger team members permanently

134. **A change request is approved through the project's governance process. What should the project manager do next?**
   a. Implement the change immediately and update documents later so delivery is not delayed
   b. Update the relevant plans, baselines, and communications before coordinating implementation
   c. Ask the sponsor to announce the change so the team understands its importance
   d. Treat the change as minor if it does not affect the end user directly

135. **A vendor submits deliverables that meet most requirements but fail one critical acceptance criterion. What should the project manager do?**
   a. Accept the deliverables because most of the work is complete, and corrections can come later
   b. Reject the deliverables and request correction based on the agreed acceptance criteria
   c. Replace the vendor because missing one critical criterion shows unreliability
   d. Ask the sponsor whether the criterion can be waived to protect the schedule

Case study 14 : National digital identity program

A national government is implementing a digital identity program to provide secure authentication for public services, banking, healthcare, and travel. The solution includes biometric verification, mobile ID apps, service-provider APIs, and integration with multiple ministries. The program is politically sensitive and highly visible because it affects millions of citizens and raises public concerns about inclusion, privacy, and state use of personal data.

During testing, biometric devices show inconsistent accuracy for some enrollment conditions, the cybersecurity team warns about mobile-app vulnerabilities, and privacy groups challenge the proposed data-retention model. Several ministries demand customized workflows, while the vendor requests more time to stabilize the biometric engine. Regional offices also say the training materials are too technical for frontline enrollment staff.

The sponsor wants to announce the program during an upcoming national event, but readiness remains uneven. The project manager must balance political expectations, technical stability, privacy compliance, adoption, and multi-agency coordination.

136. **Biometric devices show inconsistent accuracy during pilot enrolment. What should the project manager do first?**
    a. Approve the rollout because enrolment success is already above 90%
    b. Facilitate a technical root cause analysis to determine whether the issue is device calibration, environment, or matching logic
    c. Replace all biometric devices immediately
    d. Reduce biometric checks so enrolment can proceed more quickly

137. **Privacy groups raise concerns about how citizen data will be retained and used. What should the project manager do first?**
    a. Reduce retention immediately so the concerns go away before launch
    b. Conduct a privacy impact assessment to determine required controls and policy changes
    c. Ask the sponsor to reassure the public that all privacy concerns are already managed
    d. Delay the program indefinitely until every external concern is resolved

138. **The cybersecurity team flags vulnerabilities in the mobile ID app. What should the project manager do?**
    a. Conduct a security impact assessment to determine what fixes are required before release
    b. Ignore the issue temporarily because the national event date cannot be moved
    c. Reduce app features, so the vulnerabilities affect fewer workflows
    d. Delay the entire program until every security concern is fully resolved

139. **Several ministries demand customized onboarding and identity-verification workflows. What should the project manager do?**
    a. Approve all requests so each ministry gets exactly what it wants
    b. Reject all requests because standardization is more efficient
    c. Evaluate the impact on value, consistency, and implementation effort before prioritizing
    d. Ask the vendor to decide which workflow variations are easiest to support

140. **The vendor requests more time to stabilize the biometric engine. What should the project manager do first?**
    a. Approve the request because biometric stability is too important to challenge
    b. Reject the request because the national announcement date cannot change
    c. Assess the impact on schedule, dependencies, and launch commitments before deciding
    d. Ask the sponsor to decide whether the delay is acceptable

141. **The sponsor wants to announce the program during a national event, but the pilot still shows 3 critical mobile-app vulnerabilities and training completion of only 68%. What should the project manager do?**
    a. Approve the announcement because enrolment success is already 94%
    b. Present the readiness data transparently and recommend messaging that matches the actual status
    c. Ask the vendor and training team to accelerate so the original announcement remains accurate

d. Delay all public communication until the full national rollout is complete

142. **Regional offices say the training materials are too technical for frontline enrollment staff. What should the project manager do?**

a. Ask staff to adapt because public-sector systems are naturally complex

b. Tailor and simplify the training materials to the needs of frontline users

c. Delay rollout until every region can attend the same advanced workshop

d. Reduce the system scope, so training becomes easier

143. **Integration with the healthcare ministry is delayed, and dependent workflows may slip. What should the project manager do first?**

a. Continue all dependent work unchanged, so delivery momentum is preserved

b. Assess the impact on sequencing, dependencies, and alternative work paths before deciding

c. Replace the integration team because the dependency now threatens the launch

d. Remove healthcare-related workflows from the release immediately

144. **Citizens demand more transparency about how identity data will be used. What should the project manager do?**

a. Publish clear communication materials explaining the purpose, protections, and governance of data use

b. Reduce data collection immediately before understanding the actual concern pattern

c. Ask the sponsor to reassure the public at the event without changing project communications

d. Delay rollout until public support is unanimous

145. **Which issue in the pilot metrics should the project manager treat as the most urgent blocker before broader rollout?**

a. Enrolment completion success at 94%, because it is 4 points below the target

b. Biometric verification accuracy at 96.5% because it is below the quality target

c. Critical mobile-app vulnerabilities because the target is zero, and unresolved security issues threaten the whole release

d. Frontline training completion at 68% because training is well below the target

146. **Multiple ministries request different reporting formats for identity verification and enrolment. What should the project manager do?**

a. Approve all report variations because each ministry has unique governance needs

b. Reject all format changes so the reporting model stays simple

c. Evaluate the impact and standardize where possible, while allowing justified differences

d. Ask the sponsor to decide which ministry's format should become the national standard

147. **The mobile app crashes under load during pilot testing. What should the project manager do first?**

a. Approve rollout because national-event pressure is too high to miss the date

b. Reduce app functionality immediately so the crashes stop

c. Facilitate load-testing and performance analysis to identify the bottleneck before selecting mitigation

d. Replace the mobile vendor because production-quality apps should not fail under load

148. **Citizens say the enrolment steps are confusing and difficult to follow. What should the project manager do?**

a. Ask citizens to adapt because national ID processes are inherently complex

b. Simplify and clarify the enrolment communications and guidance materials

c. Reduce identity checks, so the workflow feels faster

d. Delay the rollout until every enrolment path is redesigned

149. **The sponsor asks for daily progress updates during the final pilot weeks. What should the project manager do?**
   a. Reject the request because daily reporting will create too much overhead
   b. Tailor the communication cadence and content to sponsor needs while keeping reporting sustainable
   c. Ask the vendor to provide all updates directly to the sponsor
   d. Reduce testing so the team has time to prepare the daily updates

150. **Data migration reveals duplicate citizen records in the pilot environment. What should the project manager do first?**
   a. Continue migration because duplicates can be cleaned up after broader rollout
   b. Replace the migration team because duplication should not happen at this stage
   c. Facilitate a data-quality analysis to identify the source and scope of the duplication problem
   d. Reduce the number of migrated fields so reconciliation becomes easier

Case study 15: National healthcare telemedicine platform

A national health authority is implementing a telemedicine platform to support remote consultations, digital prescriptions, AI-assisted triage, and care coordination across hospitals, pharmacies, insurance providers, and regional clinics. The platform is intended to expand access, reduce in-person congestion, and improve continuity of care, especially in underserved areas. However, stakeholder needs differ sharply: physicians want clinically safe workflows, rural clinics struggle with bandwidth limitations, pharmacies need reliable prescription integration, and insurers demand accurate, real-time claim validation.

During testing, video consultations drop frequently in low-bandwidth regions, the AI triage engine misclassifies a small but meaningful set of symptoms, and the cybersecurity team flags vulnerabilities in the prescription-generation module. The sponsor wants to accelerate rollout to address rising patient loads before winter, while the vendor requests more time to stabilize the video engine. The project uses a hybrid approach: regulatory, security, and integration controls are managed predictively, while patient-facing workflows and dashboards are refined iteratively.

The project manager must balance clinical safety, access, privacy, technical reliability, and schedule pressure.

151. **Doctors say the consultation interface is unintuitive and slows clinical work. What should the project manager do first?**
   a. Tell the doctors that workflow disruption is expected in any digital transition
   b. Conduct usability workshops and collect targeted clinical workflow feedback
   c. Reduce the number of telemedicine features so the interface becomes simpler immediately
   d. Ask hospital leadership to require adoption without further changes

152. **Video consultations frequently drop in low-bandwidth rural regions. What should the project manager do first?**
   a. Reduce video quality for all users so the issue disappears consistently
   b. Facilitate a technical analysis of bandwidth, session handling, and fallback options
   c. Delay the entire rollout until every region can support stable high-definition video
   d. Replace the rural-clinic equipment before investigating the problem further

153. **The AI triage engine misclassifies a small but meaningful set of symptoms. What should the project manager do?**
   a. Continue the rollout because a small error rate is acceptable in early deployment
   b. Reduce AI usage immediately and rely only on manual triage from now on
   c. Facilitate a clinical and technical deep-dive to determine whether the issue comes from training data, logic, or workflow design
   d. Replace the AI vendor because patient trust depends on visible action

154. **The cybersecurity team flags vulnerabilities in the prescription-generation module. What should the project manager do first?**
   a. Conduct a security impact assessment to determine the severity and required fixes before release
   b. Ignore the issue temporarily because patient demand is rising and access is the top priority
   c. Reduce prescription functionality so fewer workflows are exposed
   d. Delay the entire telemedicine program until every security item is closed

155. **Pharmacies request additional integration features for refill synchronization. What should the project manager do?**
   a. Approve the request immediately because pharmacy integration is central to continuity of care
   b. Reject the request because the current release scope is already committed
   c. Evaluate the impact on value, dependencies, and release objectives before deciding
   d. Ask the sponsor to decide because pharmacies are an external stakeholder group

156. **Insurance providers demand real-time claim validation within teleconsultation workflows. What should the project manager do?**
   a. Ignore the request because telemedicine should focus only on care delivery
   b. Evaluate feasibility, value, and dependency impact before deciding whether to include it now
   c. Reduce insurance integration so the platform remains clinically focused
   d. Ask the vendor to decide whether the request is easy enough to implement

157. **The vendor asks for more time to stabilize the video engine. What should the project manager do first?**
   a. Approve the delay because video reliability is clearly more important than timing
   b. Reject the request because winter demand requires the original date
   c. Assess the impact on schedule, dependencies, and rollout commitments before deciding
   d. Ask the sponsor to choose between delay and reliability

158. **The sponsor wants to accelerate rollout before winter demand peaks. What should the project manager do?**
   a. Approve the acceleration and ask care teams to absorb the operational risk temporarily
   b. Reduce testing so the schedule can be protected
   c. Review constraints and negotiate trade-offs such as phased rollout, narrower scope, or revised timing
   d. Ignore the request because business timing should not affect project decisions

159. **Based on the telemedicine pilot quality snapshot, which issue should the project manager treat as the most urgent blocker before broader rollout?**
   a. Video session completion at 92%, because access failures affect care continuity
   b. AI triage accuracy at 93.5%, because clinical quality is below target
   c. Two critical prescription-module vulnerabilities, because the target is zero and unresolved security issues can block safe release
   d. Rural-clinic training completion at 64%, because adoption readiness remains low

160. **Rural clinics ask for lower-bandwidth consultation modes and simpler training materials. What should the project manager do?**
   a. Reject the request because the platform strategy is built around full-feature video care
   b. Tailor the solution and enablement approach to rural connectivity and user needs
   c. Delay the rollout until all clinics can support the same high-bandwidth experience
   d. Remove advanced consultation features from the platform entirely

Case study 16: Smart agriculture irrigation network

A national agriculture ministry is deploying a smart irrigation network using soil-moisture sensors, automated valves, weather-based irrigation scheduling, and mobile dashboards for farmers. The solution is intended to reduce water waste, improve crop reliability, and support drought resilience across thousands of farms with very different soil conditions and connectivity levels. Farmers want clear and practical guidance, while regional officers need reporting that supports water-allocation policy and environmental compliance.

During pilot testing, moisture sensors show inconsistent readings across soil types, weather data integration fails during storms, and the automated valve controller still needs more testing. The sponsor wants to accelerate rollout before the next planting season, while environmental regulators request clearer documentation on water-usage optimization. Farmers say the dashboard is too technical, and several regions ask for offline access because connectivity is intermittent.

The project manager must balance seasonal value, farmer adoption, data quality, environmental compliance, and rollout timing.

161. **Moisture sensors show inconsistent readings across different soil types. What should the project manager do first?**
   a. Replace all sensors because inconsistent readings mean the hardware is unreliable
   b. Facilitate a root cause analysis to determine whether calibration, installation, soil characteristics, or processing logic is causing the issue
   c. Reduce sensor usage so fewer inconsistent readings affect the dashboard
   d. Continue rollout and correct the readings after more seasonal data is collected

162. **Farmers say the dashboard is too technical and difficult to use. What should the project manager do?**
   a. Ask the farmers to adapt because digital agriculture tools are naturally complex
   b. Simplify the dashboard language and design based on targeted user feedback
   c. Remove advanced features immediately so the interface looks simpler
   d. Delay rollout until every region agrees on one common dashboard preference

163. **Weather-data integration fails during storms, when accurate irrigation guidance is most important. What should the project manager do first?**
   a. Replace the weather-data provider because storm failures are unacceptable
   b. Facilitate a technical analysis to determine whether the issue is provider availability, network resilience, or integration logic
   c. Remove weather-based scheduling from the current release
   d. Continue the rollout and warn farmers that storm guidance may be unavailable

164. **Regional officers request additional reporting features for water-allocation decisions. What should the project manager do?**
   a. Approve the features because policy reporting is central to the ministry's mission
   b. Reject the request because the release scope is already committed

c. Evaluate the impact on value, implementation effort, and release objectives before deciding

d. Ask the vendor to decide which reports are easiest to build

165. **The vendor says the automated valve controller needs more testing before broader rollout. What should the project manager do first?**

a. Approve the additional testing time immediately because water-control reliability is critical

b. Reject the request because planting-season timing is more important than more testing

c. Assess the impact on schedule, dependencies, and seasonal commitments before deciding

d. Ask the sponsor to decide whether reliability or timing matters more

166. **Environmental regulators request documentation on water-usage optimization and environmental benefit. What should the project manager do?**

a. Integrate the documentation work into the plan and adjust activities if needed

b. Delay the documentation until after the first planting season, so operational value can be demonstrated first

c. Ask the vendor to respond independently so the schedule stays protected

d. Reduce the environmental reporting scope so compliance becomes easier

167. **The sponsor wants to accelerate rollout before the next planting season. What should the project manager do?**

a. Approve the acceleration and ask the field teams to absorb the delivery pressure

b. Reduce testing so the schedule can still be achieved

c. Review constraints and negotiate trade-offs such as phased rollout, limited regions, or revised timing

d. Ignore the request because seasonal pressure should not affect project decisions

168. **Farmers in low-connectivity areas request an offline mode for the dashboard. What should the project manager do?**

a. Approve the feature immediately because adoption depends on access

b. Reject the request because offline support adds too much complexity

c. Evaluate feasibility, value, and implementation effort before deciding

d. Ask the vendor to decide whether offline mode is practical

169. **Based on the irrigation pilot dashboard, which issue should the project manager prioritize first before broader rollout?**

a. Moisture-reading consistency at 91%, because inaccurate data affects irrigation decisions directly

b. Automated valve success rate at 93%, because failed execution undermines reliability

c. Weather-data availability during storms at 89%, because missing data during high-risk conditions weakens scheduling confidence

d. Farmer dashboard adoption is at 62%, because low adoption prevents the solution from delivering the intended field value at scale

170. **Farmers request printed quick-reference guides in addition to the app. What should the project manager do?**

a. Reject the request because printed materials are inconsistent with a digital strategy

b. Provide printed materials and tailored guidance where they improve adoption and usability

c. Delay the rollout until every region can use only the digital materials successfully

d. Remove advanced features so the printed guide becomes unnecessary

171. **The chart shows both SPI and CPI trending downward over time. SPI falls well below 1.0, indicating worsening schedule performance, while CPI moves toward 0.90, showing weakening cost efficiency. The best PMI-style response is to analyze the trend, identify root causes, and reforecast outcomes before choosing corrective actions.**

A project manager reviews the SPI/CPI trend chart and sees SPI decline from 0.92 to 0.84 over the last three reporting periods, while CPI declines from 0.96 to 0.90. What should the project manager do next?

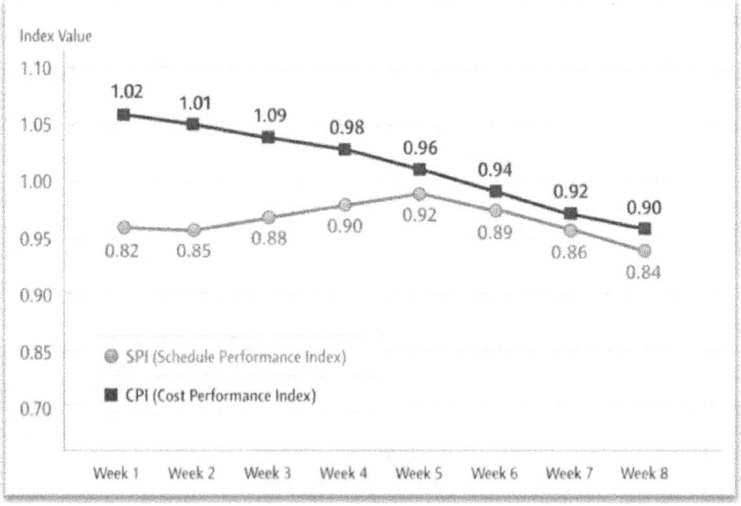

Figure 11.1: *SPI-CPI trend chart*

a. Escalate immediately because both indicators are below 1.0
b. Analyze the trend, identify root causes, and update the forecast before recommending action
c. Reduce the scope immediately because the schedule and cost are both deteriorating
d. Ask the sponsor to choose whether cost or schedule should be prioritized

172. **The heat map shows the relative exposure of five risks. The highest-priority risk is the one in the highest combined probability and impact zone. A risk in a very high probability and high impact zone should typically be prioritized ahead of a low probability but very high impact risk because overall exposure is greater and more immediate.**

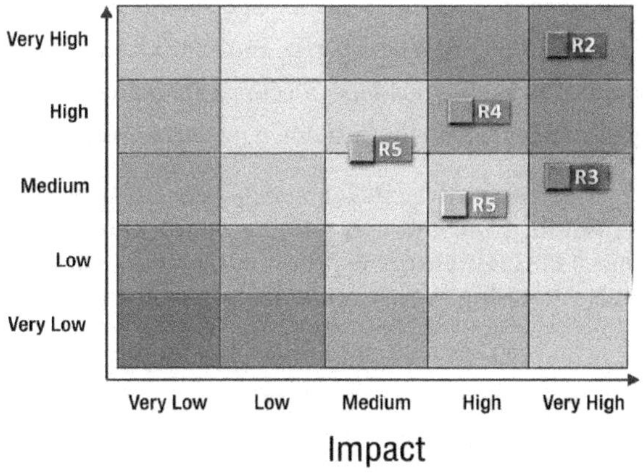

Figure 11.2: *Risk heat map*

A project manager reviews the risk heat map and notes that R2 is plotted at very high probability and high impact, while R3 is plotted at low probability and very high impact. Which risk should the project manager prioritize first?

a. R3, because impact is always more important than probability

b. R2, because its overall exposure is higher due to the stronger likelihood of occurring

c. Both risks are equal, because any risk in a red zone should be treated the same

d. Neither risk until the sponsor decides which one matters more

173. **The burndown chart flattens after the middle of the sprint, and the velocity bars decline across recent sprints. Together, these patterns suggest that the team is struggling with delivery flow, capacity, or blockers rather than facing a one-time variance. The strongest PMI response is to inspect the cause with the team, adjust planning, and improve flow rather than simply push the team harder.**

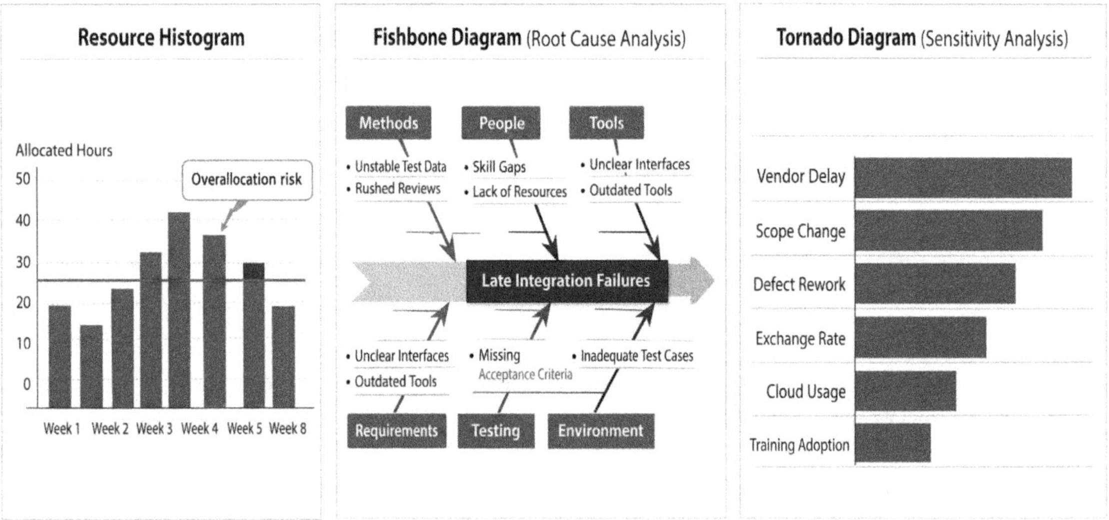

Figure 11.3: *Burndown and velocity chart*

A project manager reviews the burndown and velocity chart and sees the actual burndown flatten after Day 6 while team velocity drops from 34 to 23 over recent sprints. What is the best next action?

a. Increase the sprint commitment so the team can recover lost delivery faster

b. Meet with the team to inspect blockers, reassess capacity, and adjust future sprint planning

c. Escalate to the sponsor because the team is no longer meeting expectations

d. Replace underperforming team members so the burndown returns to target

174. **The dashboard shows only 35% supportive stakeholders, with 20% resistant and 15% unaware. Communication timeliness is declining, and end-user training completion is far lower than sponsor-office and PMO readiness. The strongest PMI response is to prioritize targeted stakeholder engagement and end-user readiness rather than simply increasing generic communication volume.**

Stakeholder engagement dashboard		
Indicator	**Status**	**Direction**
Supportive stakeholders	35%	Needs improvement
Resistant stakeholders	20%	Reduce

Stakeholder engagement dashboard		
Indicator	**Status**	**Direction**
Unaware stakeholders	15%	Reduce
Communication timeliness	Declining	Improve
Sponsor-office readiness	88%	Strong
PMO readiness	84%	Strong
End-user training completion	61%	Needs improvement

A project manager reviews the stakeholder engagement dashboard and sees declining communication timeliness, only 35% supportive stakeholders, and end-user training completion at 61%. What should the project manager prioritize next?

a. Increase the number of weekly status emails sent to all stakeholders

b. Focus on targeted engagement for resistant and unaware groups while strengthening end-user training and benefit communication

c. Ask the sponsor to announce that the project will proceed regardless of stakeholder sentiment

d. Stop stakeholder reporting until training completion reaches the target

175. **A bar chart compares schedule variance across five workstreams: Integration (-12 days), testing (-4 days), Training (-9 days), Procurement (+2 days), and Reporting (-3 days). Which conclusion is most appropriate?**

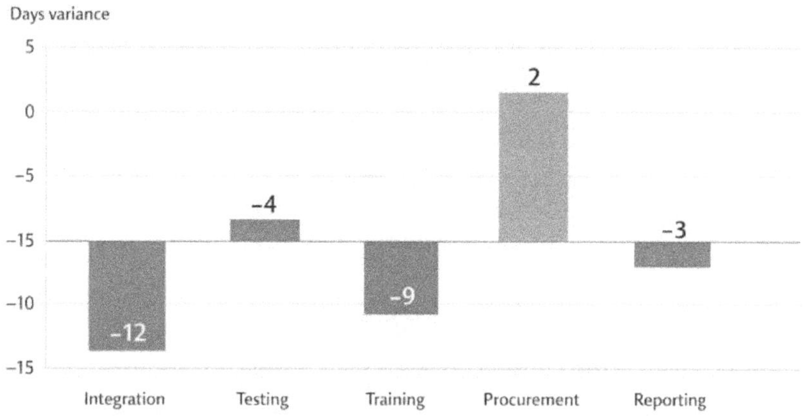

***Figure 11.4:** Schedule variance by workstream*

a. Procurement should be prioritized because a positive variance means it is the most unstable

b. Integration is the largest schedule concern and may also be affecting downstream workstreams, such as testing and training

c. Reporting is the highest risk because it has the smallest negative variance and may be hidden

d. Testing should be escalated first because quality work is always more important than schedule variance

176. **A line chart shows actual defect closure tracking below the forecast for four consecutive weeks, and the gap widens each week. What is the best interpretation?**

a. The team is recovering because both lines continue moving downward over time

b. The forecast is no longer reliable because the delivery system is underperforming relative to plan and needs reassessment

c. The issue is minor because actual closure is still improving, just more slowly than expected

d. The sponsor should be asked to choose a new target immediately before the team reviews the trend

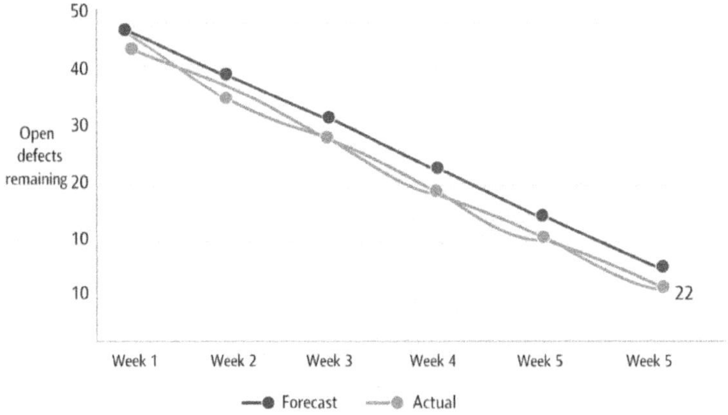

Figure 11.5: Defect closure – Forecast vs. actual

177. **A pie chart shows stakeholder sentiment by share of influence: Supportive 40%, Neutral 25%, Resistant 20%, and Unaware 15%. Which action is most justified?**

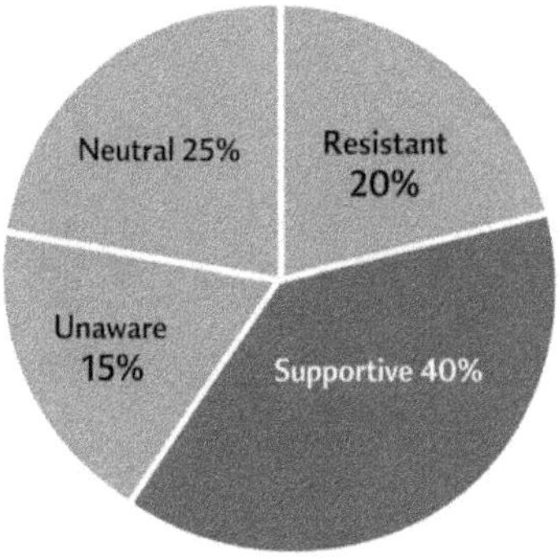

Figure 11.6: Stakeholder influence distribution

a. Focus only on the largest slice because supportive stakeholders already control the outcome

b. Prioritize conversion of resistant and unaware stakeholders because together they represent 35% of influence that could materially affect outcomes

c. Ignore neutral stakeholders because they are not currently creating visible resistance

d. Treat all groups equally because pie charts do not show urgency

178. **A scatter plot shows that teams with lower training hours per person have consistently higher error rates, while teams with more training show fewer errors. What is the strongest interpretation?**

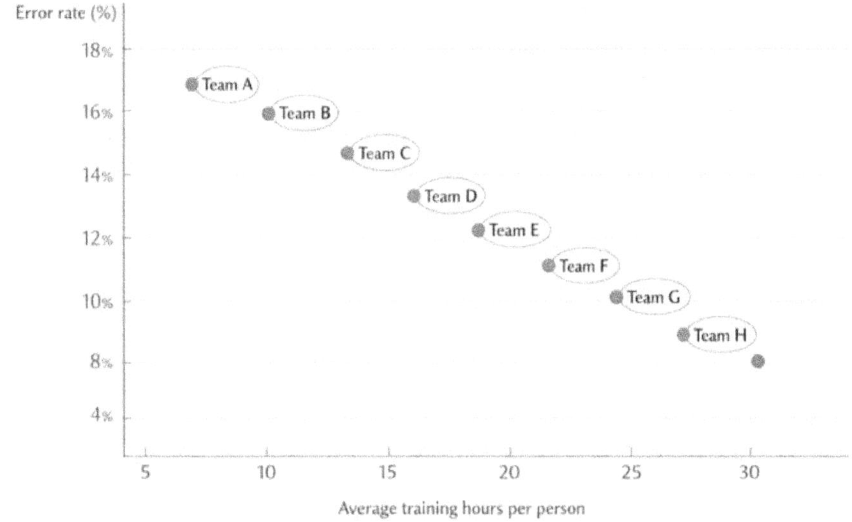

Figure 11.7: *Training rate vs. error rate*

a. Training is likely a meaningful factor in performance quality and should be investigated as a lever for reducing errors
b. Error rates can be ignored because scatter plots do not prove causation
c. The highest-performing team should be copied exactly without any further analysis
d. Training should be paused so the project can verify whether errors decline naturally over time

179. **A stacked column chart compares defect composition across three releases and shows technical defects decreasing, but configuration and data-mapping defects increasing steadily. What is the best conclusion?**

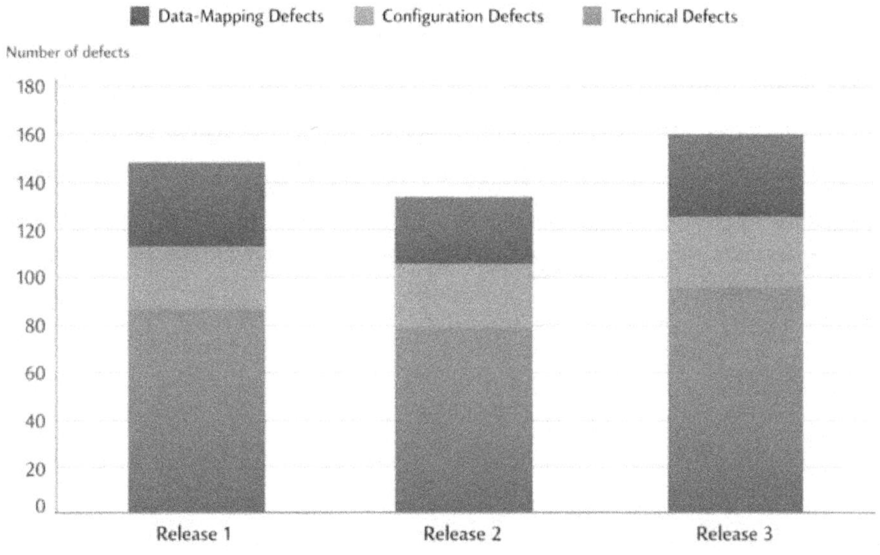

Figure 11.8: *Defect composition by release*

a. Overall quality is improving because one defect category is decreasing
b. The project should shift attention toward environment/configuration and data-governance controls because the defect mix is changing
c. Technical defects remain the only meaningful concern because they were originally the largest category
d. The release process should be accelerated because the team has already solved the hardest issues

180. **A run chart of cycle time shows one sustained sequence of eight points above the median after a process change was introduced. What should the project manager infer first?**

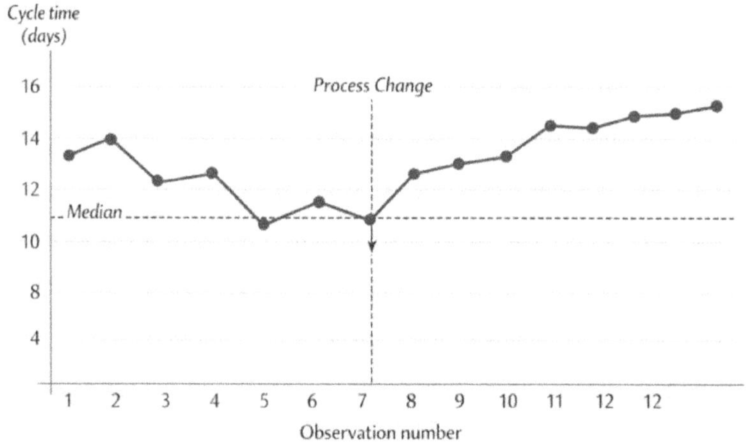

Figure 11.9: *Cycle time run chart*

a. The process is stable because all points are still within historical extremes
b. The shift suggests a likely special-cause change in the process, so the recent change should be reviewed for impact
c. The team is improving because cycle time data is now more consistent than before
d. The median should be ignored because run charts are useful only for schedule reporting

References

1. A Guide to the Project Management Body of Knowledge (PMBOK® Guide), Seventh Edition.
2. A Guide to the Project Management Body of Knowledge (PMBOK® Guide), Eighth Edition.
3. Project Management Institute (PMI) Examination Content Outline (ECO) for the PMP® examination.
4. Project management standards, principles, and good practices relating to predictive, adaptive, and hybrid delivery.

Answers

Q. No.	Answer
1	b
2	c
3	a
4	b
5	c
6	b
7	a
8	c
9	a
10	b
11	b
12	b
13	b
14	c
15	b
16	a
17	b
18	b
19	b
20	b
21	b
22	b
23	a
24	a
25	c
26	b
27	b
28	b
29	b
30	b
31	b
32	b

Q. No.	Answer
33	c
34	a
35	c
36	a
37	a
38	b
39	a
40	c
41	a
42	a
43	c
44	b
45	b
46	a
47	c
48	a
49	b
50	c
51	b
52	b
53	b
54	b
55	a
56	b
57	a
58	b
59	a
60	c
61	b
62	b
63	a
64	b

Q. No.	Answer
65	b
66	b
67	a
68	b
69	c
70	b
71	b
72	b
73	c
74	a
75	a
76	b
77	c
78	b
79	b
80	c
81	b
82	b
83	b
84	a
85	a
86	b
87	c
88	b
89	b
90	c
91	b
92	b
93	b
94	c
95	b
96	b

Q. No.	Answer
97	b
98	b
99	b
100	c
101	b
102	b
103	b
104	c
105	a
106	b
107	b
108	c
109	c
110	b
111	b
112	a
113	b
114	c
115	b
116	c
117	b
118	b
119	b
120	c
121	a
122	a
123	c
124	b
125	b
126	b
127	d
128	b

Q. No.	Answer
129	c
130	c
131	c
132	b
133	c
134	b
135	b
136	b
137	b
138	a
139	c
140	c
141	b
142	b
143	b
144	a
145	c
146	c

Q. No.	Answer
147	c
148	b
149	b
150	c
151	b
152	b
153	c
154	a
155	c
156	b
157	c
158	c
159	c
160	b
161	b
162	b
163	b
164	c

Q. No.	Answer
165	c
166	a
167	c
168	c
169	d
170	b
171	b
172	b
173	b
174	b
175	b
176	b
177	b
178	a
179	b
180	b

CHAPTER 12
Practice Set -4

Introduction

This collection of questions is designed with care to help learners explore the practical aspects of project management. Here, you will find a range of scenarios that reflect the real-world challenges and situations project managers often face.

As learners engage with this question set, they will not only test their knowledge but also explore how to apply essential project management principles, tools, and techniques in everyday situations. Each question is crafted to spark critical thinking and encourage learners to reflect on their experiences, making the learning process both meaningful and relevant.

This question set is more than just a test; it's an opportunity for learners to grow and enhance their skills. By thoughtfully considering each question, learners can connect theoretical concepts to practical applications, gaining insights that will benefit them in their future projects.

As learners navigate through the questions, they will develop a stronger foundation in project management practices, preparing them to tackle challenges with confidence and creativity.

Objectives

The objective of this practice set is to cultivate disciplined judgment, strengthen analytical thinking, and enhance the ability to evaluate project and program situations with clarity, balance, and confidence. It is intended to help readers assess trade-offs thoughtfully, apply sound decision-making under pressure, and improve readiness for scenario-based evaluation and complex leadership challenges in professional practice.

This question bank has been developed to strengthen scenario-based judgment across leadership, delivery, governance, risk, and value realization. It presents realistic project and program situations in predictive, agile, and hybrid environments, enabling readers to refine the judgment required to determine the most appropriate course of action in complex professional contexts.

The scenarios that follow are intended to help readers identify the most appropriate response by considering context, stakeholder impact, governance expectations, delivery priorities, and long-term value.

Case study 1: Project Aura

The scenario context: You are the project manager for *Project Aura*, a USD 45M strategic initiative for a global manufacturing conglomerate. The objective is to deploy a generative AI-driven energy optimization grid across 40 legacy manufacturing plants to meet the board's aggressive new ESG sustainability targets by Q4.

The environment is highly volatile. Your project team operates in a hybrid model: the GenAI data science team is fully remote (based in Silicon Valley), while the plant operations teams are entirely on-site across the Midwest, managed by veterans who have run these plants manually for decades. The project charter mandates that the AI model must dictate real-time power distribution and predictive maintenance, effectively stripping the plant managers of their traditional autonomous override capabilities. The business environment demands sustainability, but the People Domain is a powder keg of resistance.

1. **A project manager is leading the deployment of an AI-based energy optimization system across manufacturing plants. During planning, the lead architect wants to use a sensor layout generated by an AI model. A plant manager says vibration in one area will damage the sensors and rejects the design. The sponsor wants the layout finalized by Friday. What should the project manager do first?**
   a. Escalate the disagreement to the sponsor immediately.
   b. Approve the architect's design because it supports the project objective.
   c. Facilitate a joint review of the physical conditions and design assumptions with both stakeholders.
   d. Split the layout evenly between the AI design and the plant manager's preference.

2. **During execution, an AI model recommends shutting down a plant for 48 hours to recalibrate carbon-capture filters. If the shutdown does not occur, the project will miss a sustainability KPI. The plant manager says the shutdown will trigger a major client penalty. The sponsor is unavailable. What should the project manager do?**
   a. Authorize the shutdown because sustainability is the project objective.
   b. Quantify the trade-off and present a recommendation to the appropriate governance body.
   c. Log the issue as an accepted risk and continue operations.
   d. Submit a change request to remove the plant from scope.

3. **An AI maintenance system is generating false anomaly alerts at three plants. Crews investigate and find nothing wrong. They are frustrated and say they may stop using the dashboard next week. Which two actions should the project manager take? (Select two)**
   a. Revert all three plants to the legacy system until the model is perfect.
   b. Implement a temporary human review step before alerts reach the crews.
   c. Require crews to continue responding to all false alerts to train the model.
   d. Communicate transparently about the issue and the corrective plan to the crews.
   e. Wait for a full root cause analysis before addressing user concerns.

4. **A project team has worked mandatory overtime for six weeks to meet a board deadline. Velocity has dropped sharply, one engineer snaps at a teammate, and several team members report exhaustion. What should the project manager do?**
   a. Offer bonuses for team members who maintain velocity.
   b. Reprimand the engineer and redistribute work from absent team members.
   c. Facilitate an immediate team health discussion and advocate for a timeline or scope adjustment.
   d. Increase monitoring of daily task completion.

5. **At project closure, the new AI system is technically deployed, but many plant managers are using manual override daily. As a result, the expected business value is tracking well below target. The sponsor wants to close the project tomorrow. What should the project manager do?**
   a. Refuse closure until adoption reaches 100%.
   b. Close the project and record the gap as an operational failure.
   c. Document the adoption gap, hand over value tracking to the operational owner, and recommend follow-up change management.
   d. Disable the manual override before closure.

Case study 2: Project Merger Catalyst

The scenario context: Your organization, a mid-sized regional financial services firm (USD 2.3B in assets), has just acquired a smaller fintech startup (USD 300M in assets) known for cutting-edge digital banking and alternative lending products. The board has mandated a rapid IT integration—complete system unification within 9 months, to unlock USD 15M in annual cost synergies and capture the acquired company's innovative customer base before competitors poach them.

However, the cultural and technical environments are radically misaligned. Your firm runs a fortress of legacy mainframe systems with a 15-year technical debt backlog and a risk-averse compliance culture. The acquired fintech startup operates on cloud-native microservices, ships code daily, and has a *move fast and break things* ethos. The regulatory environment is intense: you are subject to dual oversight from the Federal Reserve, the FDIC, and state banking commissions. Any system integration failure could trigger a Consent Order or worse.

You are assigned as the *integration program manager*. Your executive sponsor is the **Chief Integration Officer (CIO)**, who is under intense board pressure to deliver the synergies on time. Your team is a hybrid structure: legacy system architects from your firm, agile developers from the fintech, and a compliance officer who is visibly terrified of regulatory backlash.

6. **In an IT integration program after an acquisition, the acquired company's CTO wants to replace most legacy systems quickly, while the existing enterprise architect wants a phased hybrid approach due to regulatory risk. The sponsor tells the program manager to create unity. What should the program manager do first?**

   a. Establish a decision committee limited to legacy architects and compliance staff.

   b. Facilitate a joint architecture workshop to build a shared roadmap based on business and compliance needs.

   c. Propose a 50/50 split between new and legacy systems.

   d. Recommend delaying the integration for six months.

7. **A regulator announces a focused examination of an in-flight IT integration program in eight weeks. The project is slightly ahead of schedule. What should the program manager do?**

   a. Accelerate the project to finish before the examination begins.

   b. Pause execution for several weeks and focus only on documentation readiness.

   c. Maintain execution pace and create a parallel regulatory-readiness workstream with proactive engagement and documented governance decisions.

   d. Reassign the best technical resources fully to compliance support.

8. **During integration testing, customer data does not synchronize reliably between two banking systems, affecting 2.3% of transactions. Which three actions should the program manager take? (Select three).**

   a. Convene the relevant technical, compliance, and business stakeholders to assess the risk and define decision thresholds.

   b. Unilaterally accept the defect because agile delivery expects some tolerance.

   c. Consider a phased rollout only if risk is understood and controlled.

   d. Keep frontline support staff unaware of known issues until go-live is complete.

   e. Escalate appropriately if proceeding with known transaction risk requires higher-level authorization.

9. **A board asks to accelerate an integration program from nine months to six months, even if testing is reduced. Analysis shows the remaining security and regulatory validation cannot be compressed safely. What should the program manager do?**

   a. Commit to the six-month target and try to recover later.

   b. Perform a compression analysis showing what can and cannot be accelerated and the associated trade-offs.

c. Offer a minimum viable launch without first analyzing regulatory and security constraints.

d. Reduce testing on the cloud layer because it is less risky.

10. **At program closure, the integration is technically complete, but customer churn means Year 1 value is below the original business case. The sponsor wants to close the effort. What should the program manager do?**

a. Close the program and treat customer churn as entirely outside project responsibility.

b. Keep the program open for six more months until the value target is reached.

c. Close the program, document the value gap and lessons learned, and establish clear operational ownership for continued tracking and action.

d. Conduct a blame review and escalate accountability findings to the board.

Case study 3: Project Verdant Transition

The scenario context: You are the program manager for Project Verdant Transition, a **United States Dollar (USD)** $120M, 36-month initiative to decarbonize a legacy coal-fired power generation facility and transition it to renewable energy (solar and wind). The project is mandated by the board's bold new **Environmental, Social, and Governance (ESG)** commitments, which promise to achieve net-zero carbon emissions by 2035. The initiative has strong institutional support from activist shareholders, the CEO is personally championing the effort, and the company has made public commitments to stakeholders and regulators.

However, the plant currently employs 1,200 workers, many of whom are third-generation energy sector employees. The facility is the economic anchor of a declining Rust Belt town (population 45,000). The transition will eventually eliminate 600 of those 1,200 jobs over 18 months as the coal operations shut down and renewable infrastructure comes online (renewable operations require fewer personnel due to automation).

The town's mayor, the union leadership, and local economic development officials are understandably alarmed. They are pressuring your organization to commit to a *just transition* plan, retraining programs, wage guarantees, and local hiring for new renewable roles. Simultaneously, your **Chief Financial Officer (CFO)** is skeptical about the retraining costs (estimated USD 25M over two years) and is asking whether this is a *corporate obligation* or an *optional social responsibility*.

Your team includes a diverse mix: sustainability experts excited about the climate impact, engineering teams concerned about technical execution, HR professionals facing the moral weight of workforce reduction, and a government affairs officer navigating the political minefield with elected officials.

11. **A program manager begins a stakeholder session for a power plant transition initiative. Union leaders ask whether displaced workers will receive guaranteed job placement and wage protection. The CFO warns the PM not to promise anything because costs are not yet approved, while the mayor says permits may be delayed without a credible workforce plan. What should the program manager do first?**

a. Create a joint task force with union, company, and local government representatives to develop a workforce transition plan for board review.

b. Tell the union the company supports workers but defer any concrete planning until cost analysis is complete.

c. Guarantee placement and wage protection for all affected workers immediately.

d. Direct the union to work with government agencies because workforce support is outside project responsibility.

12. **A steering committee debates whether to fund a USD 25M workforce transition plan or reduce it to USD 8M. The CEO asks whether this is a project management cost decision or a corporate strategy decision. What should the program manager do?**
    a. Recommend the full USD 25M plan as a project cost and include it directly in the baseline.
    b. Recommend a partial funding model and shift the remainder to public agencies.
    c. Explain that the funding decision is strategic and present the trade-offs of each option for executive decision-making
    d. Recommend the USD 8M option to preserve shareholder value.

13. **Midway through the transition program, many retrained workers are declining renewable-energy roles due to cultural mismatch, relocation concerns, and identity loss. The staffing plan is now at risk. Which three actions should the program manager take? (Select three).**
    a. Escalate the staffing gap and request the contractor budget only.
    b. Work with HR to redesign onboarding and support for transition cohorts.
    c. Offer a temporary wage premium as the primary solution.
    d. Reassess the staffing timeline and discuss a realistic workforce ramp-up with the sponsor.
    e. Commission a structured study to better understand barriers to role acceptance.

14. **A sponsor asks whether the program can recover the schedule by compressing construction and reducing a previously announced workforce hiring commitment. Analysis shows that acceleration raises safety and defect risk, while reducing hiring would break public transition commitments and trigger labor conflict. What should the program manager do?**
    a. Recommend both changes while minimizing public discussion to reduce risk.
    b. Provide a candid assessment of the risks and recommend against both changes, while proposing a transparent governance discussion on realistic timing.
    c. Suggest a smaller compromise in both schedule compression and hiring reduction.
    d. Present both options neutrally and avoid giving a recommendation.

15. **At program closure, the environmental transition is complete, but workforce outcomes are below target, and union grievances remain active. The sponsor wants to close the project and move on. What should the program manager do?**
    a. Close the project and hand workforce issues entirely to HR operations.
    b. Close the project and establish an oversight structure to continue tracking worker outcomes, grievance resolution, and lessons learned.
    c. Keep the project open until all grievances are resolved and all workers are stably employed.
    d. Close the project and issue a report with recommendations only.

Case study 4: Project Mosaic

The scenario context: You are the program manager for Project Mosaic, a USD 85M, 42-month digital transformation initiative at *Mercy General Healthcare System*, a large non-profit network of 12 hospitals and 60+ outpatient clinics serving 2M+ patients annually across a rural and semi-rural five-state region.

The initiative's core objective is to implement an integrated **Electronic Health Record (EHR)** system enhanced with AI-driven **Clinical Decision Support (CDS)** tools, systems that provide evidence-based treatment recommendations to clinicians in real-time. The business case is compelling: improved patient outcomes through standardized care protocols, reduced administrative burden (estimated USD 35M annual savings), and enhanced ESG positioning (reducing medical errors and healthcare disparities through AI).

However, the organization's culture is deeply clinician-centric and traditional. Your system includes physicians and nurses with 20 to 40 years of experience who have built their careers on clinical judgment and intuition. Many have explicitly stated: *I didn't spend 30 years learning medicine to let an algorithm tell me what to do.* Additionally, Mercy General operates on razor-thin margins (typical for non-profits) and is already understaffed, with nurses working 60-hour weeks, and physician burnout at 65%. The EHR implementation requires significant time investment from these already-exhausted teams.

Your executive sponsor, the **Chief Medical Officer (CMO)**, is a 62-year-old internist who privately confesses to you: *I'm not sure AI in patient care is the right path.* However, the board is pressuring me to *modernize or die,* and our competitors have already implemented similar systems. *I'm backing this project, but I need you to make sure we don't destroy the culture we've spent decades building.*

The project also carries a hidden sustainability constraint: Mercy General's board has committed to reducing its carbon footprint by 40% by 2032. The massive data centers required for the EHR and AI infrastructure will increase the organization's energy consumption by 22% unless you implement aggressive carbon-mitigation strategies (renewable power contracts, edge computing, data optimization). This was not explicitly stated in the project charter, but it is lurking in the background as a business environment constraint.

16. **Senior clinicians say an AI-enabled clinical support system may erode professional judgment and create liability concerns. What should the program manager do first?**
    a. Provide technical reassurance and issue a governance document explaining override rights.
    b. Launch a clinical-technical co-design effort so clinicians help define where AI advice is appropriate and how performance will be governed.
    c. Start with administrative functions only and delay clinical use until later.
    d. Make AI features optional and reward early adopters.

17. **An AI-enabled healthcare platform will significantly increase energy consumption and threaten a broad carbon-reduction commitment. What should the program manager recommend?**
    a. Accept the increase as the cost of clinical modernization and offset it later.
    b. Ask the board to lower its carbon target.
    c. Propose a carbon-conscious technology strategy combining mitigation actions, phased funding, and technical optimization to support both modernization and sustainability goals.
    d. Limit rollout to a few hospitals until renewable infrastructure improves.

18. **An AI clinical decision-support tool has shown bias in recommendations, and clinicians are also overwhelmed by the EHR data-entry burden. Which three actions should the program manager take? (Select three).**
    a. Disable the AI tool across all sites immediately until retraining is complete.
    b. Commission an independent assessment of algorithm fairness and remediation needs.
    c. Work with frontline clinicians to simplify workflows and reduce documentation burden.
    d. Keep the AI visible in advisory mode only while avoiding governance escalation.
    e. Escalate the issue to the appropriate quality and compliance governance body as a patient-safety risk.

19. **A union claims that an EHR rollout redistributed work to clinicians and created unsafe staffing conditions. Project data shows workload is up, and expected safety improvements have not yet materialized. What should the program manager do?**
    a. Commission an independent staffing and workload assessment, then use a joint task force to address validated issues.
    b. Reinvest administrative savings directly into staffing without further analysis.
    c. Add more automation to reduce clinical workload further.
    d. Roll back the system at the affected hospital until concerns are resolved.

20. **At project closure, the healthcare transformation is technically complete, but some outcome targets are below the original business case, and workforce trust remains fragile. What should the program manager do?**
   a. Close the project and hand all remaining outcome tracking to operations only.
   b. Close the project and establish a time-bound post-project office to track outcomes, workforce stability, and lessons learned.
   c. Keep the project open until all business-case targets are fully met.
   d. Launch a Phase 2 initiative immediately to close the remaining gaps.

21. **During a cloud migration program, an audit finds that 23 applications were migrated with inconsistent security settings and some do not meet the approved baseline. The CISO wants immediate remediation of all 23 applications, while the sponsor is concerned about cost and delay. What should the program manager do?**
   a. Remediate all 23 immediately and delay the program as needed.
   b. Prioritize remediation based on risk level and agree a governed plan for lower-risk items.
   c. Request a blanket waiver for all 23 applications until after program closure.
   d. Halt the entire migration and audit every migrated application before proceeding.

22. **A senior developer misses standups and submits poor-quality code. In a private conversation, the developer explains there is a family health crisis. What should the project manager do first?**
   a. Put the developer on a formal performance plan.
   b. Offer flexibility, adjust commitments, and discuss support options.
   c. Reassign the developer's work without discussion.
   d. Escalate immediately to HR and remove the developer from sprint work.

23. **A digital transformation program is 60% complete when the organization acquires a competitor, and executive leadership wants to redirect resources to integration work. The current program also includes public commitments to investors. What should the program manager do?**
   a. Continue the current program as planned and treat the acquisition as separate work.
   b. Present portfolio-level trade-offs and options to the executive steering committee for decision.
   c. Halt the current program immediately and shift all resources to the acquisition.
   d. Promise both efforts can proceed in parallel within the same budget and timeline.

24. **Midway through an infrastructure modernization program, the team discovers that the original requirements do not include a new federal compliance mandate and several missed business needs. What should the project manager do next?**
   a. Add the compliance requirements immediately and defer the business needs to Phase 2.
   b. Stop the program for several months and redo all requirements from scratch.
   c. Run a focused requirements recovery effort, prioritize gaps, and take the impacts through formal change control.
   d. Absorb the new requirements without formal change control because they are strategic.

25. **Two development teams integrate their work and discover a major architecture mismatch caused by separate assumptions and poor coordination. Both team leads blame each other. What should the project manager do first?**
   a. Conduct a formal blame-oriented root cause analysis and assign responsibility.
   b. Facilitate a blameless retrospective focused on process gaps and prevention actions.
   c. Pause the program for two weeks and force a detailed architecture rewrite.
   d. Assign all future decisions to a separate architecture authority.

26. **A CTO wants to pivot an e-commerce platform from Kubernetes to serverless after hearing industry trends have shifted. The architect says the current design still fits the business needs, and changing now would require major rework. What should the project manager recommend?**
    a. Pivot immediately to serverless because the market is moving that way.
    b. Conduct a trade-off analysis comparing business fit, cost, performance, and schedule impact before deciding.
    c. Stay with the current design and refuse to consider any architecture change.
    d. Use both architectures in parallel without further analysis.

27. **A configuration management system pilot reveals that maintaining the data manually will create high ongoing operational costs, while automation would require extra budget and time. What should the project manager do?**
    a. Deploy the manual solution and accept the ongoing operational burden.
    b. Stop deployment and build the automation immediately without further analysis.
    c. Present a total-cost-of-ownership comparison of manual, automated, and alternative approaches for the sponsor's decision.
    d. Reduce scope to only critical infrastructure and ignore the wider business case.

28. **A distributed infrastructure team is struggling because decisions are lost, meetings are chaotic, and key updates are missed. One leader wants strict protocols, while an engineer says that would be bureaucratic. What should the project manager do?**
    a. Impose strict communication controls on all channels and meetings.
    b. Leave communication informal and trust the team to self-coordinate.
    c. Establish lightweight communication basics such as a decision log, shared agendas, and a clear channel for critical announcements.
    d. Split responsibility for formal and informal communication between two team members.

29. **A board is concerned that a competitor has announced a more advanced EHR platform while your healthcare deployment is already underway. Switching would add major cost and delay. What should the project manager do?**
    a. Pause immediately and evaluate switching to the competitor platform.
    b. Continue without evaluating because too much has already been spent.
    c. Conduct a comparative assessment of business fit, upgrade path, total cost, and implementation impact before escalating the decision.
    d. Pilot both platforms in parallel across different hospitals.

30. **During the current sprint, users report a serious UX issue in a feature released four sprints ago. Fixing it will require 15 story points, but the team is already fully committed to the sprint. What should the project manager do?**
    a. Add the work now and expect the team to absorb it without changes.
    b. Defer the issue automatically to the next sprint.
    c. Assess business impact with the product owner and decide what work should be reprioritized if the fix is urgent.
    d. Remove 15 story points from the sprint backlog without discussion.

31. **A program sponsor has become disengaged from a manufacturing system transformation because they feel uncomfortable with the technical subject matter. What should the project manager do first?**
    a. Replace the sponsor with a more technical executive.
    b. Meet privately with the sponsor, reaffirm the value of their operational expertise, and provide briefings in business language.
    c. Reduce the sponsor's role and let technical leads make most governance decisions.

d. Bring in an outside consultant to act as interim sponsor.

32. **A customer data platform initiative is technically compliant with privacy rules, but the privacy officer warns that the design collects far more personal data than is necessary for the intended use. Marketing wants the broader data set for AI-driven targeting. What should the project manager recommend?**

    a. Proceed as designed because the broader data set is not illegal.

    b. Redesign the solution completely to collect only the minimum data for all use cases.

    c. Propose a segmented architecture that separates core operational data from marketing data with purpose-based governance controls.

    d. Defer AI features entirely until a later phase.

33. **During data migration testing, the team finds that 12% of customer records are incomplete or inconsistent. Cleaning all records before go-live would delay the release significantly. What should the project manager do?**

    a. Migrate all records now and clean them later.

    b. Delay the entire release until every record is corrected.

    c. Use a phased migration strategy: move the clean records first and remediate the problematic set before migrating them.

    d. Use AI to auto-correct the problematic data after migration.

34. **Middle managers are quietly resisting an agile transformation because they feel it threatens their authority. The sponsor wants to use performance management to force adoption. What should the project manager recommend?**

    a. Escalate to HR and discipline managers who do not comply.

    b. Create an inclusion plan that involves middle managers in designing the new operating model and clarifies their future role.

    c. Ignore the resistance and let results convince them over time.

    d. Pause the transformation until every manager fully supports agile.

35. **A telecom billing upgrade cannot safely modernize every interface within the original timeline. Some interfaces are critical for launch, while others mainly support downstream analytics. What should the project manager recommend?**

    a. Keep the original date by reducing testing and using overtime.

    b. Extend the full timeline until every interface is complete.

    c. Phase the launch by completing critical interfaces first and scheduling secondary interfaces in a later wave with temporary fallback support.

    d. Keep the legacy billing system for several more years and defer modernization.

36. **Several vendors announce API changes that are backward compatible for now, but will lose support within 12 months. The current roadmap is already full. What should the project manager do?**

    a. Migrate all vendor APIs immediately and deprioritize current work.

    b. Defer all migrations to a later technical debt project.

    c. Assess the impact of each API change, migrate the highest-risk ones within the current project, and document a governed remediation path for lower-risk items.

    d. Ask all vendors to extend their support deadlines before taking action.

37. **After a major release, the team is exhausted from an intense 10-week push. leadership wants to celebrate with bonuses and recognition, but team members also ask for a more sustainable pace. What should the project manager do?**

    a. Focus only on rewards and recognition for the extra effort.

    b. Celebrate the achievement and also reset expectations for a sustainable pace in upcoming work.

    c. Skip the celebration and focus entirely on capacity planning.

d. Pause all work for two weeks before planning next steps.

38. **A digital transformation roadmap was built for a stable organization, but leadership now plans several acquisitions over the next 18 months. What should the project manager do?**

a. Continue the roadmap unchanged and handle acquisitions later.

b. Pause the program and redesign everything for acquisitions immediately.

c. Run scenario planning, identify which architecture components must support acquisitions, and redesign only those impacted areas while keeping the rest moving.

d. Recommend delaying the acquisitions until the transformation is finished.

39. **An automation program finds that many existing automated tests now generate false positives because the framework did not adapt well to application changes. What should the project manager do?**

a. Ignore the false positives and keep increasing automation coverage.

b. Refactor the entire framework immediately, regardless of impact.

c. Assess which false positives cause the highest business impact and prioritize targeted refactoring accordingly.

d. Lower the automation coverage target and move on.

40. **A global team across the US, Europe, and Asia-Pacific is experiencing friction because decisions are made in one time zone, and other teams feel excluded. What should the project manager do?**

a. Centralize decisions in one office to avoid delays.

b. Schedule all critical meetings so every region can attend in real time.

c. Create an asynchronous decision process with a shared decision log, defined ownership, and time-boxed opportunities for input before finalizing key decisions.

d. Consolidate the team into a single time zone over time.

41. **A financial system upgrade program requires failure analysis for 50+ critical components. A full analysis will take 12 weeks and delay the program, while the sponsor asks for a lighter approach. What should the program manager do?**

a. Complete the full analysis for all components before proceeding.

b. Analyze only the 15 highest-risk components and defer the rest until after go-live.

c. Define acceptable risk thresholds with risk and audit leaders, prioritize analysis for unacceptable-risk components, and get governance approval for any deferred items.

d. Hire external specialists to accelerate analysis and proceed once they finish.

42. **A data center consolidation program discovers that one regulated customer segment must keep data in specific regions, reducing projected savings. What should the project manager do?**

a. Ask customers to waive the residency requirement so full consolidation can proceed.

b. Use a hybrid model that consolidates non-regulated workloads, keeps regulated workloads regional, and updates the business case for approval.

c. Consolidate everything anyway because the savings justify the risk.

d. Exclude the regulated segment entirely and leave its legacy environment unchanged.

43. **A grid modernization program depends on scarce specialized talent. Recruiting enough experienced people will take months and may cause cost overruns. What should the program manager do?**

a. Extend the timeline and wait for recruitment to complete naturally.

b. Build an apprenticeship pipeline only and rely on new graduates for staffing.

c. Use a combined strategy of upskilling current staff, building university partnerships, planning phased staffing, budgeting for premiums, and escalating the talent risk.

d. Recruit aggressively at any cost to preserve the original timeline.

44. **A cloud migration program finds inconsistent configurations across the first 30 migrated applications. The architecture lead wants enterprise standards, but the sponsor worries about delay. What should the project manager do?**

a. Continue migrating and remediate everything after the program ends.

b. Pause all migrations until comprehensive standards are fully documented and approved.

c. Define a minimum set of mandatory standards now, apply them to future migrations, remediate the most important gaps in the first 30 apps, and refine the full standards in parallel.

d. Review each migration case-by-case through a governance board instead of creating standards.

45. **An AI lending model shows strong predictive accuracy overall but appears to perpetuate historical bias. The board has committed to responsible AI, but leadership is under pressure to launch quickly. What should the project manager do?**

a. Launch now and fix the bias later in a future phase.

b. Delay launch immediately and fully retrain the model before any release.

c. Commission an independent fairness assessment, determine whether the bias creates material harm, and then decide on remediation or controlled launch with governance based on the findings.

d. Reframe the tool as advisory only and launch without further analysis.

46. **A disaster recovery design offers synchronous replication with zero data loss but added latency, asynchronous replication with no latency but possible data loss, and a hybrid option. What should the project manager do?**

a. Choose synchronous replication because zero data loss is always required.

b. Choose asynchronous replication because performance matters most.

c. Quantify the business impact of latency and potential data loss, evaluate the hybrid option, and present the trade-offs to business and risk stakeholders for decision.

d. Implement the hybrid approach immediately without further analysis.

47. **An EHR rollout is creating alert fatigue and workflow disruption. A few missed alerts suggest patient-safety risk, but a full pause would also be disruptive. What should the program manager do?**

a. Pause all further rollout immediately until the system is fully redesigned.

b. Continue rollout everywhere with extra monitoring only.

c. Analyze whether the problem is caused by system design, implementation, or training, optimize at current sites, and continue only in small phased cohorts if the issues appear remediable.

d. Require human validation of all alerts before clinicians see them.

48. **An ERP implementation is nearing go-live, but master data queries take 5 to 6 seconds because the system contains too much historical data. Fixing it pre-go-live requires extra cost and delay. What should the project manager do?**

a. Go live as planned and optimize performance later without analysis.

b. Delay go-live immediately and archive the old data before launch.

c. Quantify the business impact of the performance issue, compare that impact with the cost and delay of fixing it now, and present the options to stakeholders for decision.

d. Add a temporary cache and assume the problem is solved.

49. **A system integration program finds repeated discrepancies between vendor API documentation and actual behavior, causing delays and rework. What should the project manager do?**

   a. Threaten contract penalties unless vendors fix all documentation immediately.

   b. Accept reverse engineering as normal and add engineers to handle it.

   c. Classify discrepancies by severity, escalate the most critical issues with evidence, document actual behaviors and workarounds, and make API governance part of ongoing vendor management.

   d. Redesign the solution to avoid APIs and use batch files instead.

50. **An agile organizational transformation is creating anxiety, decision paralysis, and micromanagement. leadership says people should simply accept the change. What should the project manager recommend?**

   a. Increase communication and transition support but keep the pace unchanged.

   b. Pause the transformation for six months.

   c. Accelerate the change so people move through resistance faster.

   d. Assess change capacity and distress by group, provide targeted support, slow noncritical changes where needed, and use organizational health indicators to guide pace.

51. **During aviation certification testing, an upgraded navigation system shows a rare edge-case failure under specific atmospheric conditions. Regulators say certification can proceed either by fixing the defect or by implementing a reliable fallback to the legacy navigation system when the condition is detected. The sponsor prefers the mitigation to avoid an 8 to 12-week delay. What should the program manager do?**

   a. Recommend the mitigation immediately because it is cheaper and faster.

   b. Recommend a full re-engineering fix because aviation defects must always be eliminated.

   c. Confirm regulatory acceptance criteria, assess the reliability of the fallback mechanism, and present the trade-offs for the decision.

   d. Request an exception from the regulator because the failure is very rare.

52. **An organization changes strategy mid-year and asks whether two active projects still support the revised direction. Which two actions should the project manager take first?**

   a. Continue both projects until the next annual planning cycle.

   b. Reassess strategic alignment and expected benefits with governance stakeholders.

   c. Cancel both projects immediately because the strategy has changed.

   d. Present options such as continue, pivot, pause, or close based on value and impact.

53. **A utility modernization program may be affected by new grid regulations expected in six months, but the exact requirements are uncertain. The sponsor asks whether the program should delay work until the rules are final. What should the project manager do?**

   a. Continue unchanged and react only after the new rules are published.

   b. Delay the whole program until regulatory clarity is available.

   c. Identify the most regulation-sensitive components, build flexibility into those areas, monitor developments closely, and define triggers for plan changes.

   d. Ask the regulator to publish the rules early for the project's benefit.

54. **A benefits review shows slower value realization than expected because users are adopting the new tool inconsistently and managers are still measuring old behaviors. Which three actions are most appropriate?**

   a. Reassess benefit assumptions and adoption barriers.

   b. Align operating measures and incentives to the new behavior.

   c. Keep the project open indefinitely until benefits reach the target.

d. Assign post-project ownership and follow-up actions.

e. Remove benefits from the business case because the project delivered the scope.

55. **A marketing platform program assumed all brand divisions would use standardized workflows, but the business now wants more brand-specific differentiation. What should the project manager do?**

a. Enforce full standardization across all brands.

b. Allow each brand to customize everything freely.

c. Distinguish which capabilities truly require differentiation, define a standardized baseline, and allow controlled modular customization above it.

d. Launch a standardized solution now and decide on customization later without analysis.

56. **An HR platform consolidation program finds duplicate records, conflicting employee data, missing fields, and inconsistent formatting across legacy systems. Full cleanup before go-live would take 8 to 12 weeks. What should the project manager do?**

a. Proceed with all data issues unresolved and clean everything later.

b. Delay go-live until all data issues are fully corrected.

c. Classify data issues by business impact, remediate critical issues before go-live, and implement controls to catch and resolve lower-priority issues after launch.

d. Outsource all decisions to a third party to accelerate cleanup.

57. **A principal engineer who owns critical compliance and security knowledge gives three weeks' notice after accepting another job. The sponsor asks whether the organization should try to convince the person to stay. What should the project manager do?**

a. Offer a large retention bonus immediately.

b. Accept the resignation and do nothing beyond routine offboarding.

c. Respect the decision, seek a longer transition if possible, organize structured knowledge transfer, and adjust plans to mitigate the departure risk.

d. Accelerate delivery to finish the engineer's work before departure.

58. **A telecom modernization program discovers that the first 25 upgraded sites have 15 to 20% higher latency because of an integration design flaw. The remaining 25 sites are not yet upgraded. What should the project manager do?**

a. Continue using the flawed design for the remaining sites and remediate everything later.

b. Halt all work and remediate every completed site before proceeding.

c. Assess the business impact, apply the corrected design to future sites immediately, and phase remediation of the completed sites based on risk and traffic impact.

d. Record the issue and accept degraded performance until a later cycle.

59. **A financial services transformation program may be canceled if the company is acquired, but the acquisition is uncertain and may take over a year. What should the project manager recommend?**

a. Continue the full transformation as planned and ignore the acquisition scenario.

b. Halt the transformation until the acquisition is resolved.

c. Identify which components remain valuable whether or not acquisition occurs, continue those now, and defer acquisition-sensitive work until uncertainty reduces.

d. Ask the potential acquirer to guarantee continuation of the program.

60. **A government IT modernization program may face budget cuts next year. The sponsor asks whether the team should accelerate spending now or remain conservative. What should the project manager do?**
    a. Spend as much as possible now across all planned work before funding is reduced.
    b. Maintain the current pace and react later if cuts occur.
    c. Prioritize the most critical work for earlier funding, prepare scenarios for different cut levels, and build contingency plans for each case.
    d. Reduce current spending and hold back budget informally for later needs.

Case study 5: Project Momentum

The scenario context: You are the program manager for Project Momentum, a USD 185M organizational transformation initiative at a 50-year-old manufacturing company. The initiative is designed to fundamentally shift the organization from a traditional, hierarchical, command-and-control management structure to an agile, self-directed, cross-functional operating model. The transformation spans all 8,000 employees across 12 manufacturing facilities and corporate functions.

The strategic imperative is clear: traditional manufacturing is losing market share to agile, innovative competitors. The company's board has determined that survival requires transforming how the organization makes decisions, manages projects, and innovates. The transformation is expected to enable faster time-to-market, higher quality products, and improved employee engagement.

However, the transformation is profoundly disruptive to the organization's identity. The company was built on stability, predictability, and clear hierarchies. Plant managers have managed their facilities autonomously for decades. Directors and Vice Presidents have derived authority from their position in the hierarchy. A shift to agile, self-directed teams represents a fundamental loss of power and identity for mid-management and senior leaders.

Your executive sponsor is the **Chief Operating Officer (COO)**, a 64-year-old operations veteran who intellectually understands the need for agile transformation but is emotionally conflicted about dismantling the hierarchical system he built his career within. Your transformation team includes change management experts, agile coaches, and organizational development specialists. However, the transformation is facing significant headwinds from plant managers and mid-level leaders who perceive it as a threat.

61. **Pilot agile teams in two manufacturing facilities are showing good results, but plant managers keep overriding team decisions and requiring approvals. The COO says the transformation will fail if teams are not trusted, while agile coaches say plant managers fear losing control. What should the program manager do first?**
    a. Direct plant managers to stop intervening and treat resistance as a performance issue.
    b. Pause the pilot and provide focused coaching to help plant managers transition from command-and-control leadership to enabling team autonomy.
    c. Replace the resistant plant managers with leaders who already support agile.
    d. Let plant managers keep final review authority while teams make recommendations.

62. **During the broad rollout of an agile transformation, the sustainability team reports an 8% increase in carbon footprint due to more travel, meetings, and coordination. The board has a net-zero commitment, while transformation leaders argue that reducing collaboration will harm agile effectiveness. What should the program manager recommend?**
    a. Accept the carbon increase and offset it through unrelated sustainability initiatives.
    b. Reduce meeting frequency and travel broadly, even if agile effectiveness declines.
    c. Analyze which agile practices create the most value versus carbon impact, redesign lower-value high-carbon practices, and add carbon tracking to the operating model.

d. Pause the transformation until a carbon-neutral agile model is designed.

63. **An agile transformation is progressing unevenly across facilities. Sites with empowering leaders are thriving, while sites with traditional leaders are resisting the change. HR says some leaders may be able to develop, and others may not. Which three actions should the program manager take?**

    a. Replace all struggling facility leaders immediately with external hires.

    b. Create a differentiated leadership development strategy that coaches high-potential leaders and transitions low-fit leaders into other roles when appropriate.

    c. Accept uneven progress and allow struggling sites to evolve at their own pace indefinitely.

    d. Conduct a leadership capability assessment and be transparent about expectations in the transformed organization.

    e. Build cross-facility mentoring networks so that strong transformational leaders support struggling leaders.

64. **Near the end of an organizational transformation, finance reports that operational improvements are real, but financial ROI is only about 40% of the original business case projection. The CFO questions whether the transformation was a strategic mistake, while the COO says benefits may simply be slower to materialize. What should the program manager do?**

    a. Declare the transformation unsuccessful and recommend redirecting funds elsewhere.

    b. Wait 2 to 3 years and see whether financial benefits improve.

    c. Validate operational gains, analyze the causes of the ROI gap, update the benefits trajectory, and assess whether strategic advantages still justify the investment.

    d. Cut remaining transformation work and redirect half the budget to short-term financial optimization.

65. **At transformation closure, the organization has adopted agile ways of working, but leaders worry the culture may regress without ongoing support. The COO is choosing between disbanding the transformation team or creating a permanent capability function. What should the program manager recommend?**

    a. Disband the transformation team because the project is complete.

    b. Keep the entire transformation team permanently as a center of excellence.

    c. Assess which capabilities are needed to sustain gains, create a smaller permanent capability function for those needs, and define value-focused metrics and governance.

    d. Keep the full transformation team for another year, then decide later.

Case study 6: Project Resonance

The scenario context: You are the program manager for Project Resonance, a USD 320M cross-border healthcare system integration initiative. The program involves integrating two independent healthcare networks: Chart-Health (a 200-bed hospital network in the Midwest) and Regional-Care (a 150-bed hospital network in the Northeast). The integration is designed to create a combined health system that can negotiate better payer rates, share best practices in clinical delivery, and achieve cost synergies through operational consolidation.

However, the integration is highly complex due to regulatory fragmentation. Each state and region has different healthcare regulations, licensing requirements, and payer relationships. The combined entity must maintain compliance across multiple regulatory jurisdictions while achieving operational synergy.

Additionally, clinical governance is complex. Chart-Health has a reputation for cutting-edge cardiology and orthopedic programs; Regional-Care is known for oncology and primary care. The integration requires aligning clinical protocols, combining medical staff (which are often competitive and territorial), and managing patient care continuity during the transition.

The integration is also facing external pressure: a third, larger health system (National-Health) has announced plans to acquire Chart-Health independently. If National-Health acquires Chart-Health, the Resonance integration becomes impossible, Chart-Health would be absorbed into National-Health's system instead. The window to complete the Resonance integration before National-Health's acquisition attempt is approximately 12-18 months.

Your executive sponsor is the combined organization's newly appointed **Chief Executive Officer (CEO)**, who was hired specifically to lead the integration. She is an experienced health system executive but is new to both organizations and lacks deep relationships with the clinical leadership at either Chart-Health or Regional-Care.

66. **In a cross-border healthcare integration, senior physicians from two networks are territorial and skeptical of combining clinical programs. The CEO says the leaders are protecting turf instead of thinking about the shared mission. What should the program manager do first?**
    a. Form a steering committee of senior physicians to decide the integration strategy.
    b. Ask the CEO to impose clinical protocols and structure decisions directly.
    c. Facilitate a joint clinical leadership forum to co-design a best-of-both model that explicitly recognizes each network's strengths and shared ownership
    d. Keep separate clinical governance for two years and defer protocol integration.

67. **Two healthcare networks in different states are integrating, but state regulations require different governance structures. Legal says the strictest compliant structure will add major cost and complexity. What should the program manager do?**
    a. Accept the most complex legal structure immediately because it is clearly compliant.
    b. Pursue regulatory exceptions in both states.
    c. Analyze the regulatory intent, explore alternative compliant operating structures, and compare the cost and value of full versus partial integration before recommending a path.
    d. Delay the integration until regulators issue joint guidance.

68. **During EHR integration, two hospital networks discovered incompatible patient identifier systems. A full conversion would require 24-48 hours of downtime, which clinicians say is unsafe. Which three actions should the program manager take?**
    a. Delay integration immediately for 8–10 weeks and perform a full conversion before go-live.
    b. Implement a temporary record-linking workaround without further analysis.
    c. Conduct a technical review to evaluate safer conversion approaches and quantify downtime risk versus workaround risk.
    d. Use a temporary record-linking workaround only if it is formally assessed and a later permanent conversion path is planned.
    e. Establish a joint clinical-technical working group to evaluate patient safety trade-offs and recommend the best path.

69. **A healthcare system integration will create about 300 redundant positions. leadership is weighing generous voluntary severance against more traditional layoffs, while clinical leaders warn against any workforce action that could harm patient care. What should the program manager recommend?**
    a. Use generous voluntary severance for all affected roles.
    b. Implement lower-cost layoffs with basic outplacement support.

c. Differentiate by role: prioritize redeployment for clinical roles, use voluntary severance selectively for administrative redundancy, provide development paths where possible, and communicate the transition transparently with strong support.

d. Delay all workforce decisions for 6 to 12 months after go-live.

70. **At closure of a healthcare integration, clinical outcomes and competitive position are strong, but financial synergies are only about 70% of the original projection. The CEO asks whether the integration should be judged a success or a failure. What should the program manager do?**

a. Declare the integration unsuccessful because financial ROI is below target.

b. Declare the integration successful based only on clinical outcomes.

c. Conduct a strategic value assessment that validates clinical and competitive gains, analyses the financial shortfall, updates the benefits trajectory, and documents lessons learned for future integrations.

d. Launch a Phase 2 cost-optimization initiative immediately without further analysis.

71. **A hospital system plans to deploy an AI model to predict patient readmission risk. Validation shows 89% accuracy overall, but only 73% for Black patients and 76% for Hispanic patients because the training data reflects historical documentation inequities. The CFO wants to launch now and fix bias later, while the CMO warns this may worsen inequitable care. What should the project manager do?**

a. Launch now because overall accuracy is high, and improve fairness later.

b. Delay launch until the model can be retrained and the disparity is reduced to an acceptable level.

c. Remove race from the model and launch immediately.

d. Launch only in departments with the best documentation quality.

72. **A program manager finds that junior developers and developers from underrepresented backgrounds wait much longer for code review approval than senior developers, even when the measured code quality is similar. The engineering manager says the extra scrutiny is normal for less experienced staff. What should the project manager do?**

a. Accept the disparity because junior developers should face stricter review.

b. Replace the engineering manager immediately.

c. Validate the review data, establish objective review criteria, train reviewers, and implement structural controls such as blind reviews where appropriate.

d. Ask junior developers to be more patient because fairness concerns are subjective.

73. **A utility modernization program will deliver renewable-energy infrastructure first to wealthier areas because those upgrades are cheaper and easier. Later-wave customers in lower-income areas will face higher costs and delayed benefits. Regulators only require net-zero progress, not equal distribution. What should the project manager do?**

a. Proceed unchanged because the plan is the most cost-efficient.

b. Immediately redesign the program so that lower-income areas are upgraded first.

c. Conduct an energy-equity impact assessment, explore pricing or rollout options that reduce inequity, and present the trade-offs for the decision.

d. Create a separate ESG-funded program for lower-income areas and leave the main plan unchanged.

74. **Three legacy-system experts are nearing retirement during a mission-critical banking migration. When the PM proposes formal knowledge transfer, the experts say the organization ignored their expertise for years and now wants to extract it only because they are leaving. What should the project manager do?**

a. Require knowledge transfer as a condition of continued employment.

b. Offer money only and let HR manage the rest.

c. Acknowledge past undervaluation, involve the experts in designing a respectful transfer plan, and offer appropriate recognition and transition support.

d. Accept the knowledge loss and rely on external consultants later.

75. **A government cloud modernization program complies with current federal standards, but future guidance may soon require stronger encryption and tighter data residency. The CIO wants to continue as planned, while the CISO worries the solution may need costly redesign later. What should the project manager do?**

a. Proceed with the current design and ignore possible future changes.

b. Delay the program until all future standards are finalized.

c. Assess the likelihood and impact of the coming changes, design flexibility where cost-effective, and choose the lowest-risk option based on evidence.

d. Over-engineer the solution now to exceed all anticipated future standards.

76. **Junior developers learn that some contractors with similar day-to-day responsibilities appear to be paid more. The CFO says contractor rates look higher only because employees also receive benefits, and internal compensation is structured differently. Morale is dropping because employees perceive the situation as unfair. What should the project manager do?**

a. Ask employees to accept the disparity because the company's compensation logic is sound.

b. Increase employee pay immediately without further analysis.

c. Conduct a transparent total-rewards analysis, explain the findings, and work with HR on any changes needed to address true inequity.

d. Replace contractors with cheaper employees as soon as possible.

77. **A supply chain digitization platform was designed for a global supplier network, but executives now believe nearshoring may shrink and simplify the supply base over time. Significant redesign now would be expensive, but ignoring the trend may reduce strategic fit later. What should the project manager do?**

a. Continue unchanged because too much money has already been spent.

b. Redesign the platform immediately for nearshoring without further analysis.

c. Assess how likely the supply chain shift is, evaluate how adaptable the current platform is, and present options comparing redesign now versus adaptation later.

d. Build two platform variants in parallel to hedge the uncertainty.

78. **In a government digital transformation, employees over 50 are struggling much more than younger employees with the new system. An older employee says the issue is not the ability to learn, but that the system has poor accessibility and usability. What should the project manager do?**

a. Provide extra age-targeted training only.

b. Accept that older employees will always struggle more and increase help-desk support.

c. Assess both training and usability factors, implement targeted accessibility improvements, and involve affected users in validating the changes.

d. Redesign the entire system immediately without further analysis.

79. **A financial trading platform has a rare defect that may duplicate a trade under very specific conditions. The chance is very low, but a duplicate trade could cause major customer loss. Fixing the defect will delay launch by 3–4 weeks. What should the project manager do?**

a. Launch now because the defect is too rare to matter.

b. Delay launch automatically because no known defect is acceptable in finance.

c. Quantify the expected value of the defect, compare it with the cost of delay, and evaluate mitigations such as monitoring and controls before deciding.

d. Apply a temporary workaround immediately and launch without further analysis.

80. **A restructuring program will close regional offices and affect 400 employees. HR proposes an enhanced support package with severance, relocation, and career-transition help, but the CFO says the support cost will materially reduce the program's net savings. What should the project manager recommend?**

a. Minimize support to maximize savings.

b. Keep the full support package without further analysis because dignity matters most.

c. Assess the full organizational impact, including retention, reputation, legal risk, and culture, and use that analysis to recommend the appropriate support level.

d. Offer better support only to top performers.

Earned Value Management data set

Use the chart and assume that at Month 6, **Planned Value (PV)** = USD 600k, **Earned Value (EV)** = USD 480k, **Actual Cost (AC)** = USD 560k, and **Budget at Completion (BAC)** = USD 600k, unless stated otherwise.

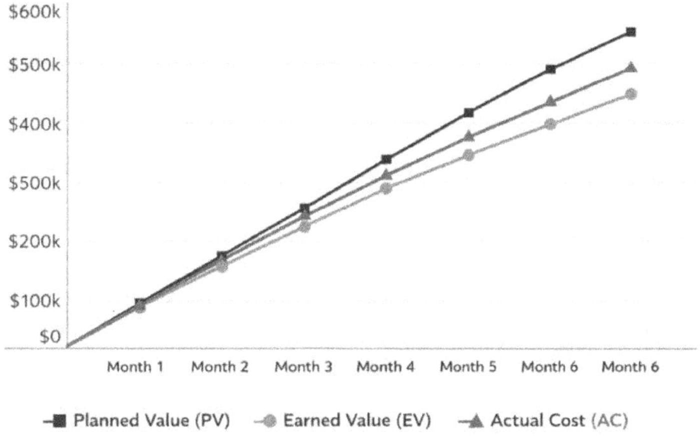

Figure 12.1: EVM

81. **At Month 6, the project has PV = USD 600k, EV = USD 480k, and AC = USD 560k.**

What do these values indicate?

a. Ahead of schedule and under budget

b. Behind schedule and over budget

c. Ahead of schedule and over budget

d. Behind schedule and under budget

82. **Compute the schedule variance (SV) at Month 6.**

a. +USD 120k b. -USD 120k

c. +USD 80k d. -USD 80k

83. **Compute the cost variance (CV) at Month 6.**

a. -USD 120k b. +USD 120k

c. -USD 80k d. +USD 80k

84. **Compute the schedule performance index (SPI) at Month 6.**

a. 1.17
b. 0.80
c. 0.86
d. 0.93

85. **Compute the Cost Performance Index (CPI) at Month 6.**

a. 0.86
b. 0.93
c. 1.17
d. 0.80

86. **Using the formula EAC = BAC / CPI, estimate the Estimate at Completion (EAC).**

a. Approximately USD 643k
b. Approximately USD 698k
c. Approximately USD 560k
d. Approximately USD 600k

87. **Using ETC = EAC - AC and the EAC from the previous question, estimate the Estimate to Complete (ETC).**

a. Approximately USD 83k
b. Approximately USD 138k
c. Approximately USD 200k
d. Approximately USD 40k

88. **Using VAC = BAC - EAC, estimate the Variance at Completion (VAC).**

a. Approximately +USD 43k
b. Approximately -USD 98k
c. Approximately -USD 140k
d. Approximately +USD 140k

89. **The sponsor says, "We must finish by Month 6 with the original scope." What is the best immediate project manager action?**

a. Ask finance to re-baseline immediately
b. Validate EV measurement, confirm remaining scope, and present corrective options with impacts
c. Stop work until a change request is approved
d. Replace the entire team

90. **Which statement best explains why EV is less than PV at Month 6?**

a. The team is spending too little
b. The project has completed less accepted work than planned by this point
c. The budget was set too high
d. Procurement has not started

91. **At Month 6, EV is depressed because several deliverables are 95% complete but not accepted due to quality gates. What is the best next step?**

a. Redefine acceptance to count partial completion as done
b. Expedite quality validation and remove bottlenecks while keeping acceptance criteria unchanged
c. Ignore EV and report only AC because it is more concrete
d. Cancel quality gates to recover the schedule

92. **A functional VP says the chart proves the team is inefficient and demands overtime. What is the best servant-leadership response?**

a. Approve overtime immediately to improve SPI
b. Facilitate a root cause analysis and collaborate on sustainable adjustments before committing to overtime
c. Escalate the VP to HR
d. Remove the scrum master to increase accountability

93. **If management wants a forecast that considers both cost and schedule performance, which formula is most appropriate?**

a. EAC = AC + (BAC - EV)
b. EAC = BAC / CPI
c. EAC = AC + (BAC - EV) / (CPI × SPI)
d. EAC = EV - AC

94. **Using EAC = AC + (BAC - EV) / (CPI × SPI), estimate EAC.**

a. Approximately USD 643k
b. Approximately USD 698k
c. Approximately USD 735k
d. Approximately USD 817k

95. **Your program has strict regulatory deadlines, and the chart trend is unacceptable. Which is the best first escalation package?**
    a. A request to re-baseline with no analysis to save time
    b. A variance analysis, root causes, recovery options, and a decision request tied to governance thresholds
    c. A message blaming the vendor and asking for more budget
    d. A slide showing only CPI to keep it simple

96. **A stakeholder proposes hiding the EV shortfall until the next steering committee meeting to avoid panic. What should you do?**
    a. Agree because transparency can wait
    b. Report accurately per governance, explain the drivers, and propose corrective actions
    c. Report only the PV line
    d. Stop using EVM because it creates conflict

97. **What is the most defensible interpretation of CPI less than 1 in this context?**
    a. The project is getting more value per dollar than planned
    b. The project is spending more than the value of the work earned
    c. The project has a schedule problem only
    d. The BAC is wrong by definition

98. **If you can only pick one immediate lever to move the project out of the "over budget and behind schedule" quadrant, what is best to focus on first?**
    a. Increase reporting frequency only
    b. Remove the primary constraint preventing work from being accepted, then reassess staffing and cost controls
    c. Cut all training and quality activities
    d. Freeze stakeholder communications

99. **A vendor change increases cost but improves throughput, likely raising EV faster. Which metric best shows whether the trade is paying off month over month?**
    a. PV only
    b. AC only
    c. CPI and SPI trend together
    d. BAC only

100. **Which action best aligns with PMI-style governance when adverse EVM trends persist for two reporting cycles?**
    a. Re-baseline immediately to make metrics look better
    b. Continue as-is because EVM is lagging and will self-correct
    c. Trigger the defined variance thresholds, implement approved corrective actions, and update forecasts including EAC and ETC
    d. Stop tracking PV to reduce noise

Cumulative flow diagram interpretation

The CFD (*Figure 12.2*) is for an agile team across the last 8 sprints. Notice the sharp widening of the *Testing* band (rising WIP there), a slowly growing *To Do* backlog, and a flattening *Done* slope in recent sprints.

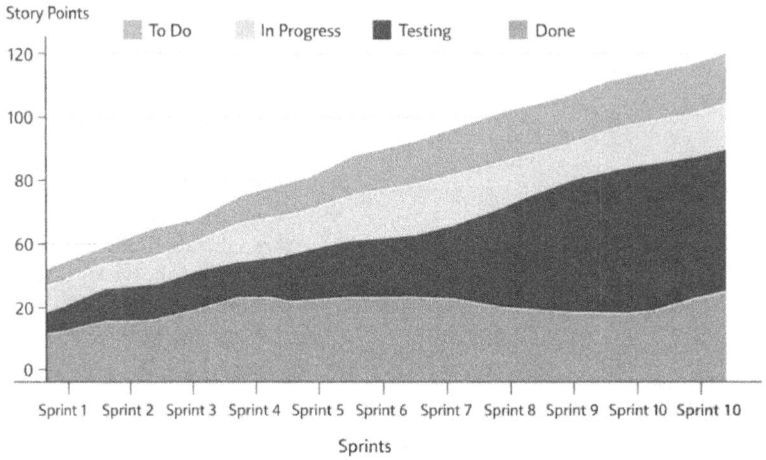

Figure 12.2: *Cumulative frequency diagram*

Use this diagram to answer the following question:

101. **Based on the CFD, what is the clearest signal?**
    a. Throughput has increased steadily
    b. A testing-stage bottleneck is growing because WIP in testing is increasing
    c. To Do is being cleared faster than planned
    d. Cycle time is decreasing

102. **Which single metric would best quantify the observed bottleneck?**
    a. Cumulative PV
    b. Work in progress (WIP) in testing over time
    c. Number of developers assigned
    d. Total story points in Done this sprint

103. **If average throughput falls while testing WIP rises, which is the likely effect on lead time?**
    a. Lead time decreases
    b. Lead time increases
    c. Lead time stays constant
    d. Lead time becomes irrelevant

104. **According to Little's Law, which action should reduce lead time most directly?**
    a. Increase WIP in testing
    b. Decrease throughput
    c. Reduce WIP in testing or increase throughput out of testing
    d. Increase To Do backlog

105. **The Testing band grows because items accumulate waiting for QA. Which immediate experiment is most appropriate to validate the root cause?**
    a. Add a strict WIP limit to testing and measure changes in cycle time
    b. Double the team size across all functions immediately
    c. Stop writing tests to speed delivery
    d. Remove the Definition of Done to mark items as Done earlier

106. **Which policy change is least likely to relieve the bottleneck sustainably?**
    a. Introduce pair testing and automation to increase throughput

b. Temporarily reassign developers to testing tasks for focused swarming

c. Increase the testing WIP limit to allow more concurrent testing

d. Implement a pull policy with explicit WIP limits and class-of-service rules

107. **If you measure flow efficiency, which result indicates a lot of waiting time relative to active work?**

a. Approximately 90%

b. Approximately 50%

c. Approximately 10%

d. Approximately 100%

108. **The team introduces test automation, raising testing throughput by 25% but increasing cost slightly. Which CFD change should you expect next?**

a. The Testing band widens further

b. The Testing band narrows, and the Done slope steepens

c. The To Do band expands only

d. No change to the Done slope

109. **Which KPI pair best tracks improvement after interventions?**

a. Number of meetings and sprint length

b. Testing WIP and average cycle time for items that go through testing

c. Developer headcount and sprint goal count

d. Story point estimates only

110. **Management wants a fast fix: "Add more people to testing." What risk should you call out immediately?**

a. Adding people may increase coordination overhead and context switching, worsening cycle time despite higher staffing

b. More people always reduce lead time without trade-offs

c. Hiring solves bottlenecks instantly with no measurement needed

d. Staffing changes are the only lever for flow problems

111. **Which visualization update to the CFD would help diagnose whether failing tests or test queueing is the main issue?**

a. Add a separate band for rework/defect fix within testing or annotate blocked items

b. Remove the To Do band entirely

c. Combine testing and In Progress into one band without labels

d. Change colors only

112. **The team enforces a testing WIP limit and sees throughput improve, but discovers recurring regressions requiring rework. Which next step is best?**

a. Add automation for regression tests and shift some testing activities earlier in the flow

b. Remove the WIP limit since regressions persist

c. Increase sprint length to allow more rework

d. Ignore regressions and push work to Done

113. **Which indicator is a leading signal that the testing bottleneck will start to impact delivery next sprint?**

a. Increasing testing WIP

b. Historical total actual cost

c. Past sprint velocity only

d. Number of retrospective actions closed last month

114. **Stakeholders demand more predictability. Which policy change improves predictability most reliably?**

a. Implement explicit WIP limits, stabilize work intake cadence, and measure cycle time distributions for forecasting

b. Accept any incoming urgent work and reprioritize ad hoc

c. Remove daily standups to reduce interruptions

d. Increase story point sizes to hide variability

115. **Which experiment would help determine whether testing capacity or test process design is the main constraint?**
    a. Run a short trial increasing testing capacity only, and a separate trial improving process only, then compare results
    b. Change both capacity and process permanently at the same time
    c. Fire the QA lead immediately
    d. Stop all testing for one sprint

116. **If the CFD shows steady To Do growth plus a wide Testing band while Done remains flat, which strategic option addresses scope and schedule together?**
    a. Implement a formal class-of-service policy with an expedited lane, a fixed-scope minimum, and negotiated descoping for lower-priority work
    b. Push more items into the sprint without changing flow policies
    c. Increase estimation granularity only
    d. Stop tracking. Done to reduce apparent failure

117. **The product owner suggests breaking large stories into smaller slices to reduce testing time per item. What effect should you expect on the CFD, all else equal?**
    a. More items moving through testing, but average cycle time per item decreases, and Done may improve
    b. The Testing band will necessarily widen forever
    c. To Do will disappear instantly
    d. No impact on throughput or cycle time

118. **Which analysis best helps forecast when the backlog will be cleared, given the current throughput?**
    a. Monte Carlo simulation using historical throughput and cycle-time distribution
    b. Only looking at today's backlog size without throughput data
    c. Counting team members and doubling it
    d. Removing estimates and guessing

119. **The team measures a higher median cycle time for items that pass through testing. Which statistic is most useful to track changes over time?**
    a. CFD only
    b. Cycle time histogram and a rolling median or percentile for items that include testing
    c. Burnup chart only for the added scope
    d. Pie chart of team sentiment

120. **Governance asks how to prevent similar bottlenecks program-wide. Which combination is most effective?**
    a. Standardize WIP limits, invest in cross-functional skills, promote automation, and require flow metrics reporting at program reviews
    b. Centralize all testing to a single silo and increase handoffs
    c. Mandate overtime across teams without measuring flow
    d. Remove CFD reporting to simplify dashboards

121. **A team's CFD shows that the Testing band is shrinking, but the Done band is still not growing as expected because business acceptance takes too long after testing completes. What should the project manager do first?**
    a. Increase the testing WIP limit again to keep testers busy
    b. Work with business stakeholders to streamline acceptance criteria and reduce approval delays
    c. Ask developers to mark items as Done when testing finishes
    d. Stop tracking the Done band because it is outside team control

122. **A portfolio leader wants every agile team to use the same WIP limit, regardless of product complexity or team structure. What should the project manager recommend?**
    a. Standardize one WIP limit for all teams to simplify governance
    b. Let every team choose any WIP level without review

c. Establish governance principles for WIP limits, but allow team-level calibration based on context and observed flow data

d. Remove WIP limits entirely and rely on sprint capacity

123. **A scrum team consistently meets its sprint goals, but the CFD shows To Do growing faster than done for three consecutive sprints. What is the best interpretation?**

a. The team is overperforming because sprint goals are met

b. Local sprint success may be masking a broader throughput problem or uncontrolled scope intake

c. The backlog is healthy because more ideas are entering the system

d. The CFD is less reliable than the sprint burndown for this purpose

124. **A regulatory project uses agile delivery, and governance requires forecast confidence for a fixed deadline. Which approach is best?**

a. Commit to the deadline using only average velocity from the last two sprints

b. Use historical throughput and cycle-time data to create a probabilistic forecast range, then review scope and risk options with governance stakeholders

c. Revert immediately to predictive delivery because regulation and agile are incompatible

d. Promise the full scope and manage risk informally after the commitment is made

125. **A team introduces an expedited lane for production defects, and soon nearly half of the incoming work is marked expedited. What should the project manager do?**

a. Accept it because urgent work should always bypass normal flow controls

b. Review the criteria for expedited work, limit its use to truly critical items, and analyze why so many items require acceleration

c. Remove the expedited lane entirely and process everything in FIFO order

d. Increase overall WIP so expedited items do not affect other work

126. **Two teams share the same testing environment, and both show growing testing queues on their CFDs. One sponsor suggests assigning time slots based on the seniority of the project. What should the project manager do instead?**

a. Allocate the environment permanently to the larger project

b. Use a transparent service policy with clear priority rules, environment scheduling, and metrics to manage the shared constraint across both teams

c. Ask each team to solve the problem independently

d. Increase both teams' WIP limits so they can keep working while they wait

127. **A Kanban team's throughput is stable, but stakeholders complain that delivery is unpredictable because a few items take much longer than the rest. What should the project manager analyze first?**

a. Average throughput only

b. The distribution of cycle times and the causes of outliers

c. Story point estimates for all completed items

d. Team utilization percentages

128. **A product owner wants to improve flow by stopping all retrospective actions that do not show immediate throughput gains. What should the project manager advise?**

a. Focus only on actions that raise throughput this sprint

b. Balance short-term flow improvements with actions that improve quality, sustainability, and future predictability

c. Replace retrospectives with additional planning meetings

d. Measure only Done and ignore team health indicators

129. **An enterprise PMO wants a single dashboard for agile teams. Which metric set is most useful for system-level flow governance?**

a. Team happiness only

b. Velocity only

c. Throughput, WIP, cycle time distribution, aging work, and defect escape trend
d. Budget burn only

130. **A team improves throughput significantly for two sprints after interventions, but escaped defects also increase. What should the project manager conclude?**
   a. The intervention succeeded because throughput is the primary goal
   b. The intervention likely improved speed at the expense of quality, so the team should rebalance flow and quality controls
   c. Escaped defects are unrelated to agile flow changes
   d. The team should double down on the intervention because defects can be fixed later

131. **A hybrid project has strong sprint execution, but change requests from a governance board take four weeks to approve, slowing delivery. What should the project manager do first?**
   a. Stop using change control because agile teams adapt continuously
   b. Work with governance stakeholders to define faster approval paths for low-risk changes while preserving control for higher-risk items
   c. Ask the team to implement changes before approval to maintain velocity
   d. Reclassify all changes as defects to bypass the board

132. **A sponsor wants to add scope mid-project because the team is under budget so far. What should the project manager do next?**
   a. Approve the scope increase because the budget remains available
   b. Assess impact on value, schedule, risk, and dependencies before taking the request through the proper governance path
   c. Reject the request because the scope must never change after baselining
   d. Ask the team to absorb the work informally to avoid paperwork

133. **A vendor insists that a critical integration issue is outside its statement of work, while the internal team argues that the vendor's design caused the problem. What should the project manager do first?**
   a. Threaten legal action immediately
   b. Review the contract, technical facts, and acceptance criteria jointly with procurement and technical leads to determine responsibility
   c. Accept internal ownership to preserve the relationship
   d. Pause the project until the dispute resolves itself

134. **A project's risk register contains many high-probability, low-impact risks and one low-probability, catastrophic risk. Resources are limited. What should the project manager prioritize?**
   a. Only the high-probability risks because they are more likely to happen
   b. The catastrophic risk, while also assigning proportionate responses to clusters of smaller risks
   c. All risks are equally because prioritization is subjective
   d. No action until risks become issues

135. **A team delivers incrementally, but users say the product still feels fragmented and difficult to adopt. What should the project manager do?**
   a. Increase sprint speed to deliver more features faster
   b. Work with product and UX stakeholders to validate end-to-end user journeys and prioritize cohesion improvements
   c. Ignore the feedback because increments were delivered as planned
   d. Delay all releases until every feature is complete

136. **A project is tracking on schedule, but the defect escape rate is rising. The sponsor says quality can be fixed after launch. What should the project manager do?**
   a. Agree, because schedule performance is currently strong

b. Present the quality trend and the likely business impact, then recommend corrective action before launch decisions are finalized

c. Reduce quality reporting to avoid distracting the sponsor

d. Ask the team to work overtime quietly to hide the issue

137. **A benefits review shows that the project delivered all committed outputs, but the expected savings are not appearing because business units are still using old processes. What should the project manager do before closure?**

a. Keep the project open until all savings appear

b. Document the adoption gap, assign benefit ownership, and ensure an operational plan exists to complete the transition

c. Close the project and remove savings from the business case retroactively

d. Hold the delivery team responsible for post-project business-unit behavior

138. **A critical stakeholder repeatedly misses governance meetings and later objects to decisions already made. What should the project manager do first?**

a. Remove the stakeholder from the governance structure

b. Meet with the stakeholder to understand the pattern, confirm expectations, and adjust the engagement approach if needed

c. Ignore later objections because the stakeholder was absent

d. Escalate immediately to the executive sponsor without discussion

139. **A release train has many dependencies, and one team is consistently late delivering components. What should the program manager do?**

a. Publicly identify the team in executive dashboards to increase pressure

b. Facilitate dependency mapping, identify the recurring cause of delay, and agree on cross-team corrective actions with transparent tracking

c. Allow each team to manage dependencies independently

d. Remove all integration testing until the late team improves

140. **An executive wants weekly status reports reduced to one green-red summary to save time. The project has emerging scope, vendor, and quality risks. What should the project manager recommend?**

a. Replace all reporting with a single status color each week

b. Keep concise executive summaries, but retain enough supporting analysis to make risk and decision implications visible

c. Stop reporting until major issues occur

d. Report only the schedule trend because it is easiest to read

141. **A hybrid team is debating whether to treat a recurring production problem as a defect, a process issue, or technical debt. What should the project manager do first?**

a. Classify the problem correctly because the response path depends on its nature and urgency

b. Call it technical debt to avoid immediate work

c. Call it a defect to force priority

d. Escalate to the sponsor without analysis

142. **Mid-project, a new sponsor replaces the original sponsor and questions the entire business case. What should the project manager do next?**

a. Defend the original business case and continue without change

b. Pause all work immediately until a new charter is issued

c. Reconfirm strategic objectives, current value delivered, and available decision options with the new sponsor and governance stakeholders

d. Ask the team to avoid direct contact with the new sponsor until they settle in

143. **A release has met all test exit criteria, but frontline users report the solution is difficult to use in real-world conditions. What should the project manager do?**
   a. Launch anyway because exit criteria were met
   b. Validate the user feedback, assess business impact, and decide with stakeholders whether usability remediation is required before rollout
   c. Ignore the reports because they are subjective
   d. Blame the business analysts for incomplete requirements

144. **A project manager discovers that key assumptions documented early in planning are no longer valid. What should the project manager do first?**
   a. Ignore the change because assumptions are only for planning
   b. Update the assumption log, assess impact on plans and risks, and communicate needed actions
   c. Replace the original planner
   d. Convert all assumptions into issues immediately

145. **A project is under intense executive pressure to demonstrate visible progress, and the team proposes starting low-value work because it is easier to complete quickly. What should the project manager do?**
   a. Approve the work because visible activity will reassure stakeholders
   b. Recommend prioritizing the highest-value feasible work, even if progress appears slower at first
   c. Split the team between low-value and high-value work equally
   d. Stop all work until the pressure subsides

146. **A team uses velocity for planning, but a manager wants to compare teams by velocity to judge performance. What should the project manager say?**
   a. Velocity is a relative planning measure and should not be used to compare team performance across teams
   b. Higher velocity always means better performance
   c. Velocity should be standardized company-wide before comparison
   d. Velocity is mainly a budget metric

147. **A customer requests a feature that conflicts with an approved architectural principle designed to reduce long-term operational complexity. What should the project manager do?**
   a. Approve the feature because the customer is always right
   b. Reject the request automatically because architecture principles cannot change
   c. Assess the customer value and the long-term architectural impact, then route the decision through the appropriate design and change governance path
   d. Ask the development team to implement the feature quietly and hide the exception

148. **A team's burndown looks healthy, but users say the most important capabilities are still missing. What is the best explanation?**
   a. Burndown alone does not show whether the highest-value work is being completed
   b. Burndown always proves value delivery
   c. Users are usually wrong about priorities late in delivery
   d. The sprint backlog should never include high-value work first

149. **During implementation, a regulator asks for evidence of decision traceability on high-risk changes. What should the project manager provide?**
   a. A summary email saying the team used good judgment
   b. The change history, decision records, approvals, rationale, and links to affected baselines or artifacts
   c. Only the final approved schedule
   d. A verbal explanation during the audit meeting

150. A large transformation is delivering many local improvements, but executives say enterprise behavior is not changing. What should the project manager recommend?

a. Continue with isolated team improvements and wait longer

b. Assess whether governance, incentives, leadership behaviors, and operating policies are aligned to reinforce the desired enterprise change

c. Replace all local managers who resist the transformation

d. Stop measuring organizational outcomes and focus only on project outputs

151. A portfolio review shows three active projects competing for the same scarce cybersecurity specialists. All three are sponsor-priority initiatives. What should the project manager do first?

a. Ask each sponsor to negotiate directly with the specialists' manager

b. Escalate the shared resource conflict through portfolio governance with an impact-based comparison of options

c. Split the specialists evenly across all three projects, regardless of need

d. Delay the lowest-budget project automatically

152. A project is meeting output milestones, but customer adoption remains low because frontline managers are not reinforcing the new process. What should the project manager do?

a. Close the project because deliverables are complete

b. Work with operational leaders to identify adoption barriers, reinforce ownership, and define post-project actions to improve uptake

c. Ask the technical team to add more features to drive adoption

d. Escalate the frontline managers for noncompliance immediately

153. A supplier repeatedly misses delivery dates, but contract penalties have not changed behavior. What should the project manager do next?

a. Continue issuing penalties and wait for improvement

b. Review performance data, identify root causes with procurement and the supplier, and decide whether corrective action, incentive redesign, or replacement is warranted

c. Ignore the delays if the project can still recover later

d. Transfer all remaining work to internal teams immediately

154. During planning, a key stakeholder says the project should maximize speed, while another says the project should optimize maintainability and long-term cost. What should the project manager do first?

a. Choose the objective supported by the sponsor alone

b. Document the competing success criteria and facilitate alignment on decision priorities before detailed planning continues

c. Plan for maximum speed and address maintainability later

d. Create two different plans and let the team decide which to follow

155. A team reports that a quality gate is slowing delivery, but quality data shows defect escape is rising whenever the gate is bypassed informally. What should the project manager do?

a. Remove the quality gate to protect the schedule

b. Keep the gate, analyze why it is slow, and improve the process while preserving the control objective

c. Let each team member decide whether the gate is needed

d. Stop measuring escaped defects because they discourage the team

156. **A transformation sponsor wants to declare success early because visible morale and market perception are improving, but measurable business outcomes are still uncertain. What should the project manager recommend?**

a. Announce success immediately to build momentum

b. Distinguish between leading indicators and realized benefits, and report both transparently

c. Delay all communications until final benefits are achieved

d. Remove benefits metrics from governance until later

157. **A product owner keeps accepting urgent work directly from executives, disrupting sprint commitments and confusing priorities. What should the project manager do first?**

a. Instruct the team to reject all new executive requests

b. Work with the product owner and governance stakeholders to clarify intake rules, escalation paths, and decision rights for urgent work

c. Remove the product owner from the role

d. Ask executives to communicate only through email

158. **A change initiative has strong executive support, but middle managers are quietly deprioritizing it in staffing and local decisions. What should the project manager do?**

a. Assume executive support will eventually override local resistance

b. Identify where local incentives and operating measures conflict with the change, and work with leadership to realign them

c. Replace the middle managers who resist

d. Increase promotional messaging about the change vision only

159. **A major dependency is at risk because another program's milestone may slip by one month. What should the project manager do first?**

a. Add contingency cost to this project immediately

b. Confirm the dependency risk with the other program, assess impact scenarios, and develop coordinated response options

c. Assume the delay will happen and re-baseline now

d. Escalate to the board before speaking with the other program team

160. **A regulatory submission deadline is fixed, but several low-value features are consuming team capacity needed for compliance-critical work. What should the project manager do?**

a. Keep all work in scope because stakeholders already expect it

b. Reprioritize around compliance-critical scope and negotiate deferral of lower-value features

c. Increase overtime across the team for the rest of the project

d. Ask compliance to relax the deadline

161. **A team wants to skip a retrospective because delivery pressure is high. What should the project manager do?**

a. Skip it because delivery always comes first

b. Keep a focused retrospective to identify one or two high-value improvements that can reduce future pressure

c. Cancel all ceremonies for the rest of the release

d. Replace the scrum master to allow the request

162. **A customer says a deliverable meets the formal requirement but not the intended business need. What should the project manager do first?**

a. Reject the complaint because the requirement was met

b. Validate the gap between requirement interpretation and user need, then determine whether correction is a defect, enhancement, or scope change

c. Approve a redesign immediately to satisfy the customer

d. Ask QA to sign off again

163. A sponsor asks for a forecast that shows only the "most likely" completion date, but delivery data is highly variable. What should the project manager do?

a. Provide a single date to avoid confusion

b. Present a forecast range with confidence assumptions and explain the variability drivers

c. Refuse to provide any forecast

d. Use the earliest plausible date to demonstrate confidence

164. An executive asks why the team is spending time on stakeholder mapping instead of "just building." What should the project manager say?

a. Stakeholder mapping is optional and mainly for documentation

b. Stakeholder mapping reduces delivery risk by clarifying influence, expectations, resistance, and engagement needs before issues escalate

c. Building first is always better because feedback can come later

d. Stakeholder mapping matters only in very large programs

165. A project is under budget because several planned risk responses were never needed. What should the project manager do with the unused contingency?

a. Spend it on nice-to-have features before finance reclaims it

b. Report the status transparently and follow the organization's governance rules for contingency and reserve management

c. Reclassify it as operational savings immediately

d. Distribute it across the team to boost morale

166. An implementation partner says a late design decision by the client is the reason the schedule has slipped, but the client says the partner failed to raise risks early. What should the project manager do?

a. Accept the client's view because they pay for the work

b. Facilitate a fact-based timeline review of decisions, notifications, obligations, and mitigation opportunities before assigning accountability

c. End the relationship immediately

d. Ignore the disagreement and push both sides to work harder

167. A project has many cross-functional handoffs, and delays often occur because no one sees the full end-to-end process. What should the project manager do?

a. Add more status meetings only

b. Facilitate end-to-end process mapping and identify where ownership, queueing, or decision delays occur

c. Ask each function to optimize its own part independently

d. Reduce communication to prevent overload

168. A project's formal communications are clear, but rumors are spreading because leaders are inconsistent in informal conversations. What should the project manager do?

a. Ignore informal communication because only official channels matter

b. Align leaders on key messages, expected language, and escalation paths so formal and informal communication reinforce each other

c. Stop all informal communication across the program

d. Publish more documents without engaging leaders directly

169. A pilot has shown positive results, but scaling will require more governance, more support staff, and process changes. What should the project manager do before recommending enterprise rollout?

a. Assume the scale will behave like the pilot and proceed quickly

b. Assess scalability assumptions, support model needs, governance implications, and total cost before confirming rollout readiness

c. Repeat the pilot indefinitely

d. Leave scaling decisions to operations only

170. **A project delivered the expected capability, but downstream teams say they were not prepared to support it operationally. What should the project manager do?**
  a. Close the project because delivery is complete
  b. Confirm the operational readiness gap, complete or strengthen transition and support handoff actions, and capture lessons for future deployments
  c. Transfer the issue entirely to the service desk
  d. Ask the sponsor to lower support expectations temporarily

171. **A board asks whether a large transformation should continue as one integrated program or be split into smaller waves because execution risk is rising. What should the project manager do?**
  a. Keep the current structure because changing the program design will create confusion.
  b. Split the program immediately into smaller waves without further analysis.
  c. Assess whether the risks are driven by scale, sequencing, governance, or dependencies, and then present restructuring options with trade-offs.
  d. Pause all deliveries until the board decides on the new structure.

172. **A project is delivering to plan, but stakeholder confidence is declining because leaders feel they are hearing surprises too late. What should the project manager do first?**
  a. Increase the amount of status reporting without changing content.
  b. Meet with key leaders to understand where confidence is breaking down and adjust risk, issue, and escalation communication accordingly.
  c. Ignore the perception because objective performance is still strong.
  d. Replace the communications lead immediately.

173. **A sponsor wants to accelerate value realization by launching before all support processes are fully ready. Operations says they can absorb the gaps temporarily. What should the project manager do?**
  a. Launch now because early value always outweighs readiness concerns.
  b. Refuse any launch discussion until every support process is complete.
  c. Assess which support gaps are acceptable for controlled launch, what mitigations are required, and whether the remaining risk is within governance tolerance.
  d. Ask operations to sign a blanket acceptance and proceed.

174. **A program has too many committees, causing slow decisions and duplicate reviews. What should the project manager recommend?**
  a. Add one more oversight committee to coordinate the others.
  b. Map decision rights, remove overlapping forums, and redesign governance so each decision has one clear path and owner.
  c. Let teams bypass committees when deadlines are tight.
  d. Keep the structure because more oversight always reduces risk.

175. **A release is likely to miss its date because one third-party dependency is unstable. The third party is strategically important, and relationship damage would be costly. What should the project manager do first?**
  a. Publicly blame the third party in governance meetings to create pressure.
  b. Build a workaround secretly in case the third party fails.
  c. Engage the partner with evidence, assess contingency options, and escalate the dependency risk through the appropriate commercial and governance channels.
  d. Remove the dependency from the scope and hope users will accept the gap.

176. **A project dashboard shows all milestones as green, but frontline feedback and defect data suggest rising operational risk. What should the project manager conclude?**

    a. The dashboard is correct because milestones are the best health indicator.

    b. The project is healthy and user concerns can be addressed later.

    c. Milestone status may be masking deeper quality or readiness issues, so the PM should integrate outcome and risk indicators into governance reporting.

    d. Frontline feedback is too subjective to influence status.

177. **A transformation depends on local leaders changing long-standing behaviors, but they are waiting for more detailed central instructions instead of acting. What should the project manager do?**

    a. Provide a complete rulebook covering every local decision in advance.

    b. Clarify the non-negotiable outcomes, decision boundaries, and support available so local leaders can act with confidence.

    c. Replace the local leaders with transformation specialists.

    d. Pause the transformation until every local leader is fully aligned.

178. **A key business unit says a planned process standard will reduce its flexibility and local competitiveness. The enterprise sponsor says standardization is necessary for scale. What should the project manager do?**

    a. Enforce the standard because enterprise scale is always more important.

    b. Let the business unit opt out to preserve goodwill.

    c. Analyze which parts truly require standardization and which can allow bounded local variation, then govern the exceptions explicitly.

    d. Delay the entire standardization effort until all business units agree.

179. **A program shows strong early adoption, but support tickets reveal that users are relying on workarounds to complete critical tasks. What should the project manager do next?**

    a. Treat adoption as success and ignore the workarounds.

    b. Investigate the workaround patterns, assess associated risk, and prioritize fixes or process changes where they threaten value or control.

    c. Ban all workarounds immediately.

    d. Ask users to submit enhancement requests after closure.

180. **A project uses a new vendor because their proposal is innovative, but their delivery governance is immature. What should the project manager do?**

    a. Trust innovation and keep governance light to avoid slowing the vendor.

    b. Add disproportionate control to every work item immediately.

    c. Tailor governance to the vendor's maturity by increasing review frequency, decision traceability, and early quality checkpoints while the relationship stabilizes.

    d. Replace the vendor before delivery begins.

References

1. A Guide to the Project Management Body of Knowledge (PMBOK® Guide), Seventh Edition.
2. A Guide to the Project Management Body of Knowledge (PMBOK® Guide), Eighth Edition.
3. Project Management Institute (PMI) Examination Content Outline (ECO) for the PMP® examination.
4. Project management standards, principles, and good practices relating to predictive, adaptive, and hybrid delivery.

Answers

Q. No.	Answer	Q. No.	Answer	Q. No.	Answer	Q. No.	Answer
1	c	27	c	53	c	79	c
2	b	28	c	54	a, b, d	80	c
3	b, d	29	c	55	c	81	b
4	c	30	c	56	c	82	b
5	c	31	b	57	c	83	c
6	b	32	c	58	c	84	b
7	c	33	c	59	c	85	a
8	a, c, e	34	b	60	c	86	b
9	b	35	c	61	b	87	b
10	c	36	c	62	c	88	b
11	a	37	b	63	b, d, e	89	b
12	c	38	c	64	c	90	b
13	b, d, e	39	c	65	c	91	b
14	b	40	c	66	c	92	b
15	b	41	c	67	c	93	c
16	b	42	b	68	c, d, e	94	c
17	c	43	c	69	c	95	b
18	b, c, e	44	c	70	c	96	b
19	a	45	c	71	b	97	b
20	b	46	c	72	c	98	b
21	b	47	c	73	c	99	c
22	b	48	c	74	c	100	c
23	b	49	c	75	c	101	b
24	c	50	d	76	c	102	b
25	b	51	c	77	c	103	b
26	b	52	b, d	78	c	104	c

Q. No.	Answer
105	a
106	c
107	c
108	b
109	b
110	a
111	a
112	a
113	a
114	a
115	a
116	a
117	a
118	a
119	b
120	a
121	b
122	c
123	b

Q. No.	Answer
124	b
125	b
126	b
127	b
128	b
129	c
130	b
131	b
132	b
133	b
134	b
135	b
136	b
137	b
138	b
139	b
140	b
141	a
142	c

Q. No.	Answer
143	b
144	b
145	b
146	a
147	c
148	a
149	b
150	b
151	b
152	b
153	b
154	b
155	b
156	b
157	b
158	b
159	b
160	b
161	b

Q. No.	Answer
162	b
163	b
164	b
165	b
166	b
167	b
168	b
169	b
170	b
171	c
172	b
173	c
174	b
175	c
176	c
177	b
178	c
179	b
180	c

Index

www.ingramcontent.com/pod-product-compliance
Lightning Source LLC
LaVergne TN
LVHW081736071126
851857LV00042B/1889
9788167080011